VEDIC ASTROLOGY TRANSIT GUIDE FOR 2018 - 2019

A Reference Book of Detailed Interpretations for Major Transits and Events!

Revised Edition

By Barry Rosen
Compiled by Jamie Bateman

www.appliedvedicastrology.com

Acclaim for Vedic Astrology Transit Guide for 2018 - 2019

"Barry Rosen's brilliant text is a practical guide for any practicing astrologer. His book provides extensive research on the world of Jyotish as well as a detailed analysis of the planetary transits of 2018. My prediction is that it will become a classic cornerstone for any Vedic Astrology library."
- **Dennis M. Harness, Ph.D.** – *President Emeritus, American College of Vedic Astrology*

"This is an amazing, well-written book, gives deep insights into coming trends. It uses dasha periods and transits which are Vedic astrology tools that are extremely accurate for predicting future events. Barry also gives practical tools to deal with difficult transits to help you move gracefully through your life."
- **Michael Mastro,** *Vastu Consultant, Vedic Astrologer, Author*

"Barry Rosen lifts the spirit of Jyotish to new heights with his latest offering. From the practical considerations of how to plan your year to the spiritual well-being always imbibed in his work; Barry inspires and comforts the soul."
- **Gary O-Toole,** *Timeline Astrology*

"This almanac is truly a masterpiece and labor of love. Barry is a gifted astrologer and writer. I have written yearly forecasts for over 30 years and understand the work, knowledge and dedication involved. It is so complete with everything a beginner or advanced student of astrology would need. The references to the planet's transit through the signs, Nakshatras, aspects, dates and times, plus their interpretations is fantastic. He even covers the effects these will have on individual countries. I am sure I will be referring to this manual frequently throughout the year."
Joni Patry, *Author and Vedic Astrologer*

"Barry Rosen's reference work is comprehensible for those with minor astrological backgrounds and is also useful for professionals as a yearly transit and progression guide. As a Neo-Vedic astrologer, Barry also uses the outer planets to help track world events both in finance and on the political and economic scene. Definitely a book to have on your shelf."
– **Juliana Swanson,** *Neo-Vedic Astrologer at Astral Harmony*

"Barry Rosen's masterwork is a must - have for the serious student of Vedic astrology. The beauty, complexity, and perfection of this wonderful science of light is further illuminated in this well written and clearly detailed catelogue of the year ahead. Never stop learning. Go deep. Buy the book. Invest in your scholarship from a master with lifetimes of expertise."
- **Tom Yaroschuk,** *Level II Graduate, American Academy of Vedic Art & Science*

www.appliedvedicastrology.com
support@fortucast.com
Office: 928-284-5740 ext. 5000 or 5983

LEGAL

Vedic Astrology Transit Guide For 2018 – 2019
A Reference Book of Detailed Interpretations for Major Transits and Events for the Year!

Copyright © 2018 Barry Rosen

Religion & Spirituality, Astrology, Calendars, Planners

All rights reserved. No part of this book may be reproduced in any manner whatsoever, or stored in any information storage system, without the prior written consent of the publisher or the author, except in the case of brief quotations with proper reference, embodied in critical articles and reviews.

Compiled by Jamie Bateman

Cover and interior design by Jamie Bateman

Images, artwork and articles: Copyright © Barry Rosen

All quotations remain the intellectual property of their respective originators. All use of quotations is done under the fair use copyright principal.

Library of Congress Control Number:

ISBN: 978-0-692-06131-2

Printed in the United States of America

Disclaimer: This publication is sold with the understanding that the author is not engaged in rendering psychological, medical, or other professional services. If expert assistance or counseling is needed, the services of a competent professional should be sought.

Table of Contents

LEGAL 2
OFFERING OF ACKNOWLEDGEMENT AND GRATITUDE 8
INTRODUCTION 11
DEALING WITH DIFFICULT TRANSITS WITH TRUE GRIT AND DISCIPLINE 14
RESPONSIBILITY, JYOTISH AND TRANSFORMING KARMA 16
SECRETS OF TIMING 19
HOW ASTROLOGICAL TIMING WORKS AND HOW IT IMPACTS YOUR CHART 21
COSMIC TIMING: USING INDIAN TIME CYCLES TO PIN DOWN THOSE ELUSIVE LIVE EVENT 23
QUICK GUIDE TO YOUR DASHA PERIOD 27
SUN PERIOD: FAVORABLE AND UNFAVORABLE 28
MOON PERIOD: FAVORABLE AND UNFAVORABLE 29
RAHU PERIOD FAVORABLE AND UNFAVORABLE 30
JUPITER PERIOD FAVORABLE AND UNFAVORABLE 31
SATURN PERIOD FAVORABLE AND UNFAVORABLE 31
MERCURY PERIOD FAVORABLE AND UNFAVORABLE 32
KETU PERIOD FAVORABLE AND UNFAVORABLE 33
VENUS PERIOD FAVORABLE AND UNFAVORABLE 33
DIG BALA AND MARANA KARAKA STHANA OR BEST AND WORST HOUSE PLACEMENT FOR PLANETS 35
UNDERSTANDING PLANETARY OPPOSITIONS AND OPPOSING SIGNS 37
GUIDE TO PLANETARY ASPECTS: UNDERSTANDING THE QUALITIES OF PLANETARY ASPECTS 42
UNDERSTANDING PLANETARY COMBUSTION: PLANETS TOO CLOSE TO THE SUN 45
PERIODS OF PLANETARY COMBUSTION: CAZIMI 46
SECRETS OF RETROGRADE PLANETS 50
GUIDE TO RISING SIGNS: NEW LIGHT ON ZODIACAL SIGNS ARIES – PISCES 53
Hidden Flaws By Rising Sign: The Achilles Heel 57
HIGHLIGHTS OF THE YEAR BY RISING SIGN: PLANNING YOUR YEAR 64

JANUARY 2018 65
FEBRUARY 2018 66
MARCH 2018 66
APRIL 2018 67
MAY 2018 68

JUNE 2018	68
JULY 2018	68
AUGUST 2018	69
SEPTEMBER 2018	69
OCTOBER 2018	70
NOVEMBER 2018	70
DECEMBER 2018	70
HIGHLIGHTS OF THE YEAR: 2018	71
GLOBAL AND ECONOMIC OUTLOOKS FOR 2018 THE YEAR OF VILAMBA	76
2018 - 2019 GLOBAL AND POLITICAL OUTLOOKS: *POLITICAL AND GEO - COSMIC OUTLOOK FOR 2018*	80
THE UNITED STATES IN A RAHU PERIOD: DECEMBER 2015 – 2033	100
ASTRO-FINANCIAL OUTLOOK: LOOKING AHEAD INTO 2019 – 2023	103
LOOKING AHEAD: 2020	104
THE 33 - 38 YEAR CYCLE: 2020	105
HISTORY OF THE 33 - 38 YEAR CYCLE:	105
OUTLOOK FOR 2020 CYCLE	106
THE 20 - YEAR CYCLE: SATURN CONJUNCT JUPITER	107
2018 ASTRO-FINANCE OUTLOOK (Revised January 18, 2018)	108
TRANSITS FOR THE YEAR: BY RISING SIGN	115
TRANSITS IN 2018 BY: RISING SIGN OF SIGNIFICANCE	117
2018 LEO RISING: TRANSITS OF THE SUN	127
2018 CANCER RISING: LUNAR ECLIPSE GUIDE and GUIDE TO FULL and NEW MOONS	139
2018 ECLIPSE GUIDE: ASPECTS AND ECLIPSES	142
ECLIPSE GUIDE FOR 2018	144
2018 LIBRA AND TAURUS RISING: TRANSITS OF VENUS	149
GEMINI AND VIRGO RISING: TRANSITS OF MERCURY	169
CAPRICORN AND AQUARIUS RISING: TRANSITS OF SATURN	179
Saturn in Sagittarius and Mula Nakshatra:	188
Understanding the 7.5 Years of Saturn in Connection with Transits Through the Constellation: Sade Sati	190
Saturn in Purva Ashadha Nakshatra:	193
Saturn: Enough Doom and Gloom Already!	195
Saturn/Ketu Connections 2018: Cleaning Up the Past	197

Saturn Retrograde: 200
Focus on Saturn at Work: Grumbling and Complaining 203
Saturn and Fear of The Future: Trust In The Divine 204
2018 AQUARIUS RISING: MORE TRANSITS OF SATURN URANUS INTO ARIES: THE FIRE OF SURPRISE 206
2018 GUIDE TO THE NODAL TRANSITS: RAHU AND KETU 208
RAHU AND KETU IN CAPRICORN/CANCER: YOUR GUIDE FOR THE NEXT 18 MONTHS 211
RAHU AND KETU IN CAPRICORN/CANCER: YOUR GUIDE FOR THE NEXT 18 MONTHS 213
A GUIDE TO RAHU/KETU: GOING THROUGH THE HOUSES 215
2018 RAHU ASPECTS 227
KETU IN SHRAVANA: SPIRITUAL AWAKENING AND MATERIAL CONFLICTS 234
2018 PLANETS CONJUNCT KETU 236
THE SNAKE IN TIME: KALA SARPA YOGA IN TRANSIT 2018 239
2018 SAGITTARIUS AND PISCES: TRANSITS OF JUPITER BY RISING SIGN OR MOON SIGN 241
JUPITER IN SWATI NAKSHATRA: LIBRA 6.40-19.59 245
2018 SAGITTARIUS AND PISCES RISING: JUPITER IN LIBRA 245
FOCUS OF FESTIVALS: VEDIC HOLIDAYS 254
Vedic Holiday: Makara Sankranti - A New Beginning 254
Vedic Holiday: Maha Shivaratri - Overcoming Darkness and Ignorance 254
Vedic Holiday: Holi - Festival of Love and Colors 256
Vedic Holiday: Spring Navaratri - Chaitra 257
Vedic Holiday: Navaratri - Journey toward Enlightenment 258
Final Note 265
ABOUT BARRY ROSEN: CONFESSIONS OF A JYOTISH ENTHUSIAST: THE WIZARD BEHIND THE CURTAIN IN THE LAND OF OZ 266
Jyotish Star of The Month 268
BIBLIOGRAPHY 273
Supplemental: Vedic Astrology Material 274
Retrogression Report for United States 2018 EST 286
Sign Ingresses 291
KARAKAS AND SIGNIFICATIONS 296
Signs and House - Polarity 298
NAKSHATRA (LUNAR MANSIONS): SHAKTI POWER AND KEY MEANINGS 302

AUTHOR BIOGRAPHY: ABOUT BARRY ROSEN 305

OFFERING OF ACKNOWLEDGEMENT AND GRATITUDE

I stand on the shoulders of my great teachers and I particularly want to acknowledge:

Sanjay Rath	Komilla Sutton,
Bill Levacy	Juliana Swanson
Robert Koch	Dennis Harness
Andrew Foss	Zoran Rosavliveic
Robert Hand	Gordon Brennan
Joni Patry	Marc Berkowitz
Alan Annand	Christina Collins

For their guidance and support over the years and the wisdom in their books.

Special Thanks to:
Jamie Bateman for her help with editing and writing and rewriting. So grateful!

Special thanks to my wife Bonnie who sacrifices time with me so that I can be writing. We are only as great as the women behind us!

And of course, to my spiritual Gurus over the years including Maharishi Mahesh Yogi who got be involved in meditation and to Sri Sri Ravi Shankar and their lineage through to Brahmananda Saraswati.

Jai Guru Dev
Victory to the Big Mind! May we never get caught up in ego and remain here to serve.

PREFACE

The ocean of Jyotish is infinite. This book started out to be about 75 pages and has expanded greatly over the past few weeks. I realize that this is not exhaustive, but I have focused on highlights. I would like to cover the astrology of 40 countries and spend two hours writing about each country, but time prohibits that.

I have covered all the major transits of the year and when I thought it was important, I discussed nakshatras, but I have not discussed all the nakshatra transits. My work with aspects is far from exhaustive and those will be kept up on my daily blog at Applied Vedic Astrology.

As a Neo-Vedic astrologer, I think the outer planets are important and because of my 30 years of experience, I cannot ignore them in mundane astrology as they govern world trends and politics and are very important for countries. I included articles about them.

My experience dictates that if they have a strong 2-degree impact to planets in your natal chart by conjunction or aspect, that they also have a strong influence and that influence will also show up in transit particularly if there is a natal signature. I have chosen to use True Nodes vs. Mean nodes from my years of experience watching conjunctions and trines to transiting planets. It is thought that Ketu is headless and cannot cast aspects but does influence planets strong within 3-5 degrees with a conjunction. My experience also shows that Ketu trines can be important because they are conjunctions in the D-9 chart if they fall in the same navamsha pada. I have chosen not to include the Ketu trines in the almanac.

My hope is that you use this book to cut the puppet strings of the planets that influence your emotions and psychology and that prevent you from being free. You are so much bigger and more powerful than all the planets so use this knowledge to become freer and become the great Divine Being that you are!

All love and light and blessings for you for the New Year!

Barry Rosen -
January 19, 2018
Stay in touch with our daily updates and forecasts on Facebook at <u>Barry Rosen</u>, <u>Astro-Yoga</u> and <u>Spiritual Astrology and Financial Astrology</u> by Barry Rosen

DISCLAIMER:

The information is this book is general and may not apply to your personal chart. As with my daily columns, I have to paint broad-brush strokes around general psychology and planetary significations to benefit the most number of people. If you need personal insights, please sign up for a reading with me at my Applied Vedic Astrology website.

Astrology shows multiple possible paths of action and is not fatalistic. Any knowledge from this book is the summation of probabilities based on ancient methods and records from many years of my training and expertise.

However, as an interpreter, I make no guarantees regarding the accuracy or consequence of any aspect of the reading and cannot be responsible for any interpretation or action that follows. You have your own free will so please take responsibility for your life.

This knowledge is not a substitute treatment for professional, financial, medical, and/or legal advice.

As a professional astrologer, I always seek to provide my best interpretation, but you always have free will to pursue your best outcomes. As always, I bless you with success and deep knowledge

INTRODUCTION
THE PURPOSE OF ASTROLOGY: CUTTING THE PUPPET STRINGS BEYOND ASTROLOGICAL BYPASSING

My orientation with work is to help you see the emotional and psychological strings that are running your life. The planets impact our thoughts and emotions most and if we understand what is happening, we do not have to buy into the self-deprecation of Saturn or the rashness and anger of Mars. We can catch the thoughts as they manifest, observe them, and banish them.

Back in the 80's I used to tell Saturn that he could go, that I did not need have his fear and I would feel a sigh of relief. We are more powerful than the planets if we are regular in our meditation and spiritual practices and we can be a master and not a victim. Astrology was never intended to strike fear into our hearts or make us very stuck. Jyotish means light and the light of knowledge should free us from the grip of our thoughts and emotions but we have to be aware and observe.

I find that astrology gets misused very much. Sometimes on the Western circuit, it becomes a media type-play to expect the next catastrophe. This week we have Mars conjunct Uranus and some unexpected violence, accident or fire will flare up, but it will only impact your chart if you are in a malefic Mars period or if the transit is impacting a key area of your chart and you have that karma to work out. Eventually in 5 years, even if it does manifest, you will see it as a blessing.

I have moved a bit more beyond predictions or gloating if predictions are correct because even the best astrologers can only be 70% correct, as there is always some level of free will in terms of how we react to a situation and make new choices.

I find that the astrology will bring up lessons and tendencies for us to learn and if we get it right, we may not have to suffer but if we are oblivious to the signals, then we get a hard hit.

How many of you use astrology and intellectual constructs to bypass the hard work that it takes to transform your soul and consciousness? Do you use astrology to over-intellectualize or blame the circumstances in your life?

I have to admit that this happens to me, much too often. My friend Kara coined the term; "*Astrological Bypassing*" and it struck a deep chord. Astrological bypassing is rampant in our community. We may blame the planets if we do something wrong or hurt another: "*Oh it was Mars aspecting Mercury.*"

We may accept the responsibility for picking a fight or arguing and then apologize. Do we find solace in knowing that Saturn is going over our natal moon and creating depression or do we do something about it like mediation, yoga and service to transform it? Do we avoid doing something because we are in a bad period or bad transit and does this avoidance prevent deep lessons? Sometimes a real challenging life situation does this for us in an intense, dramatic way and helps us shift. It can be painful but sometimes it takes something dramatic to bring the necessary growth.

Steven Stuckey, an insightful colleague, observed, that do we use astrology to avoid the drama of surprise, which often creates the greatest growth for us:

"I believe we need to be cast out into the unknown, so to speak, so that we don't have any "idea" of what is going to happen next, so that something new (i.e., beyond thought) can come to us. Going into the 'darkness' is very important for spiritual life and sometimes we may not quite get there with total abandon, since we have become a bit too 'intelligent' for our own good, and know when a difficult transit, (which often brings a spiritual experience along with it) is going to leave orb. So, the potential of the intensity of the moment, which is needed for transformation, can sometimes be lost."

My own sense is that Jyotish throws "*light*" on our shadows and helps us remove the "*self-blame*" and the "*self-shame.*" If we can see that the puppet master is pulling the strings on our emotions and thought, then we can step back and stop blaming ourselves.

This can create a moment of Zen observation that enlightens us to see that we are not thoughts or emotions or ego. In a sense, this is a Gyana technique to free ourselves from the bondage that normally grips us. I have used this technique daily for years to create freedom because I know when the shadow will pass and what is causing it. I still have to do the work on myself, but I can be kinder to myself and not beat myself up as much.

Sometimes we get a bit too fated by what the stars suggest but for spiritual seekers and those involved in long-term spiritual practice, I suspect our consciousness is more flexible.

My friend, Juliana Swanson noted that:

"When we wake up, we realize we are multidimensional and at any given time, there are many possibilities. There are unlimited possibilities seen in the fact that every astrological combination is good for something and bad for something and has a higher, versus a lower expression, depending on the consciousness of the person."

Our consciousness is more powerful than the planets because Divinity resides within us and we lessen that Greatness when we become a victim of the planets.

I am reminded of a seminal work, by Robert Augustus Masters, *Spiritual Bypassing: When Spirituality Disconnects Us From What Really Matters*. The work focuses on when spiritual beliefs allow us to avoid dealing with painful feelings, unresolved wounds and developmental needs in order to duck uncomfortable feeling in favor of more "*seemingly enlightened activity.*"

On one level, I understand the value of spiritual practice as a way of transforming karma through meditation, service work and spiritual knowledge. It is a healthier way of doing so, rather than traditional addictive behaviors that are used to avoid painful feelings. Still, can we really become Whole and "*enlightened*" without looking at our shadows?

One of my great teachers always reminded me "*mud is endless.*" Spiritual practice and spiritual organization allow us to cope with psychological scarring but require digging into our wounds at times to transform, release and make us whole. How do we balance the good of spiritual practice and excessive bypassing of feeling? Somehow, we need to find balance.

In the end, for those on a spiritual path, Vedic astrology can create a deep transcendence and shed light on difficult situations. If we use that light to eliminate our shadows, we are can have immense growth. I suspect that ultimately, I lean toward spiritual practice as a way to get through life without digging up the muddy waters. Focused attention on spiritual life and doing good for others gives us an opportunity to increase our awareness. If we let our mind concentrate on something more positive than the regrettable past and allow ourselves to live in the present moment with more joy and presence, we will experience a higher quality of life.

DEALING WITH DIFFICULT TRANSITS WITH TRUE GRIT AND DISCIPLINE

Some people are afraid to go out of the house because of bad transits. Transits are only 20% of forecasting. If you are running a bad cycle and have the same bad transit, then it is a tornado warning and you do not schedule a picnic, but instead, plan and take precautions and continue to live, act and go through any challenge that happens.

For example, the upcoming solar eclipse will impact you most if you are running a Sun or Rahu period or if you have Sun/Rahu as a signature in your natal chart or if you have planets within 5 degrees of Leo 5. Otherwise, it may be just an emotional bad day.

My writings try to give us perspective and probably 60% of the year there is something challenging happening in the stars but there are always movements of grace. Even this year with the difficult Rahu/Ketu conjunction, Jupiter and Venus are holding down the fort as much as they can.

My forecasts are general but their impact on your specific life has to be diagnosed and properly evaluated by a professional astrologer. My intent is not to frighten you or advise you to bunker down but rather to recommend that you have an umbrella handy if it is going to rain.

We should not use astrology to prevent us from acting and moving forward with our lives but we can use astrological forecast to "*see*" the puppet masters that are tugging our emotional and psychological strings and rather than hide our head in the ground like an ostrich, if we understand what is happening in the stars, we can avoid bad decisions, move beyond their grasp and transcend their influence.

I find that 95% of my mental and emotional noise disappears with spiritual practice and I am able to move forward as a result. Sometimes when things get rough, we get undisciplined and skip our spiritual practices. This is like taking our coat off in the middle of a hard freeze in winter. It gets more challenging. By being more disciplined with diet, good habits, yoga, exercise and meditation when the planetary weather is rough, you can avoid or minimize the adverse effects.

The value of spiritual practice during difficult times is that it should empower you with inner strength to move forward and blow away the adverse planetary smoke and help you to adjust and make better decisions.

Integrate spiritual practices into your life by always being realistic and practical. A famous Arab quote says: "*Pray to Allah but tie up your camel.*"

My colleague, Sam Geppi has a useful spiritual reminder about difficult transits:

"Challenging times are where spiritual muscles are stretched and worked out, and these opportunities are not to be avoided if one seeks advancement. Moksha isn't a pretty process, it involves letting go and can be painful."

We need not fear karmic lessons. That is why we are here. One of Paramahansa Yogananda's most advanced disciples, Gyanamata, wrote beautifully:

"*I have come to measure spiritual advancement, not alone by the light that surrounds one when he meditates or by the visions he has of saints, but by what he is able to endure in the hard, cold light of day.*"

We can make difficult transits easier by helping others, donating to charity, doing special Vedic ceremonies and spiritual practice but some of it just requires getting through it and learning our life lessons so that we can become free. Go forth with courage!

Do your spiritual practices! Act! Have the courage to face your challenges! Know that God's grace is supporting you to unmask a higher self-realization and reach the light.

Do not use astrology to bypass your karmic destiny or avoid your challenges. It is not meant to be used in that way. You have nothing to fear and are always intimately taken care of by the Divine.

RESPONSIBILITY, JYOTISH AND TRANSFORMING KARMA

Jyotish means, "*light*" and the practice of Jyotish is shining light on what is hidden. Revealing the Puppeteer play of stings tugging at our emotions and psychology makes us realize that the planets are hard at work spinning their webs of illusion. In reality, there may not be anything there but a game of "*smoke and mirrors.*" When we recognize these "*shadow*" patterns, we have the opportunity to take responsibility and create positive shifts in our lives by taking directed action when we use this newfound awareness.

Thoughts that are erratic or blocked by self-doubt are often the root cause of our problems. People think that mantras and Vedic ceremonies are magic bullets but that is not totally the case. Mantras and ceremonies are prescribed to loosen the grip of mind illusions so that we can then take new action without being manipulated, controlled or feeling victimized.

Mantras and ceremonies should create good health, power of speech and action to construct new directions in our life so that we are empowered. Sometimes clients would like a magic bullet to lift the problems and sometimes that can happen with grace if you have a Sat Guru and are blessed. More often than not, the client has to actively make major changes in their life to recreate their life.

This is no easy task and requires huge willpower, motivation and a strong ability to change. Without spiritual practice, service, the company of spiritual people and support this can be difficult to accomplish. Ideally, we have to own the responsibility of our own suffering and do something to change it.

For modern Western clients, I like to recommend donations that are specific for the karma involved. If we can do service work or donate to charities related to the problems in our life, we are re-addressing past karma very directly.

Jupiter/Rahu afflictions, which may cause problems with luck in this life, may mean that you were not a good parent to your children in past lives or that you were not respectful of Gurus. Donating to support children or teachers and doing volunteer work for agencies like scouting and Big Brother/Little Sister on a Thursday, ruled by Jupiter, may be a way of addressing that past karma.

One can start seeing all karma in a chart in this way and by being more specific in seeing the karma on a microscopic level, one can suggest a more specific remedy that will be stronger depending on the planet's sign, aspects and nakshatra.

My financial astrology course recently had a lesson on this and is quite fascinating and it makes good karmic sense. Rather than blame the planet, learn what lessons you did not master in the past and get it right this time. It's like that wonderful Bill Murray movie, Groundhog Day (1993). Get out of your nightmare by being kinder and help others and then you will not suffer. The planets just want us to get it right this time, so we do not have to wake up in the same nightmare every morning like Bill Murray.

Difficult transits can increase fear, anxiety and tension depending on where they fall in the chart, which creates a lot of tension, and dealing with regrets of the past and deep emotional psychological churning that you may feel as if you cannot get a handle. Swimming in the sea of transits can feel like being in a Scorpion swamp. Do we run off to take shelter?

Most of world will have a few drinks, take some drugs, smoke a pack of cigarettes or eat themselves into a numbed-out stupor. That can work for a bit but it is destructive and takes you out of your deepest being. If you are on spiritual path, what do you do? Those of us on a spiritual path have to go through these moments in time, acknowledge them and feel them deeply. The process of feeling them can facilitate their deep release.

What are we afraid of? Are we really those stupid feelings and emotions or something bigger? Go deep into them and the attention of your consciousness will facilitate their release.

We can always do a bit of spiritual or astrological bypassing and that can help too but remember you are so much bigger than your emotions. If a storm is happening be like Billy Buddy in the Herman Melville's classic. Strap yourself to the mast and go through it! In the end, you will find that your eternal Self is so much bigger than a few waves and in fact, you are the waves and you are ocean! How can you be afraid of the very water that you are made of? Stay strapped to the mast, whatever storms come, say, I am here and let them come through me. How can we run away from a tiny emotion? What power can it really have over us? Don't the storms make you a deeper and a more powerful person? Embrace. Realize that you are unchanging, and nothing can touch you. You are invincible. Merge with the water and become One.

So, if you are not able to do that you can always do the following:

1) This is a time to be disciplined about your meditation practice and yoga and other spiritual practices because these lighten the burden and give us more strength to deal with everything. The tendency is to skip that which is good for us.
2) Donate time and money to help those in need. This is one way to address karma and by getting out of our own stuff, we feel better and move through our own karma.
3) Be disciplined with diet and exercise. The tendency is to use food to cover up difficult emotions or skip exercise because we feel tired or lazy. So much illness (6th house) can be overcome if we are disciplined doing what is good for uu.
4) Avoid addictive behaviors and non-life-supporting actions, especially now. The tendency is to escape but usually this leads to more difficult problems.
5) Spend time with spiritual knowledge, attend spiritual gatherings and hang around positive people that uplift you.

6) Do transformational healing work to move through these energies. T

The transits will pass. Embrace yourself, embrace the storm, embrace your emotion and just be!

Please see the appendix course listings if you would like to explore traditional Vedic mantras, Yagyas, Pujas and other remedies with Applied Vedic Astrology.

SECRETS OF TIMING

I live in a community where people are involved in Vedic knowledge and most of the community has had one or more readings. Many of the people I have talked to have been jaded about their readings because they have not been accurate or there was a cultural difference between the person giving the reading and the client. The reading was "lost in translation." Even the best astrologers in the world may only be 70% accurate because there is some level of free will and spiritual people are aware to make better choices.

It is possible to get very specific information out of a chart that is very precise. I often tell people that true Vedic astrology is like reading strands of DNA if you go deeply enough with it and I find that Western psychology and Western astrological approaches are very useful for helping people reveal their patterns.

My initial background in financial astrology and timing markets and mundane events has taught me a lot about timing and people. Very specifically, about how events manifest in life. Observing daily dashas for 25 years and transits has helped understand how karma manifests and some of the common mistakes that astrologers can make.

ALTERNATE UNIVERSES: Firstly, I do not think that everything in our life is written in stone and can be predicted with 100% accuracy. I often think there are alternative universes available that our free will and intention can shift karma. It's a bit like that movie *Sliding Doors* with Gwyneth Paltrow. She meets one boyfriend when she catches the train and meets someone else when the doors close and she misses the train. Other science fiction writers have played with this theme of multiple possibilities. When we are aware of the problem and choose not to repeat the same mistake, we can create an alternative universe. I often see in charts that the dasha period will set up a school to bring up the issues but with meditation, service, awareness and poise, we can make new choices and create an alternative universe.

While some karma is very hard and does have to hit us, as we meditate and do good deeds and become more conscious and aware, I think karma comes back more softer and that we are given schools to karma to work out and choices to make. Often, I think the astrology sets up a situation and how we act up on it this time is dependent on our judgment and free will. Often clients want us to give a definitive yes or no that it will go this way and the best astrologers can be is 75%.

More often than not, we can see the karma coming up but how you deal with it is up to you. Even if there is a health condition coming up, if it is connected to the 6th house, through discipline and diet and awareness we can change the outcome. Eight house karmas can be more difficult and more acute but even 8th house issues are beckoning us to transform and transcend and if are on top of what we need to do for certain areas of our life, they do not have to hit us. I think there are early warning systems available but once in a while stuff hits us out of the blue. When we are aware of the problem and choose not to repeat the same mistake, we can create an alternative universe. I often see in charts that the dasha period will set up a school to bring up the issues but with meditation, service, awareness and poise, we can make new choices and create an alternative universe. Hence, awareness from a reading may allow us to see our blind spots.

TRANSITS ARE ONLY 20% OF TIMING: The Vedic Mahadasha system and dasha systems are based on signs (Rashi Dashas) and give us a contextual rotation of periods in our life for things to manifest and transits trigger those events within the context. Western astrologers are not aware of the larger cyclical context.

If you are running a very good Jupiter period and have a bad Saturn transit, it may be a minor bump in the road and it will not be devastating. If you are in a difficult Saturn period and have a difficult Saturn transit at the same time, it may throw you for a loop. Dashas and larger periods are 80% of timing and you need an accurate birth-time rectified to the minute to get a good prediction. Every minute off may impact timing by 3 – 4 days. Some studies reconciling birth certificate times with actual births show that hospitals can be 30 minutes off. Some countries, like India and Germany of course, are more accurate about getting the timing right.

Transits are key when a transit and dasha coincide. If you are running a Mars/Mercury period or a Mercury/Mars period and there is a Mars/Mercury planetary war, then there will be a huge impact to your chart but in another period and if Mars or Mercury does not rule you it may not mean much.

THE DIVISIONAL CHARTS: Too many people get caught up in the main chart (Rashi chart) but it is important to look for a manifestation in the divisional charts. If career is strong in the natal chart but is blocked in the D-10 or career chart, then it manifestation may not happen. (Vice-versa.) A strong divisional chart will not yield results if the natal chart is blocked. Some astrologers do not like to use divisional charts because of inaccurate birth times but there are simple techniques to rectify a chart quickly and be able to get the more microscopic information. They are vital information for uncovering the layers of karma or strands of DNA that will manifest.

ASTRO-LOCALITY: I recently wrote an article on how moving far away enough from where you are born can change your chart and create a new rising sign with some different problems. Many astrologers fail to take this into account, but we are not the same person when born in India and the living in the US. We may have some of the same natal chart karmic patterns, but material work manifestations may be very different. I moved 1800 miles from my birth city of Chicago, Illinois to Sedona, Arizona in 1997 and went from Scorpio 7 degrees to Libra 20 degrees with an exalted Saturn at Libra 27. My life changed dramatically, and it was not just being in a new city that was the impact of being Libra verses Scorpio.

KARMA SHIFT: I do believe in karma shifts, which means if we were meant to get a bullet in the head, then with good deeds, charity work, service and meditation, maybe the bullet goes through our hat or grazes us. The more conscious we are, the more we can shift karma.

BLIND SPOTS: A good astrologer should throw light on our schools of karma and help us see unconscious patterns that we are blind toward. 12th house karma represents our blind spot because the 12th house is right before sunrise where we are blinded by glare of the rising sun and cannot see clearly. So, give astrology a chance from another perspective. It should do a lot more than predict the future and remember you do have free will so a reading may change your outcome!

HOW ASTROLOGICAL TIMING WORKS AND HOW IT IMPACTS YOUR CHART

1. There are multiple levels of applying transits to your chart. First, 80% of timing is connected to the planetary period you are in. If your period is good, a bad transit may be a bump but if it is a bad period and you get a bad transit it can be amplified.

2. With transits, the most impact comes if there is a direct interaction with another natal planet in your chart.

3. Let's look at an example from the Mars/Ketu conjunction in 2017.
    a. The Mars/Ketu conjunction was at 12 degrees of Aquarius so if you have key planets from 9 - 15 degrees Aquarius, like other malefics, it will have more of an impact, particularly if it is your natal Sun, Moon or Ascendant or another key malefic like Saturn or Rahu.

4. The dasha cycle or planetary period running is 80% of timing and transits are 20%. If you are currently running a Ketu/Mars period or Mars/Ketu then the impact of that transit would be more intense or if you are running a Rashi Dasha for Aquarius, you will be more aware of feeling the effects.

5. Ninety-degree aspects to the same planets in Taurus at 9 - 15 degrees, Leo at 9 - 15 degrees or Scorpio at 9 - 15 degrees in your natal chart could also be more dramatic.

6. If the two are both happening at the same time it is a double hit and something major may happen, but it would depend on what house is being hit and what rising sign you are and then you might need remedial measures like mantras, Yagyas or be more alert and careful.

7. If you have a signature of Mars/Ketu in your natal chart then when it happens in transit, it is more significant.

The mind tends to take 20% of our fear and exaggerate it. Fear is false evidence appearing to be real, and 99% of what we fear may happen, does not occur. You are safe and intimately taken care of by the Divine, so do not be afraid.

Karma can be averted through meditation, service work, charity, and awareness. Getting caught up and apprehensive about major events that might happen based on planetary significations in the sky is not useful.

My work is not meant to scare you but rather make you aware of the influences of the Puppeteer planets and how they impact your mind and emotions by pulling on your "*strings*." This is the illusion or 'Maya.'

Meditation, yoga and service to others will help you move beyond the noise of your emotions created by the planets and moved you beyond the Maya and into personal empowerment.

Based on our experiences, interpretations and perceptions of life events, we automatically judge our adventures as good or bad but all the events that happen in our life are for our growth. Jupiter teaches us by experience, that we should re-label these "challenges" and understand that they provide a chance to learn, expand and grow.

Mars/Ketu may create a lot of anger and frustration in some areas of our life depending on where they hit our chart but, in the end, the way through it is by acceptance and patience. So, don't go flying off the handle, stuff food into your system or hide in your addictions. This will block your ability to effectively handle the transit oppositions.

COSMIC TIMING: USING INDIAN TIME CYCLES TO PIN DOWN THOSE ELUSIVE LIVE EVENT
By Barry Rosen

Below is a brief introduction to Indian Sidereal Astrology on how I became acquainted with it.

EARLY RESEARCH BEGINNINGS
I first became interested in Indian astrology in 1985, when a Jyotishi (Vedic astrologer) told me that I was finishing up a twenty-year Venus cycle, and that my life would completely change in one year when I would enter a new six-year Sun cycle. I was told that I would become famous, make great advances in my career, change professions and locations, and emotionally change from a depressing period, into one that was more jubilant and optimistic. And surprisingly, one year later, that is exactly what happened. I went from being an instructor in film studies in Bloomington, Indiana to studying Vedic astrology, investments and commodities, and moving to southeastern Iowa. My ability to forecast my own life and those of my friends very accurately led me to apply Vedic astrology to the markets and became an especially exciting connection!

The Western Zodiac vs. the Indian Zodiac
Vedic astrology is over 10000 years old and has its foundation in ancient science. Parashara, a great seer or ancient scientist, intuited the laws of space and time responsible for the evolution of human consciousness and recorded his findings in a book called the Brihat Hora Sastra. As with all knowledge in book form, over time, the knowledge became fragmented and lost, when it migrated to various other cultures and became distorted. In its purest form, however, Indian astrology has always been acknowledged for its predictive abilities, whereas, Western astrology (with the notable exception of Medieval astrology) has excelled in its analytical and psychological insights.

The first major difference between Vedic and Western astrology lies in the calculation of the longitude of the planets. Ancient Indian astrologers observed that the equinoxes and solstices moved backward by one degree every 72 years, an astronomical phenomenon now known as "*precession.*"

Over time, this has resulted in a difference of slightly over 23 degrees between the tropical Zodiac, used by Western astrologers, and the sidereal Zodiac, used by Vedic astrologers. In essence, the two systems differ in their choice of a zero point for Aries - the Western system uses the position of the spring equinox, while the Indian system uses a fixed star. Thus, when the Sun is moving into Aries according to the Western system, it is still at 6 degrees Pisces in the Indian system.

Planetary Periods: Beyond Transits

A dasha is a period of time during which one's life is influenced or governed by a particular planet. For example, the shortest period, the Sun period, lasts for six years, while the longest period, Venus, lasts for twenty years. These cycles unfold in a fixed sequence and comprise 120 years before they repeat and begin again.

The Dasha Cycle Order:
- Ketu: (Moon's South Node) 7 years
- Venus: 20 years.
- Sun: 6 years.
- Moon: 10 years.
- Mars: 7 years.
- Rahu: (North Node) 18 years.
- Jupiter: 16 years.
- Saturn: 19 years.
- Mercury: 17 years.

Where the cycle begins is based on what lunar mansion or constellation the moon is in at the time of birth. For example, when soybeans started trading in 1936, the moon was in the constellation (nakshatra) of Orion or Mrigashira, which is ruled by the planet Mars. Thus, a sequential enfoldment of cycles began with a seven years Mars period followed by Rahu (North Node of Moon), 18 years, then Jupiter's 16-year period, and into its current period, etc.

If beans had begun trading a day later, then the cycle would have begun from the next constellation, which is ruled by Rahu know as Swati or Betelgeuse. The number of degrees the moon has transited through a nakshatra will determine how much time is left in the initial cycle. Thus, if the moon were in the final degree of the constellation, the initial cycle will begin in the last section of the cycle. (Software is available for rapid computer calculation of these cycles)

Within major cycles are sub-periods or sub-cycles that also unfold in a set sequential pattern. The sub cycle begins with the planet ruling the major cycle and then continues in sequence. For example, the current Saturn period (*at the time of this article publication. — Ed.*) for soybeans started with a Saturn/Saturn period in September 1979, and continued with a Saturn/Mercury period in September 1979 followed by a Saturn/Ketu period, etc.

The major Saturn cycle will finish in 1996 and then soybeans will move into a major Mercury cycle starting with Mercury/Mercury, Mercury/Ketu, Mercury/Venus, etc.

In order to properly use the Indian time cycles and their smaller periods, one must have the exact time of the start of the first future's contract of a commodity. Each minute that one is off can lead to changing the prediction low or high by 4 days. This concept also applies to the location and time of birth of the native in the natal chart, which is in direct correlation with the rising sign on the ascendant.

O'Non and Remnick illustrate the importance of the exact time using a brilliant analogy from physics: *"To launch a rocket ship to the moon, knowledge of the precise angle, time, and location of the launching on earth are necessary. If it is launched at a slightly different time and angle, it will miss by 30,000 to 40,000 miles."*

Predicting the effects of the period is based on the natal chart placements at the time of birth. The positive or negative nature of these periods depends on the placement of the planet by house position, the houses he owns, the houses he aspects, the planets that aspect him, and the sign that he is in.

For example, in a person's natal chart that has Jupiter in Cancer in the 9th with Scorpio rising, a speculator Jupiter period lasting 16 years would expect astounding results, since Jupiter owns the 5th and the 2nd (speculation and accumulated wealth) and is exalted in the house of good luck and good fortune.

Indian astrology is especially fruitful for looking into one's own chart and seeing what periods and transits will bring the most good luck and good fortune. My own experience has supported this notion. Even when timing is correct, if my own chart suggests losses or obstacles in the cycles, I inevitably get caught in trading the wrong direction or missing out an opportunity.

In Indian astrology cycles are stronger than transits and aspects. This concept can explain why some Western astrologers are frustrated in their analyses. According to Indian astrology if the underlying period is positive, then bad transits or aspects will only have a minor negative effect; if the underlying period is negative, even good transits or aspects may not make a dent.

APPLICATION OF THE INDIAN CYCLES TO STOCKS

What is extraordinarily exciting about using dashas or time cycles for prediction is that it allows one to know the exact date that cycles change, to label them, and to quantify whether they are strong ups, minor ups, strong downs, or sideways. If one studies history, patterns and cycles and is familiar with the rules for predicting and interpreting the Indian dasha or time cycle system, the mysterious cycles which seem to govern events manifestations in the material world, is no longer a mystery. The Indian time cycle analysis is a genuine solution to forecasting because it can predict the future, not just suggest it from the past.

CONCLUSION

Anyone attempting to uncover the mysterious laws of nature that underlie, and influence events will be rewarded and intrigued by the depths of Vedic astrology. The study of Vedic astrology leads not only to knowledge of economic laws, but ultimately to knowledge of the Self.

Understanding one's Indian cycles and transits is more important for timing system than just using transits. A combination of the two is astoundingly useful and leads to an awe-inspiring appreciation of the order of natural law. While no astrological system should be used 100% to time event entries and exits, a combination of astrological and technical signals and a knowledge of personal patterns can certainly stack the odds in one's favor and lead to the answer of one of man's greatest metaphysical questions — the relationship between his own consciousness and the universe.

QUICK GUIDE TO YOUR DASHA PERIOD

The term "*Dasha*" in Sanskrit is used to describe the planetary period that is running at a specific time and shows when the effects or significations of a planet will manifest in a person's lifetime.

Each dasha is controlled by one of the nine planets who controls the quality of the fruits harvested based on the position of the planet in the natal chart i.e. sign, house, yoga, nakashatra and aspect.

There are many dashas systems within Vedic astrology with at least 32 of them mentioned by Parashara. The Dasha Paddhati is unique to Vedic astrology and it not found anywhere else. One of the most common dasha systems is the Vimshottari Dasha based on the number 120, assuming that the maximum duration of one's life will not go past 120 years of age. This is a composite time span of all nine planets. The year of the Vimshottari dasha is 365.25 solar days, the time it takes the Sun to return back to its original starting point from the previous year.

The Moon also plays an important role in the dasha system. This is where the lord of the nakshatra is determined based on the placement of the Moon in the one of the 27 lunar mansions known as nakshatras at the time of birth. The sign, navamsha or D-9, and the nakashatra placement of the Moon is the basis for determining the timing of life events such as health, wealth, happiness, activity, general well-being and whether the dasha period will be beneficial or not.

Each dasha period has a main period followed by several sub-periods. For a more in-depth discussion and fascinating look at predicting life events, visit Applied Vedic Astrology for the *Secrets of Timing Your Life 2: Planetary Periods and Dashas* course where we dive deep into how major events unfold and how to time daily events and plan things appropriately.

Below is a quick guide to key issues that can arise in a dasha period. They are sorted by favorable or unfavorable. If the planet is good for the rising sign and is well placed, it will give good results and if the planet is an enemy for the rising sign and poorly placed, it will give unfavorable results.

SUN PERIOD: FAVORABLE AND UNFAVORABLE

Sun periods are favorable when they supported by his planetary friends, the Moon, Mars, and Jupiter and when he is in the sign of Leo or Aries. The Sun is also happy when he is in good living quarters and enjoys being in the 3rd, 6th, 10th and 11th house. He is also happy in the 5th sign of Leo wherever it falls in the zodiac.

When the Sun is strong, his royal qualities emerge, and he acts like a king! He conducts his affairs with a sharp, intuitive mind that yields confidence, so he leads with creative authority balanced with a healthy respect for his needs and those of his people while also promoting the value of freedom. He is not so much concerned with the materiality of life but rather seeks to independently actualize his spiritual and political goals.

Filled with vitality, his ability to organize allows him to lead his government with generosity, inspiring those around him, bringing honor and admiration.

You will find this friend, supportive father, and confident king living or near wooded areas. See his eternal flame that lights the way and leads all out of the darkness.

The Sun is weak when he is receiving aspects from his enemies (Saturn, Venus, Rahu, and Ketu) or living in their uncomfortable signs. He does not enjoy living in the sign of Libra in the zodiac or the 12th house where he loses much of his luster. In these conditions, he cannot focus on his eternal being. He may suffer from heart and eyesight problems; high fevers, ulcers. When the Sun is debilitated and in an unfavorable condition, his ability to shine is muted and his ability to express his power and strength is blocked. He's eclipsed from fulfilling his goals and will exude arrogance, condescension and may become boastful. He will not like his employees or servants and will be power hungry, and pompous. He becomes obsessed with his career as his life pursuit and will often over spend.

MOON PERIOD: FAVORABLE AND UNFAVORABLE

Moon periods are favorable when she is at home in Cancer and Taurus. She loves her home and family where she can be the 'Cosmic mother' and a good parent to all by exercising her skills as a loyal partner who lives a life full of compassion, kindness, emotional nurturing, patience, and the fullness of love! She has a great imagination, heightened sensitivity and often experiences an expansion of consciousness resulting in psychic experiences, which makes her highly intuitive as well as a good listener.

She is graceful and has a strong desire to explore the meaning of life and existence. Anyone around the comforting glow of the Moon would agree that with her steady flow of emotions, she is thankful in her nurturing spirit and kind to all she encounters. She carries herself as a Queen as she observes all her mental emotional chatter and recalls her unchanging nature.

The Moon is badly placed when she is in the 8th house or afflicted by her enemies, Saturn, Mars, Rahu and Ketu. If she is waning or dim her ability to illuminate is weak and she does not like living in the signs of Scorpio, Aquarius or Capricorn where she feels depleted of her precious light.

When she is weak, the Moon is miserable and forlorn. The Queens crown is worn with a heavy heart and she may be overly dependent, clingy, hypersensitive, moody and filled with self-pity. This will lead her to choose dysfunctional friends and partners and promote mood swings or dry emotions. She may develop hoarding tendencies or worry that her loved ones will abandon her. She may suffer from coldness, lung problems, nervous or emotional issues, mood swings, insomnia, excessive mucous, and depression. These conditions may cause her to withdraw, isolate and clam up, failing to express herself or emotions.

MARS PERIOD FAVORABLE AND UNFAVORABLE
Mars periods are favorable when he lives in the signs of Capricorn, Aries, Scorpio, and Leo or when he is receiving a gaze from his friend Jupiter or he is living in the 10th house.

A happy Mars surges into new action with great joy and dynamism! He is eager to serve humanity and with childlike joy, gushes forth in search of growth, movement and change! His desire for fresh karma and his love for adventure leads fills him with inner vitality that needs to be expressed and with his own initiative that isn't reckless, selfish, or destructively angry, he pursues his goals to attain higher states of yogic siddhis, or surge into the fields of science, military, engineering, geology — hoping to make discoveries that will lead to rewards.

Mars is unhappy in the sign of Cancer or receiving aspect glances from Mercury, Saturn, Rahu or Ketu or he is combust by the Sun (unless Cazimi) or in the 7th house where his life force energy is weak. He's reckless and filled with agitation and anger. With animal passion, he may resort to childlike outbursts, bloodshed, and battle cries. He becomes destructive in his thinking and actions. He's uncooperative, selfish, and self-centered. His arrogant nature causes him transforms him into a saboteur where he becomes hostile in relationships and may be impulsive in his sexual advances, leading to sexual conquests. He cheats to get results, which may force litigation. This saboteur behavior may result in abortions, war-like engagements and explosions, loss, suffering, injuries, problems with fire, accidents and health issues (bleeding, surgery, acute infections, liver and gallbladder disorders, toxins in the blood, venereal disease, stroke or heart attack).

RAHU PERIOD FAVORABLE AND UNFAVORABLE

Rahu periods are favorable when he lives in the signs of Gemini, Virgo and Taurus. He enjoys living in the 3rd, 6th, 10th and 11th house of the zodiac and when he is aspected by his friends, Venus or Mercury and Jupiter who helps him to behave and calms his recklessness.

Rahu is full of ambition! When he is at his best, Rahu is creative and artistic seeking ways to turn his inner suffering into Divine manifestation by adapting and accepting the changing nature of his karmic situation. He wants to learn wisdom from every situation he encounters and learn to detach so he can understand his inner eternal reality. Recognizing that living life to the full gusto with dynamic experience, Rahu seeks material success and will ultimately bring latent jewels of expression into your experience through unexpected opportunities for enjoyment in the form of luxuries, friendships, and honors from the state, and recognition of merit. Rahu's goal is to give you gains of material success, so you can learn to detach from them as you learn the futility of the material world being a black hole of *"never enough."* His message is to learn Divine Wisdom from every situation and let go of attachment to the material in favor of your own endless supply of the Divinity that is within the self.

Rahu is unhappy in the houses of Scorpio and Sagittarius or if he is connected to the 1st, 2nd, 4th, 5th, 7th, 8th, 9th, and 12th houses. If he's aspected by enemy signs or stars connected to Saturn, Sun, Moon, or Mars, especially the 9th house, it can be a particularly unfavorable period for him.

When Rahu, is unhappy this karmic axis, feels constrained by forces beyond his control. He is overpowered, overwhelmed and victimized. This is a psychologically intense time for him, and due to his shadowy maneuvers, he suffers the mental anguish of sorrow, and is filled with frustration, bereavement and disappointment. This leads to feelings of dejection and depression, which may create problems with fears and phobias. Feeling empty, and tinged with dissatisfaction, he will often turn to drugs and other addictive behaviors to fill the void of never having enough. The victim of bad company, he may experience theft, loss of wealth, abandonment, and loss of prestige. He will have problems with foreign travel and challenges when traveling abroad. Ultimately, he may become anti-social and steer towards transformation, but he must learn to recognize boundaries, or he will surely suffer difficult to treat health disease, host a weak immune system, experience problems with pollution, suffer from bad dreams and fright or become manic-depressive.

JUPITER PERIOD FAVORABLE AND UNFAVORABLE

Jupiter periods are favorable when he is in Cancer, Pisces, Sagittarius and living in the signs or constellations of his friends: Mars, Moon and Sun. He loves living in the 1st house (Dig Bala) and is happy in the 2nd, 4th, 5th, 7th, 10th, 9th and 11th houses.

Jupiter has a great desire for power, higher status and egoist expansion. He delights in public decorations and throwing lavish festivals, especially if the social gatherings are for his meritorious deeds connect to philanthropy! Please do bring gifts! Attached to material and personal relationships, especially children, Jupiter delights in material affluence and social eminence. He loves community and enjoys discourse, especially about religious and philosophical topics. He will be happy to be your teacher and guide a spiritual pilgrimage in hopes of growth-producing, horizontal expansion of consciousness as you meditate together and experience a detachment from the material. His creed is to help those in need by using his gains and expanding his life in celebration and joy!

Jupiter is constricted when he is in the sign of Capricorn or enemy houses such as Virgo, Gemini, Taurus, Libra or Aquarius. He doesn't enjoy living in the 3rd, 6th, 8th, or 12th house. A planet of expansion, Jupiter feels his energy takes on a level of superficiality in these placements and he is stuck in spiritual materialism. Surprises, sudden expenditures, loss of money unhappy events, are easily passed over with grace as he works to preserve his reputation. He may suffer health issues related to being overweight, high cholesterol, a weak liver, benign tumors or hormonal imbalances.

SATURN PERIOD FAVORABLE AND UNFAVORABLE

Saturn periods are favorable when he is comfortable in the signs of Capricorn, Aquarius, Libra, and Taurus. He enjoys being in the 3rd, 6th and 11th houses and also loves receiving aspects from Jupiter, Venus and Mercury.

Saturn takes great pleasure in overseas travel and seeks prestige from international organizations. He also is not opposed to assisting people in need of having governmental charges dropped. A proponent of psychological transformation, Saturn enjoys exploring deeper insights of the inner workings of the Divine process in accelerating spiritual growth and does his best work by lifting the material veil to prepare us for spiritual change as he trusts the process of loss and turns his sights on the Divine for change.

When Saturn is afflicted and weak he finds himself living in the houses of Aries, Cancer, Leo or Scorpio. He is weak in the 1st, 3rd, 6th and 11th as well as when he is receiving negative glances from his malefic enemies, Mars, Ketu, Rahu and the Sun.

When Saturn is weak, he feels unsupported, lonely, abandoned and forsaken. He wonders if he's been marooned and this leaves him emotionally dry with melancholy. Persecuted by the state, he is robbed of material gifts and devoid of sensual gratification, he fears for his future. This leads him to suffer health problems including low vitality, weak digestion (he just can't stomach these things), constipation (he's can't seem to get moving) pain, arthritis, and tumors and feeling old.

The best affirmation for Saturn is: "*I am not rushed, I accept delays and setbacks, I work hard, and I handle my life responsibly.*"

MERCURY PERIOD FAVORABLE AND UNFAVORABLE

Mercury periods are favorable when he is in the houses of Gemini, Virgo and Libra. He is particularly strong in the 1st and 10th house or when he receives supportive aspect glances from his friends Venus and Jupiter. If he is close to heat the Sun, it's not a problem for him as he is the messenger of the King and used to being in the presence of the Sun, so he doesn't get burned.

Mercury has a sharp intellect that energizes his mind with curiosity! He loves to explore and hopes to uncover the mysteries of the Universe. Using discrimination, he overcomes many situations as he seeks profitable business partnerships and expansion in foreign lands. He enjoys monetary, literacy and social rewards for his work and is highly skilled in accounting, law, communication, public speaking, business, writing and higher education.

A frequent flyer traveler, Mercury, as a messenger, encounters a lot of people during his travels. Always interested in learning and expanding his knowledge about the human experience, he manages to balance his heart and intellect to integrate all of his good experiences to uncover priceless nuggets of wisdom that he can share in his many modes of expression whether written, speech, music, film, art, sending a letter, an email, a text, a dream, a hunch, a phrase on a billboard sign, sending a Morse code or smoke signal - Mercury will always find a way to deliver his message!

When Mercury is weak, you will find him in the signs of Pisces, Aries, or Scorpio, the 4th house or the 7th house. He may also be aspected by his enemies, Mars, Saturn, Jupiter and Ketu.

When Mercury is unhappy he broods and spends a lot of time in his head thinking and failing to act. He becomes an anxious hypochondriac. The intellect starts to dominate his feelings and he waffles back and forth when trying to make decisions. That leaves Mercury spaced out, checked out and worn out with mental fatigue. His relationships suffer as he seeks satisfaction with multiple spiritual partners that are idealized and too practical for him. He seeks solace in many spiritual paths, which are unsatisfactory, and he slips into depression. Other health problems with cough, allergies and speech defects affect him and he may develop nervous disorders.

KETU PERIOD FAVORABLE AND UNFAVORABLE

Ketu periods are favorable when he is in the signs of Pisces, Scorpio, and Sagittarius. He also enjoys being in the 6th and 11th house as well as being aspected by beneficial friends, Jupiter, Mercury and Venus.

Ketu is blind but still has the third sight of higher, occult knowledge when strong. He has a love for meditation and astrology. As a seeker of enlightenment, Divine Wisdom and esoteric studies, he retreats from the material world to honor his passions and opens the portals of the deeper truths and hidden mysteries to of life by initiating us into the mysteries of existence. He can bring honor and status as well as travel to foreign countries.

When Ketu is weak, he is sitting in the house of Gemini or Taurus; receiving malefic glances from the Sun, Mars, Saturn and the Moon. Ketu also finds himself in the unfavorable 2nd, 8th and 12th houses.

Ketu debilitated is always seeking to change direction. He feels disillusioned with life and questions reality. This creates emotional knots and distortions, leaving him feeling unsettled. He dwells on the mistakes of the past and in deep isolation, he isolates himself or spends him time with undesirable people that could cause him humiliation or lead to his imprisonment. He wants to give up all material attachments and rush off to the ashram and practice spiritual escapism. He is very judgmental towards materiality and will give you gains but he will take away what is given within 7 years to teach the lesson of non-attachment to desires. When weak, he suffers from mysterious and hard to diagnose diseases, cancer, infections, and he is prone to receiving wrong surgeries.

VENUS PERIOD FAVORABLE AND UNFAVORABLE

Venus periods are favorable when she is living in the signs of Pisces, Libra, and Taurus and Cancer. She is particularly strong in the 4th house but does worse in the 6th, 7th and 10th houses. She loves receiving friendly glances from her aspecting friends, Mercury and Jupiter.

Venus loves to socialize in the material world and enjoys harmonious relationships. She has lots of friends and spends her time painting, composing poetry, singing, dancing, attending fine art performances and enjoys fine dining, good wine, sexual play and physical comforts in luxurious living spaces that are sensual. She is gratified and balanced. When Venus is happy she fulfills wishes. Venus is a lover of LOVE!

When Venus is unhappy, you will find her in the 3rd, 6th, 7th or 10th house. She may also be in the houses of Virgo, Scorpio or Aries. Mars, Ketu and Sun may send malefic aspect glances her way and weaken her energy.

Depending the house of Venus' depletion, she will be unhappy in her work, lack purpose, and host a lazy professional life. She will find herself picking bad relationships, ill-suited mates because of her low self-esteem and that will lead to broken romances, unorthodox relationships, possible problems with impotency, or hyper sex drive where she leaps into intimate relationships too quickly. This creates mental unhappiness, dissipation of life force and over-sensitivity. She finds work distasteful and may be dominated by her loved-ones. She may lack staying power and have poor grooming habits. Health problems will arise in the kidneys, bladder and reproductive areas and she may suffer miscarriage or have problems conceiving.

Special thanks to Bepin Bihar for his great insights and teaching on the qualities of Dashas.

DIG BALA AND MARANA KARAKA STHANA OR BEST AND WORST HOUSE PLACEMENT FOR PLANETS

Certain planets do not do well in certain houses because their significations bring out their worst qualities and these placements can get ignored sometimes but they have a deep suffering quality that can bring out more karmic challenges than what follows conventional practice.

The opposite case is that planets that have Dig Bala gain strength from certain houses.

Here is a quick guide for best house placement and worse house placement.
Note: These house places in the natal chart, moon chart or other divisional charts (Vargas) will elicit results for those specific charts.

Sun: in the 10th house is best. Sun thrives in activity, in seeking status and being recognized so Sun in the 10th house has the highest energy. Sun in the 12th house is the most challenging placement because the Sun is hidden, unnoticed and feels abandoned, unsupported and secretive. This may have been a result of an unavailable father and leads to poor self-confidence, heart problems, health problems and breathing problems.

Moon: in the 4th house is the best placement for the moon where happiness reigns, mother is at home and in the heart. Emotional support is full and one feels nurtured, affectionate, content and with expanding, full feelings. Moon in the 8th house is the most challenging as the emotions are stuck, repressed, dry or not experienced. This can lead to shyness, distance from mother, sexual extremes, jealous, intense desire to be loved and dangers from water accidents.

Mars: does best in the 10th house where it is innovative, smart, cheerful, quick to get results, self-sufficient at work and where status, action and recognition occur. Mars has the most difficultly when placed in the 7th house where sexual conquest, ego and force overtake duty and service. This often leads to fights in relationship at work, selfish partners, aggression, disputes and reproductive problems.

Saturn: does best in the 7th house where it has Dig Bala and this is the natural 7th sign of the zodiac, Libra, where diplomacy and skill at the workplace bring rewards. It produces practical business people who are loyal and dutiful in partnerships. Saturn has Marana Karaka Sthana (MKS) and is at its worse in the 1st house (connected to the 1st sign of the zodiac Aries) where fear in the head takes over grounded diplomacy. This position creates selfishness, depression, isolation, slow physical development and low self-esteem.

Jupiter: has Dig Bala and does best in the 1st house where wisdom, joy and generosity create great status, generosity and luck with children, wealth, good coaches and teachers. Jupiter does worse in the 3rd house where wisdom is lost in a Kama play of sexual pleasures and games. It leads to low energy, poor attention, boredom, and lack of resources and poor attention to detail.

Mercury: does best in the 1st house where intellectual prowess and reason lead to success and good cheer. Mercury here is conscientious, principled, ethical, good at speech, math and writing. Mercury does worse in the 7th house or the 4th house. In the 4th house the intellect destroys the emotional contentment of happiness and prevents expression of feeling. In the 7th house it becomes the immature child/prince having love affairs with no thought to the ethical consequences. It also makes one too critical of partners and does not allow love to flow smoothly.

Venus: does best in the 4th house of happiness, home and contentment where it creates love of family, nurturing and love of elegant homes. When it is in the 6th house (i.e., 6th sign like Virgo) where it creates conflicts with partners (partner as enemy) and has a perverse love of fighting, it has difficulty. The 6th house is the house of celibacy and Venus is more at home in its sexual energy and this leads to problems.

Rahu: does well in 10th house where it gains status at work but in the 9th house it is considered the worse placement or Marana Karaka Sthana where it usurps father, Guru, bosses and traditional religion in a rebellious innovation. It is a schemer here holding onto private, bizarre philosophies rather than embracing the traditional.

Ketu: does well in the 12th house where it has a natural placement for Moksha and may bring a mystical element to sexual expression. Ketu dies in the 4th house where happiness and contentment take it off the path. Early unhappiness from the mother may lead to broken homes, problems with homes, vehicles or irregular heartbeats.

Of course, these rules are general and will be colored by sign, planetary aspects, nakshatra placements and other associations. A planet exalted or in its own sign in MKS (Marana Karaka Stana) may have a better chance at overcoming a poor placement like having Sun in the 12th house in Leo but the planet may still lack poor judgment and not get through it as the 12th house placements are often life-long journeys.

If the owner of the house where the planet is placed is afflicted, suffering may be more intense such as Sun in the 12th and aspected by Saturn and or Rahu may even create an "*almost*" deep curse. The remedy for these poor placements of Marana Karaka Sthana is to worship the ruler of the Karaka of the house that is involved. So, if Mars is in the 7th house, then one needs to worship Venus, the karaka for the 7th house to overcome the relationship problems.

Special thanks to Sanjay Rath from his wisdom in bringing MKS to the forefront of Vedic Jyotish studies. I have elaborated on his general house guidelines to flesh them out in psychological and spiritual detail.

UNDERSTANDING PLANETARY OPPOSITIONS AND OPPOSING SIGNS

Note on How to Use This: THE MOVEMENTS OF THE NODES, THE FULL MOONS AND THE OPPOSITIONS OF THE OUTER AND INNER PLANETS CAN YIELD MUCH RICHER INFORMATION USING THE BELOW ANALYSIS.

I learn a great deal from Western astrologers and their psychological orientation and find that bringing their concepts into Vedic astrology is very helpful for understand basic archetypal impulses of the human psyche. While the material below is basic, it is worthy of review with a Vedic twist.

Basic natural house oppositions between the natural houses of the zodiac (Pisces as the natural 12th house and Virgo as the natural 6th house) set up basic archetypal tensions that we all go through in our life. The value of the material below is seen most through the transits of Rahu and Ketu since they are always in opposition tugging and pulling between desire and letting go, "*I want,*" and "*I do not want.*" Rahu and Ketu create this pull for one and a half years during its transits.

We also see this energy at Full Moons for a few days each month when the Sun and Moon are in opposing signs. Less frequently, we will get it between the outer and inner planets.

The 7th house aspect of any planet creates a desire for the opposing sign that is being aspected. For example, Saturn's aspect on the 7th house has a decaying or negative impact on that house. Mars's 7th house aspect causes us to fight and protect the house where the energy falls, which means those houses, are under attack. Jupiter's 7th house aspect is immortal nectar and creates value, respect and dignity for that which it aspects and purifies it. Mercury's 7th house aspect will give knowledge and information and learning about the house that it aspects. Moon's 7th house aspect will often create obsessions with obsessions with the house that is being influenced and aspected.

Below is a basic guide to remembering house and sign oppositions:

Aries/Libra or 1st house/7th house.
This is the basic relationship axis, where Aries and the 1st house represent "*self*" and Libra and the seventh house represent "*other*." Where Aries - 1st house is about self-assertion, Libra - 7th is about compromise. People born with planets in both Aries and Libra or both the 1st and 7th need to learn the balance between these two needs and it is the perpetually in a dance with Mars wanting to be the hero and go it alone and Venus and Libras who always have to do it together.

Taurus/Scorpio or 2nd house/8th house.
This polarity deals with material manifestation (Taurus and the 2nd house) versus spiritual transformation (Scorpio and the 8th house). While Taurus - 2nd house deals with matter, personal values, material goods, possessions, and security, Scorpio - 8th house rules the destruction of material (Ketu), and change/transformation. Ketu is often forgotten as the secondary owner of Scorpio with its mystical and spiritual nature to wander in search of enlightenment, which is so opposed to the earthiest sign of Taurus and its desire to bathe in the sense and accumulate more. When Rahu goes through Taurus and Ketu through Scorpio, this opposition will be strongest, and we will see this again **September 2020 - March 2022.**

Gemini/Sagittarius or 3rd house/9th house.
This is a mental axis, where Gemini and the 3rd house represent the "*lower mind*" and Sagittarius and the 9th house represent the "higher mind" mind and the wisdom that spirituality and religion brings to the table. Gemini and the 3rd house rule curiosity and logical thinking. Sagittarius and the 9th house rule a broader way of thinking — the quest for the meaning of why we are here in is search for the Divine. Inherent in this conflict is the opposition between the logic of Mercury and the 3rd house and the faith and dogma of Sagittarius in the 9th house. It is playing out strongly now between the US sign of Sagittarius and the war with the media represented by Gemini with transiting and weak Saturn in Sagittarius fueling the decaying flames.

Cancer/Capricorn or 4th house/10th house.
This connection highlights the private life, domesticity and the need for a home base reflected in the nurturing (Cancer and the 4th house) versus the public life, career, reputation, and accountability (Capricorn and the tenth house). Cancer and the 4th sign are connected to attachments and love, while Capricorn rules achievements and rewards/punishments. This is the archetypal conflict between being out in the world and wanting to be secure at home. Ketu moved into Capricorn in September and Rahu moved into Cancer, so this has stirred up the desire the peak in housing prices and the desire for home and security while Ketu will create less of an attachment to work and rising in one's career.

Leo/Aquarius or 5th/11th house.
We are always juggling the balance between individual status and fame (Leo and 5th house) and humanitarian service and groups. (Aquarius and 11th house.) Leo and the 5th house rule creative self-expression and the boost to the individual ego that we receive through pleasure and romance, while Aquarius and the 11th house rule the groups and service to humanity. It seems that we are always fighting between ourselves and our personal glory and the need to serve society and do humanitarian work for selfless service. Rahu transiting Leo and Ketu in Aquarius has stirred that pot for this in **2016 - 2017** but it ended in September when the nodes transited into Cancer/Capricorn. Ketu in Aquarius was causing people to run away from groups in favor personal advancement.

Virgo/Pisces or 6th/12th houses.

This polarity is the service axis, and it deals with the balance between day-to-day functions and routines, physical health, work and the need for order (Virgo and the 6th house), spiritual health, transcending the material world, and the infinite (Pisces and 12th house). Virgo and the 6th house rules our tools and techniques that we use to deal with day-to-day life, while Pisces and the 12th house rule the tools that we use to deal with our spirituality and our desire for Moksha and to find God. We are often at odds between the drudgery of going to work every day and our desire for our highest calling to realize God.

2018 Planetary Oppositions

DATE	TIME EDT	PLANETS	SIGNS
APRIL 17	02:59	VENUS/JUPITER	BETWEEN ARIES AND LIBRA
MAY 08	20:39	SUN/JUPITER	BETWEEN ARIES AND LIBRA
MAY 23	01:54	MERCURY/JUPITER	BETWEEN ARIES AND LIBRA
MAY 26	02:40	VENUS/SATURN	BETWEEN GEMINI AND SAGITTARIUS
JUNE 05	21:47	MERCURY/SATURN	BETWEEN GEMINI AND SAGITTARIUS
JUNE 15	12:54	VENUS/MARS	BETWEEN CANCER AND CAPRICORN
JUNE 21	12:54	VENUS/MARS	BETWEEN CANCER AND CAPRICORN

2018 Planetary Oppositions

DATE	TIME EDT	PLANETS	SIGNS
JUNE 23	05:24	MERCURY/PLUTO	BETWEEN GEMINI AND SAGITTARIUS
JUNE 27	09:28	SUN/SATURN	BETWEEN GEMINI AND SAGITTARIUS
JULY 05	07:49	MERCURY/MARS	BETWEEN CANCER AND CAPRICORN
JULY 12	06:01	SUN/PLUTO	BETWEEN GEMINI AND SAGITTARIUS
JULY 24	15:23	VENUS/NEPTUNE	BETWEEN LEO AND AQUARIUS
JULY 26	07:49	SUN/MARS	BETWEEN CANCER AND CAPRICORN
SEPTEMBER 07	22:14	SUN/NEPTUNE	BETWEEN LEO AND AQUARIUS

2018 Planetary Oppositions

SEPTEMBER 12	05:01	VENUS/URANUS	BETWEEN LIBRA AND ARIES
SEPTEMBER 13	21:32	MERCURY/NEPTUNE	BETWEEN LEO AND AQUARIUS
OCTOBER 10	13:35	MERCURY/URANUS	BETWEEN LIBRA AND ARIES
OCTOBER 23	20:46	SUN/URANUS	BETWEEN LIBRA AND ARIES
OCTOBER 31	04:45	VENUS/URANUS	BETWEEN LIBRA AND ARIES
NOVEMBER 30	21:12	VENUS/URANUS	

GUIDE TO PLANETARY ASPECTS: UNDERSTANDING THE QUALITIES OF PLANETARY ASPECTS

The lights that planets throw around the sky are called aspects and there are two types of these "*glances*." The one glance that people understand the most is the aspect gaze from planet(s) to another planet(s) or planet(s) to signs and houses. This article is intended to discuss the qualities of planetary aspects to help you understand the quality of a planets aspect gaze.

Often an astrologer will say that a planet has a benefic, meaning good or malefic, meaning bad, aspect on a house or planet but Vedic astrology is so much more precise!

An aspect from the Moon is connected to desire while an aspect from Venus may suggest love of something. We all need to learn to be more specific in our language when describing what planetary glances mean.

Aspects glances or gazes from planet(s) to other planet(s) and houses, represent karma that wants to deliver a manifestation(s) into the material realm and the nature or signification(s) of the planet, whether a benefit, hindrances or annoyance, delivers that karma.

BENEFIC ASPECTS: JUPITER, VENUS AND MERCURY

Benefic aspects from Jupiter, Venus and a benefic Mercury (i.e., Mercury connected to benefic planets OR signs - Mercury can also be a mild malefic) create positive experiences and malefic aspects create unhappy experiences. The planet(s) house, sign and Nakshatra placement is the storage container where the karma is kept and shows the nature of desire.

For example, Venus in Virgo, in the 3rd house, a house of Kama and passions would have a strong stored up energy for sexual desire. Its aspects on the 9th house of Pisces, ruled by Jupiter, would possibly indicate, especially with Jupiter's placement, a sexual relationship with a teacher or Guru, assuming Venus has additional malefic energy besides the highly charged sexual energy of Virgo.

Note: The benefic and malefic qualities of planets are discussed in general terms and it should be noted that not all planets are benefic or malefic for every ascendant rising sign. For example, Jupiter is a great malefic and Saturn a great benefic for Taurus ascendant rising signs.
In general, the benefic planets (Venus, Jupiter, and Mercury) create good desires:

Venus: show what we love or desire and what we love, we wish to possess. Venus aspecting the 2nd house may show what we love to eat or its aspects on the 12th house show that we love foreign travel or ashrams or even our love of sleep. Venus usually shows love of material possessions such as cars, houses and dresses so Venus in the

4th house will create love of beautiful and luxurious homes. Venus always aspects the 7th house from itself so it always creates a desire to find a partner and love in our life. Venus aspecting the 9th will show a great love of father and Guru.

Mercury: provides informational reconnaissance to provide knowledge and learning about something. Mercury is the student ready to learn and wherever his aspects land is where he desires knowledge. It creates a place for our favorite subject of learning. So, Mercury aspecting the 12th house will create a desire to study spirituality, and meditation. A Mercury aspect or association with the Moon will create a desire to study psychology and the nature of the human mind. A person with Mercury aspecting Rahu might desire to study viruses or specific diseases. Rahu in the 8th house may have a strong desire to study astrology if it is connected to a Mercury ruled house like Gemini or Virgo. (You get the idea).

Jupiter: shows all the good karma that we have done and remind us that when we continue to do charity, service and philanthropy in this life, we create new karma for the future. Jupiter's aspects show that which we value in life and that which we respect. Jupiter can purify any area that his aspects touch. One will value whatever houses Jupiter touches, so Jupiter in the 1st house, aspecting the 7th is a wonderful placement for relationships where one values, honors and treasures, the spouse. Whatever planets Jupiter aspects, he will honor and value. Jupiter aspecting Saturn will lead one to honor and respect his employees and Jupiter aspecting Mars will mean that he will honor soldiers and policeman and treat his enemies with dignity. Jupiter aspecting Venus means he will honor his spouse and have great value for her.

Here is a quick summary of the types of desires involved:
Sun: Desires related to soul, career, good fortune, father and that which we consider worth living for. Sun aspects are not malefic but creates burning, cruelty, selfishness and egotistical acts.
Moon: Desires mind, family, home, mother, obsessions of the mind.

Mars: Desires conflict, power, ambition, property, siblings — that which is worth fighting for. Mars aspects cause fighting, debts, fires and accidents when Mars is afflicted but when Mars is strong, it may bring out the highest aspect of the fighter to serve, protect society and country.

Mercury: Desires speech, communication, learning, profession, wealth, friends and relatives. Mercury aspects show what one wants to learn and understand.

Jupiter: Aspects indicate desires for knowledge, good fortune, spirituality, values, children, teachers or gurus. Jupiter aspects show what one values and respects.

Venus: Aspects show desires for love, enjoyment, sex, comforts and relationships to beloveds, wife and sisters.

Saturn: Aspects indicate desires related to one's weaknesses, blocks, suffering and hard work. Saturn aspects cause weakness, suffering, poverty and illness.

Rahu: (North Node) Aspects indicate desires for enjoyment, manipulation, and ambition. Rahu causes shocks, cheating and losses. Most people do not know that Rahu has a sneaky 30 degrees or 2nd house aspect on planets from itself aside from its trinal aspects. (A Rahu aspect the 1st, 5th, 9th from itself and also has the sneaky 30-degree aspect as stated above)

Ketu: (South Node) Does not have desires so he has no aspects. Many think the trinal aspects are important within 2-3 degrees and they are because that would create a conjunction in the D-9 or navamsha chart and have an important impact in creating deep past life regrets, past life karma or creates a black hole with the planet that is being affected. (Ketu has no aspects)

Note: Most of you know that Jupiter aspects the 1st, 5th and 9th house from itself and Mars the 4th, 7th and 8th house from itself and Saturn the 3rd, 7th and the 10th house from itself. Other planets (Sun, Moon, Venus, Jupiter, and Mercury) the 7th house from itself but most of us do not think about the qualities that the planets create through their glances or that the energy that they throw is really dependent on being 3-5 degrees in conjunction or in aspect to have a major impact. Special thanks to Sanjay Rath and Zoran Radosavljevic for their insights on this material.

UNDERSTANDING PLANETARY COMBUSTION: PLANETS TOO CLOSE TO THE SUN

At various times of the year, planets in the sky may fall behind the Sun and may not be visible due to the blinding energies of the Sun. This is called combustion or not visible in the sky. This is one of the more difficult events in Vedic astrology particularly when this happens within 2-3 degrees as the significations of the planet are destroyed and the darker energies of the combust planet may arise. If you are born with planetary combustion then when it happens in transit, it is particularly activated. Still if the combust planet is the ruler of your chart, you will always feel a strong impact from the combustion in transit particularly when it is within 2 – 3 degrees. As always there are so many combinations and exceptions.

In natal charts less than 10 degrees is usually a problem but any planet within 1 - 4 degrees is particularly damaged. Then there is the odd case of Cazimi from Medieval astrology where a planet within 40 minutes of the Sun goes into the heart of the Sun and is very energized by it in a positive way. However, there are a few parameters for natal charts that are known as saving factors for the planet. Sometimes a planet can perform very well in the horoscope if there are other ameliorating factors.

These include:
- If combust, a planet is occupying its own or exaltation sign in the horoscope.
- If combust planet is getting a strong benefic aspect from Jupiter, Mercury or Venus.
- If combust planet is sitting in the house where it gets directional strength like Mercury and Jupiter in the 1st house, Moon and Venus in the 4th house, Saturn in the 7th house and Mars and Sun in the 10th house.
- If combust planet is exalted and well placed in divisional charts (Specially in D-9 & D-60).
- If combust planet is retrograding in horoscope.

PERIODS OF PLANETARY COMBUSTION: CAZIMI

A planet, when it is too close to the Sun in conjunction by degrees is drained of its energy and considered to be 'combust' or weaker by the Sun's intense energy rays, hence, it is 'combust.' Combustions within 2 - 4 degrees of the Sun causes planets to lose their energy and planets within 1 - 2 degrees are considered by some to be completely combust, in theory, destroyed and unable to produce any of their qualities, however, there is a unique condition that occurs when a planet is with 40 minutes of the Sun which is called Cazimi when the planet receives the Sun's Divine energy by infusion.

Cazimi combustion can spiritualize individuals as it takes away material manifestation and the light of the Divine is infused into the soul with combustion.

Retrograde Mercury is not combusted because it is behind the Sun's disc.

Retrograde Venus is combusted but not combust when it is in forward motion within 8 - 10 degrees of the Sun.

Mars does not become as vulnerable to combustion because fire does not extinguish fire. Still depending on the sign and other aspects and other planets involved, it can increase volatility and blow out Mars.

Saturn Combustion: Can bring out the darker qualities of Saturn. In the early stages, it may promote hard work, efficiency, clarity and reliability at work but as it gets closer to the can make work intense, cause problems between bosses and co-workers, mistreatment by employers and resistance to authority. On an emotional level, it can hurt confidence and bring on depression.

In Ayurveda, Sun/Saturn combination if in your natal chart in the 4th, 5th or 10th or 11th houses, may raise blood pressure and if severely afflicted can lead to heart problems so go easier with exercise and avoid stressful conditions that may affect your heart. This might impact Virgos, Leos, Pisces and Aquarians rising or Sun signs more. Go easier if you have heart or high blood pressure problems the next few weeks and visit your doctor to monitor it if it seems to be acting up.

Sun also rules health for everyone, and I notice the Saturn affliction can hurt the immune system which is also why a lot of flu seems to break out with this combustion combination. Products like Colostrum can enhance your immune system. Get plenty of rest and keep your immune system strong by cutting down on sugar.

If you are born with the Sun very close to Saturn in your natal chart within a few degrees, this signature could lead to over-responsibility and taking on too much work and this could stress your heart and circulatory system so lighten up if you are start pushing yourself. If you are running a Sun/Saturn period or a Saturn/Sun period and have a tight signature in your natal chart, this transit may be most difficult.

Saturn cuts off the energy of the Sun and restricts its ability to shine so you may feel lonely and cut-off or inclined to break relationships or quit work because of a conflict with a supervisor. This can lead to depression. The anecdote for Saturn is always Venus so women, relationships, singing, food, music and dance all help lighten Saturn so avoid isolation.

This is a time to be disciplined about your meditation practice and yoga and other spiritual practices because these lighten the burden and give us more strength to deal with everything. The tendency is to skip that which is good for us when we are challenged but that's like taking off a winter coat when it's below zero.

Donate time and money to help those in need. This is one way to address karma and by getting out of our own stuff, we feel better and move through our own karma.

Be disciplined with diet and exercise. The tendency is to use food to cover up difficult emotions or skip exercise because we feel tired or lazy. So much illness (6th house) can be overcome if we are disciplined doing what is good for us.

Venus Combustion: Can raise jealous issues so remember to praise and appreciate others at this time, help them, applaud their success and good fortune. This conjunction can also lead to manipulative energy in relationships, cause annoyances, friction and problems so remember to accept people with all their imperfections or you will likely be seething with anger.

While combustion is one of the most damaging things for a planet in Vedic astrology, it turns out total combustion within the last degree is a blessing. The exact conjunction of the Sun with Venus can be a really good thing and is called Cazimi and comes from medieval astrology and is used to refer to planets that are so close to a conjunction with the Sun that they are "*in the heart*" of the Sun. They actually become energized by the Sun and their most positive qualities come out.

Venus Cazimi should be a great day for creativity, artistic development and love. It may increase socializing, luxuriating, going out for fun and amusement. If you are a woman, it may create incredible magnetism and make you Queen for a day and you will attract men more easily. It's a good day to hit the drawing board if you are an artist. This fulcrum point will last just a day and then the problem issues with Venus combust returns so be sure to watch the transit degree points.

Taurus and Libra rising signs in Vedic astrology may continue to experience intense fatigue as the Sun moves toward Venus so get extra rest and watch over-eating or zoning out watching too many movies or you will get exhausted. Take care of the reproductive organs as problems can happen during this transit. If you are feeling friction, take a walk and get out the house rather than get into battle with your partner.

The best outlet for Venus frustrated energy during combustion periods would be to do some wild dancing, take a craft class, sing loudly with the radio turned up or go on a wild shopping spree or create a massive artistic dinner with friends that you are not likely to get into fights with.

Mercury Combustion: Can create a very busy, buzzy and frustrated mind with some agitation. When Mercury is beneficially supported by the Sun in Cazimi it can create deep analytical abilities, shrew business practices and good financial planning so maybe a good day for bookkeeping but as the strength of the Mercury wanes away when combust (check transit combustion dates), one will have to manage money more carefully and make sure that ethics return to business. Mercury transits are quick. Retrograde Mercury combustion is not much of a problem except within a few degrees in transit.

Find time for meditation and ways to quiet the mind. The cobra pose and the shoulder stand in yoga can quiet the mind a bit and balance Mercury. Be patient with angry communication from others and technology problems and know that it will lift. Retrograde Mercury combustion is probably about 75% less difficult and can be discounted.

Jupiter Combustion: Can burn up its significations so things like the liver, which is ruled by Jupiter, may have more problems functioning. Jupiter rules optimism and judgment and when it gets too close to the Sun, it can be falsely optimistic about something or be too critical or judgment. Be realistic and check your facts careful and lighten up on people if you are feeling heavy. The exact conjunction of Sun and Jupiter can be really powerful for the Sun and Jupiter as the Sun will take on all of Jupiter's energy and feel uplifted by generosity, confidence and expansion.

Avoid heavy and oily foods — especially at night — which are hard to metabolize and use liver tonics and lemon in water in the morning to tonify the liver. This is a good time for Panchakarma at the Ayurveda clinic or a simple diet of rice and dahl to give your liver a rest. So, stay on top of liver health and check your facts carefully and avoid false optimism so that you will not get disappointed.

Conditions of Planetary Combustion

Planet	Degree	2018 Periods of Combustion		
MOON	UNDER 12 DEGREES FROM THE SUN			
MARS	UNDER 17 DEGREES FROM THE SUN			
MERCURY	UNDER 14 DEGREES FROM THE SUN AND 12 DEGREES IF IN RETROGRADE MOTION	27 JANUARY TO 05 MARCH 25 MARCH TO 08 APRIL 24 MAY TO 18 JUNE	01 AUGUST TO 16 AUGUST 27 JANUARY TO 05 MARCH 05 SEPTEMBER TO 11 OCTOBER	21 NOVEMBER TO 02 DECEMBER
JUPITER	UNDER 11 DEGREES FROM THE SUN	12 NOVEMBER TO 9 DECEMBER		
VENUS	UNDER 10 DEGREES FROM THE SUN AND 8 DEGREES IF IN RETROGRADE MOTION	28 NOVEMBER 2017 TO 19 FEBRUARY 2018 21 OCTOBER TO 31 OCTOBER 28 NOVEMBER 2017 TO 19 FEBRUARY 2018		
SATURN	UNDER 15 DEGREES FROM THE SUN	04 DECEMBER 2017 TO JANUARY 07, 2018 16 DECEMBER 2018 TO JANUARY 19, 2019 04 DECEMBER 2017 TO JANUARY 07, 2018		
CAZIMI	PLANETS WITHIN 40 MINUTES OF THE SUN			

SECRETS OF RETROGRADE PLANETS

I frequently get questions about retrograde planets and they are often misunderstood because everyone always thinks of Mercury retrograde as being universally bad and that is not true for everyone. Mercury went retrograde on December 3rd, 2017 so hopefully, you got your ducks in a row. It is thought if the retrograde planet is the owner of the chart, then it becomes stronger for the person but makes them more *"reflective"* psychologically. The houses, nakshatras and signs of the retrograde position in the natal chart are key and then in transit, if it is in the natal chart, it gets triggered in transit.

Retrograde planets are brighter and closer to the earth. So, they are focused on the past and the disappointments and abuses they suffered. This makes them look within and they become confused about moving forward but they don't want to go backwards so this creates a situation of deep introspection. So, this creates a planetary influence of thinking rather than doing that happens according to the planet that is retrograde. For example, if Saturn is retrograde, one may a lot about spirituality but only in the reflective sense rather than actually practicing it.

Some general things you can say about retrogrades:

- The planet's energy may reverse, pulling the energy back into the sign that it is retrograding into.
- There are more medical problems from retrograde planets in Ayurveda.
- The flow of the planet's normal energy is disrupted and the house that the planet occupies will be affected and not work fully.
- The houses that the planets own will also be weaker.
- The significations that the planet or house produce become a source of confusion and is surrounded by stress and difficulty but because the retrograde planet is closer to Earth, it shines brighter and illuminates the internal, psychological aspect of how the quality of the signification feels, hence, its force of intelligence becomes very developed because it is 'reflecting.'
- Note: The Sun and Moon never retrograde.
- Retrograde makes the planet stronger which does not always mean better.
- Retrograde malefics like Saturn and Mars may have more strength to cause more harm unless they are the chart lord and then they are better for the person, in which case they may make the person inwardly reflect to find ones' true source of strength.
- Planets that are exalted and retrograde may become passive and thus are conducive to material or spiritual achievements in life if they are in the 1st, 4th, 7th or 10th houses.
- Dasha periods of debilitated or exalted retrograde planets deliver results during their dasha periods. This is good for spiritual advancement.
- Some special rules apply to combust retrograde planets as they can accelerate spiritual growth during their dasha periods.

- Note about the outer planets: Pluto, Neptune and Uranus are in retrograde motion approximately 5 months every year.
- Parashara indicates that a retrograde motion will reverse the effect of an exalted or debilitated planet but that is controversial.
- Exalted Retrograde Saturn acts debilitated — not totally true. The reality is that an exalted Saturn will still externally produce good results such as good technical competence, making one clever, focused, well-organized, faithful, practical and good in foreign connections but internally, a person may have the debilitated qualities of Saturn including some depression, self-deprecation, fear and feeling frustrated even if outwardly things go well. There becomes a schism between the outer and inner realities.
- Retrograde planets must be present in the natal chart to manifest their qualities during retrograde transits but may not show their problems when direct in transit.

Some general qualities of retrograde planets in a natal chart:

Mars: Less inclined to act. Procrastinators. Avoids conflict. Doesn't compete. Avoids battles. Avoids confrontation. May be hotheaded or excessively competitive with a chip on their shoulder.

Mercury: More intuitive people and reverses Mercury's normal logical mind. Non-linear thinkers. Doesn't feel heard or understood. Hesitates to speak his or her mind. Doesn't have clarity. Not sure how to express ideas or oneself. May stutter.

Jupiter: Creates bargain hunters and people who help the disadvantaged and weak. Searches for the 'inner guide or teacher.'

Venus: Reverse sexual norms and they could become celibate, frigidity in women or some tendency toward gay/bi sexual or being at odds with traditional marriage and partnering.

Saturn: Renunciate, monastic, self-isolating; alone; rejects others so they will not be rejected; grim, depressed. Fear of time, death, decay, loss, separation, disease, transitions and infirmity.

Uranus: An abrupt, forceful or extreme change that is unconventional

Neptune: Inner fears about making dreams a reality, keeps ideas hidden, practices escapism, may be deceptive and wear a mask to fit in.

Pluto: Inner fears about suppression and authority, phobias, manipulation, betrayal, the realms of the taboo, sexuality, death, will be in denial, strives for security, and wants to be in control, scared of transformation and change.

As always there are many factors that govern judging every planet including how many benefic and malefic aspects associations there are to the retrograde planet, placement in the D-9 chart, nakshatra influences, houses involved, and houses owned but these are some general guidelines.

Special thanks to Bill Levacy, James Braha, Sanjay Rath and Sam Geppi for some of their insights on this material.

GUIDE TO RISING SIGNS: NEW LIGHT ON ZODIACAL SIGNS ARIES – PISCES

From our first glimpse into astrology from the newspaper, we became proud to pronounce our Sun sign and say, *"I am an Aries,"* and read about our transits.

Zodiacal signs also fascinate us but do we know their true meaning and power, energy or Shakti? The point of this article is that we get too attached to thinking we are one sign.

We are not just our rising sign or our Sun sign or our Moon sign but in the Vedic system, when we look at the Divisional charts or the Vargas, the rising signs there also reveal the depths of our personality around those issues of life. So, if our rising sign in the D-10 career chart is Pisces, it reveals that we may have great talent and knowledge in business, which is something we might not normally think about. We also are many signs in the zodiac and our planets are scattered across the entire zodiac.

The article below is to help you learn a quick vocabulary for translating signs in your chart and their power, energy or Shakti and to remind you that you embrace the entire Universe and not just one small section of the zodiac. You are the Universe and Vedic astrology should help you embrace your infinity and not confine you into one small section of the sky.

Below is a quick table of key words, purposes and energy Shakti or power that can help you translate zodiacal signs wherever they appear in your chart. At some point, I will need to write a series of articles about each sign, but I wanted to give you a quick guide to help translate key and often unnoticed qualities.

Realize that whenever you have a planet placed here it brings out hidden Shakti or energetic power of that sign and empowers the planets whether they are connected to your Sun rising, Moon rising, Ascendant rising sign, Arudha lagna (or how we appear to others) or rising sign in any divisional chart rising sign (Varga). For people who practice astrology, the challenge is often to translate these abstract symbols into something deeper and expressive that clients can understand.

Below is a guide for the Shakti of each sign to help you translate.

Aries: Key word for Aries Shakti is creativity and it has the power to dominate life. Those of you knowing Bharani Nakshatra (Aries 13.20-26.40) can remember this very powerful creative energy. Planets placed in this sign in any part of your chart create ego identification so that is part of the challenge with this sign. Wherever there is an Aries, there is also a dominant energy toward major activity in life. Aries are actually very emotional because it is the sign before Taurus, where emotions are full. I actually find many talented artists come out of Aries particularly if they have Venus placed here as the sign brings out their creative talent.

Taurus: The Shakti of Taurus is that it gives power to bring wealth, social success, prosperity and enjoyment. For Vedic lovers, it is connected to Krishna. The key word to remember here is Blessings and it is easy to remember the blessings of Venus who brings material prosperity to us. Planets placed in Taurus in any part of the chart bring blessings, but we of course have to consider all the other aspects of interpretation that we know as Jupiter in Taurus may bring blessings of teachers but will also bring problems with obesity.

Gemini: Planets placed in Gemini anywhere in the chart is the need for Shakti creative energy or they get stuck in idleness. Hence when you see a planet anywhere in the chart connected to Gemini, you need to recommend being active and focused and then the planet will blossom. This sign also may show the path or direction in life, so it is a key signature in people charts for giving them focus for life purpose. Planets placed in Gemini anywhere in the chart may reveal the focus that the person needs to take to move forward in their life. Hence my Jupiter in Gemini, even in the stuck 8th house, gets activated when I teach and gives wisdom and it fulfills my life purpose.

Cancer: The Shakti of Cancer is to bring the blessings of the Divine Mother or Gurvi to our lives. Planets placed here show our best friend, those who can provide healing and care for us. If you have Venus anywhere in Cancer or in any Varga chart, then women, spouses and artistic expression provide healing Shakti for that area of life. Thus, if you had Venus in Cancer in the 9th house in your D-10 chart, then you might attract a female boss that actually supports you at work.
The ways that you can use and translate this are endless.

Leo: The Shakti of planets placed in Leo show what we know, naturally learn, read or where our hidden talents to express knowledge come. If you have Mercury in Leo then you have the power to express great knowledge and are a great teacher or speaker. Leo brings the blessings of Lord Shiva and the desire to transcend into the infinite and merge with the Universal transcendental soul, Shiva. The 2nd half of the zodiac has more karmic challenges than Shakti although Libra and Pisces, the natural benefics of course offer brighter spots.

*My goal is to help you develop a deeper and richer vocabulary to quickly describe and translate the meaning of signs, in whatever part of the zodiac they appear in the chart rather than to get caught using astrological clichés.

Virgo: Whenever a planet appears in Virgo in any sign of the zodiac it is a Shakti for striving to be better, improve or be pure. Being the natural 6th house of the zodiac, it means that we need discipline around regular work, health and diet to prevent illness and we also need to develop skills to work with people so that we do not develop enmity with co-workers at work. The challenge is Saturn and wanting too much perfection in the world and being too hard on oneself and one's weaknesses. There can be too much self-deprecation and continual beating oneself up or focusing too much on one's shadow/dark side or a continual focus on always wanting to be better (perfect) but that can become a good quality. I have Virgo rising in the D-9 chart and am amazed that so many of these qualities are the core of my soul's journey. Key words to remember are purity and improvement.

Libra: Wherever Libra falls in any rising or Varga chart, it brings the Shakti blessings of prosperity and Lakshmi, the grace to end conflicts. Venus has trouble with Mars. Mars produces creativity by wanting to fight and express its ego and leave its mark on the world to gain status. The Shakti of Venus is that if it can end conflict, it can bring prosperity, growth and fulfill desires and help distribute resources. Still the dark side is intense psychological brooding, particularly in Chitra or Swati nakshatras where there is never happiness. Artistic creativity has to replace sexual energy for balance to prevail here.

Scorpio: If we see Scorpio in any part of a chart, it is connected to the 8th sign of the zodiac, the Shakti of transformation, and deep past life karma which can bring deep suffering to one's life. Planets placed in Scorpio may experience deep cruelty from the darker side of Mars and may seem rather fallen.
Scorpio is co-owned by Ketu, the mystical headless wonder that takes us toward enlightenment and the key in Scorpio is finding spirituality and transformation to transmute that dark energy. Ketu may want to take everything from us to point us toward Moksha, so it sometimes can create poverty and loss — completely opposite of the material abundance that Taurus brings.

Scorpio anywhere in the chart even when blessed by Jupiter or Mars in its own sign can still cause deep problems that are hard to remedy. Still I think Jupiter and the grace of the Guru can bring the most support to Scorpios and provide the grounding needed to balance out the dominance of the space element that Scorpios have.

Sagittarius: The 9th natural sign of the zodiac brings lessons around the Shakti belief, dogma and blind faith. The Shakti of Sagittarius is that planets placed here show dogmas and rules but will bring luck if we follow our dharma and will bestow deep wisdom if we can follow our path and purpose. The curse of Sagittarius is that it will create war and conflict in order to uphold its belief and fundamentalist values. The US being Sagittarius rising is a difficult example of this. Sagittarius has problems with Vishnu and Mercury, so it has difficulty with communicating in relationships.

Capricorn: Wherever Capricorn appears as a rising sign or in a Varga chart or in other places of the chart, there is no joy but the Shakti of hard work, which creates deep, suffering. If you have Capricorn rising in the D-10 chart or if you are Aries rising where Capricorn rules the 10th, this may seem even stronger. The 10th natural sign of the zodiac owned by Saturn is experience deep toil, lack of hope and faith, receive little support except through their own efforts and experience great pain and suffering. The challenge here is joy. There is little awareness and sometimes planets placed here have no choice but to toil and work hard in order to move out of or cover up their pain. The weakness for Capricorn is Jupiter, as it needs to learn integrity and ethics in business practice or suffer like Capricorn rising Bernie Madoff did with his investment Ponzi schemes.

Aquarius: Aquarius is the 2nd most difficult sign to have anywhere prominent in ones' chart, as it is ruled by the Shakti of suffering Saturn and Rahu, which is the seat of desire. Rahu gives and then takes away so we are reminded that we are here to find the Divine. Aquarius is on the opposite side of the zodiac from Leo, the giver of light and it tends to take away the material, creating great pain and suffering from the losses that arise. Aquarius is a bitter enemy with the moon and mother so issues around maternal care, nurturing and food become prominent. Whenever the rising sign in any Varga chart has planets in Aquarius this creates suffering and loss in this area. Devotion to Shiva and to meditation and offerings to Shiva dispels the suffering of Aquarian Karma.

Pisces: Pisces is the natural 12th sign of the zodiac connected to Moksha and enlightenment. Its Shakti is that it brings the blessings of Saraswati, the Goddess of Wisdom that brings Knowledge of the Self. Planets placed here or anywhere in any of the charts show great talents and knowledge. But being the natural 12th house, it requires dedication to service and sacrifice to bring out its power. Pisces rising has difficulty with the Sun, the natural 6th house from Pisces so father issues and issues with authority and bosses become a natural problem.

All blessings to my Jyotish Gurus, particularly Sanjay Rath and Komilla Sutton for their depth of understanding for these subtle principles and their continued love and guidance. Special thanks to Zoran Radosavljevic for his insights into the signs derived from Sanjay Rath's talks.

Hidden Flaws By Rising Sign:
The Achilles Heel
Andrew Foss and Barry Rosen

This article is based primarily on a lecture given by Andrew at the Spring 2015 BAVA International Conference as also notes made by Barry at this and other lectures by Sanjay Rath and Bill Levacy. It introduces and explains the traditional concept of an inherent issue for each sign.

Our rising sign, which is called the Lagna in Vedic astrology, represents our personality, our temperament, disposition, tendencies, confidence, self-love and self-esteem and its afflictions reveal our inherent internal struggles. If the owner of the rising sign is strong and well placed in his own or exalted sign or in friend's houses or aspected by benefics, then he brings out his best qualities. More often than not, because we are human and working on perfecting our life, there is some affliction to the rising sign or its owner and therefore, the more challenging qualities come out.

There is also an inherent flaw or Achilles' heel for each rising sign. The more complex rising signs that are owned by Mercury, Jupiter and Saturn have life-long issues related to one of the planets. These are Gemini, Virgo (Mercury), Capricorn and Aquarius (owned by Saturn) and Sagittarius and Pisces (owned by Jupiter). Libra owned by Venus also comes into this group.

There are core life-lessons associated for these signs due to the placement of the key planet for the sign and the houses they own. By complex, we mean that the symbol associated with the sign is complex. For example, Gemini is thought of as two people while Aries is a single animal.

The planet associated with this flaw is often the owner of the sixth or twelfth house but sometimes the seventh house is also involved so the relevant issues are challenges around habits, sacrifices and relationships. This often manifests as a life-dominating issue for these rising signs that often plague the person most of their life. The signifiers or karakas of these planets and their extended values become major life issues and themes for a person.

Part 1 of this article is about the more complex rising signs below. The other rising signs will be covered in Part 2 and their issue is related to a tattva or element.

The flaws are applicable to these signs wherever they fall in the chart. Therefore, they also affect the Sun and the Moon Lagnas. These are also key Ascendants in Vedic Astrology. The Sun sign is of particular interest to the Western astrologers. This article only considers sidereal astrology but it could likely be applied to tropical also as the root of the flaws is the psychology of the sign as an influence on human life.

Part 1: Problem Planets By Sign:

Jupiter Owned Signs:

Pisces: Consider Pisces rising with an afflicted Jupiter. One may think the person has problems with confidence, restlessness, Utopian thinking, poor planning and their ability to put plans into action. Internally this is very connected to their relationship with their fathers as they have problems with authority figures. The Sun is the natural sixth house lord which teaches lessons about staying humble and since Pisces/Jupiter so often gets involved in teaching and counseling, their challenge is to do this with humility. This is particularly a problem if a person has the Sun in the first house of Pisces. Pisces people are wise, and one does not expect them to be egotistical, but they often admit that this is an issue they struggle with.

Sagittarius: If Jupiter is afflicted in their charts, we normally think of the challenges of this rising sign as being connected to being too religious, fanatical, pushy, greedy, having problems taking orders or listening to others advice and being too quick tempered. Mercury, the seventh lord, wants to talk and debate. Thus, Mercury becomes the issue for Sagittarius. Mercury is the Badhaka for this sign, so allowing others' opinions can be seen as a threat. Many religious leaders are famously intolerant. By not understanding and being conscious of this flaw, they can be blocked in finder their Higher Self, as well as, potentially doing much harm to society. The difficulty is that the Badhaka is very difficult to understand.

Saturn Owned Signs:

Aquarius: If Saturn and/or Rahu are afflicted, we normally think of this rising sign has having self-esteem problems in not recognizing their own talents, being too unconventional and outspoken, having problems with routine, being isolated and depressed, paranoid or hiding their misery behind a fake smile. The Achilles' heel for this rising sign is the sixth house lord, the Moon. This sign has major problems around their mother and issues around food, nurturing and the complexities of the mind.

Capricorn: If Saturn is afflicted, we normally think of the inherent problems of this rising sign as having problems with being suspicious, selfish, not making friends, having time constraints, being gloomy, being overly concerned with security and not being a good partner in relationship. The Achilles' heel for this rising sign is Jupiter, which naturally owns the third and twelfth houses for this sign, giving Capricorns problems with Gurus, children and being truthful in business. Bernie Madoff is an excellent example of poor ethics in business with his Ponzi scheme, which misused other people's money. He also had major problems with his children. It seems that the nature of Capricorn and business is that it is always a bit on the edge in terms of ethics, particularly if Jupiter is afflicted or poorly placed in a chart. Their lifelong challenge is having good judgment about what is right and ethical in business.

Venus Owned Signs:

Libra: If Venus is afflicted, we normally think of the challenges of this rising sign as sneaking away from conflict, being too charming or manipulative and capricious, waiting too long to act or being too much of a yes person and chameleon and not exerting one's self. Mars is the Achilles' heel planet for this sign and if badly afflicted it may create people who need to rule or dominate others and who have major issues with sexual restraint and ambition and overexerting power. A famous example in history is the violent nature of Alfried Krupp of the Third Reich as well as Adolf Hitler himself. They both had Mars in Aries in the 7th. Under Alfried, his companies used slave labor supplied by the Nazi regime and thereby also became involved in the Holocaust, assigning Jewish prisoners from concentration camps to work in many of its factories. Libras seek balance and fairness but if this gets warped, they can be very cruel.

Mercury Owned Signs:

Virgo: If Mercury is badly afflicted and poorly placed, we normally think of Virgos as having problems with being too emotionally uninvolved, having high expectations, being worried and depressed and frustrated and skeptical, finding fault with everything and being a bit lonely and monastic. Saturn is the problem planet for Virgos as it naturally owns the fifth and sixth houses creating issues around traditional beliefs, hard work, and obsessions with purity and cleaning, endless service, shyness and health issues.

Gemini: If Mercury is poorly placed or afflicted, we naturally think that this rising sign has problems with being indecisive, hasty, too cunning, not finishing what they start and talking their way out of being responsible. Their Achilles' heel planet is Venus, which naturally owns the 5th and 12th houses, connected to Venus' romance and relationship issues. If Venus is poorly placed or afflicted than this can lead to sexual obsession, frustration in romance and problems with relationships. Their life-long search is their quest for getting love and also doubting their partners: *"do they really love me?"* Relationship issues continue to challenge them throughout their entire lives. The desire for affection is often thwarted.

These flaws are inherent in the signs and cannot be removed but, if understood, they need not ruin our lives or those around us. Knowledge, as the Bhagavad Gita teaches, is the greatest purifier. Denial is something, which humans have made into an art form, but it only means that we will be born again to try to learn the same lesson. No one is flawless, but honesty, humility and kindness leave no room for the flaws to function. Everyone has the capacity to express these positive qualities, if we do not convince ourselves we are better off indulging our flaws. In fact, if we take the flaws as gifts from God as Guru, to help us develop humility and grace, then we already have achieved a great deal.

Part 2: Secret of The Elements

Fatal Flaws of The Elements:
Aries has problems with water or Jala, the water element, and hence they may have difficulty with emotion, love, food and connecting to the public. Venus and the Moon

become difficult planets for them, creating relationship problems unless the Moon and/or Venus is well placed in the chart or if the fourth, eighth and twelfth houses offer some compensation. The antidote is connecting more to Mother Divine energy through mantras or worship. If Mars or the first house is afflicted, the Aries rising people have to be careful with impatience, selfishness, "*I want it now,*" arrogance, recklessness, and leaving tasks undone.

Taurus: has problems with the fire element or Agni; hence, they have a problem with 'get up and go.' The fire planets, Sun, Mars and Ketu have their issues but are essential for accomplishing anything. Taurus is known for being the earthiest of the signs and the most grounded. They can get stuck with the tendency to hold onto money or material things in their life. Taurus needs help with the fire signs and fire signs and fire planets and if they are well placed then this helps. Lots of fiery and vigorous aerobic exercise is important to get this sign moving. There can be a tendency toward heaviness, depression and melancholy and one can sense why Jupiter here might cause problems with weight gain, or even diabetes despite being an auspicious planet in an auspicious planet in an auspicious planet in an auspicious sign. Taurus has to be careful with sweets if Jupiter is afflicted. Jupiter is afflicted. Jupiter or Venus afflicted in the chart can create stubbornness, inflexibility, greed, laziness, self-indulgence, ultra-conservative positions, intolerance and over-accumulation.

Cancer: This rising sign has problems with the earth element and hence with material success and structure and manifesting in the material world. Hence a strong balance of well-placed planets in Capricorn, Taurus and Virgo can be helpful to offset this latent flaw. A well-placed Venus or Saturn can offset this imbalance particularly if they are well aspected or are in Taurus or Capricorn. Cancers have to actively focus on saving money and getting motivated for worldly success. Often, they would rather just meditate and bathe in the wonders of the spiritual world. If the Moon or the first house is afflicted, Cancers have problems with being too dependent or clingy, hoarding, hypersensitivity, moodiness, winsomeness, abandonment and picking dysfunctional friends and partners. Forcing themselves to get grounded in the material world is essential so doing earthy activities like building and carpentry and gardening is helpful. Increasing the fire element through active and fiery aerobic exercise is important to get the solar plexus enlivened and get the fire moving.

Leo: Leos have problems with the air element or Vatta, hence Saturn and Rahu need to be strong or strengthened in their charts. Archetypically, the King needs good servants to be successful and needs a good relationship with Saturn and yet Leos have the most difficulty with Saturn. Health and longevity can be an issue if Saturn and Rahu are not well placed in the natal birth chart. If the Sun is afflicted or the first house is afflicted, Leos may have to deal with vanity, arrogance, boasting, condescension, domineering personalities or traits, having problems with subordinates, being power hunger, work-alcoholism by letting career take over their lives, which create imbalances. Increasing the water element and cooling off the heat by swimming can be helpful. It may be wise to not overdo intense aerobic activity to make sure the air element does not get out of balance. Of course, it all depends on the individual chart. Exercise is good, but one should not get dehydrated or depleted.

Scorpio: has a problem with space or Akasha and has difficulty holding everything together as they have a strong ability to intuitively go into the ether realm and deeply connect and expand their consciousness. Their strong quest for Moksha needs the Divine connection to remind them that all is well and God and the Divine are taking care of them. Jupiter is the remedy for this affliction, as they need the Guru and knowledge. This helps to gather and ground consciousness, bringing things together, taking them out of meditative isolation. Community becomes important to prevent isolation and being alone. Pisces and Sagittarius need to be strongly prominent in the chart and Jupiter connected to Mars or Ketu to re-balance this affliction. If Mars, Ketu or Scorpio is afflicted, there will be problems with being too critical, possessive, vengeful, hypersensitive, controlling, grim, being victimized in relationships, overworking and excessive worry. Grounding and earthy activities, like gardening is essential for them and even something like light weight-training can help combat the lightness that can overtake them. Yoga is grounding and helpful.

Again, charts are very individual, and we do not ever want to stereotype people by sign but sometimes it is a way of putting one's finger right away on a core problem of a person's entire life. We hope the reader finds this knowledge as enlightening as we did.

Special thanks go to the teachers whose insights into these rising signs is the basis of this material.

Andrew Foss has a PhD in Computing Science and is also an Oxford physics graduate with publications in Nature and other leading scientific journals. He is the author of the acclaimed book and ebook series *Yoga of the Planets.* He enjoys a deep love of music, art and poetry and has more than 30 years' experience studying and teaching the Vedic wisdom around the world. He is the Founding President of the BAVA, Editor of the *BAVA Journal Gochara* and is a certified Jyotish Pandit and Jaimini Scholar, the highest professional certifications in Vedic Astrology involving about a decade of intensive study. He has developed the unique, easy and powerful software Shri Jyoti Star that has become the first choice amongst Vedic Astrologers around the world. He teaches and consults in Jyotish. Web site VedicSoftware.com, YogaOfThePlanets.com email Andrew @ vedicsoftware.com, phone 0207-193-7517 or +1-202-657-5432.

The Achilles' Heel For Each Sign

Planet	Sign
MOON	AQUARIUS
MARS	LIBRA
MERCURY	SAGITTARIUS
JUPITER	CAPRICORN
VENUS	GEMINI
SATURN	VIRGO
SUN	PISCES

The Achilles' Heel For Sign Flaw: Element

Sign Flaws Connected To The Elements

TAURUS	FIRE
CANCER	EARTH
LEO	AIR
SCORPIO	SPACE

**Note: As Discussed In The Text Article "Hidden Flaws By Rising Sign: The Achilles Heel" by Andrew Foss and Barry Rosen

Ascendant Sign Planet Ruler

Planet	Sign
SUN	LEO
MOON	CANCER
MERCURY	GEMINI / VIRGO / URANUS
VENUS	TAURUS / LIBRA / NEPTUNE
MARS	ARIES / SCORPIO / PLUTO
JUPITER	SAGITTARIUS/PSICES
SATURN	CAPRICORN / AQUARIUS / URANUS

North and South Nodes Sign Ruler

Sign Flaws Connected To The Elements

RAHU
*AQUARIUS IS OFTEN THOUGHT TO HAVE A PRIMARY RULER WITH RAHU

KETU
*SCORPIO IS OFTEN THOUGHT TO HAVE A PRIMARY RULER WITH KETU

**Note: As Discussed In The Text Article *Hidden Flaws By Rising Sign: The Achilles Heel* by Andrew Foss and Barry Rosen

Special Vedic Astrology Planetary Aspects

Planet	Aspect
SUN	7TH HOUSE
MOON	7TH HOUSE
MERCURY	7TH HOUSE
VENUS	7TH HOUSE
MARS	4TH, 7TH, 8TH HOUSES
JUPITER	5TH, 7TH, 9TH HOUSES
SATURN	3RD, 7TH, 10TH HOUSES

North and South Nodes Aspects

Planet	Aspect
RAHU	5TH, 7TH, 9TH *30° ASPECT FROM ITSELF OR THE 2ND HOUSE FROM ITSELF
KETU	NO ASPECTS

HIGHLIGHTS OF THE YEAR BY RISING SIGN: PLANNING YOUR YEAR

So, to summarize the high points and low points for the year for you, I have outlined the stronger months for success and the periods of challenge for the first the quarter of **2018**.

So the transits of the ascendant lord are the most important for gauging what issues will come up in your life and they are always contextual to the larger cycles or dashas that you are running.

Here is a quick guide by rising sign to key events this year that will impact you.

Aries and Scorpio: Ruled by Mars:
Mars in Scorpio **January 16th - March 7th** is really your best time for self-confidence and health and Aries are dealing with 8th house transit and while meditation will be supported, without using the energy to transform your deep issues it will be challenges. Mars in Sagittarius is conjunct Saturn and Mars in Capricorn this year from **May 2 – November 5th** has a number of bumps with the Ketu conjunction and the retrograde. May is pretty clear for moving forward with lots of energy and **October15 - November 5th** will be better. December yields another Saturn aspect in Aquarius. So jump on February, March and May to get the most done.

Capricorn and Aquarius: Ruled by Saturn and Rahu co-ruling Aquarius
Capricorn is going through a difficult 12th house transit, which can bring up foreign journeys, expenditures, visits to ashrams and some deep psychological churning. Constellation of Mula until **March 3rd** will bring up regrets from the past and deep emotional healing and then retrograde **April 17- September 6th** will slow things down. Constellation of Purva Shadha **March 3 - June 4th** and connection with Venus is much better. Be patient with delays this year   Aquarius Rising has an 11th house transit which can lead to slow and steady increases of income, benefits from new age groups, technological advances but still the pesky aspect from Saturn into Aquarius can still create self-doubt or low confidence at times so remember your positive self-talk.

Venus Related Signs: Taurus and Libra Rising
So the transits of the ascendant lord are the most important for gauging what issues will come up in your life and they are always contextual to the larger cycles or dashas that you are running. Here is a quick guide by rising sign to key events this year for Libra and Taurus rising, owned by Venus that will impact you.

The best transits of the year for Venus this year are in Capricorn, Pisces, Taurus, Gemini, Cancer and Libra. Venus stays in Libra for 5 months from September to the of the end of the year. Hence, **March, May** and **September** through **December** will be very strong months for Venus ruled signs like Libra and Taurus.

Mercury Related Signs: Gemini and Virgo Rising
It is a difficult year in that Mercury is afflicted by Ketu in Capricorn by a Saturn aspect in Aquarius. March is good with the Venus exalted conjunction but then April difficult without it in Pisces. Aries is always difficult but is an 11th house transit for Gemini. Taurus is the best transit of the year for Virgo being unafflicted and in the 9th house and a friend's sign. Gemini is mixed with the Saturn aspect from Sagittarius this year. Cancer retrograde has to deal with eclipse energy and Rahu for a few months. Leo transits are mixed and a 12th house transit for Virgo. Virgo transit is great but will have brief moments of the 10th house aspect from Saturn and Mercury in Libra is pretty unafflicted and with Venus and is one of the better transits of the year and Mercury in Scorpio is always a bit tricky but at least not Saturn conjunction this year.

Leo Rising:
Capricorn is difficult this year with the eclipse into **January 31st**. Aquarius gets hit by the Saturn aspect. Pisces is great for spirituality but has to fight a bit with Venus for space. Aries is always a great time for leadership and confidence and is always the best transit for Leos of the year. Taurus is mixed but usually strong and unafflicted this year. Gemini is troubling this year with the Saturn aspect. Cancer is difficult this year with Rahu and the eclipses. Leo is always a strong time to be home and Virgo has only a brief affliction from Saturn. Libra is always a low time for the year and Scorpio is unafflicted this year and Sagittarius moves back toward the Saturn conjunction this year.

Cancer Rising:
Watch the **January/February** transits and **July/August** transits and aspects and watch all the eclipses carefully in **January/February** and **July/August**. The moon moves too quickly for me to write about it.

JANUARY 2018

Venus remains combust until **February 9th,** so relationships stay on edge a bit and one has to be patient with partners. Venus goes into Capricorn on **January 13th** and that is a friend's sign, but it will still make Venus ruled signs cautious about relationships and searching for the truth.

Mars is fairly strong connected to Jupiter and then in its own sign, so action can move forward with courage and success. It moves into Scorpio on **January 16th** and it is one of the better transits of the year for Mars being unafflicted and in its own sign.

Mercury will be a bit more optimistic and have support in communication in Sagittarius but is still afflicted by Saturn into **January 12th** making computer and communication stuff a bit more challenging.

Saturn is getting stronger but is still is dealing with past regrets in the nakashatra of Mula.

Jupiter is strong in its own constellation and continuing the buoyant expansive energy, which is leading to new highs in the stock market and continued buying.

The total lunar eclipse/Super moon on **January 31st** is at 18 degrees Cancer and will impact Cancer and Capricorn rising for a few weeks into **February**.

FEBRUARY 2018

Sun is in Capricorn is not happy about moving into conjunction with Ketu into February 2nd which will create increasing edginess and being forced into working on past karma and just working hard. By **February 6th**, he moves into the constellation of Dhanistha (Capricorn 23.20-Aquarius 6.40) into a friend's sign and will strength.

The partial solar eclipse into **February 15th** is at 4 degrees Aquarius and will impact Leos and Aquarius rising greatly.

Saturn throws a 60-degree aspect onto planets in Aquarius and hits Venus on **February 14th** at the solar eclipse and then the Sun on **February 25th**. Mercury, on **February 21st** is showering some winter depression and fear but promoting hard work and focus.

Mars squares Mercury into **February 28th** with a 4th house aspect is causing arguments and disputes so Virgo and Gemini rising should be cautious driving the week of **February 26 - March 2nd** and watch out for the other guy. Use February to get your communication and writing projects in order as Mercury will spend over 2 months in Pisces in **March, April** and into **early Ma**y.

With Jupiter direct still in **February**, stay on top of business expansion and marketing. Work extra hard here as Jupiter Retrograde starting **March 8th** until **June** throws a whole wrench into the works around this so get your projects done in **January** and **February**.

Before Mercury goes into Pisces on **March 1st**, make sure you are on top of computer and communication and writing projects because they will take 2 - 3 times as long to complete during the next few months. Venus will cancel the debilitated Mercury in **March** but it only helps a little and **April** is a mess with it.

MARCH 2018

March is one of the better months of the year with Venus moving into exaltation in Pisces until **March 26th** and this uplifts relationships, buying, energy and overall ease and comfort for all.

Mercury goes into Pisces and this means that Virgos have to work three times as hard on relationship issues and Gemini rising three times as hard to get status at work. There will be glitches in communication now for a few months.

Saturn moves into Venus's nakshatra of Purva Ashadha (Sagittarius 13.20-26.40) until **June** and this will really uplift Saturn's energy and make-work more successful and smoother and finally lift the veil of Mula and regrets of the past.

Jupiter goes retrograde on **March 8th** and Mars moves into Sagittarius that day.

While very expansive that week for getting a lot done and feeling great with the Jupiter station, you will have to get ready for delays in marketing and expansion for the next 4 months.

Mars in Sagittarius will first be in Mula Nakshatra ruled by Ketu until **March 30** forcing Aries and Scorpio rising to deal with past regrets and cleaning up the past and moving toward deeper spiritual experience. With Mars in a separate constellation from Saturn, the impact of the **April 2nd** conjunction will probably not be felt strongly until **March 27th** when they get closer together.

The Vedic New Year starts **March 18th** and that day will imprint the yearly future for the world.

Venus moves into Aries on **March 26th** and then into conjunction with Uranus on **March 28th** and usually the shift from Pisces to Aries for Taurus and Libra rising is rather dramatic after the energetic high of the past month.

APRIL 2018

Everyone is still dealing with the delays and frustration of the Mars/Saturn conjunction which peaks on **Monday, April 2nd** but its influence may not be done until **April 13th** even though they will stay in the same sign until early **May**.

Sun into exaltation on **April 13th** is always my favorite for the year in renewed optimism, leadership and confidence and the Jupiter opposition helps this year. While it can create relationship tensions between the natural 1st house of Aries and the natural 7th house of Libra, it is always a bright spot for the year.

Venus in Aries until **April 19th** is never happy here and afflicted a bit by the Sun and makes relationships a bit tenser. The 12th house transit from Taurus is also tough for that rising sign. Opposition with Jupiter can fan expansive buying and overspending but still creates relationship tensions.

Pluto stations into **April 21st** and is always intense. Mars conjunct Pluto into **April 26th** is always explosive for personal anger, world anger and can trigger earthquake activity. Mercury hits its exact point of debilitation on **April 26th** and finally moves out of debilitation and saves our computers going into Aries on May 9th.

Saturn goes retrograde **April 17th** and that may start to slow things down a bit so get used to it through **September 6th**.

Even retrograde planets have their benefits, I do find retrograde Saturn being more intense for bringing suffering, health issues. Sagittarius, Gemini and Virgos will feel it most.

MAY 2018
Mars enters Capricorn on **May 2nd** and will give a nice shot of energy and feelings of relief getting away from Saturn. It is still far enough from Ketu until Memorial Day not to be too disturbed. With the exalted Sun here, this month can provide lots of energy the first half to get a lot done and achieve great status.
Venus is also happy in Taurus until **May 14th** so the first few weeks of **May** are a time to push the envelope and make great strides in your work.

Saturn is still happy in Venus's nakshatra of Purva Ashadha until **June 4th**, which will support work with more ease even if Saturn is retrograde.

JUNE 2018
June is a more troubling month starting off with the Mars/Ketu conjunction exact into **June 9th** so watch the repressed anger and find a way to release with exercise or screaming in an empty car or room or pillow. Mars goes retrograde on **June 26th** until **August 27th** and this can increase energy for Aries and Scorpio rising but the retrograde still can prevent action from happening. The Ketu conjunction becomes even more maddening.

Mercury in Taurus and Gemini provide a nice lift for Gemini rising and Virgo rising after a pretty difficult first part of the year with Mercury hit by Saturn and debilitated in Pisces for over 60 days.

Early **June** is always great with Sun in Taurus having natural Dig Bala for Leo rising and providing success at work.

Venus is hit by a Pluto opposition into **June 5th** but gets into the friendly sign of Cancer by **June 8th — 26th** where it can relax a bit and is unafflicted.

JULY 2018
July starts out optimistically with a Jupiter trine exact into **July 5th** so the holiday may seem more joyful. Afflicted Mars opposing Mercury into **July 5th** will require careful driving and looking out for those drivers who drank too much around the holiday.

Jupiter goes stationary direct on **July 10th,** so those delayed business-marketing projects can move full steam ahead!

Minor solar eclipse on **July 12th** at Gemini 27 degrees may upset digestion but not a huge thing unless you are Leo rising.

Mercury goes retrograde in Cancer on **July 25th** for a few months so get those books done early and be mindful of computer issues. Lunar eclipse on **July 27th** at 11 degrees Capricorn is a bit problematic with Mars there.

Sun gets hit by conjunction with Rahu into **July 28th** and that may create strong ambition but can lead to toppling from status.

AUGUST 2018

Venus goes into Virgo on **August 1st** so a definite time for Libras to retreat, wind down and go on a meditation retreat. There is less energy here, so it's time to rest. Avoid over-sexual stimulation and be patient with partners who are less than perfect.

Final eclipse of the year on **August 20th** at 25 Cancer is relatively minor but still Leos have to watch digestion, stay rested and in good health during this 12th house transit and eclipse. It's not a good month to book a foreign trip for Leos despite the desire. Meditate at an ashram instead.

Uranus stations and goes retrograde on **August 7th** and that can bring strong and unexpected action for share markets or surprises in the world. Given the rebellion energy up from Ketu/Mars, we have to worry about riots with Mars still too close to Ketu the first few weeks of the month.

Mars goes direct **August 27th** and will be out of range from Ketu so there will be some energy to move forward ahead with projects.

SEPTEMBER 2018

September Venus is going into Libra for 5 months bringing peace to the summer turmoil, but Mars still has to get by Ketu and it is not clear until the 2nd week of **October** so there is still seething anger that may be more capable to express now with the forward motion. Last conjunction of Mars/Ketu is into **September 26th**.

Mercury goes into his exalted sign of Virgo on **September 19** and after a brief hit from Saturn into **September 23rd**, it will gain power until **October 6th** there but will move into the happy sign of Libra where artistic and creative speech and writing can emerge. **October** is a good month for creative writing.

OCTOBER 2018

Jupiter moves into Scorpio **October 11th** but is sandhi in late degrees **October 7 - 15th** and this can impair judgment and slow down the liver so make sure to take care of your live with drinking fresh lemon water every morning.

Venus goes retrograde **October 5th** and then gets too close to the Sun and this can mess with relationship energy and create anger. See Applied Vedic Astrology for more information about this. Venus does not go direct until **November 16th** and is combust until **October 31st** and hidden by the Sun.

Sun in Libra the 2nd half of **October** is always a tough time until **November 6th** particularly and overall into **November 17th** when confidence and status and health can suffer a bit.

NOVEMBER 2018

Mars goes into Aquarius **November 6th** and finally gets away from Ketu but then gets hit by a 60-degree aspect from Saturn on **November 27t**h creating more stress and frustration after an already difficult year.

Sun moves into Scorpio on **November 17th** providing relief for Leos after a tiring October. Venus goes direct **November 16th** and can finally enjoy Libra until the end of the year. Mercury goes retrograde **November 16th** in Scorpio giving us another 60 plus days in this churning emotional sign of the zodiac.

Jupiter gets combust by the Sun into **November 12 - December 9th** fueling false optimism but at least it is in Scorpio.

DECEMBER 2018

Mercury goes direct **December 6th** making sure that better delivery for those Christmas presents will come.

Sun goes into Sagittarius on **December 15th** fueling Christmas optimism and shopping but has to deal with sharing space with Saturn.

problems, anxiety, fatigue, stress, which goes with Christmas anyways. This is a repeat of Christmas 2016.

Mars goes into Pisces on **December 23rd** and can finally relax a bit after its tough battle with Saturn, Ketu and Saturn connected signs.

Mercury ends the year going into Sagittarius right before midnight Eastern Time.

HIGHLIGHTS OF THE YEAR: 2018

***Note:** Dates and times listed using the Sidereal zodiac and are Eastern Standard Time (EST)
**To convert to your time zone: timeanddate.com

MARS/SATURN CONJUNCTION:
APRIL 3, 2018

The impact is particularly strong **March 27 - April 7th** when Mars moves within 3 degrees of Saturn's energy. During these two weeks, it is as if we are getting closer to the flame of fire; when you are in the same room of the fire, it is more intense compared to being downstairs.

The tendency is for anger and frustration to bubble up and you may snap at people. Resentment may flow through the mind. Delays, obstacles and indecision may bubble up in the volcanic cauldron of Sagittarius. Jupiter's energy soothes it a little and if you channel the energy into humanitarian service it can become a positive.

Staying on top of your meditation, yoga and spiritual practices during the month of **April** can help you stay balanced and grounded. Take it slow and easy. Exercise patience and awareness to avoid accidents and angry flare-ups.

Give people the benefit of the doubt for mistakes that happen and be forgiving rather than fly off the handle. This is a 2-week period to practice mindfulness and observe what is happening in the mind and body so stay balanced and do not overreact. Find a way to laugh at situations and practice mindful presence and patience. If you do not stay on top of sleep, and instead, you indulge in bad habits that are not good for you, and you are not mindful, Mars conjunct Saturn may seem rough and frustrating.

MARS IN CAPRICORN:
**MAY 2ND, 2018 - NOVEMBER 5TH, 2018
RETROGRADE AND CONJUNCT KETU**

Mars spends over 6 months in Capricorn its sign of exaltation. The month of **May** is rather unafflicted, however, after **mid-October**, pesky Ketu afflicts the transit.

When Mars is strong, it has great stamina, high energy, and courage and is hard-working. He won't be defeated!

He can be charming, cunning and good at taking risks.

Afflicted, Mars can be impatient, quick to anger and deceptive, does not complete work, and is arrogant and combative.

That is the energy of the transit when Mars goes retrograde on **June 26th - August 27th.**

Retrograde Mars is less inclined to take action and a person needs a fire under them to get something done. There can be a lot of procrastination. Hence, it can be a bad time for starting new projects or doing business projects. There still can be a lot of energy but it you may feel block at times. Getting plenty of exercise and movement is important during Mars retrograde.

The wrong signs, and exalted malefics lend more harm than good, so Libra and Taurus may feel it strongly. Capricorn and Cancer rising and Sagittarius rising with Mars owning the 12th will feel this strongly too. Aries will do best with Mars in Aries for career and Scorpio rising will plough through problems. Virgo and Gemini will be challenged with Mars and Mercury being bigger enemies. Pisces will do the best with the 11th house transit.

When a planet transits its exaltation sign, and is retrograde, it brings with it a sense of the planet being in debilitation; frustrating our plans with unforeseen delays, and many more twists and turns to negotiate. There is outward energy to get stuff done but the inner anger and frustration might feel like there is a block in place and if when we feel blocked, we may not act. So, we have to watch sudden angry outbursts with retrograde Mars.

MARS CONJUNCT KETU:

Mars will first approach Ketu in early June in Capricorn. On the highest level, in the sign of Capricorn, the Mars/Ketu conjunction encourages us to work hard at business but often we are frustrated or blocked leading to deep-seeded anger and resentment.

If you watch small kids in a playground, they get angry, fully express it and then go back to being normal. Anger is a natural emotion that is often an expression of an unfulfilled desire. Kids are great about it but we tend to repress our anger until it explodes and that is dangerous.

As I have said before, transmute the anger by doing charity work and channel the energy into positive social service rather than raging at things that you cannot control.

This conjunction challenges us to be happy with our own power and leadership and this may be the case particularly among women, so express it now if it comes up.

This transit supports mathematics and engineering so this is the time to go deep into invention mode.

For Scorpio and Aries rising, it will foster spiritual experience and intuition, as Ketu is the most spiritual planet. This is an excellent time for a meditation retreat or extra spiritual practice. Other activities may be frustrating.

Overall, this conjunction is very difficult for the planet and is a signature for violence and terrorism. It is thought that when Mars is retrograde/exalted that it acts like a debilitated planet and would have an impact more subjectively in terms of seething anger.

The race riots in St. Louis a few years back and in September in Milwaukee were recent examples of the Mars/Ketu aspects. 9/11 also happened during a Mars/Ketu conjunction in Sagittarius.

Find another way to express your feelings in a positive way. Write letters, do posts on Facebook or call your Congressperson. In the extreme, this aspect can lead to accidents, fires, burns and explosions if the energy is not released. Be careful around your home and while driving around those key dates. Even if you are alert, others may not be as aware or mentally present in the moment.

The bright side of the conjunction of Mars/Ketu is that it forces us to face our unconscious fears and repressed angers, so we can look at them and transform them.

Capricorns and Aquarians need to find an outlet to unlock pent-up anger or it will explode. Exercise and healthy competition is one way to let off steam.

Ultimately terrorism and war-like events of craziness will fan the flames of irrational fear that the media will use as energy to whip us into a frenzy and inspiring our leaders to put motions into place to impede human rights and try to control us through fear. "*The Deep State*" continues working on a soft coup with the electoral voters and if that fails they may turn up the heat.

Usually yoga and exercise are good to get things moving but be gentle on yourself as too much will increase the air element or Vata and create more anxiety. Use the Nike slogan, "*Just Do It,*" to get moving as Mars/Ketu can create very sluggish and lazy energy, making it hard to get started again.

The exchange of houses between Saturn and Mars, two tamasic planets can also make things hard to get started and get through.

Capricorns, Aquarians, Scorpios, and Aries will probably be most affected by this transit and people having key planets in Capricorn/Cancer will be affected most as will people running Mars/Ketu periods or Ketu/Mars periods.

If you are running those periods and they are connected to difficult houses (4th, 6th, 8th, or 12th) in Capricorn, then be particularly careful driving.

Otherwise nothing will get triggered. The best way to work through this challenging transit is to stay alert, aware. Don't get lazy by repressing or stuffing any feelings that come up during these brief moments in time. Remember, you are not your emotions and you are empowered to choose how you will best respond to challenging situations. You have the tools and advance notice of the stars to prepare you for handling this Mars/Ketu highlight.

VENUS IN LIBRA:
SEPTEMBER 2, 2018 - JANUARY 2, 2019

Venus moves into Libra on **September 2nd** and will remain there 4 months providing peace and a breather from the Mars/Ketu tensions.

This placement is a life saver and brings all kinds of wonderful energies including elegance, being well-respected, artistic creativity, balance in thought and deep, good intuition, passion, enthusiasm, comfort, luxury and humanitarian enterprises.

Of course, Libra rising will feel this most as it is a Malavya Yoga, but Capricorns and Aquarians will benefit greatly from it as well as Geminis and Virgos.

Enemies of Venus, like Mars, Jupiter and the Sun may have challenges with this transit. Scorpios have to watch expenditures and sexual indulgences. Leo, Taurus and Aries rising get 3rd, 6th and 7th house transits of Venus, which are more challenging.

Still a deeper sense of ease and comfort will come, as it's such a contrast for Libra rising going from the deep debilitation of Virgo the previous month to the comfort of being home. More harmony in relationships should be felt unless you have any natal malefic planets in Aries or Libra causing problems. Ah, the break that refreshes!

Venus goes retrograde **October 5th - November 16th** and is combust **October 21st - 31st.** Venus is actually spiritualized by being so close to the Sun, although, some of its outer values and significations are challenged.

The exact conjunction on **October 26, 2018** can actually be a good thing by infusing Venus with the Sun's Divine rays and making it a star! Oprah Winfrey has this configuration in the 2nd house of her natal chart. Still, the time before and after the conjunction is more problematic.

Sun/Venus combustion can raise issues of jealousy. Remember to praise, appreciate and help others at this time by applauding their success and good fortune.

This energy would normally produce strong, passionate expression such as creative expression for artists but with the afflictions, can lead to major relationship outbursts. For example, if sexual/creative energy is not allowed to express itself it can lead to major conflicts.

The best outlet for frustrated energy would be to do some wild dancing, take a craft class, sing loudly with the radio turned up, create a massive artistic dinner or go on a wild shopping spree with friends that are not likely to end in a conflict or fight.

The conjunction can also lead to manipulative energy in relationships, causing annoyances, friction and problems. Remember to accept people with all their imperfections or you will likely be seething with anger.

Take care of your reproductive organs as problems can happen during this transit.

If you are feeling friction, take a walk and get out the house rather than get into battle with your partner.

Taurus and Libra rising signs in Vedic astrology may continue to experience intense fatigue as the Sun moves toward Venus into **October 26th** and it will not be free until after **October 31st** so get extra rest. Don't over-eat or zone out by watching too many movies or you will get exhausted.

I personally find the Venus/Retrograde combust period one of the more difficult transits to deal with because it requires more patience to cope with people and their imperfections.

GLOBAL AND ECONOMIC OUTLOOKS FOR 2018
THE YEAR OF VILAMBA

The New Year in Vedic Astrology Starts
March 17th, 2018

Whereas western culture delights in January New Year predictions, the Vedic New Year calendar is often run for the new Moon in **March** after the spring solstice for the capital city of a country. Because the New Year begins after sunrise, Vedic astrologers will assign the ruler of the day to be ruler of the year and because the new moon is after sunrise, the Sun is the ruler of the Year. The chart is cast the capital city of your country for the new mono and predictions for the New Year are made accordingly.

In the Vedic calendar there is a deity or god that governs each year and they rotate each year for 60 years and they are connected to the Jupiter and Saturn returns, and that suggests that just like last time, Jupiter was in Libra and Saturn in Sagittarius. Hence, we are going to have influence like we had in 1958 - 1959.
This is year, **March 17, 2018** at 9:12 a.m. EDT, the chart for Washington, DC is the Year of Vilamba. You can run your capital at the new moon after the spring equinox.

Here is what the Vedic texts say if you were born this year, which last was seen between **March 1958 - 1959**: "*The native whose birth occurs in the 'Samvatsara' of 'Vilamba' is deceitful, extremely avaricious or greedy, lazy, phlegmatic (that is, his predominant humour is Phlegm), weak, fatalist and has the habit of speaking without purpose, serviceable, defeated by his wife, contented, keeps his thoughts secret, and is of restless nature.*" (*Note: These Vedic texts never seem kind in these descriptions. – Ed.*) In any case it would continue the theme of political greed, smoke and mirrors and the inability to plough through difficult global political problems, which is not what we need in our troubled world. Kick the budget and the tax problems down the road until our future generations are so chained with debt they will be forced to work elsewhere. We can look back in time and see what past Vilamba years were like.

In world history, the Spanish-America war began in **April 1898** and continued into the end of the year. This was also during the 3rd year of the US Rahu period. Russia prevented Finland from becoming autonomous in **February 1899** and one has think of Ukraine. The satellite Sputnik 2 (launched **November 3, 1957**) disintegrates during reentry from orbit in **April 1958**. Castro's invasion of Havana began that year. **In** Lebanon**, 5,000** United States Marines landed in the capital Beirut in order to protect the pro-Western government there. In 1959, at Cape Canaveral, Florida, the first successful test firing of a Titan intercontinental ballistic missile was accomplished. The Tibetan uprising erupted in Lhasa when Chinese officials attempted to arrest the Dalai Lama. Alaska and Hawaii were granted statehood during the Year of Vilamba.

If any theme emerges, it seems to be that of war and blocking of freedom for countries wanting to become independent occurred. Obviously, Korea has to be on our mind this year with Saturn in Sagittarius promoting fear from opponents and I think that the

Ukrainian situation could escalate this year, but I will have to look at their chart in more detail.

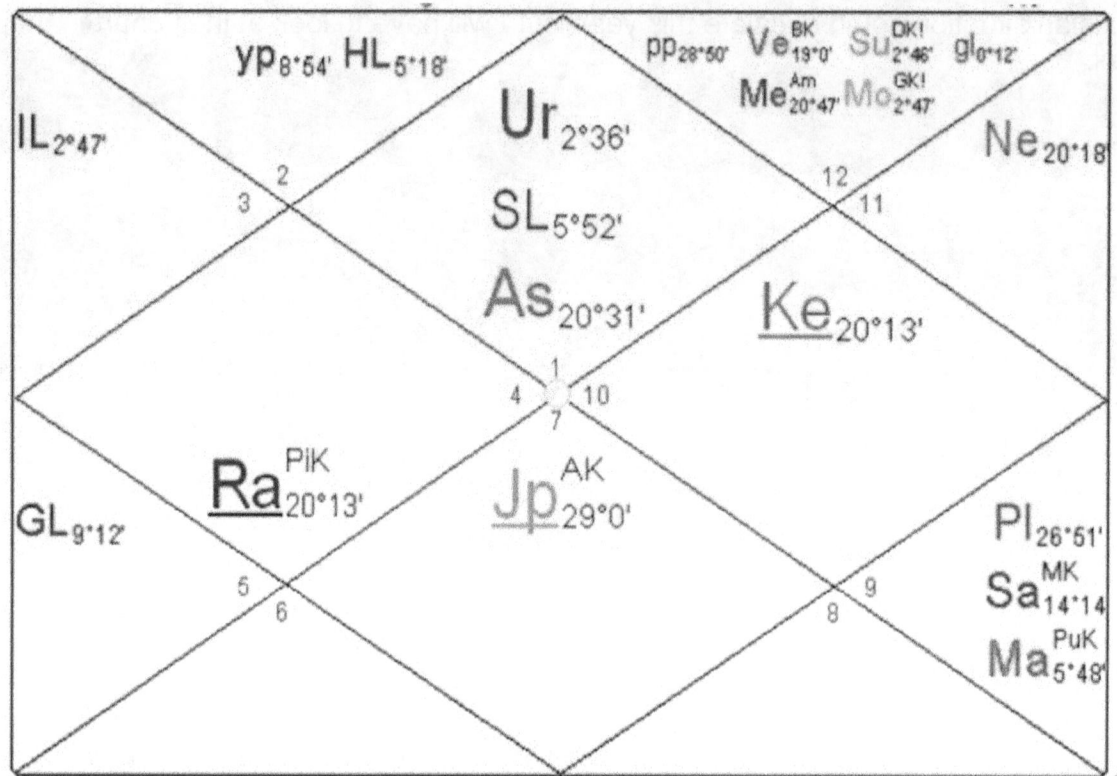

Chart of the Year of Vilamba for the United States

The chart for the US that day is as above for **March 17, 2018:** Note the ruler of the day is the Sun because the new moon occurs after Sunrise and thus Sun in the 12th house becomes the major influence for the year. The lord of the chart is Mars conjunct Saturn within 9 degrees in the war-like sign of Sagittarius and the 9th house dealing with foreign countries. All of this suggests strong desire for war.

Jupiter is retrograde and sandhi at the end of the sign in Libra and not of much help as the depositor for Sagittarius. Four planets are in the 12th house of Pisces including an exalted Venus with Rahu in the 4th house creating an unsettled feeling of peace and contentment on the year. The ruler of the Year, the Sun, is placed in the 12th house, which is the most difficult placement for the Sun suggesting that the world will not see the US in a positive light or it will become less important or it will quest after power to be seen and express itself and fail.

We should note that in the US chart, the Mars/Saturn conjunction in early **April** is in the US 1st house aspecting the US house of enemies and this would greatly increase fear and war tensions for that time window. Given the parallels with the Spanish - American War of 1898 in that Year of Vilamba, one has to think a war by spring seems rather ominous but is something that we do not want to put too much attention on. We wonder if Iran will be more of a target than North Korea with olive branches happening with North and South Korea around the Olympics at publication. Will the US continue to be frustrated?

Will the Mars/Saturn conjunction and all the planets in the 12th house create a lot of frustration regarding foreign affairs? Seems that way but maybe the exalted Venus in the 12th can rescue the situation and prevent major problems. Will Venus have enough of a strong benefic influence to prevent war?

The Mars/Saturn conjunction is a signature for frustration. Aries wants to fight but Saturn will block. Will the rest of the world be able to block war and leave the US in a smoldering situation?

Other country charts will have different rising signs and put the planets in different houses. For North Korea and Japan, Jupiter goes into the 1st house and creates a much better annual chart for them. Rahu plagues the European countries in the 1st and Ketu in the 7th suggesting continuing wrangling over the EU problems and this is true for the UK.

Saudi Arabia and Israel and Turkey come out Leo rising with the Sun in the 8th house, which means the country needs to set up major transformational energy but seems rather vulnerable. Turkey and Israel seem particularly India and Pakistan come out to be Virgo rising with Sun, Venus, debilitated Mercury and the Moon in the 7th house suggesting conflicts and uneasy but at least protected by the exalted Venus.

Of course, these annual charts are always secondary information in the context of the natal charts, which we will discuss in more detail below.

2018 - 2019 GLOBAL AND POLITICAL OUTLOOKS:

POLITICAL AND GEO - COSMIC OUTLOOK FOR 2018

While the media spins end of the world scenarios and political decapitation for Trump, I doubt we will see either of those in 2018. Trump is in a Jupiter period and Jupiter in Libra is still rather positive for the world economy so at least through **October** the mania should continue.

The partisan fighting and scandals are not likely to end soon but what else is new as the continual battle of Mad Magazine's Spy vs. Spy is likely to continue to sell more cable subscription and continue addiction to scandal on phony news.

On a global level, those worried about pandemics can probably wait for **April/May 2019** as we start moving closer to the Saturn/Pluto/Ketu conjunction and Saturn will still be casting a 10th house aspect onto the sign of Virgo which is always connected to national health. Still with the Saturn/Sun conjunction at the winter equinox, flu season may be particularly bad this year and already many deaths are happening, but it is not a pandemic but a bad flu season.

EARTHQUAKES:
Saturn/Rahu and Saturn/Jupiter aspects tend to trigger earthquakes and we do not have the Saturn/Rahu opposition until **May/June 2019** and it is happening connected to the US sign of Sagittarius.

For earthquakes on a minor scale, we always watch Mars/Uranus aspects—particularly oppositions. Most notably we have the Mars/Uranus squares from Capricorn to Aries on **May 16th** and repeating **August 1st** in retrograde motion and then again into **September 18th** in direct motion. Capricorn and Aries are both movable signs so pronounced earthquake activity on the planet are likely during those times.

POLITICAL UNREST:
Still war cycles increase from **March to early June** and in **June** it looks like there could be a trigger event with the Mars/Ketu conjunction on **June 9th**. The military-industrial-complex is always itching and pushing us in this direction, so this is not hard to predict.

WOMEN'S RIGHTS:
Jupiter in Libra and then Venus in Libra for 5 months will allow women to continue to come into power in **January - February 2018** as more speak up against continued disgust for predatory action that will lead to more resignations.

April and May seem like particularly strong months for women to have their voices heard and gain more equality. We will see continued support with Jupiter in Scorpio bringing out secrets around predatory behavior.

COUNTRY TRENDS:

Countries on the horizon this upcoming year for particular challenges include Australia, Israel, and Turkey. Israel of course, with the New Jerusalem capital. Turkey has been a mess for years and its societal structure is breaking down. Australia has had a huge housing bubble crunch that is likely to end. New leadership there is turning against Islam too. We are limited on what we can do but I have been able to cover the following:

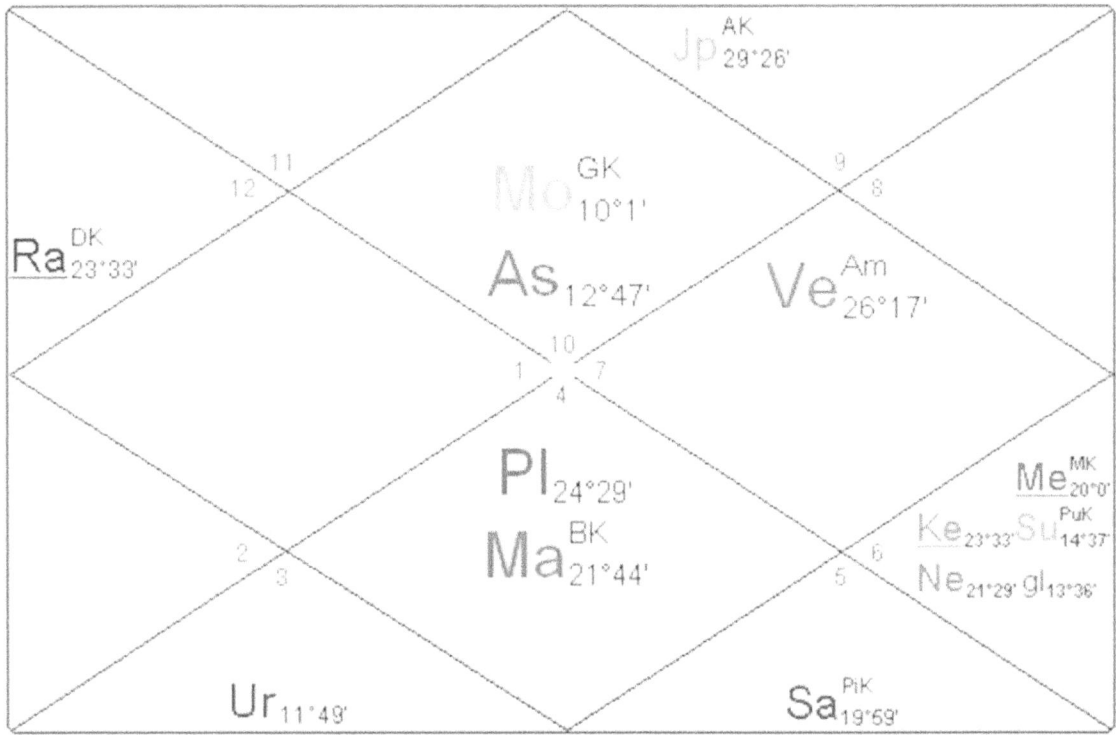

CHINA: (October 1, 1949, 15:15, Peking, China)

China is a Capricorn country and began Saturn/Jupiter period on **March 14, 2017** with Mercury major period starting in **September 2019** with Mercury in their 9th house in Virgo. I am a bit concerned around Sade/Sat for China which has her moon in the first house in Capricorn in Shravana nakshatra which means Saturn's transit in Mula this year in the 25th nakshatra is particularly difficult for China with major changes happening. China's fragile economic system is built on more debt than the US and we wonder if a major Chinese meltdown in their stock market will spark big changes.

With Mars/Ketu transiting through Capricorn from **June - October**, expect violence and unrest and more aggression popping up around the South Sea territorial problems. China has continued its expansion in the Asian Pacific by turning the South China Sea into an anti-access and area-denial zone controlled by the Chinese military through a network of artificial islands. In addition, Beijing has also expanded its maritime, airlift, and amphibious capabilities, and is actively working to shift the balance of power in the Pacific, a region that it describes as lying within its sphere of influence, through its naval power dominance in the area. With Mars and Ketu in Capricorn, expect this to continue.

In diplomatic and economic terms, China continues to follow a finely balanced foreign policy, while providing a slight diplomatic support to Russia. This calibrated approach allows Beijing to contest US dominance in some regions, most obviously in the Middle East, while avoiding an open confrontation with its main economic partner.

Still there is something non-trustworthy about them as recent satellite photos showed them selling oil to North Korea despite the ban.

Expect some huge shift in US/China relations with the Saturn/Jupiter conjunction in **December 2020** and expect the combination of the US rising sign being debilitated in Capricorn in contrast to Saturn being in the Chinese ascendant will complete a shift in Chinese global dominance.

China's future in the world looks bright. In the Mercury period starting in **September 2019,** they should clean up the environment, make advances in education and start leading the world. Long-term investment in China after any 2018 fall-out would be advised.

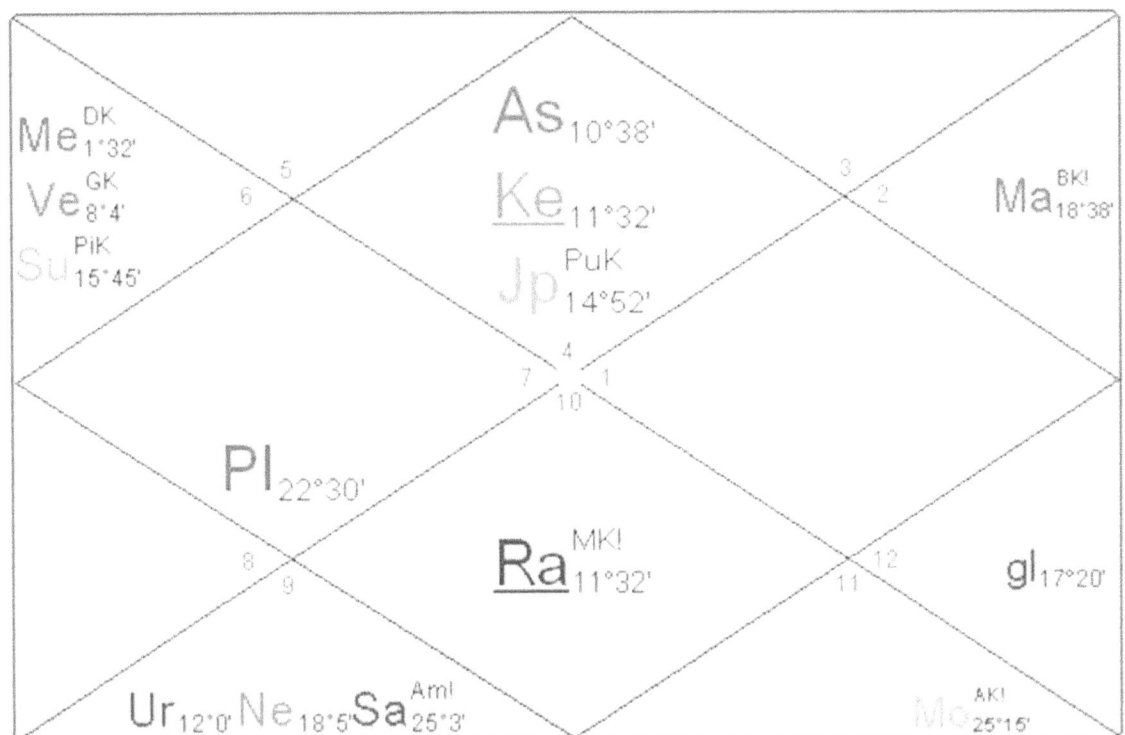

GERMANY: (October 3, 1990, Midnight, Frankfurt am Main)

Germany is a Cancer rising country with the ascendant at 10 degrees with natal Ketu in the 1st house and Rahu in the 7th house. Rahu will transit in Pushya and Rahu will be over its ascendant. Watch **November** of this year when Rahu goes over its ascendant. The migrant crisis is likely to peak then but Germany seems unable to shift its liberal policies, which are destroying its culture.

European nations like Germany will continue to be challenged by foreign immigration this year with so many Cancer rising charts and Rahu transiting their 1st house.

When Rahu moves into Gemini in **March 2019**, I wonder if more European nations will follow Austria and Hungary's recent leads and move toward anti-Islamic politicians and legislation. I have to think that Europe is in great danger if they do not stem this tide.

Mars/Ketu in the 7th house will increase its aggressive tensions and fears around Russia and lead to defense increases. Germany is also in a Saturn/Jupiter period and will enter Mercury in **March 2019** with Mercury in the 3rd house. This may help lift Germany out of the weight of the past.

I do fear that the migrant crisis will hurt the country greatly in the Mercury 12th house period where foreign dominance becomes stronger.

Continue ECU tensions are likely to continue with Rahu in the 1st house and Ketu in the 7th house in transit with things unlikely to be resolved.

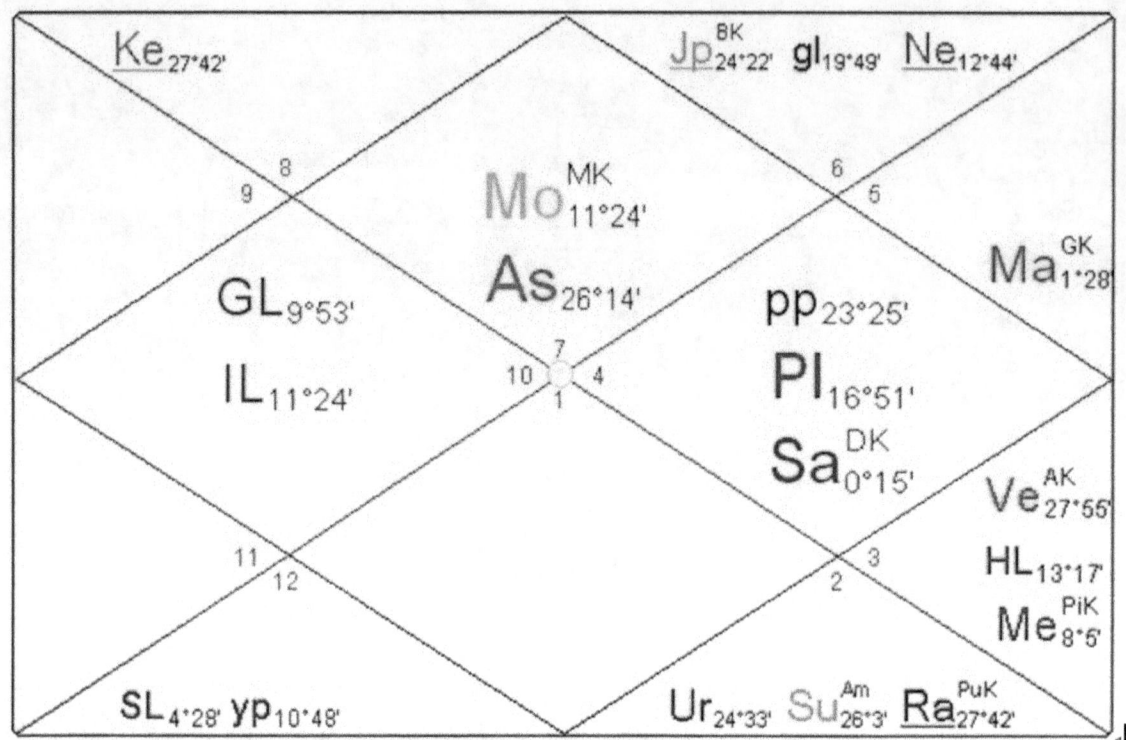

ITALY: (June 10, 1946, 18:10, Rome)

Italy is in a Ketu period until **June 2018** for this Libra rising country. Political chaos there may finally get resolved this year if the time of this chart is correct. Venus is in the 9th house in Gemini and would suggest a much better period coming. Still, the chart suggests a major banking crisis coming within a few years.

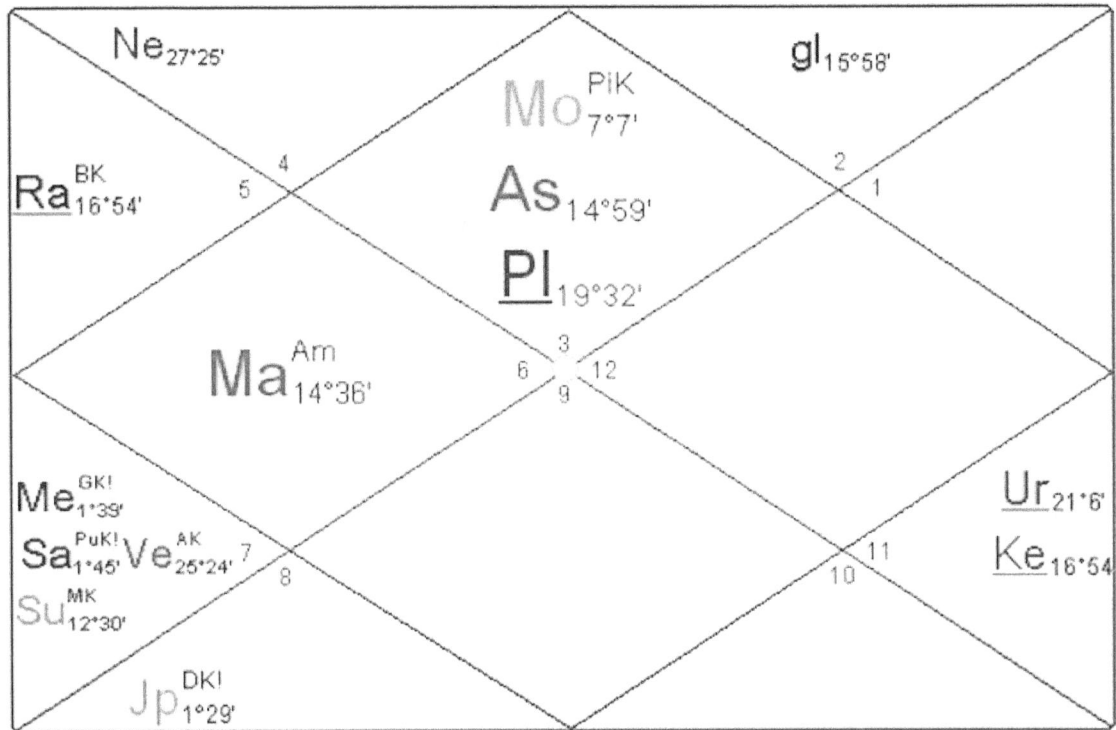

TURKEY: (October 19, 1923, 20:30, Ankara)

The New Year for Turkey is troubling this year and they have been in the news. Their natal chart has Mercury, Venus and exalted Saturn in the 5th house with a Venus major period ending **March 2020** followed by a debilitated Sun period starting with Sun in the 5th house.

Saturn now transiting their 7th house is interested in boundary setting and there is major political realignments happening. I have to think their quasi-dictator is in trouble as the Sun major period starts but then again that can lead to taking more control due to fear.

Political analysts note that: *"Due to the rapidly developing situation in the region and the failed military coup attempt in July, Erdogan's Turkey has become a reluctant ally of the Syrian-Russian-Iranian alliance in the Syrian war. Examples of this, such as the success of the Astana talks on Syria, the Russian-Turkish S-400 deal, and the Turkish-Iranian-Iraqi cooperation to counter the formation of an independent Kurdish State in northern Iraq by the Kurdistan Regional Government showcase this changed geo-political landscape."*

During 2018, Turkey will remain a key player in the ongoing Syrian crisis, and an ally (if a reluctant one) of the Iranian-Russian-Syrian alliance in the region. Ankara has few options remaining aside from developing its coordination with this bloc.

The current US foreign policy towards northern Syria and Iraq is frankly incoherent, with Turkey (being a NATO member and the most powerful US partner in the Eastern Mediterranean), no longer considering the US as a reliable ally in its strategic planning.

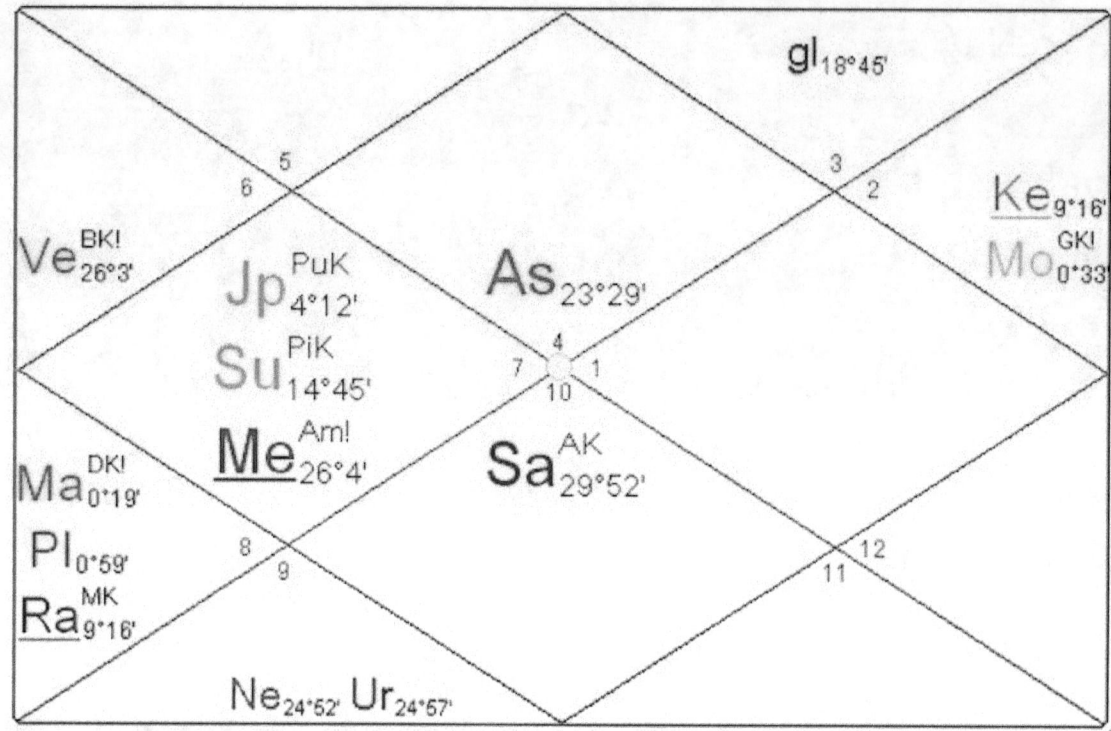

EUROPEAN UNION: (November 01, 1993, Midnight, Brussels)

This Cancer rising chart is also subject to the intense bickering of Rahu transiting the 1st house and Ketu transiting the 7th house. Mars in Capricorn for 5 months is going to intensify the aggressive nature of the EU wanting to control partners this year. Rahu in the 1st can want to overpower its opponents and the EU has continued to almost move into a dictatorship in the number of rules imposed on members and they are rebelling. EU is running a Rahu /Jupiter period with Rahu in the 5th house and Mars will transit over natal Saturn in early **November**. Rahu/Saturn period has Saturn in the 7th house and fear of enemies and then Rahu transiting into the 12th house in **March 2019**, should start shaking up this union and wondering if the Saturn/Pluto/Ketu/Jupiter transits through their 7th house into **2020 - 2021** will lead to dissolution. It's not looking good here. I think the migrant crisis is a real problem.

Political analysts note: "*In the European Union, we can observe the continued decline of the institutions of the European bureaucracy. Crises such as those we see in Catalonia, as well as the inability of the European leadership to successfully deal with the migration flow from North Africa and the Middle East are clear signs of this continuing decay. In an attempt to control these problems, the EU has intensified attempts to develop a joint security system and to lay the foundation for the creation of a European army.*

These efforts, however, could come too late. If the EU is unable to find a way to consolidate its member states in 2018, we can expect to witness further fragmentation in the future."

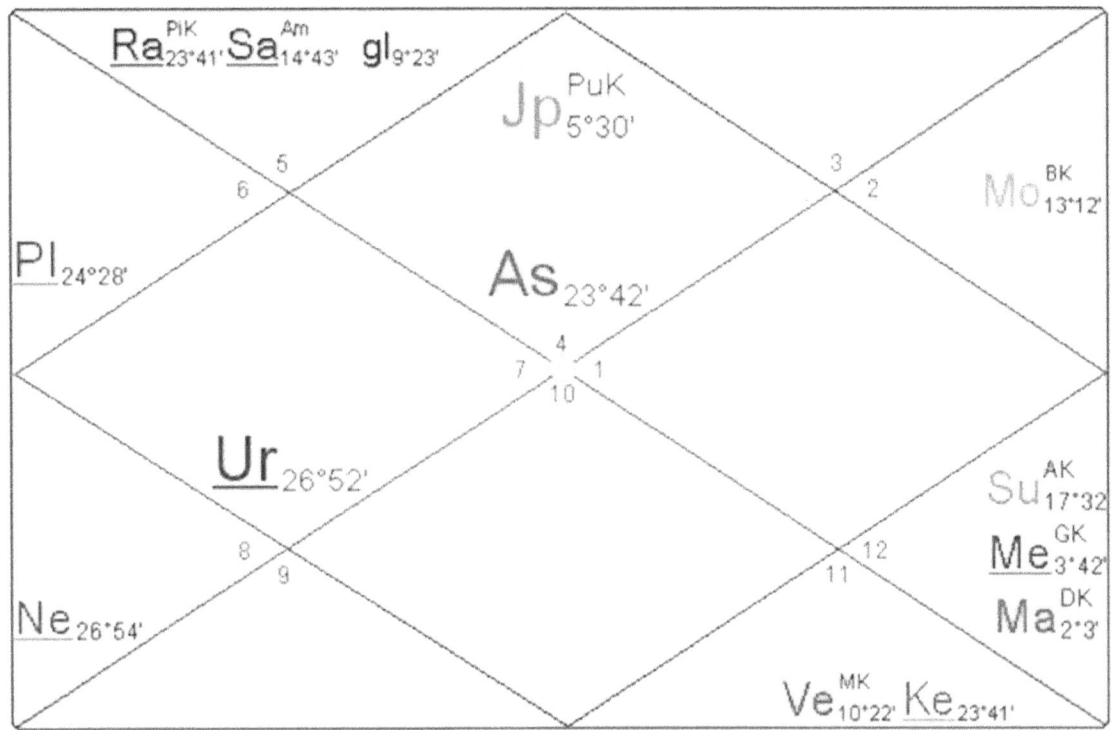

IRAN: (April 1, 1979, 15:00, Tehran)

This Cancer rising country with an ascendant at 23 degrees Cancer has just been having Rahu go over its ascendant, so the recent unrest makes sense given the radical and revolutionary nature of Rahu. It would seem to calm down as Rahu moves away from the ascendant. It has an exalted Jupiter in Cancer and is in a Jupiter/Ketu period and it seems like it knows who they are and what is right. Unfortunately, Jupiter that strong can be too fundamentalist. The challenge is also the Rahu/Ketu transits that will continue to be a problem until **March 2019**.

Political analysts note that: Iran has also strengthened its positions in the region over the last ten years. It has reinforced its air defense with the Russian-made S-300 systems, strengthened its armed forces and got combat experience in Syria and other local conflicts. Tehran also strengthened its ideological positions between the Shia and even Sunni population, which live in the region.

Considering these circumstances, initial expert opinions indicate that Israel would decide to participate in a large-scale conflict in Lebanon only in the case of some extraordinary event. However, the growing Arab-Israeli tensions and the tense Israeli-Hezbollah relationship are moving this extraordinary event ever closer.

Nonetheless, Israel will continue local acts of aggression conducting artillery and air strikes on positions and infrastructure of Hezbollah in Syria and maybe in Lebanon. Israeli Special Forces will conduct operations aimed at eliminating top Hezbollah members and destroying the movement's infrastructure in Lebanon and Syria. Saudi Arabia will likely support these Israeli actions. It is widely known that Riyadh would rather use a proxy and engage in clandestine warfare.

With Jupiter in the first house so strongly, I doubt that Iran will be toppled despite its enemies ganging up on it. The July eclipses could certainly trigger something and when Saturn goes into Capricorn in **2020**, I suspect Iran will have more of its hands full.

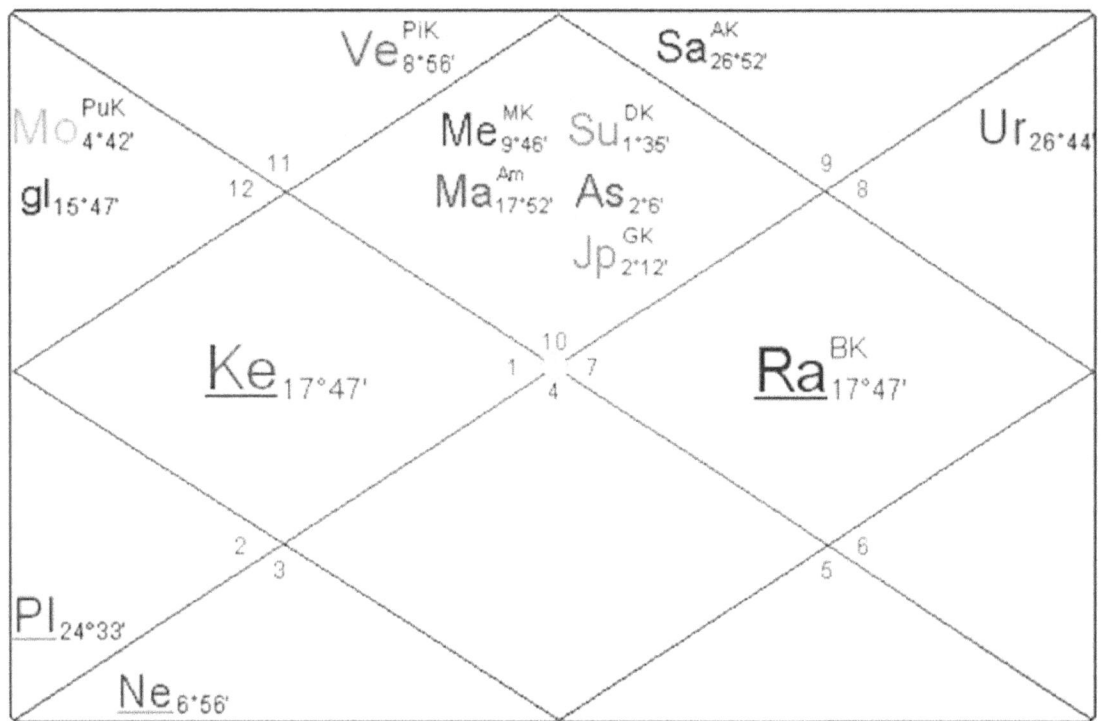

SAUDI ARABIA: (January 15, 1902, 06:45, Riyadh, Saudia Arabia)

Saudi Arabia is another big country in the news, this Capricorn rising country also having major Rahu/Ketu transits and Saudi Arabia has 4 planets in Capricorn including, Jupiter, Mars, Rahu and Sun. Expect more fireworks here with the eclipses going on in their axis and Mars/Ketu conjunctions happening here this summer.

They do go into a Saturn major period in **February 2020** and with Saturn going into Capricorn, one would expect stability to emerge by then but before the end of Jupiter/Rahu, it should shake things up.

Oil tends to fall in Saturn periods, as was the case in Rahu/Saturn in 1993 and Jupiter/Saturn in **2005 - 2006** so Saturn major period may mean the end of the oil era?

Political analysts note that: *"All these took place amid the developing crisis in Saudi Arabia where Crown Prince Mohammed bin Salman had launched a large-scale purge among the top officials, influential businesspersons and princes under the pretext of combating corruption.*

According to the experts, the move is aimed at consolidating the power of the crown prince and his father, King Salman. In general, the kingdom is seeking to shift its vector of development and to become a more secular state. In 5-10 years, it can even abandon Wahhabism as the official ideology. At the same time, Saudi Arabia is involved in an unsuccessful conflict in Yemen and a diplomatic crisis with Qatar. This situation fuels tensions and a competition for resources among the Saudi clans. As a result, the Saudi regime and the Saudi state in general, are now, in a weak position."

These are the key reasons why Saudi Arabia prefers to avoid an open participation in new conflicts. Additionally, there is always a chance, that for example, of conflict in Lebanon, the main combat actions could be moved to the Saudi territory.

Russia and Iran are also not interested in this "*big new war*" because such a conflict in the Middle East will pose a direct threat to their national security.

During the coming year we can expect to see both Israel and Saudi Arabia continuing their diplomatic and military efforts to deter Iran and Hezbollah.

Riyadh will continue its efforts to turn Yemen into a puppet state, but is unlikely to achieve any notable successes, leaving the Houthis and their missile arsenal as a constant threat to Saudi Arabia.

Israel and Saudi Arabia will also continue their building of a broad anti-Iranian coalition, with the support of the Trump administration, while Israeli forces will continue conducting their limited military operations against Hezbollah targets in Syria and Lebanon. In general, the chances of a new regional conflict will remain high.

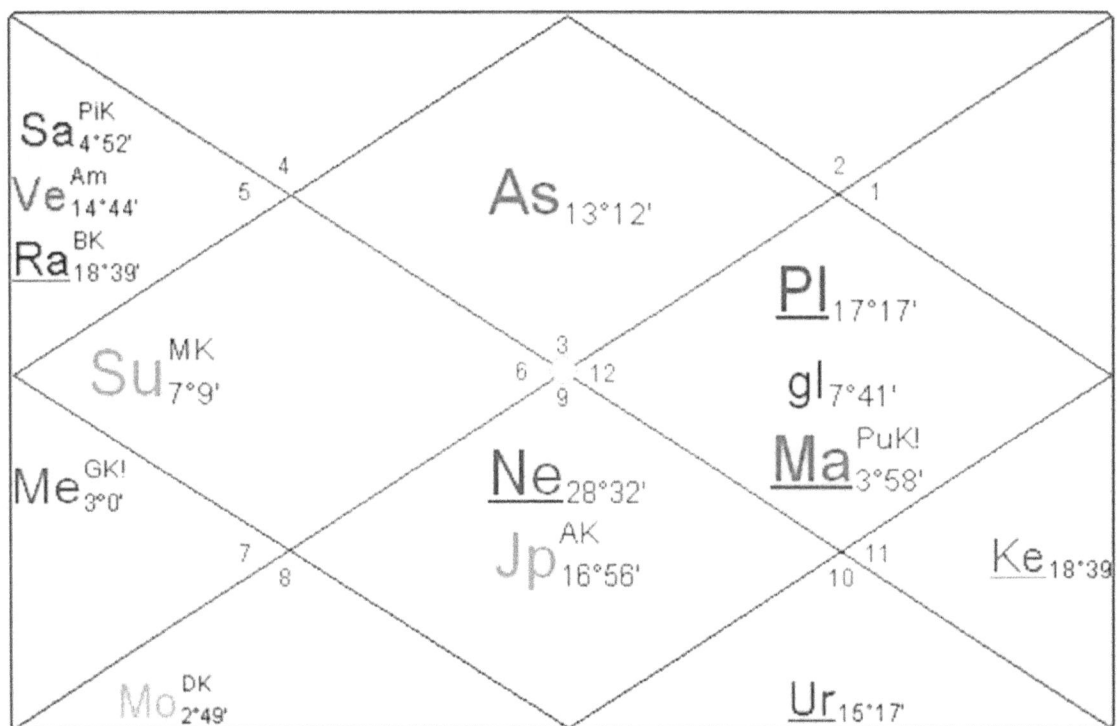

VENEZUELA: (September 22, 1830, Midnight, Caracas)

This Gemini rising country is completing Sade Sati with its Scorpio Moon in the final section for Sade Sati with the transit of Saturn into Purva Ashadha (Sagittarius 13.20-26.4) **March – June**, which should really accelerate the crisis. Sun/Saturn period ending in **February 2018** should go into a better Sun/Mercury period but then the January total lunar eclipse is visible in the area and should spark a major crisis in **February**. I am not sure how the people can survive there unless they overthrow their corrupt ruler.

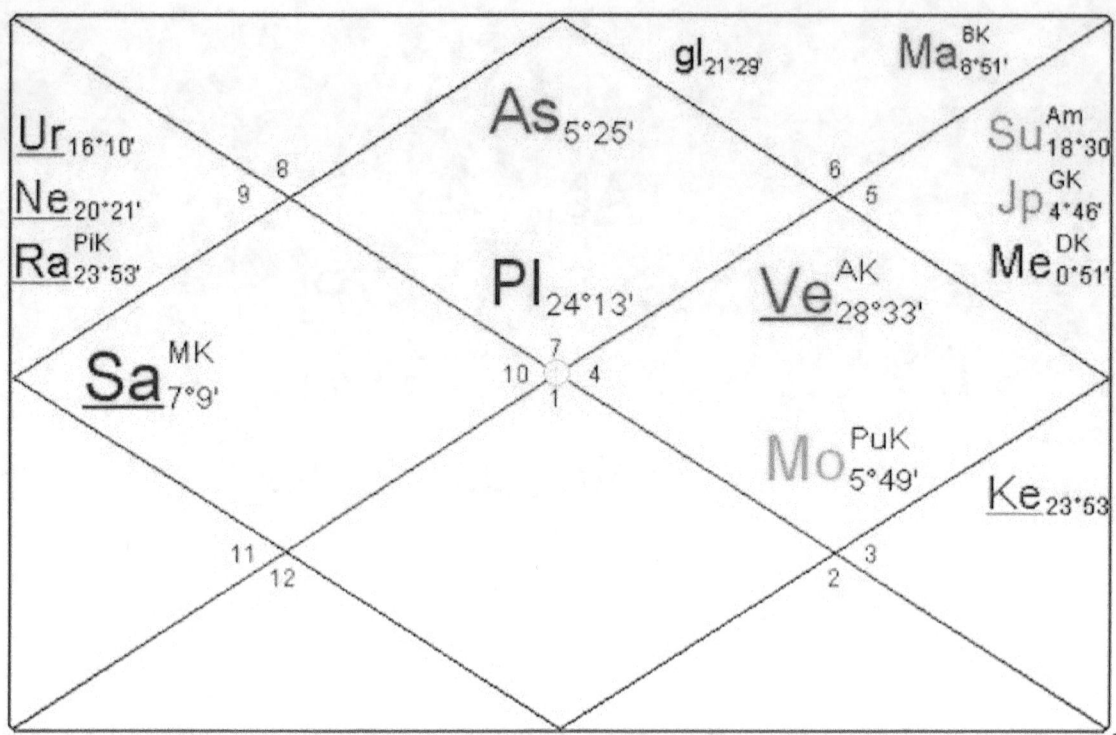

RUSSIA: (September 5, 1991, 10:30, Moscow)

This Libra rising country with retrograde Venus in Cancer in the 10th house is in the news every day. Jupiter transiting the 1st house is giving them great status this year until October. Moon in Cancer at 5 degrees will get hit late in the year by Rahu and stir things up a bit. There are some movements not happy with Putin but skeptical he can be usurped. Venus 5 month stay in Libra will be a big support for Russia to move its agenda forward this fall.

Russia is currently in a Mercury/Rahu period with Mercury in the 11th house and Rahu in the 3rd house and Mercury/Jupiter **2019 - 2021** looks more troubling for this country but I am not suggesting nuclear war but problems with enemies.

Mars aspects Rahu in this chart and it is making the country more aggressive and fearful. The Mars aspects on Rahu in transit this year from **April - November** are not going too helpful.

Big shift in Chara Dasha **September 2018** to Capricorn period that is connected to the 4th house and 9th house should improve foreign relationships, as should the Venus transit in Libra.

Debilitated Rahu in Sagittarius in the 3rd house aspected by Mars in the 12th house is a problem but more so in a Mars period. With Mercury/Rahu going on until **February 2019**, we have to assume that their war-like aggressive energy will increase. Political analysts note the increasing influence of Russia on the Middle East:

"The rapidly developing relations between Russia and Egypt have been overshadowed by the more prominent relationships between Russia and Syria, as well as Russia and Iran. Nevertheless, the Russia-Egypt relationship deserves closer scrutiny because, unlike the country's relations with the other two Middle Eastern powers, it concerns a country that until recently appeared to be firmly in Western orbit. The abrupt shift of its geopolitical vector toward Eurasia therefore represents a far bigger change for the region than Russia's successful support of the legitimate Syrian government, or the close relationship with the Islamic Republic of Iran, both of which have been on the Western "*enemies list*" for decades. The reasons for this shift are twofold and have to do with the way Western powers interact with Middle Eastern powers in the context of a systemic economic crisis, as well as with Russia's demonstrated attractiveness as an ally.

These events have led to strengthening economic ties and military cooperation between both sides. Recent negotiations to build Egypt's first nuclear plant, as well as those allowing Russian and Egypt joint use of each other's air space and military bases are perhaps the most noticeable examples of this cooperation.

With recent rumors of Russia establishing a military base on the coast of the Red Sea, in Sudan, it is easy to conclude that Moscow has become an influential power in the region, with some countries now viewing Russia as an attractive alternative to the US. With its rejection of direct cooperation with Moscow, Washington has weakened its own position in the region.

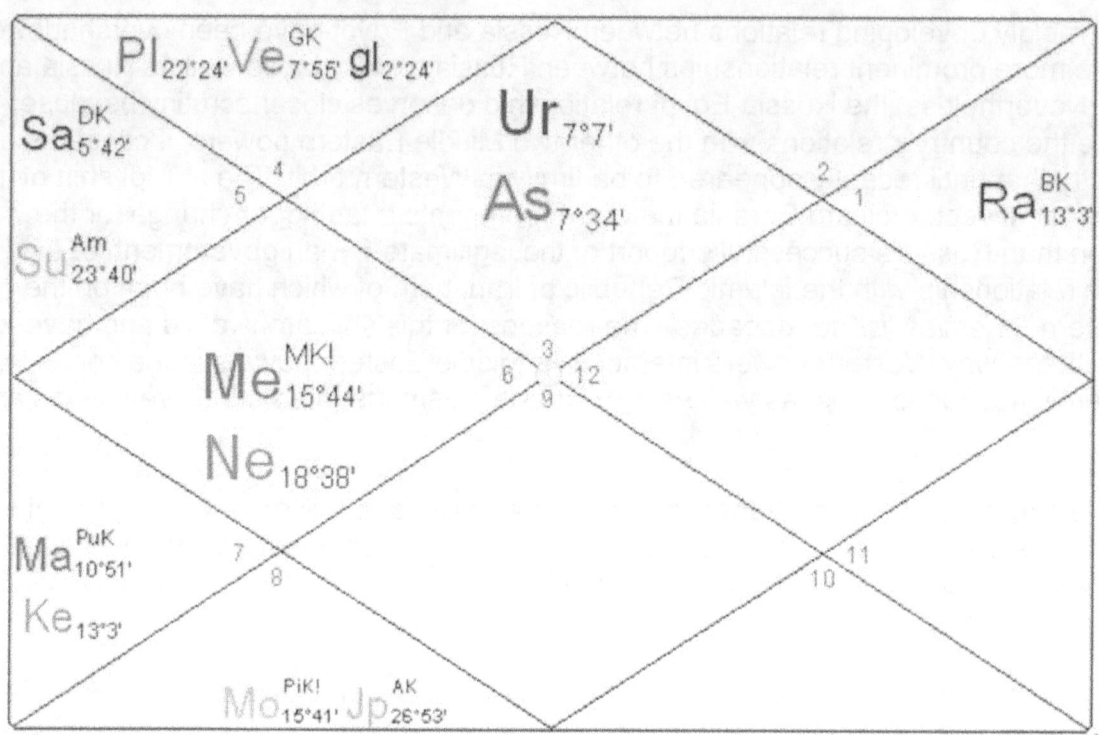

NORTH KOREA: (September 10, 1948, Midnight, Pyongyag, North Korea, unverified

I am not clear on the rising sign with no verified time, but the date is correct, and they do have a debilitated Scorpio moon creating deep insecurity as a nation. They are still in Sade Sati with the transit through Mula nakshatra into early March being a more dangerous part of their chart and then the retrograde Saturn return into Mula Nakshatra being very difficult again in **June - November**. Their annual chart cast for **March 18, 2018** is Libra rising and if they make it through the spring, they should be fine in the fall.

Jupiter in the 1st house is in their annual chart and despite world press fears that they will blow up the world, the reality is that they do not have that desire and their nuclear arsenal is a deterrent. Still, we cannot rule out a fear-based attack by aggressive countries like the United States. Russia and South Korea appear to be making progress in preventing war and Venus in Pisces this year will help in the annual chart.

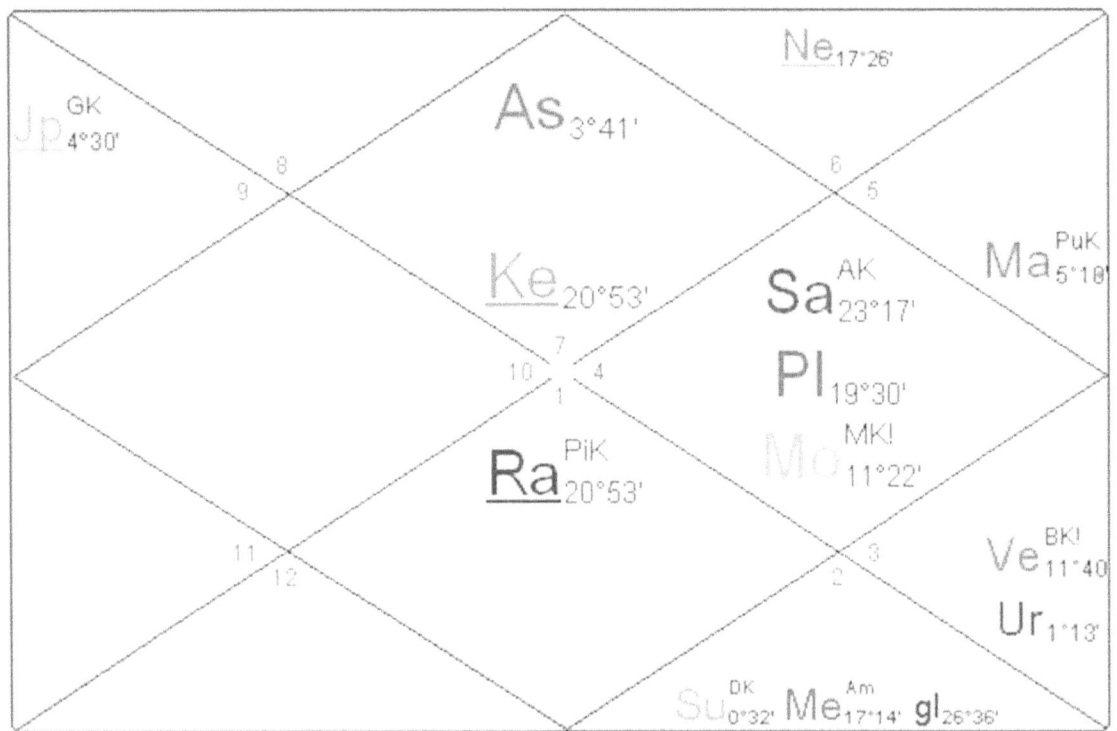

ISRAEL: (May 14, 1948, 16:37, Tel Aviv)

This Libra rising country will do better in the fall with the long transit of Venus in Libra coming. They are in a troubling Mars/Saturn period that started at Christmas with Mars in the 11th house and Saturn 12 houses away in the natal 10th house.

Their annual chart looks troubling this year with the ascendant coming out in the Leo gandanta for **March 18, 2018**. Rahu ends up in the 12th house here creating political tensions and desire for change.

Our political analysts note: 'Israel and Saudi Arabia will also continue their building of a broad anti-Iranian coalition, with the support of the Trump administration, while Israeli forces will continue conducting their limited military operations against Hezbollah targets in Syria and Lebanon. In general, the chances of a new regional conflict will remain high.

In this already unstable environment, the current US policy remains as one of the key destabilizing factors in the region. The recent US recognition of Jerusalem as Israel's capital, as well as the hostility towards the Iranian nuclear deal, continues to fuel tensions between the Israeli-Saudi and the Iranian-Hezbollah blocs.

The current US administration continues with America's consistent pro-Israeli and anti-Iranian policies in the region, inspiring both Israel and Saudi Arabia to embrace more active policies as well.

As a result of this growing US support, the Israeli military stands ready to implement active military responses to any action taken by Hamas, Hezbollah, or any of the other regional players whom Israel considers a threat to its wide range of national interests.

While the odds are low of the Trump administration being able to abort the Iranian nuclear deal, the mere fact that such attempts continue does little to contribute to peace in the region. The fact remains that Washington fuels the new cold war and perhaps even a potential hot war in the Middle East.

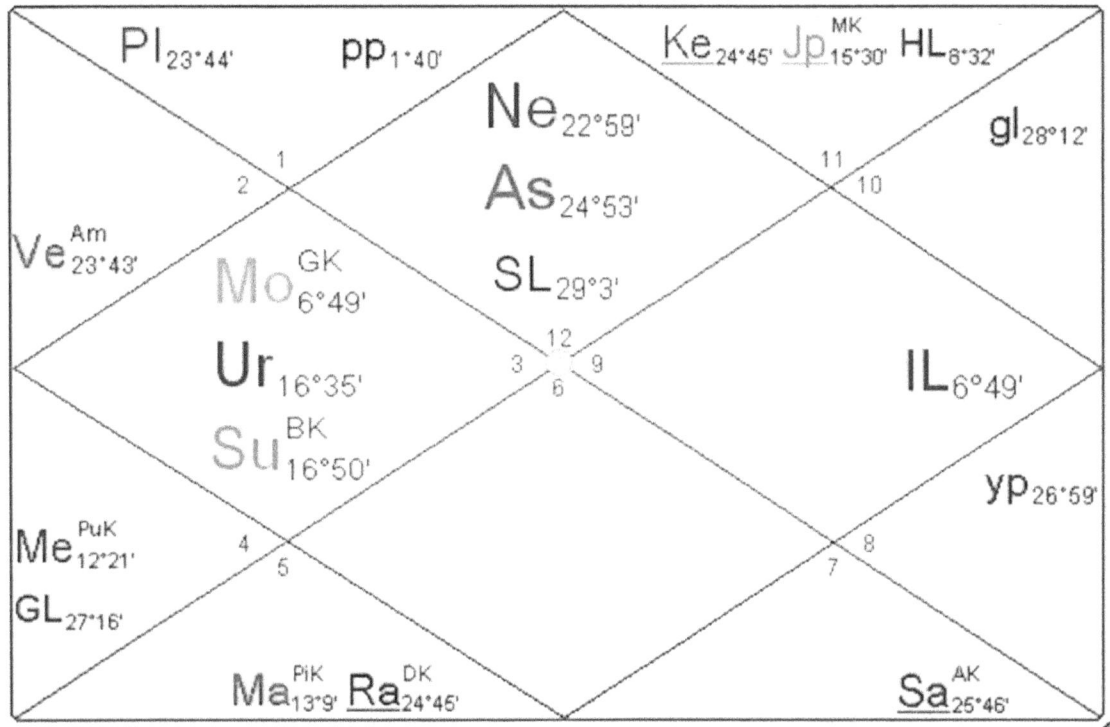

CANADA (July 1, 1867, Midnight, Ottawa)

This Pisces rising country is finishing off its Jupiter period in **April 2021,** but the chart lord Jupiter is in the 12th house, retrograde and in Rahu's nakshatra with Rahu conjunct Mars in the 6th house. Canada has not had an easy time economically the last 4-5 years. Still it has an exalted Saturn in the 8th house promoting longevity.

Jupiter is transiting the 8th house in Libra until **October**, which is still suggesting huge transformations happening in the Trudeau administration. Jupiter going into the 9th house in **October** will be more supportive for the country. Rising oil prices this year should help.

I am concerned about the end of the Jupiter period with Jupiter/Rahu starting in **November 2018** and the end of a major period is a bit problematic with Rahu afflicted in the 6th house by Mars.

I also should note that Rahu will transit over the natal Sun and Moon in Cancer in **October 2019 and April 2020** in their natal 4th house. While the housing bubble has been crumbling a bit, it would seem Rahu in Gemini in Ardra will cause some major shake-ups around housing in late **2019 - 2020**.

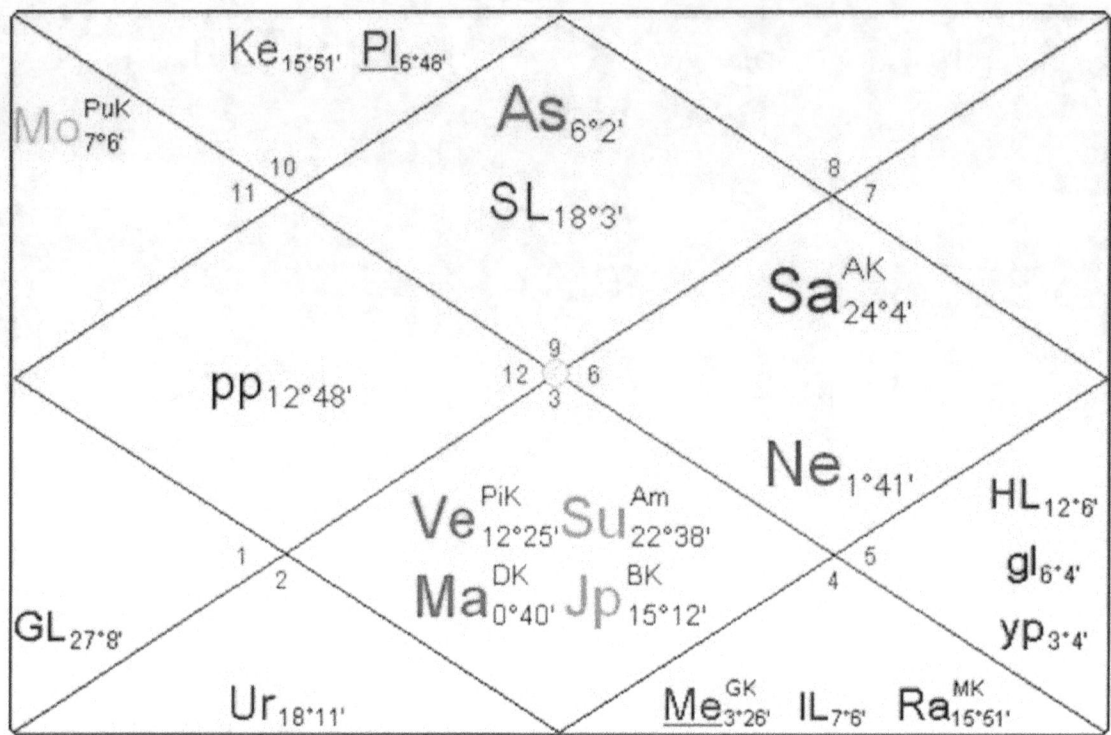

UNITED STATES (July 4, 1776, 6:17 PM, Philadelphia, PA

This Sagittarius rising country has Saturn going through its 1st house the next 2 years and its image in the world will continue to diminish. The Chinese and the Russians continue to work with the BRIC countries to derail the US dollar and pull war-mongering money out of the US treasury system.

The US is headed for one of their largest transformational periods with Saturn/Jupiter/Ketu and Pluto transiting through Sagittarius in **2019 - 2021** and the Nodal axis is triggered with Ketu going into Sagittarius in March 2019 and Rahu into the house of enemies at the same time. The big trigger should be Rahu transiting into the constellation of Ardra, **September 2019 - April 2020** and then Ketu going over the US ascendant in **May 2020**.

The current transits of Rahu/Ketu in the US 8th and 2nd house axis is going to force transformation around the US budget and debt crisis and the summer eclipses and Mars/Ketu conjunctions in the US 2nd house of Capricorn are likely to cause a crisis around US bonds and interest rates.

Jupiter in Libra in the 11th house in Vishakha nakshatra may fan continued exuberance until **October** but the 12th house transit into Scorpio in **October 2018 - November 2019** will force serious problems unless change happens, and Saturn in Sagittarius will not help matters.

I try to stay out of politics and I will not comment much on Trump, but he is in a Jupiter period and his stationary Jupiter in the 2nd house in Virgo will continue to support him through attack. Still the Annual Chart for **2020** does suggest a more humanitarian new leader will emerge for the US.

We have detailed articles below about the US Rahu period and the Saturn/Ketu/Jupiter/Pluto transits and their impact on the world and US economies.

Note: We do not have a UK chart that we trust and I have a few versions for Australia and so I will bow out on discussions there. India is always discussed so well by my colleagues there so I will also defer to their comments.

THE UNITED STATES IN A RAHU PERIOD: DECEMBER 2015 – 2033

The United States went into a Rahu Mahadasha period on **December 1, 2015** based on my rectified US Chart (**7/4/1776**, 18:17 pm, Philly and it is always controversial talking about the US chart and it's starting time).

Rahu governs immigrants and outcasts, so it would suggest a repeat of the huge influx of immigration that we saw between **1895 to 1913**. At the moment, the Trump administration has curtailed that, but world upsets are likely to continue migration in **2021** when a more liberal policy could be restored if the Democrats take back the White House.

I also expect that the US began in a Rahu Mahadasha in 1776 so prolonged revolutionary energy may boil up to throw out the leaders in power and continued dissatisfaction with government will eventually lead to something more dramatic. The battle of the conspiracy-orientated "*Deep State*," the CIA and military industrial complex and their hold on our government will continue to be a struggle over the next 7 years with Neptune in the constellation of Purva Bharapada (Aquarius 20 - Pisces 3.2).

Rahu governs technology, so I would expect huge technological advances in the period - probably even more so than we can imagine. The period has already brought self-driving cars and the industry seems determined to get the bugs out and make them a reality.

The last Rahu period, **1895 - 1913** was a troubled time for the US economy with many banking upheavals and problems with legislation around the metals industry, particularly silver. During that period, the Rahu period started in the 2nd house and we are not expecting a repeat exactly. Clearly the US is setting up for another economic crisis with the budget ceiling not under control and there are no real solutions for the economy happening so at some point between **2019 - 2023**, we could see a huge financial crisis happening.

The difference between the 1895 Rahu period and this Rahu period is that under the principle of Dasha Pravesh and running a chart for the start of the dasha period in 2015, one gets Rahu in the US 10th house in the exalted sign of Virgo so getting an exact repeat of **1895 - 1913** should not be totally in the cards.

It would be easy to predict another major war as the US is always finding a war to fight. Sagittarius rising is the most war-like sign of the zodiac having the symbol of the archer and Saturn in Sagittarius has brought its shares of wars. One would think that with Mars going into Sagittarius in **March** and joining Saturn, that we will probably attack Korea.

In the past US Rahu period the Spanish-American war did breakout in Rahu/Jupiter. The 40-year world war cycle connected with Saturn/Ketu conjunctions (think of

September 1939 for the invasion of Nazi Germany into Poland) is also happening during **September 2019** during the Rahu period and is not that auspicious. The saving grace is the Dasha Pravesh in the 10th house again with Saturn 3rd from the Dasha Lord but Jupiter 12th from the dasha lord.

Rahu periods bring political upheaval. During the last Rahu period, US President McKinley was elected and later assassinated by a Polish anarchist in 1901. Some of the transits for 2018 including Ketu in Capricorn this year also suggest great anger toward government and the Mars/Ketu conjunction this year between **June - September 2018** is likely to bring its share of angry citizens, ready to rise up! I would not be surprised to see an assassination attempt as we saw in 1981 against Regan with Ketu in Capricorn as noted by Joni Patry in her research.

The last Rahu period brought growth of labor, populism and higher tariffs and taxes. Given the coming economic problems for the US, the chances for saving the country by raising taxes seems likely as it moves toward crisis. We have also thought that as US government finances have problems, state and local governments would take over and increase property taxes to keep things going. That seems inevitable. The tax bill has started the process reducing deductions for property taxes.

The good thing about the last Rahu period was that Theodore Roosevelt brought great reform to the US, created the national park system and brought the big stick diplomacy to fight for the little man. Our work on the 2020 President Election suggests someone who will fight for the people again and maybe Elizabeth Warren or someone like her stand a chance of bringing the kind of change and populism that is needed for the move from a *corporate-topia* back to a government by the people. The fight against the "Deep State" will be long but I think that the people may have a chance with the Saturn/Jupiter/Pluto conjunction in **2020**.

Rahu is also connected to mass epidemics and the chance for a repeat of a massive problem seems strong during Rahu/Saturn, which starts in **December 2020**. The Rahu/Saturn opposition in **2019 - 2020** will fan that energy.

Rahu has a way of wanting to change outmoded aspects of society and uncovering deception. The current uncovering of the Uranium One scandal with the Clinton Foundation and much more is likely to unfold through the period. Rahu should continue to unearth the secret and shadow government that has been keeping us at war, supporting the military industrial complex and turning the CIA and FBI against their President. The drama of this will continue to unfold.

While Trump is not popular with many, he is a perfect reflection of the Rahu period being a brash ambitious President ready to take the country to war with Korea, challenging the *"Deep State"* and getting rid of corruption. The military industrial complex will not go down easily, and Trump has surrounded himself with generals as there is a huge fight going on. He has to make concessions to the Military Industrial complex or fall victim like President Kennedy did. Clearly, he has a very fine line to walk.

I find Rahu refreshing as it is into societal transformation. Clearly the outmoded institutions of society and the secret societies running the US economy into the ground with debt need reform. I suspect that a crisis between **2019 - 2020** will bring in a new leader to continue the transformation that is needed.

ASTRO-FINANCIAL OUTLOOK: LOOKING AHEAD INTO 2019 – 2023

Subscribers often want me to do long — term forecasting and I have stayed away from it over the past years because our world changes so quickly and difficult problems are being solved by new technologies. At the same time, the Central Banker/Military Industrial Complex, media whitewash continues to leave us wondering about the end game, as historically the world has never built up these unsustainable levels of debt that cannot end prettily without massive changes and reality checks that our leaders do not want to do. Even Trump's 10-year balanced budget proposal is fraught with the naïve notion that we can have 3% growth over the next 10 years, which has never happened.

No one is addressing the notion that the glories of Detroit and the wonder of the glorified industrial age cannot repeat on dreams of electric cars that run self-drive.

Meanwhile, Amazon and Wal-Mart continue to take over the world and price everyone out of business and kill main street America. We wonder why we struggle. Automation and robotics continue to make people less important and our government is supporting the oligarchy in their profitable questing at the expense of real, struggling people. We are heading toward a climax into **2019 - 2020** with regard to all of this. People are anxious now, but I suspect the real trouble will come in a few years based on larger cycles at work.

On **May 24, 2017** we began a new 140 - year cycle with Neptune entering Purbabhadra Nakshatra (Aquarius 20 - Pisces 3.20) that we have not seen since **1853 - 1859**. We will see more of its impact from **March 2018 to February 2025**. It is complex, but it is connected to schemes, inflation, conspiracies, and grand governmental plans to make everything bigger in scope.

Historically, we saw this the last time this cycle happened, in 1853. For example, in **October 1853**, on the East coast of the United States, Donald McKay launches the Great Republic, the world's biggest sailing ship, which at 4,500 tons is too large to be successful. It sank. The recent launch of the world's largest plane is a modern comparison. This cycle can inflate but, in the end, it deflates as high hopes crumble. Uber is putting cabbies out of business but losing millions on paper, as are many other Silicon Valley startups.

This new Neptune cycle that began in **mid-June 2017** will also support the film industry, raw cotton, medicine, surgical goods, tobacco, drugs, chemicals and perfumes. A smaller cycle with Jupiter in Libra from **September 2017 - September 2018** will enhance the growth in these industries so if we get stock pullbacks into **September** and **October** this year, these areas may be places to buy.

This Neptune cycle also rules socialism, so the Bernie movement will probably come back strongly from **2018** onward but it also contributes to political instability — as if we do not have enough of that!

The darker side of this cycle is secret societies and conspiracies and we have to be concerned that the *"Deep State"* will be emboldened to create more smoke and mirror deception until maybe **January 2019** when that bubble will break. For now, they will probably get more powerful.

HISTORY AND SECRET SOCIETIES:
THE FEDERAL RESERVE

Most of you know that shareholders in foreign countries, such as the Rothchilds, privately own the Federal Reserve Bank. The United States has been under economic tyranny ever since 1913 when the Federal Reserve was signed into law by then President Woodrow Wilson. In its 104-year history, any independent government or private agency has never once audited the Federal Reserve. There is a total lack of transparency where the Federal Reserve is concerned. The Federal Reserve acts as a law unto itself. It creates fiat currency out of nothing and charges the US government and therefore, the taxpayer has little interest on it.

This is a something for nothing usury at the highest level — the ultimate Ponzi scheme. The Federal Reserve does whatever it wants with regard to foreign banks with no accountability to congress or the general public. If established political, economic, and industrial social and physical infrastructures potentially fail, it's very possible that the US will break into regions and people are forced to survive in their local communities. Human society will be forced to reinvent itself. There is some kind of climax around **2019 - 2020** for this. Exactly what will happen is unclear, but I think we have another year to focus on self-sufficient agricultural in our homes with hydroponic pod gardens where you can grow vegetables in the corner of your apartment.

LOOKING AHEAD: 2020

There is a huge climax into **January 13, 2020** with Saturn conjunct Pluto when the karmic backlash of the abuse of power and the misuse of advanced technology can be the most severe. This could lead to unleashing of deadly power in the hands of organized purposeful institutionalized groups like the *"Deep State."* Still on the bright side, there is a chance to overcome our most destructive spiritual ignorance, and our deepest fears, which have manifested as the institutionalized evils of oppression tyranny and war.

Also, in **2020** there are a number of key cycles that are important, which indicate a new populist experiment in religious, economic, political and social organization with Jupiter conjunct the South node, Ketu. The alternative would be an increase in more evil, contemptuous and brazen out-of-control elitist corruption. It could also indicate hyperinflation necessitating the creation of a new, more, just, monetary system.

Many larger cycles have created a fear of closure. Many people today sense a global "end of times" feeling, particularly because of the decline of natural resources, the rapid extinction of species, and the intensification of extreme weather patterns. Will there be a new dawn following the dissolution of so much that has been taken for granted?

THE 33 - 38 YEAR CYCLE: 2020

There is a key 33 - 38-year cycle happening in **2020** connected to Saturn conjunct Pluto. This meeting of forces represents, among other things, the redistribution of power in the world or, in other words, which faction will make the decisions that affect the greater collective, whether this occurs in plain sight or behind the scenes.

From a spiritual perspective, this cycle reflects a rite of passage determining who is most qualified to be the custodian of resources, and thus regulates who will be in a position of influence. In its purest form, this cycle is one of the highest tests of integrity and morality for those in authority, along with a test of capacity and resilience. Beyond the management of power, this cycle is also about the skill to increase power and the value of resources.

This cycle reflects a lesson about the right use of power, so this cycle is also associated with corruption and abuse. Since it holds the key to the "bank coffers," it also describes the temptation to disregard moral standards and use global resources to satisfy one's greed. It would seem that there would be a climax for the IMF, the Central Banks and the Military Industrial Complex are set for a reckoning. Sooner or later, corruption is exposed, and this cycle represents the karmic consequences of misaligned actions.

Interestingly, David Rockefeller, one of the richest and most influential bankers in the world, was born under this cycle, and so was Rupert Murdoch (opposition), head of a massive media empire, and Bill Gates, founder of Microsoft (listed as the wealthiest person in the world for a number of years). Similarly, Saudi Arabia, a country that possesses some of the largest supplies of oil in the world, was established under this cycle. So, a deep complex reckoning will need to happen. Despite his seemingly philanthropic nature, Bill Gates, is spearheading dangerous vaccinations in Africa, is doing the bidding of those that favor depopulation.

HISTORY OF THE 33 - 38 YEAR CYCLE:

Looking back at previous 33 - 38-year cycles with Saturn conjunct Pluto we have always seen major events happening. One of the last times we saw this cycle was in October 1914, around the outbreak of World War I. This global conflict certainly reshuffled power dynamics by dissolving the Russian monarchy, the Ottoman Empire, and the Austro-Hungarian Empire, which led to the redrawing of national borders within Europe.

In 1931, the ½ synodic period of this cycle defined an era that included the Great Depression, which started in October 1929, and also the Geneva Convention relative to the ethical treatment of prisoners of war, which entered into effect in July 1931.

The next key part of this cycle happened in October 1947 soon after World War II ended; Germany and Japan lost military influence and dominance, and the power struggle between Capitalism and Communism gained greater intensity.

In 1947, the International Monetary Fund (IMF), whose aim is to foster global economic growth and reduce world poverty, began its operations.

The year 1947 saw the division between India and Pakistan and their establishment as individual sovereignties (today both countries have nuclear weapons); this split cost Gandhi his life. In the Middle East, Israel gained independence from the British in 1948, creating an incredibly complex power dynamic in the region with the return of the Jews' spiritual influence in the markedly Arab-dominated region. While Israel possesses few natural resources (no oil in an oil-dominated region), the historical significance and spiritual power of the land are certainly the reasons it is perhaps the reason for ongoing battles in the region, essentially for control of the holy city of Jerusalem.

The following cycle of 1982 marked a time of economic recession in the world, with the highest rate of unemployment in the US since the Great Depression. It also marked the escalation of the Cold War during the Reagan years, later leading to the collapse of the Soviet Union. Soon after the cycle last peaked, in January 1983, the Kilauea volcano erupted in Hawaii; it has become the longest-lasting volcanic eruption, still flowing in **2015**.

OUTLOOK FOR 2020 CYCLE

We can anticipate important changes in the natural resources industry, the banking system, regional and world leadership, but it is difficult at this point to anticipate what direction this powerful influence will take. We understand that the initial intention of the cycle is to increase value and empower systems, but it is easy to mismanage these influences because they demand high ethical leadership, and therefore we must consider the prospect of a severe economic recession. This has sorely been lacking due to control from the Central Bank and "*Deep State*" more interested in bankrupting us and increasing the coffers of the military industrial complex rather than provide and do basic infrastructure re-building.

We can expect rebellion on both the individual level (people leaving their workplace and reinventing themselves) and the collective level (worldwide protests demanding change). In light of growing separatist sentiment in the US, we may see the secession movement gaining greater momentum. We have to think what is happening in Venezuela as an omen of what happens when government is not responsible.

THE 20 - YEAR CYCLE: SATURN CONJUNCT JUPITER

The 20 - year cycle is very key and hits in **December 2020** and is one of the most important markers representing what direction our lives are taking, personally and socially. It often sets the tone for the "new order" we will all respond to.

The most important cycle in the 20 - year cycle will hit **December 21, 2020** at a place where economic low points hit. The cycle creates the need for new rises in consciousness, but we do not think they will come about until **2023**. The climax into **late 2020**, will force attention to practical and financial matters where the **2023** cycle will bring forth a stronger push for culture, progress, and global emancipation and total freedom from the "*Deep Sate*".

If we contemplate the whole sequence of cyclical events in the year **2020**, with its dramatic cyclical alignments, we can anticipate great intensity and changes on many levels. These events will likely have a destructive edge as a new world order is programmed — change is not always a smooth process. However, since all the year's transits culminate in **2023**, we will see new solutions and paradigms emerge. There is a promise of rebirth and a new vision that will gradually unfold in the following months and years.

Still this huge climax in **2020**, suggests major restructuring of our political and economic institutions — more so than we have seen since the end of the World War 2. Let's hope our leaders are guided to do this peacefully as was the case when the Berlin Wall came down and the Soviet bloc crumbled without any major bombs going off.

2018 ASTRO-FINANCE OUTLOOK
(Revised January 18, 2018)

Note: Markets move very quickly as do our forecasts. I have a daily financial newsletter. Stay on top of forecasts with a monthly subscription to Financial Visions into the Future or the daily ETF Timer. Both available at www.commoditytimers.com.

US STOCK MARKET: CASH S & P 500 FUTURES by Barry Rosen

BIG PICTURE: Our monthly chart pattern is suggesting a move to 2980 but it can easily be extended given the parabolic rate of advance. Next weekly chart cycle high is **June 2018**. The rate of ascent and telescoping nature of the move could take it to S & P 3038. Jupiter in Libra and in the constellation of Vishakha will continue expansive exuberance.

BREAKDOWN POINT: Market will need to take out 2190 to issue a stronger sell signal on the monthly chart. New high toward **May 2018** should go to at least 2980 if not 3038. It seems pointless to call the top of the bull at this point in time, as the easy FED money will continue to push investment bankers into their one-way greedy mode and everyone is happy, and we should be happy that pensions are protected—at least temporarily.

LARGER CYCLE SYNTHESIS: A key 12-year cycle of Jupiter **is** positive from **September 11, 2017 - October 13, 2018**, the 18.5-year cycle which we last saw in **1999-2000** was also higher for stocks and goes from **September 11, 2017 into January 2019**. The 29.5-year cycle of Saturn is also positive from **October 26, 2017**. We continue to think that the game will continue into at least June 2018 and possibly a year longer. Trouble due in the summer of 2019 for sure.

MONTHLY CHART PATTERNS: 2980 on cash is likely before this bull market ends, and some patterns point higher to 3038. It takes a long time to turn an ocean liner around in so V-tops and crashes are not to be looked for, and publications that steer you that direction are being too sensational. It's too early to declare the top of the bull market. At the moment we have a bias toward **2018** as a key high. Some cycle analysts are even seeing **2019**. We need to do more work on that year.

YEARLY OVERVIEW: (12/15) Pattern analysis has kept us out of trouble as far as getting too beared-up. As we have noted, getting to 2980 an upper target might take at least until **June 2018** and create a rather symmetrical pattern on the monthly charts. There are a lot of messy political crosscurrents over the coming years, but the stock market is the only thing making money and the game there will continue and not sure what will pop it.

We think China is very vulnerable in **2018** and then Europe, and that money will flee to the US initially. It's pointless to predict a crash or focus on one and we can only take profits at key pattern completions 2980. If we're looking for a crash, it may be more from **2019 - 2021**.

In past analogue years when the stock market topped and crashed, the market fell 50% but it's hard to extrapolate the next major fall as we are moving into the 40-year world war cycle in **2019** and the breakdown of the massive bubbles never seen before so a retest of the **2010** cycle low is a very reasonable possibility. No doubt stocks are in a bubble and until we have a real economy not based on throwing printed money into the stock market to give the illusion that everything is fine, the market may not really recover for quite a while. Still, the blow-off phase isn't quite over. It would seem that if Trump can move the US to a real economy and possibly get rid of the Fed Reserve, which is one of the wishes for one of his new cabinet members, than the stock market may not need to deflate. Given the nature of bubbles and the nature of trouble world economies and spillover impact, the chance for a sharp break between **2019-2021** seems likely.

In looking at world economic cycles, a massive cycle low centers into **January 2020** and the global financial reset may not be complete until 2023. It would be naïve to think that governments can go on supporting bubbles indefinitely before someone runs out of money or the printing presses wear out.

INTEREST RATES

MONTLY CHART: (12/15) The long bond completed a major interest rate low going back to 1980 and so this top that we put in is very significant. It's clear from the Fed's forward guidance that higher rates are coming over the next 3 years and this is good news for savers but lifts the free money that has supported the mortgage industry into recovery and has kept credit card rates down. Many feel that as rates rise, the stock market will top out within 6 months and that the larger issue of the US having to pay more interest monthly to bond holders is a huge problem for our budget. Clearly something will have to give short-term until the economy really recovers, and more tax revenues are brought in.

DOLLAR INDEX
WEEKLY CHARTS: (1/4) There has been a movement buy Russia and China and other countries to usurp the Petrodollar in place since 1973 and force oil purchase in other currencies and hence taking money away from the US. This has been happening and weakness at the beginning of the year makes us wonder if the dollar will start weakening. It is too early in the year to take a total stand.

The dollar is close to a major chart breakdown if it closes under 8900 and then projections would go to 8500 and 8100. Saturn in Sagittarius may not be great for the dollar. At this point the market at best could recovery to 9550. We had assumed that the dollar would dominate this year with Jupiter's transit in Libra in the 11th house from the

US and a strong desire to buy US stocks with dollars and we are not giving up on that, but the market needs to take out 9100 and start accelerating soon.

Saturn going over the US ascendant around 6 degrees Sagittarius has not been helping the early fall in the dollar but it will gradually move away from there and that might help matters.

YEARLY CYCLE SYNTHESIS: (12/5) The 18.5-year cycle involving Rahu/Ketu that kicked in September is supportive for the next year and 1.5 years. It's hard to see the dollar taking out 89.00 even if we get a crisis and the tides will turn and it will recover into next year but skeptical now about taking out 95.50.

MONTHLY CHART PATTERNS: We'll stay open to the long-term cycle low projection to 6650-6750 and that could take until the 2023 to come in. We do see a lot of problems for the US **2019-2021** due to the debt levels with problems likely to increase as the fallout from crude continues. Still, Europe seems like it will be in worse shape. Indeed, higher interest rates into **2018** might continue to keep the dollar stronger once we get through the fall. In addition, long-term technological and growth outlook for the US may be favorable for long-term sustained growth. How the US is going to deal with its Social Security/health care/Medicare crisis is a huge issue.

The global unraveling into **2020-2021** is going to be quite fascinating and let's hope that prudent and calm minds prevail.

EURO OUTLOOK
by Barry Rosen

OVERALL: The Euro got above 120 to start the year and may have enough of a technical breakout to project 123.56 on cash and maybe 125.50 if the dollar falls to 8800. Still we think that US fundamentals are much better than European ones and that Europe is in trouble Into **2020** with the migration crisis

YEAR CHART OVERVIEW: (12/3) While the Catalan energy has temporarily vanished, it should come back in January due to cycles and we wonder if this will have a more major impact. Greek long bonds went over 4% again and so more trouble is brewing. More and more European countries don't want to be under the control of the heavy hand of the EU, which has had a liberal migrant policy that is destroying European sovereignty. This probably may climax in **2020** when indeed when it will seem as if Europe has be invaded by the Arab world.

Longer-term, Martin Armstrong is more pessimistic about Europe and the Euro:

"We are looking at the collapse of Europe unfold much faster than anyone suspected. I have been warning that the Continental EU banks are in serious trouble. The negative interest rates have devastated Europe. While trying to stimulate borrowers who are not interested without an opportunity to make money, the ECB has wiped out savers,

pensions, and sent cash into hiding contracting the European economy – not stimulating it. I have also warned that it is the EURO, which is in serious trouble, and that BREXIT was the only way to save Britain from being dragged down under as the Euro sinks.

The Italian banks are collapsing, and the crisis is now risking bringing down the Italian government. If they do not bailout the banks, the people will be in revolution. If they bailout the banks, they can only print Euros. This starting to illustrate what I have been warning about. The EURO is in effect like a gold standard. When crisis hit, everyone had to suspend the gold standard for World Wars I and II and then upon the fall of Bretton Woods. The currencies were tied to gold which they could not increase its supply. This is the same crisis now with the EURO. Despite the EURO is really just electronic/paper, its quantity is still fixed by the EU membership. No single member state can just increase its supply unilaterally. That would be like trying to maintain a gold standard and one nation revalued its gold to three times that of what everyone else uses. That becomes impossible. The Silver Democrats nearly caused the bankruptcy of the USA for overvaluing silver relative to the world in the 19th century."

By the time this mess comes unraveled, we will see the world completely change. We're probably looking at a major world monetary reform by as early as **2019-2020**. The speed with which this is unfolding is rather incredible.

GOLD by Barry Rosen

WEEKLY CHART: (1/4) Gold is seasonally strong in **January** with Sun in Sagittarius but often fades to seasonal lows into **March and June**. Sun going into Leo is usually supportive for new rallies. Until gold takes out 1350 and 1375, it is still in a bear market, but it is looking like 1275 will not come out on dips in the spring if rallies in early winter are strong.

LARGER CYCLES: The 12-year cycle of Jupiter is positive for gold started **September 11** and runs for 13 months. The 18.5-year cycle of Rahu/Ketu that hit 1999 was bearish the first 9 months last year and that would also confirm a more major cycle low by July/August 2018. The 29-year cycle of Saturn created a spike into the end of 1987 but then gold fell about 18% in 1988. That might support a rally in **December/January** but then be a problem for first 2 quarters of **2018**. Other cycles are not supportive for gold.

The trade is looked on Bitcoin and the ease of buying and selling electronically so gold and silver continue to lose their luster. We're turning neutral now for a sluggish one-month rally.

MONTHLY CHART: (11/3) Gold failed to close above 1400 or even retest 1375 so it's still in a bear market and no one will want it if the S & P goes up to 2980 next year. We've seen gold be taken out so many times by Central Bankers that we won't get trapped. It is possible that a final bear trap next year could take gold to 1100 or lower but we think the dollar may only to 100-1 although could do more and that would not push gold that low. Still, there is a lot of competition from Bitcoin.

YEARLY CYCLE ANALYSIS: Calculating how high gold can go into **2019-2020** is tricky because we should be moving into unchartered territory and a world economic reset. Our fellow analysts throw out numbers like 3000.00, 5000.00 but it can't be calculated until we get a first major swing up over 1350 in 5 waves and for now it looks like gold may put in that monthly chart low toward 1000 or 800 because the market failed.

Analyst Martin Armstrong brings us down to earth on this matter:

"Gold would ONLY rise when it is the monetary base or the money everyone uses. That it is not. You cannot pay your mortgage in gold nor can you pay your taxes. That means it is NOT legal tender. The younger generations are into plastic, not even paper money."

This is Alice in Wonderland, plain and simple to say gold will rise to $50,000 or higher. The maximum our models project is $5,000. That is probably the point at which total chaos is unleashed anyhow and you end up with a completely new monetary system.

So, the question is rather simple insofar as gold will be the hedge against government and that means it will retain a reasonable value for the transition from the current monetary system to the next.

Therefore, what we are ultimately looking for from gold is the hedge against government to make that transition, which historically always happens. Before we get to that place, there will be trades to be had and from that perspective you can increase your gains rather than just the buy & hold. Selling at the high in 2011 and buying even here is a huge gain. The buy & hold strategy never works when it comes time for the correction. Anything beyond the sock drawer strategy fails because inevitably people cannot hold through the worst declines.

Gold bulls have been bankrupted waiting for their ship to come in, as Central Bankers don't want any competition for their worthless paper assets. Still, things are changing. There is reason to be making money on gold over the next 3-4 years, but we can't rule out some liquidation-crash happening like **2008-2009** at some point, and a buy-and-hold strategy will not work. We will again wait until this summer 2018 to consider gold if 1100 is holding.

SILVER by Barry Rosen

WEEKLY CHART: (1/4) if we're right about gold patterns, silver could recover sharply to **1795 - 1800 in January** and then still make a swan song in the summer with key weekly chart support at 1425. Market has too much competition from Bitcoin now. Given the end of bearish cycles for silver into **2018**, we won't rule out even lower prices.

MONTHLY CHARTS: With rates going up and stocks still being attractive, hard to see why metals will rally. Even if demand is there in India with their currency crisis, there are government raids and taxes to discourage metals accumulation. Given the continued war on metals by Central Bankers and even countries like Australia wanting to move away from cash and our new electronic age where economic crises can be solved by creating helicopter money and issuing debit cards, we wonder if people will return to silver. I suspect that if so we're looking more at **late 2018 into 2020** when a great economic crisis is likely to happen.

Do we go back out on a limb and say that $50.00 silver is again very possible if US stocks and the dollar were to crash at some point? Martin Armstrong' discussion of gold is relevant to silver also. Silver is more liquid for bartering and trading if we have problems. Still, we're in a new electronic age and Central Bankers have a plan with helicopter money as already thrown out by countries like Sweden where handy-dandy plastic can be handed out easily and funded with electronic air. The new age of electronic money reminds us that the governments will have new and creative solutions at their disposal. --Barry Rosen

CRUDE OIL by Barry Rosen

OVERALL: Saturn in Sagittarius is generally support for crude prices despite huge oil gluts. World powers are desperate to get prices up and prevent economies from being wrecked by deflation.

Global and economic tensions and a harsh winter will support crude this year and we could see 6750 come in during the winter and start to fuel frustration. The Saudis budget for breakeven for their economy is at 7000 and you can make sure that they will get the price up there.

WEEKLY CHART: (12/15) Brent Crude patterns into **2018** could project 9000 and would push WTI up to the 8400 region into next summer but given current fundamentals, it's hard to imagine that scenario. Strong war cycles May - October 2018 should be supportive for the complex.

The Saudis need 7000 crude for their government budget to breakeven and you have to imagine that the power brokers are hard at work here given the need for higher crude prices to make major economies work.

STATEMENT OF DISCLAIMER

FUTURES AND OPTIONS TRADING IS RISKY AND CAN RESULT IN SUBSTANTIAL LOSS. THE USE OF STOPS MAY NOT LIMIT LOSSES TO INTENDED AMOUNTS. SPREAD POSITIONS MAY NOT BE LESS RISKY THAN OUTRIGHT POSITIONS. PAST RESULTS DON'T NECESSARILY INDICATE FUTURE RESULTS. SOURCES ARE BELIEVED TO BE RELIABLE, BUT NO ASSURANCE IS MADE FOR ACCURACY.

HYPOTHETICAL PERFORMANCE RESULTS HAVE MANY INHERENT LIMITATIONS, SOME OF WHICH ARE DESCRIBED BELOW. NO REPRESENTATION IS BEING MADE THAT ANY ACCOUNT WILL OR IS LIKELY TO ACHIEVE PROFITS OR LOSSES SIMILAR TO THOSE SHOWN. IN FACT, THERE ARE FREQUENTLY SHARP DIFFERENCES BETWEEN HYPOTHETICAL PERFORMANCE RESULTS AND THE ACTUAL RESULTS SUBSEQUENTLY ACHIEVED BY ANY PARTICULAR TRADING PROGRAM.

ONE OF THE LIMITATIONS OF HYPOTHETICAL PERFORMANCE RESULTS IS THAT THEY ARE GENERALLY PREPARED WITH THE BENEFIT OF HINDSIGHT. IN ADDITION, HYPOTHETICAL TRADING DOES NOT INVOLVE FINANCIAL RISK, AND NO HYPOTHETICAL TRADING RECORD CAN COMPLETELY ACCOUNT FOR THE IMPACT OF FINANCIAL RISK IN ACTUAL TRADING. FOR EXAMPLE, THE ABILITY TO WITHSTAND LOSSES OR TO ADHERE TO A PARTICULAR TRADING PROGRAM IN SPITE OF TRADING LOSSES ARE MATERIAL POINTS WHICH CAN ALSO ADVERSELY AFFECT ACTUAL TRADING RESULTS. THERE ARE NUMEROUS OTHER FACTORS RELATED TO THE MARKETS IN GENERAL, OR TO THE IMPLEMENTATION OF ANY SPECIFIC TRADING PROGRAM WHICH CAN'T BE FULLY ACCOUNTED FOR IN THE

PREPARATION OF HYPOTHETICAL PERFORMANCE RESULTS AND ALL OF WHICH CAN ADVERSELY AFFECT ACTUAL TRADING RESULTS.
****

FORTUCAST MARKET TIMING INC., 509 N. 4th St., Fairfield, IA 52556.
PHONE: 928-284-5740 and in US: 800-788-2796.
Copyright © 2002-2017 Fortucast Market Timing. All rights reserved.

FOR OUR LATEST FORECASTS GET A SUBSCRIPTION AT

WWW.COMMODITYTIMERS.COM

TRANSITS FOR THE YEAR: BY RISING SIGN

The easiest guide to predicting your future second to considering your dasha period, is to look at the transit of your ascendant lord or rising sign through the zodiac. Transits over these points are usually quick but sometimes can be longer depending on the transit planet involved (i.e., slower moving planets and planets that retrograde during a transit period). When a planet moves through a house in the natal chart and forms a conjunction with another planet(s) in the house, it can trigger life events to manifest. The relationship between the conjunct planets will determine if the events are favorable or unfavorable depending upon their nature with one another. The planets quality and its influence is based on its strength (exalted, debilitated etc.).

Transits by unfavorable planets: A weak and unfavorable planet in the natal chart when transited by an unfavorable planet will give negative results. The timing of the effect will be at the exact degree of conjunction with effects being felt the day before or the day after unless the planet is slower moving such as Saturn, Rahu, Ketu or Mars, in which case, the effect may begin sooner or last longer than the exact conjunction.

Unfavorable current dasha: If the dasha is bad, this will amplify the unfavorable transit effects.

Unfavorable transits are also connected to the 6th house and sign of Virgo: The ruler of the sign and house, Mercury, will trigger negative events related to health, disputes, accidents, and debts but you have more control over these events and can take extra precautions by being more aware. Take care of your health, meditate, donate to charity and perform acts of selfless service and keep an eye on expense to minimize the effects. If Mercury is strong in the natal chart, the transits over the 6th house will give more positive effects because the house is strong and can offer resistance to loss, attack, disease, illness and accidents.

Unfavorable transits are connected to the 8th house and sign of Scorpio: The ruler of the sign and house, Mars and Ketu, will trigger negative events related to serious health problems, worry, fear, loss of support, scandal and bring up other karmic related challenges, etc. If Mars or Ketu is strong in the natal chart, and the house is strong, then negative transits here will have less impact. For example, there could be windfalls or unexpected gains from trusts, inheritances or insurance. Doctors could appear to help make correct health diagnosis and provide more effective treatments.

Unfavorable transits are connected to the 12th house and sign of Pisces: The ruler of the sign and house, Jupiter, will trigger events related to loss, dreaminess, disconnection, ungrounded, imprisonment, hospitalization, fines, feelings of imprisonment, slow spiritual development insomnia, trouble with foreign travel and trouble in the marriage bed. If Jupiter is strong and able to lend strength to the 12th house, the transit could create a sense of charity, self-sacrifice, movement towards spirituality, provisions against loss and legal problems fade away, gains from foreign travel, sexual relations are more pleasurable, and self-sufficiency may expand.

Planets debilitated in transit bring negative results: One exception is retrograde debilitated planets that act more positively during their transits.

Aspects by other unfavorable transiting planets also create negative events.

Mixed events can also occur when you have a good dasha but challenging transitory planet or vice versa so some effects may be overall good or not so good.

Now, let's talk about favorable events. A strong planet in the natal chart that is favorable will yield good results when transits are moving through the house by favorable planets. Current, favorable dashas will amplify favorable planetary transits.

Note: The ascendant lord going through its particular house will enliven and activate issues around that house during its transit.

TRANSITS IN 2018 BY: RISING SIGN OF SIGNIFICANCE

The transits that are the most important to follow are the ones for your rising sign and for your dasha lord.

KEY SUN TRANSITS AND ASPECTS FOR 2018

Sun conjunct Venus in Sagittarius: January 9th

The January's bright spot during this transit is the conjunction of Sun and Venus on **January 9th at 02:02**. The Sun moved into Sagittarius on Thursday, **December 15th** before the Christmas holiday and brought expansive joy for righteous action. The Sun's positive qualities have come out which included positivity, fairness, impartiality, devotions to high ideals and causes, friendliness and joyfulness, fun, sincerity.

Sun and Jupiter are good friends and have a 5/9 relationship between Sagittarius and Leo so there is a deep spiritual relationship that emerged at Christmas had an optimism that expanded life with holiday cheer which was badly needed. Leos and Aries rising did best with the transit but also Sagittarius rising if its ego didn't get in the way. Taurus, Capricorn and Gemini rising signs have more problems with this transit in their 8th, 12th and 7th house from their own sign. It was mixed for others.

The Sun is getting a roommate, with Venus moving into Sagittarius on **January 9th**. Venus and the Sun don't usually get along and in this case, they are so close together that Venus is considered to be combust from the Sun's heat, however, something wonderful happens with this conjunction called Cazimi where Venus enters the 'heart of the Sun' and becomes spiritualized and empowered rather than depleted of strength.

This spiritual union will bring expansive love to the house and gains for Taurus and Virgo that will find themselves drawn to soothing, pleasant aspects of love and enjoying sensuous romance. They may travel during this time and enjoy a love affair while on their journey. Staying focused on the 'bright side' of life, Taurus rising, and Virgos will have good earning capacity and may meet a prominent person that can help expand their spiritual horizons.

Sun and Jupiter are good friends and have a 5/9 relationship between Sagittarius and Leo so there is a deep spiritual relationship that emerged at Christmas had an optimism that expanded life with holiday cheer which was badly needed.

Leos and Aries rising did best with the transit but also Sagittarius rising if its ego didn't get in the way. Taurus, Capricorn and Geminis had more problems with this transit in their 8th, 12th and 7th house from their own sign. It was mixed for others.

Sun conjunct Ketu in Capricorn: February 3rd

This is a weird week between the eclipse with the Sun conjunct Ketu on **February 3rd.** Sun and Ketu are both fiery planets and their conjunction will increase that element. This transit brings up a lot of rajasic energy, which creates a lot of fiery energy to want to change everything. There is not enough calming satvic energy to keep one balanced. One may want to fly off the handle in all directions or lash out at a boss or supervisor or loved one if you cannot reign in this energy.

Drink coconut water or coconut milk to calm the fire. Channel the energy into exercise, drink calming herbal teas and stay away from spicy food, which will fan the flames. Find ways to ground yourself with gentle yoga, long walks in cool woods or being near more water.

As the Sun moves toward Ketu, if you have this in your natal chart within 3 degrees it will be activated, particularly if you have a birthday **February 3rd.** This can bring up past regrets and karma, blocking living in the present moment. It could lead to loss of reputation or embarrassment if you have that natal signature in your chart and you may feel unsupported from organizations or government. It could bring up difficult energy with your father and wanting to shed past dark energy here and feelings of rejection or guilt.

It may also bring up intense anger at times as both planets are on fire. If you are running a Sun/Ketu or Ketu/Sun period these issues will come up for a major crisis to reinforce your whole identity.

Be alert while driving as if you are in a Sun/Ketu or Ketu/Sun period Saturn/Ketu or Ketu/Saturn or Rahu/Ketu or Cancer, Leo and Capricorn rising, you may be more vulnerable to mishaps especially during the eclipse because the luminaries are very connected and will naturally cause more distress. My friend Christina Collins reminds us that *"the eclipses will be **January 31st** (total lunar) and **February 15th** partial solar, if you have to drive or travel, be aware of other drivers, as those with Libra and Scorpio rising are at risk while traveling because the eclipse is happening in their 4th house of vehicles. Ketu or South node will be at 20' Capricorn, and Sun and Moon 3' Aquarius. So, this is a 4th house partial solar eclipse for both rising signs. This also applies to Leo rising, as the eclipse will happen in their 6th house of accidents."*

Sun conjunct Rahu in Cancer: July 28th
Rahu in Cancer will create a strong drive for home, family life, maternal affection and will increase intuitive energies. The transit will force a need for more nurturing and caring. With Rahu in Cancer, the natural sign of the home and conveyances, watch out for toxins in the home.

It's a good time to check for Radon, get a carbon monoxide detector, and get a dehumidifier for mold or other household pollutants. Prevent bug and rodent infestations, which could rear up. That will be one way to stay on top of the transit. Make sure your vehicle is in good shape and inspected and that you are on top of maintenance.

If you have lung problems, now is the time to stay on top of them as moon/Cancer is very connected to lungs and Rahu may create problems from toxins or pollution so now may be a good time to invest in an air purifier if you are having those kinds of problems. On a mundane level, later in the transit, more compassion for the homeless and immigrants is likely to manifest.

Given the plight of migrants in the world this will be a good thing but not without its challenges given what has happened in Europe and countries like Sweden. Rahu in Cancer will probably increase the problem and bring a better solution by spring **2019** but a crisis around it will develop first.

As Sun enters into Cancer, he is eclipsed by Rahu's shadowy energy, which may cause feelings of tiredness and shifting moods. Career and finances may be erratic and there may be spats with loved ones. Problems with digestion, swelling, and water retention can occur so take care of your health by getting plenty of rest and exercise.

This eclipse will be favorable for spiritual activities and there may be benefits from work in foreign countries or unusual occupations. Some may suffer from lack of confidence or not be as self-aware during this time and feel worried, foggy and confused. There may be trouble with bosses, superiors and relationship with your father may be distant or troubled.

Sun opposition Jupiter in Aries to Libra: May 8th
Sun in Aries will oppose Jupiter on **May 8th** and it is fairly strong in transition as it moves past its exaltation point. Exalted planets are misinterpreted often, and my personal feeling is that they have too much power and do exaggerated actions that are often out of balance.

It also depends what rising sign you are for an impact but if you are born between **April 13 - May 14th**, you have the exalted Sun in your natal chart.

Mars is the only planet afflicting the Sun in this transit but he is weak in degrees, so the impact will be minimal. Mars is friends with the Sun, both are fiery, hot planets so his glance towards the Sun is much like a small wave from your neighbor a few houses up the street.

This part of the transit can bring out gains at work or add fuel to projects you may be working on but with Jupiter(R) in opposition to the Sun, this may bring up feelings of betrayal and not feeling supported by teachers and your superiors and there may be some confusion about your interests in higher education and spiritual pursuits. Issues with fathers, children and spouses could occur during this transit causing you to reflect and turn inward for solutions as you seek a fair resolution.

Don't act too rashly or get exhausted as this can increase overheating and affect your health. If you are a fire sign and have a lot fire energy, stay calm with coconut water and raw foods and avoid spicy foods. There could be problems with blood sugar and weight gain, so be mindful of over eating.

With initiative and good disposition, you can avoid any fights by using some of the Libra's charm so don't manipulate or try to be controlling but rather handle small tasks in duration and enjoy a spontaneous approach. If you start to feel a little 'heat,' cool off with exercise, walking outside in fresh air, put on music that you like and 'dance it out' or go see a movie with friends! With the Sun and Mars aspect and Jupiter opposition, it's a good idea to blow off some steam.

Still most of the transit is in good shape with increasing leadership, courage, ambition, sharp thinking, achievement, joy, strong fathering and innovation. Leos, Scorpios, Sagittarius and Cancer rising, and moon signs probably do best with the transit while Taurus rising and Libras and Virgo rising and moon signs will have more problems with it.

Still the Sun represents the Divine and will be packed with Divine power and grace from this transit and sitting in Aries, it will pack a lot of self-starting energy, so it's good time to do projects and get a lot done. It packs a lot of self-starting energy, so it's good time to do projects and get a lot done.

Sun opposition Saturn in Gemini to Sagittarius: June 27th
Sun goes into Gemini **June 15th** where the Shakti of the sign should bring out creativity, particularly for writing and computer programming but you have to make sure not to stay idle.

This is a time for clever actions while remaining structured and disciplined so don't try to do too many things at once but instead, apply your focus towards expansion.

We also get Saturn opposing the Sun on **June 27th** exactly and that will impact most on **June 25 - 29** so be careful with opposing bosses, fighting with your children or getting into tangles with IRS agents or policeman and avoid speeding as you might get caught if you have this signature in your natal chart.

The Sun is channeling Rahu's energy, and he is not happy in the sign of Gemini and in the constellation of Ardra (Gemini 6.40-20.00) where suffering can come up. Leo rising will most feel this transit but in Gemini it is an 11th house transit and will bring gains. Cancer rising will have the most trouble with this transit as it will disappear from the horizon and fail to shine.

Life is always a coexistence of opposites, bringing out our timid, light and fragile wandering qualities which seem opposed to the warrior nature of Mars but in this sense, with the Sun in Ardra, the constellation of striving for material gains, using the power of your own efforts, you do have the ability to clear emotional storms, and you can rise and shine!

So, enjoy the quest for Truth and something higher in this very pure constellation and my favorite of all, Orion, the spiritual warrior.

Sun opposition Pluto in Gemini to Sagittarius: July 12th
Sun goes into Gemini **June 27th** where the Shakti of the sign should bring out creativity particularly for writing and computer programming, but you have to make sure not to stay idle. This is a time for clever action while remaining structured so don't try to do too many things at once but instead, apply your focus towards expansion.

Over the course of twenty-five years, I have learned and experienced the power of the outer planets and would call myself a "*Neo-Vedic*" astrologer. This week we have Pluto aspects peaking with Sun squaring Pluto exactly on Thursday, **July 12th**.

So let's understand Pluto a bit more. Pluto is about power, transformation, unconscious patterns and death of old patterns.
Dennis Harness, talking about Pluto notes:

"*The discovery of Pluto in 1930 by astronomer Percival Lowell reflected the beginning of a new era of powerful dictators such as Hitler and Stalin and the exploration of nuclear energy leading to the development of the atomic bomb. Pluto themes of transformative as well as destructive power would pervade the events of the 1930s and the decades to come. At the time of this writing, the bombing of the World Trade Center and the Pentagon occurred reflecting the challenging Pluto/Saturn opposition of* **2001/2002**. *In mythology Pluto, the god of the underworld was also called Hades which means "invisible" or "to make invisible." The origins of Vedic astrology credited to the great sage Maharishi Parasara occurred at least several thousand years before Pluto and the other outer planets were "visible" to astronomers.*"

He goes on to say that Pluto is probably connected to Lord Yama:

"*In Hindu mythology, Yama is the god of death and agent of Lord Shiva. Yama means "the binder, restrainer" who keeps mankind in check….He is a deity that demands sacrifice and discipline. He decides which actions of humans bare or do not bear fruit. Yama then judges the dead whom his messengers drag before his throne. His aide, Chitragupta catalogues the karma of all human beings and replays the major life events helping the soul realize its life's work.*"

See: http://dennisharness.com/plutoneovedic.html

Politics never end so, Pluto's influence brings about strong power struggles, as we are experiencing now. Pluto rules over hidden agendas and often revenge. All the tension is a manifestation of this aspect. It will take time to sort through the huge social issues involved. The aspect continues through **October 2018** when Neptune finally goes direct after he retrogrades on **April 22nd.**

What is happening? The shadow of the ego individuality, creative energy, the will and economic inequality is coming up from the depths of the subconscious to be healed.

The shadow is becoming conscious and luckily the Divine grace of Sun is there to help heal it — it is no longer repressed.

Do we learn to move peacefully through these issues and work together to solve them or do we utilize the dark and more destructive energy of Pluto to rage and riot? It's an issue that will be with us until at least **October**.

The Sun in Gemini is about clever action and duality — basically twins or twos, pairs, partnerships. So here we can see aspects of twos in jobs, relationships, interests. Pluto, a higher octave of Scorpio speaks to regeneration, cooperation and deep transformation, which would indicate that we need to come together in partnership and equality rather than division and separation. So perhaps it's time to join hands, as Gemini would suggest, and form a partnership that is versatile, conservative, charming and polite in order to make promote positive gains.

On a personal level, this aspect is about gaining knowledge, creating and completing big unfinished projects. Use the energy to make major transformations in your life with unfinished business and seeking out new information.

So, go take a new class or attend a lecture on something that interests you. Write that book. Get involved with science and other scholarly pursuits that interest you and better yet, have a friend join you! The energy is there if you let it empower you. You may feel some confusion with education, religion or higher studies but the important thing is to start somewhere so be like Mars and take action! Try something new! Take that painting class, join the choir and sing your heart out! Have you secretly dreamed about learning to dance the tango — now's your chance!

Pluto is clearing the shadows on fear so we can step out and have the courage to transform areas of our lives that have gone dry with stagnation. He wants us to go out and live our desires with passion!

Sun opposition Mars in Cancer to Capricorn: July 26th
Mars in hard-working Capricorn, with the influence of spiritual Ketu, is the planet afflicting the Sun in Cancer during this transit. Mars is a friend with the Sun and Ketu, both fiery characters and filled with passion, so his glance towards the Sun is much like a friendly, supportive wave from your neighbor a few houses up the street. This part of the transit can bring out the heat between Ketu and Mars, increasing their energy.

Mars will have the ability to respond more quickly to demands at work but may be more annoyed, irritated, and early provoked by negativity and criticism. Emotions may run hot.

With the Sun opposing Mars in Cancer, where he is joined by Rahu who is taking on the cooling effects of Cancer's lord Moon, Mars/Ketu may find some relief from this aspect and here may be gains from work overseas or in foreign work or work at home may be more innovative.

There could be health challenges with overheating, heart problems, dryness, respiratory, stomach and constipation so be sure to make efforts to drink plenty of water, be cautious about fluid retention and swelling.

Also, be careful with knees and joints as Capricorn rules this area and with Mars wanting to go exercise and 'blow off some steam,' injuries, accidents and surgeries could be a result of an overstressed body. Meditation, breath work and easy stretches are great alternatives to heavy weight bearing activities that could over-stress joints, muscles and tendons.

Sun opposition Neptune in Leo to Aquarius: September 7th
Sun is opposing Neptune on **September 7th** in Leo to Aquarius. Sun/Neptune transits can bring up escapism or levels of spiritual strength. You may find yourself in seeking the path of least resistance or looking for ways to gain spiritual protection or guidance. This could lead to being idealistic, imaginative, or becoming artistically creative or feeling hypersensitive, scattered, indecisive and overly sentimental.

The Sun is in the constellation of Purva Phalguni and wants to create and transform. So, this transit with Neptune is about cohesion and movement in a harmonious, diplomatic way to bring about transformation but with Neptune in the sign of eccentric and often misunderstood Aquarius, the transformation may have some friction.

Positives to look forward to including a concentrated, bright Divine, nurturing, transformative energy from the Sun that is blended with Neptune's receptive, aspiring spiritual nature and enthusiasm to chase your dreams and spiritual goals.

Neptune's influence will be subtle, flexible and dynamic while taking a factual, intellectual and visionary look at humanitarian pursuits and the Sun, with his charisma will offer refined diplomacy in relationships that will be pleasing, harmonious and influential.

Negatives to watch out for include a tendency to over idealize partners and leave you open to deception and scandal. Keep yourself grounded in the real world as much as possible. Your desire to help others can easily be taken advantage of. Being extra sensitive you should avoid negative environments where arguments could be lead to a dismantling of what you're trying to build or accomplish.

Your body is more susceptible to cold and dryness due to the Suns heat, as well as gaining weight (Kapha). Nervousness could be a problem as well as sleep issues so get plenty of rest and if you feel overly stressed during this transit be sure to take time out for relaxation and stress relieving activities.

Use this transit to create and transform old habits and patterns. Avoid abusing your body with too much activity as this may lead to exhaustion. Infections and fevers are possible, and the energy may be quite intense so avoid escaping into alcohol or food binges that may temporarily lead to escape but lead to deeper complexity. This transit will affect you most if you are Scorpio or Aries rising or Aquarius or Leo rising or if you have key planets like the Sun, Moon or the ascendant at 13 - 15 degrees Aquarius or Leo.

Sun opposition Uranus in Libra to Aries: October 23rd
While the outer planets are not a traditional part of Vedic astrology, I find them important for understanding collective behavior and if they impact sensitive points in your chart within 2 degrees by transit or in your natal chart, they can be rather impactful.

As Dennis Harness has discussed: *"Narendra Desai saw an ancient Vasistha Nadi palm leaf in a museum in Madras, India, which predicted that three important grahas or planets would be discovered by the jyotishis of the Kali Yuga. The great seer Vasistha was the author of a number of hymns in the Rg Veda (dated 3000 BC) and was considered a great priest of the kings. According to the ancient palm leaf the names of the grahas or planets would be Prajapati, Varuna, and Yama."*

Prajapati is connected with Uranus and will be in opposition to the Sun on **October 23rd** at 20:46 in Aries to Libra. Dennis notes that:
"Uranus is probably connected to Prajapati is the lord of progeny and creativity. He "exerts his heat and duplicates himself" and his "divine voice sounds like thunder."

One of the translations of Prajapati is Indra, the lord of thunder and lightning. A similarity to the planet Uranus can easily be seen. Uranus represents the Prometheus myth of bringing fire to earth, the bringer of change and innovation. Uranus is often associated with heat, lightning and thunder. He was also the father of Venus, the goddess of creativity. Narendra Desai felt that Uranus was a higher octave of Mercury, the god of creative intellect. He said that a prominent Uranus was often seen in the chart of a good astrologer." (See: http://dennisharness.com/plutoneovedic.html)

So, what can we make of Sun's opposition to Uranus on **October 23rd**? Uranus is connected to surprises and the connection with Sun may bring an unexpected encounter with someone who may impact your life in a very surprising way. This may shake up your life in such a way, that it destroys the old in order to make way for the new!

This strong force has the extreme fire of Aries behind it and will help liberate you from an unwanted situation. On a personal level this transit can create a release from boundaries and restrictions or a break from limiting experience like a relationship or job.

It will create energy to implore you not to continue the same way you have been doing things.

Though technically a challenging transit, the relief from stress and tension can be very satisfying once you've survived the disorienting and intense affects that illuminate the established attitudes and patterns that are no longer serving your highest good — those out dated beliefs that have outlived their usefulness. Uranus is here to help you let go of fear and release, so let go! It shakes us loose and destroys what constricts us.

A change in beliefs or social interaction may be all it takes to act as a circuit breaker. At the deeper level, you are seeking a burst of higher awareness, to transcend your daily routine and bring on a spiritual growth spurt.

There is a conflict between the independent, practical energetic Aries self and the Divinely diplomatic Sun, who is sharing space with a highly spiritualized and refined Retrograde Venus in the harmonious, balanced sign of Libra, representing 'the other' that likes to be with others. This will add more passion and intensity to relationships where you take on the role of 'student.'

You may have a hard time adjusting to being more socially active and engaged in group spiritual pursuits as a participant rather than following a solo path and having others follow you as the leader. This is the dramatic upheaval that Uranus brings in transits with unusual role reversals. If you choose to take on this new role, it will release a lot of tension and create breaks and shift energy within your life but you have to make these breaks carefully and with a clear head.

Go with Mar's courage to make the change even if it seems disruptive. Be practical and plan. This transit has been building influence and if you are Aries or Libra rising you will be most affected by this transit or if you key planets at 01 - 11 degrees Libra.

Sun conjunct Jupiter in Scorpio: November 26th
Jupiter is conjunct the Sun on **Monday, November 26th.** This aspect has been ignored a bit with so much going on but. For Leos, the energy will be very high and charged with wisdom, confidence, enthusiasm, expansion and comfort as the Sun will take on the energy of Jupiter and they are friends, so the Sun is uplifted.

Still for Jupiter, and Pisces and Sagittarius rising, it is not a great thing. Combustion is one of the biggest afflictions for planets that really is not talked about enough as combust planets are burnt up and their significations are hurt.

The Jupiter combustion creates false optimism, which can feel great, but then reality can set in after all the false hopes.

Make practical decisions over the next few weeks and stay out of the Pisces cloud of optimism. Jupiter governs the liver and it may be afflicted these next few weeks so drink fresh organic squeezed lemon in some hot water in the morning to get that liver moving. All forms of the twist in Hatha yoga support the liver and help squeeze out toxins. You may need to do the Cow face pose (Gomukhasana) to energize the liver over the next few weeks.

The good thing about the conjunction is that those ruled by the Sun are energized greatly by Jupiter's exalted warmth and this may help leadership and self-confidence. All of this is taking place in Saturn's constellation of Anuradha (Scorpio 3.20 - 16.40), which brings in the great widow of Mitra.

Sun conjunct Saturn in Sagittarius: January 2nd
I learn a lot from my Western astrological friends. While combustion is one of the most damaging things for a planet in Vedic astrology, it turns out total combustion within the last degree is a blessing. Saturn will be conjunct the Sun in the Eastern US on **Wednesday the 2nd** at 00:49 AM EST but other parts of the world will experience it later.

The exact conjunction of the Sun with Saturn on the 2nd for the East coasters can be a really good thing and is called Cazimi from medieval astrology and is used to refer to planets that are so close to a conjunction with the Sun that they are "*in the heart*" of the Sun.

They actually become energized by the Sun and their most positive qualities come out. This will be a positive for Thursday and into about 7 a.m. on Friday when Saturn is within 40 minutes of the Sun.

An example of Cazimi is Oprah Winfrey who has a Cazimi Venus in her natal chart; it has made her an incredible star to women and brought out her acting and relationship abilities with the public to a pinnacle.

Saturn Cazimi will impact Capricorn and Aquarius rising in a positive way and also if Saturn is in your first house or if it is your Atamakaraka or planet with the highest degree. It could bring out hard work, reliability, efficiency, and good at following work instructions precisely and could bring deep meditative transcendence.

2018 LEO RISING: TRANSITS OF THE SUN

The Sun's transits are beneficial when they are 3rd, 6th, 10th and 11th houses from the rising sign or Natal Moon sign.

For Leo rising, the Sun going through the various houses from Leo enlivens and activates the significations and qualities of the house. These are issues to work on.

SUN IN CAPRICORN: JANUARY 14 - FEBRUARY 12

Sun enters Capricorn: January 14th
Sun moves into Capricorn on **January 14th** and is a bit afflicted in transit with a Ketu conjunction into **February 3rd** contributing to the **January 31st** total lunar eclipse.

Saturn and Sun are enemies and the eclipse in the sign of Capricorn may contribute to health issues for Leos with this 6th house transit and Capricorns are also vulnerable.

The Sun afflicted in Capricorn may feel that one has not done enough, overworks, and this can create self-centeredness, skepticism, and lack of humor. It may lead to poor circulation, cold hands and feet and problems with the adrenals.

This is a 6th house transit for Leos but the affliction may create too much fire energy or pitta so stay patient and cool down with coconut water. Be careful with getting into too much debt. The **January 28 - February 6th** period before and after the eclipse with the conjunction to Ketu may bring up past regrets but it may lead to some loss of status or reputation.

It can bring it up problems with one's father or lead to issues around rejection that needs to be healed.

Use this difficult eclipse time if you are Leo or Cancer rising to heal and transform this past emotional guilt and rejection.

SUN ENTERS CAPRICORN: MAKAR SANKRANTI, JANUARY 14

Sun enters Capricorn: January 14th
Sun moves into Capricorn on **Saturday, January 14th** and it is a larger event than you might imagine.

In the Vedic calendar, it is the real beginning of the New Year where the days start lengthening, and more light descends on the planet.

Surya, the Sun God, is regarded as the symbol of divinity and wisdom, and is one of the most important planets (heavenly bodies) of the zodiac and our daily lives. It represents a new kind of New Year - a "*new beginning*" for which we want to strengthen the Sun within in our lives.

Surya actually means self, representing in our Jyotish (Vedic Astrology) charts both the big Self, and our little individual egos. As The Self, or Atman, Surya stands for and represents that Divine quality that all of us have within us. Thus, it is good to give some attention to this element within us. So it represents a day to celebrate our individuality and the Divinity within.

The equivalent for Westerners would be for us to clean a closet out on Friday, **January 13th** and take stuff to the dump or give stuff to the 2nd hand store which becomes symbolic of discarding the old and then on **January 14th** to celebrate our own individuality as well as, the Divine within and revisiting our New Year's resolutions or making a list of intentions if we did not get to it on January 1st when the Western culture tends to do so.

Apart from a harvest festival, Makar Sankranti is also regarded as the beginning of an auspicious phase in Indian culture. It is said as the 'holy phase of transition.' It marks the end of an inauspicious phase, which according to the Hindu calendar begins around **mid - December**. It is believed that any auspicious and sacred ritual can be sanctified this day onwards.

It represents realization, transformation and purification of the soul by imbibing and inculcating Divine virtues. So, think of Friday and Saturday as a time to release the old, to release the past and move forward.

As my friend Daniele Lepke noted:
As we flip the calendar, we need to keep flipping our mind as well.
Often, our diaries are full of memories.
See that you don't fill your future dates with past events.
Learn and unlearn from the past and move on.
Enjoy the rich symbolism and ritual of the Makara Sankrati, the Sun moving into Capricorn. Again, a very Happy and Blessed New Year to You.

SUN IN AQUARIUS: FEBRUARY 12 - MARCH 14

Sun enters Aquarius: February 12th
The Sun will go into Aquarius on **February 12th** and stay there until **March 14th**. Leos sometimes benefit from the Sun throwing a full aspect into their own house, but it can bring up stubborn relationship issues, but loyalty always will win out.

The Sun is afflicted by Saturn's glance during this transit with that aspect peaking into **February 25th** but having a strong influence **February 22 - 28th**. One has to watch health issues during this transit and beware of rebelling against authority figures like bosses or government officials.

Aquarius is a very innovative sign but when the Sun is afflicted during this transit, if you are Aquarius rising or Aquarius Sun, it can bring up low self-esteem, lack of self-promotion, rebellious activism, depression, cynicism, gullibility, isolation. So, despite not wanting to be social, you are going to have to get out there! Venus will be supportive of relationships and prevent those energies from getting out of hand.

The Sun then moves toward conjunction with Mercury, the planet of communication, and the link between the mind and matter, exactly into February 17th around 4 degrees Aquarius. This can create a very busy and buzzy mind so watch the intensity if you are Aquarius rising or Leo or Virgo or Gemini rising within a few days of this exact aspect.

We also have a partial solar eclipse on **February 15th** and I have written about this in the eclipse section.

The first part of the transit continuing through Dhanishta (Delphini constellation, Aquarius 0-6.40) through **February 18th** and is trickier **February 12 - 15th** as the Sun is debilitated in D-9 where it lacks confidence and needs to think more of others and so it is not able to shine as much. Another reason to get out of your pity-party and go out and help others this week is to work through and get through any low self-esteem issues. Energy picks up **February 16 - 18th**. Going to spiritual services on a Sunday will uplift the energy and staying rested will be important. This is particularly relevant if you are Leo rising or have Sun in Aquarius.

As always, I try to write general forecasts for the populace, but transits are 20% of prediction and subject to the larger cycles you are running. Reading charts is like reading DNA strands and people are so unique.

SUN IN PISCES: MARCH 14 - APRIL 13

Sun enters Pisces: March 14th
The Sun in Pisces this year is relatively unafflicted with its neutral partner Mercury and enemy Venus. The Sun is happy in Pisces, but it is eight houses from its home in Leo and people born with that rising sign are still going through deep spiritual transformations. If you were born with Sun in Pisces you are generous and supporting others, peaceful, a dreamer, well liked, intuitive and cooperative.

The more afflicted side of Sun in Pisces squanders opportunities, lacks confidence, volunteers too much, has poor financial management and has foot problems. The transits with Mercury and Venus this year are not going to bring out too much of the dark side.

The first part of the transit in the first part of Pisces is in the constellation of Purava Bhadrapada, **March 14 - 17th** (Pisces 0-3.20). The constellation of Purva Bhadrapada located in Pisces is a very satvic or pure constellation in the 12th sign of the zodiac connected to cut through negativity to get to the truth. If you have your Sun in Purva

Bhadrapada and were born between **March 31 - April 12th**, you tend to be able to see both sides of an issue.

SUN IN ARIES: APRIL 13 - MAY 14

Sun enters Aries: April 13th
SUN EXALTED IN ARIES--GREAT LEADERSHIP OR OVERBEARING POWER
Sun moves into Aries, **April 14th** and is a bit weak entering the sign as it moves towards it's exaltation point. Exalted planets are misinterpreted often, and my personal feeling is that they have too much power and do exaggerated actions that are often out of balance. It also depends what rising sign you are for an impact but if you are born between **April 13 - May 14th**, you have the exalted Sun in your natal chart.

Retrograde Jupiter is the only planet afflicting the Sun in this transit and it is a friend and increasing optimism and ambition. This part of the transit can bring out winning that which was lost (in relationships) or what has outlived its purpose. This may lead one to pursue projects, people, ideas or situations that have become weak or in need of repair or rejuvenation. Later in **May**, Mars as a square onto Aries and it is a wide orb aspect and Mars is supporting its own sign.

I think the Sun in Aries will pick a lot of self-starting energy and so a good time to do projects and get a lot done.

Sun will be in the constellation of Ashwini (Aries 0-13.20) **April 14-16th**, which is known, in modern astronomy as Alpha-Arietes and Beta-Arietes near the bright star of Andromeda.

Prash Trivedi notes that the symbol for Ashwini is a horse's head representing a dauntless spirit of adventure and a headstrong nature. This transit usually fosters self-starters and energy to complete projects. It is also a very healing constellation and so there will be more energy for healing. The ruling deities are the Ashwini twins who ride in a golden chariot and shower healing energy down to the earth plane. They are the *"Physicians of the Gods"*. This is a nakshatra of initiation, revitalization and transformational healing. The ruling planet is Ketu (South Node of the Moon), which gives a mystical and mysterious bent to their life journey.

The first part of the transit is through Aries 0-3 degrees (**April 13-15**) and particularly between 0.00-0.48 is through the gandanta or karmic knot on April 13th. There is underlying strength to work out new beginnings in a new cycle of growth initiated by moving into the start of the zodiac. The energy is there to untie deep karmic knots, but frustrations will still come up strongly and given all the changes going on from the first week of **March**, there will be plenty to work on and heal. The Sun is too powerful here and Leo rising people or Aries may be too overbearing and burn others up. My exalted Sun friends who are Leo are way too intense to connect to. The ruling constellation of

Ashwini is Ketu spurring you into new spiritual growth and development. So, go forth in action with new energy!

This is a 9th house transit for Leo inspiring new spiritual adventures and deep wisdom and pursuit of knowledge. It is always a highlight of the year for Leo rising if you have no natal planets afflicting the transit.

SUN IN TAURUS: MAY 15 - JUNE 15

Sun enters Taurus: May 15th
SUN IN THE CONSTELLATION OF KRITTIKA (ARIES 26.40-TAURUS 10)
The Sun in Taurus is in an enemy's sign but has no bad aspects during its transit. If you were born with Sun in Taurus unafflicted you are artistic, good with people skills, enjoying pleasure, has stamina and a fixed purpose and has traditional values and is good with business.

Sun transits into a new constellation of Krittika known by the West as the Pleiades on **Tuesday, May 11th**. Mars and Sun are friends with Sun in Aries and it promotes courage and leadership and is good transit.

The Taurus section loses some strength and brings out the more material side of leadership and politics, but it is still strong.

Sun is strong in its own constellation although some think that it can be out of balance in this position. Sun has immense courage and confidence during this transit and can create great power to handle difficult situations. People born **May 11 - 24th** have a warm, fierce and supportive energy and know how to use their power wisely.

The first pada (Aries 27.00 - 30.00) **May 11 - 14th** is connected to Sagittarius and is a healing zone and is a place of immense strength for the warrior energy to come out and protect society and do battle for great good. Sun loses energy **May 14 - 15th** as it changes signs and is weak in degrees but then moves into the 2nd Pada, **May 15 - 17th** where the mind feels secure and nurtured. The third Pada (**May 18 - 21st**) is always the most challenging section as loss, suffering and churning of deep fires of purification can happen here. Finally, the 4th pada, (**May 22 - 24**) is owned by Pisces is particularly strong and has hidden positive qualities.

Prash Trivedi notes that Western astronomers connect this constellation with the Pleiades or the seven sisters. The ruling planet of the constellation is the Sun with Agni, the God of Fire, as the residing deity. The Shakti of this lunar mansion is 'the power to burn away the negativity to get to the truth.' Given all the smoke and mirrors with politics and the media, this energy will be welcome. It has a stronger nature for fulfilling material desires and its symbol is a razor, which cuts through the "*bull*" to get through to the truth.

The constellation allows one to go through extreme purification and get through blocks on the path.

Of course, Leos do best with the transit, as it is a 10th house transit where status and career can flourish. Cancer rising also enjoys fulfillment of desires and great friendships during this transit. Aries and Scorpios may get a bit of a relationship burn if they cannot tone down their drive for success at all costs. Geminis do well with the 10th and 11th house transits of the Sun also.

SUN IN GEMINI: JUNE 15 - JULY 17

Sun enters Gemini: June 15th
SUN IN CONSTELLATION OF MRIGISHIRA (TAURUS 23.20 - GEMINI 6.40)
Sun moves into the constellation of Orion, the warrior of the winter sky on June 8TH (Taurus 23.20-Gemini 6.40). Its symbol is the deer. Mrigishira is formed by three faint stars at the head of the constellation of Orion. The constellation is very spiritual and promotes moksha and spiritual liberation and inspires people to study religion and philosophy. The Shakti of Mrigishira is the "*power to give fulfillment*" so a good time to rub your genie's lamp and ask for a boon.

Sun is very strong in this constellation and will be prone to intellectual and spiritual exploration particularly when Sun goes into Gemini on **June 15th** but there is also a sense of comfort here. Sun goes into Gemini **June 15th** where the Shakti of the sign should bring out creativity particularly for writing and computer programming, but you have to make sure not to stay idle.

As Prash Trivedi notes, life is always a coexistence of opposites as the deer symbol brings out the timid, light and fragile wandering qualities of this constellation embody the greatest spiritual warrior heroes of the Ramayana and Gita, Hanuman and Arjuna, in the constellation's deep quest for liberation and getting to the truth of the matter. If your Sun, Moon or rising sign is in this constellation, it gives you a deep yearning for something greater in your life. The deity of the constellation is Soma, connected to the Moon and the life and vital subtle forces that are created to manifest the physiological components of enlightenment.

The Sun has the most difficulty in the constellation of Ardra (Gemini 6.40-20) **June 22 - July 6th** as it is channeling Rahu's energy and this constellation can bring storms and deep suffering and tear-drops in the quest to shed old pattern. Use this transit for transformation.
The opposition from Saturn into **June 27th** will force the issue and create tensions between bosses, workers and between self and outside authority. Not a time to fight city hall or go over the limit in a speed trap zone.

The best part of transit is a wave of relief as the Sun gets more connected to Jupiter first with a trinal aspect on **July 5th** bringing optimism and expansive energy and confidence. Then on **July 6 - July 20th**, the Sun is channeling a reflective retrograde

Jupiter's energy in the constellation of Purnavasu (Gemini 20-Cancer 3.20), where he is happy in the sign of Libra and in the constellation of Vishaka where there is a deep connection with one's soul purpose through spiritual initiation and this can come up.

Leo rising will most feel this transit but in Gemini it is an 11th house transit and will bring gains. Cancer rising will have the most trouble with this transit as it will disappear from the horizon and fail to shine. For now, enjoy the quest for Truth and something higher in this very pure constellation and my favorite of all, Orion, the spiritual warrior.

SUN IN CANCER: JULY 16 - AUGUST 16

Sun enters Cancer: July 16th
SUN IN CONSTELLATION OF ASHLESHA (CANCER 16.40 - 29.59)
Sun moves in the zodiac sign of Cancer on **Monday, July 16th**, the natural house of home and supporting the *"family."* The Sun will spend some of the first 3 days in the constellation of Punarvasu and bring light into the darkness. This is a good time to take action through your feelings.

Sun in Cancer is rather afflicted in transit this year. It is a 12th house transit for Leos suggesting a need for retreat, meditation and foreign journey. With the conjunction of Rahu on **July 29**th, and the **July 27th** and **August 11th** eclipses, there can be an identity crisis for Leos. The Rahu/Sun combination can create strong power, success and social achievement but this can lead to falls from power and status also if you strive too high. Scandal is possible and intrigue with foreigners is very possible. Even when there is success, Rahu is never satisfied and there is often inner dissatisfaction. The key is to be happy with where you are.

Mars also afflicts the Sun this month with the **July 28th** opposition creating great tension between work and home and problems. While they are friends, the connections with Rahu and the eclipse may lead to odd power struggles and violence and tension.

The end of the transit, **August 14 - 16th** is in the Cancer gandanta (Cancer 27-30) in the constellation of Hyrda (Ashlesha, Cancer 16.40-29.59) is a place where the toxins of the past are accumulating in a big knot that is difficult to untie. Deep unconscious patterns and difficult problems arise that seem daunting and filled with regrets. Remember you have the power of free will in the present moment to move through into new light and do not have to live in the shadows and mistakes of the past. Let them go. They seem tangled and difficult to deal with, but you are strong enough to get through them.

So, July and early August are difficult times for Leo rising so good to go on a meditation retreat and do the inner work as the outer ambitions may be frustrating.

SUN IN LEO: AUGUST 16 - SEPTEMBER 16

Sun enters Leo: August 16th
SUN IN CONSTELLATION MAGHA (LEO 0.00 - 0.40)
The Sun enters Leo on **August 16th** at the Leo gandanta (Leo 0.00-0.40) in the constellation of Regulus (Magha, Leo 0.00-13.20) where there is more material emphasis on life and the soul is troubled in its decision to move forward now into a more successful material life and begin a material journey through the more tamasic constellations of Magha-Jyestha that dominate into early winter.

If you were born with Sun in Leo you have strong leadership abilities, ambition, tend to think big, are independent, liberal and have great stamina. This transit is unafflicted so the Sun returns to power after the earlier eclipses in Cancer.

This is a great time to work on your Divinity. The key will be to help others and not need praise or attention. You are great, and you have to acknowledge yourself and then others will do so. Like the Leo Lion, look to the mirror and see the great Royal soul that you are. In Christian mythology, the Lion is the representative the Divine king. Rise up out of the shadows of past experience and move toward deeper spirituality by letting go of the past. You are great in your own Divinity. Do not get lost in small ego. Jai Guru Dev. Victory to the Big Mind and then let go of the little ego that wants to keep us chained to the material world.

Special thanks to Komilla Sutton and Prash Trivedi for their wonderful insights on the nakshatras and the gandanta.

SUN IN VIRGO: SEPTEMBER 17 - OCTOBER 17

Sun enters Virgo: September 17th
The Sun has an afflicted transit in Virgo this year with the 10th house square from Saturn, which is exact into **September 26th** and will have a strong influence **September 23rd - 29th** impacting health and problems with government, fathers and authority figures. The problem with this transit is that one cannot consider their own needs enough and may be taken advantage by superiors. There are disappointments with married life and some depression and one can become victimized by doing too much volunteer work.

Sun moves into the constellation of Uttara Phalguni on **Monday, September 17th** which is one of the constellations of the zodiac commonly known as the social worker that helps friends in need and has great skills in healing and counseling.

On a spiritual level, this transit will inspire compassion from the caring side of Virgo and in a sense, it is a time to reach out into the community and help the homeless and the poor and those who have been left behind. It is a time to do spiritual service work to accumulate merit to move on through your spiritual growth. It could create a turning point for you if you have been stuck in the more material aspect of artistic illusion in order to move more deeply into the Divine. Connection to Durga and the creative impulse of Mother Divine can help move through the Maya of the material world and toward moving beyond the illusion into the true nature of the Divine.

So, enjoy the third constellation in Virgo and move into your creative realms and start great projects to benefit mankind. Bring out the kind and compassionate energy of Virgo, the Divine Mother who deeply cares for her children.

Move beyond the material realm of new gadgets to the Christian ethos of helping those in need. Suns' transit here will bring out more dynamic energy to lead by example and foster compassion in a crazy world.

SUN IN LIBRA: OCTOBER 17 - NOVEMBER 18

Sun enters Libra: October 17th

Sun moves into Libra on **Tuesday, October 17t**h and stays there until **November 16th**. The Sun is moving toward the lowest point of the year of the Sun toward **October 27th** at 10 degrees Libra. The Sun governs health, leadership and confidence and self-esteem for everyone, so this transit can bring about health issues, depression, poor decisions in government and low self-esteem. The worse part of the transit is usually when the Sun is in the constellation of Swati, which is between **October 23 - November 6th**.

Currently in early Libra the Sun is still in Chitra (Virgo 23.20-Libra 6.40) and connected to his friend Mars and in a stronger part of Libra is not as bad. The transit is particularly difficult for Scorpio rising and Pisces rising as it is a 12th and 8th house transits for them. Taurus rising may have trouble with it as a 6th house transit and Leo risings will particularly feel it. It may bring up poor motivation, poor financial management, headaches and addictions.

The positive side of this transit is that it may create some people that offer good sense, support, and charm and may bring out the ability to work with others better. Libra rising and Aries rising may experience this a bit more. Gemini rising and Virgos may do ok with this transit. Bottom-line is that if the dark side comes up, find ways to do good self-talk and find the fire to move on and do great things if you feel stuck. Take care of your health this month, which means watch your diet and addictions and stay on top of your immune system.

The transit of the Sun into Vishaka nakshatra **November 6 - 19th** connects it to Jupiter and it uplifts it so the worst part is the transit in the constellation Swati when it is connected with Rahu **October 23 - November 6th**. Our Leo president, Donald Trump will probably not do well with this transit as it can bring out the darkest part of ego when the lesson is learning to work together.

For some people, the problem of a debilitated Sun is that the ego is too stuck and encrusted in its position but for more people it can create low self-esteem and depression and then the ego is not good enough.

It is all illusion. You are Divine within. Fight off the negative self-talk. Do more meditation and see beyond the puppet strings and realize your own greatness!

Sun salutations and the tree pose, and the peacock pose can support the fallen Sun this month.

This is a 3rd house afflicted transit for Libras and can create conflicts with younger siblings, neighbors or difficulties with communications. Leos should avoid angry communications or face some degree of regret.

SUN IN SCORPIO: NOVEMBER 16 - DECEMBER 15

Sun enters Scorpio: November 16th

The Sun moves into Scorpio on Friday and ends its difficult month in Libra. Scorpio is the natural 8th sign of the zodiac owned by Mars and Ketu and represents the mystery of life, sexual or kundalini energy, the occult. It is a water sign and deeply connected to intuition and higher spiritual knowledge and can bring up deep karmic and psychological releases.

Saturn is out of Scorpio and will not hinder the Sun and Mars. The owner of Scorpio is a pleasant 4 houses away in Aquarius and supporting the Sun. The first part of Scorpio is connected to the constellation of Anuradha, which runs (Scorpio 3.20-16.40) and the Sun's transit there between **November 19 - December 2nd.**

Prash Trivedi reminds us that the constellation of Anuradha is connected to Mitra, the God of Light and this transit can awaken ones' connection to the Divine. This can really enliven and awaken spiritual life. If you were born **November 19 - December 2nd**, you may have a strong spiritual inclination, which will be enlivened by this transit.

The Sun is the planet of the soul and of expressing ones' power so at this time it is very important, and the goal is not to get immersed in materialism but remember one's deep connection to the Divine and use the awakened Kundalini of Scorpio energy for higher consciousness.

Saturn's ownership of this constellation can bring great teachings of cosmic truths if you can lean to move to the highest level of knowledge of responsibility for the planet and self-realization.

Still the darker side of this transit may come out as the Sun channel's Saturn's energy I this constellation. The movement toward Saturn peeking into **January 2nd** will have an impact more when the Sun goes into Sagittarius on **December 15th**. This can bring up some conflicts with government, leadership or employers so this is not a time to avoid taxes or go into rebellion against the police.

Saturn becomes combust and burned by the Sun **December 16th** while the Sun is in Sagittarius and this may dampen Christmas spirit a bit. As the Sun gets closer to Saturn on **January 2nd** and gets impacted, the darker energy of the Sun may come out leading to jealousy, possessiveness, bluntness, scandalous behavior, cruelty, spitefulness and potential heart problems. Reproductive problems may occur as it moves to conjunction into **January 2nd**. I often find that blood pressure can go up when the Sun is approaching Saturn for some people so watch your heart health and exercise routine between **December 16 - January 18th.**

SUN IN SAGITTARIUS: DECEMBER 16 - JANUARY 14

Sun enters Sagittarius December 16th
The Sun moving into Jupiter's sign of Sagittarius on **December 16th** brings expansive joy for righteous action. One can think of the Salvation Army ringing their bells every Christmas to save the world. Sun's positive qualities are coming out with this transit in Sagittarius which includes positive energy, fairness, impartiality, devotions to high ideals and causes, friendliness and joyfulness, fun, sincerity.

Sun and Jupiter are good friends and have a 5/9 relationship between Sagittarius and Leo so their is a deep spiritual relationship that emerges at Christmas and an optimism that expands life with holiday cheer. It is badly needed. Leos and Aries rising do best with the transit but also Sagittarius rising if its ego does not get in the way. Taurus, Capricorn and Gemini rising will probably have more problems with this transit as it is an 8th, 12th and 7th house from its own sign. It is mixed for others.

This year, Saturn's presence in Sagittarius, spoils this transit so there may be a bit more fear, tension, fanaticism, tensions between employees and employers and tensions with government authority. Watch for the exact conjunction into **January 2nd**.

The first part of the Sun's journey is in the asterism of Mula, the constellation ruled by Ketu that focuses on mystical power to ruin or destroy and break things apart.
The first 3 degrees of this star are a vulnerable area **December 15 - 17**, but the Sun is still exalted in the D-9, Divisional chart here and can handle the transformation that it requires of the soul.

Mula, (Moo'la), occupies Sagittarius (0-13.20) (**December 15 - 28**) and means a bundle of roots. As Charlotte Benson, notes, the purpose of this star is to remain rooted in the physical world, while having high aspirations to achieve liberation.

The goddess of this constellation is the challenging, Niritti, the demon goddess of negation and transformation. Her painful influence provokes humanity to radically change its essential nature.

Ketu, who is not happy in the business sign of Capricorn, rules this constellation. The Sun's transit through this territory now is a bit angrier and it is no wonder that the warring factions of government are rearing their heads to roar even more.

Still, a time for holiday joy but not without some needed spiritual transformation. Good time to get your meditation and yoga in and stay rested and balance to ward off the angry snapping and seething anger that may progress by Christmas.

Stay rested and keep your immune system strong with the Sun moving toward Saturn into **January 2nd, 2019** and this will not help this transit. As I have written before, keep your immune system strong by taking Collustrom or other boosters, stay away from sugar and focus on warm and unctuous foods that reduce the Vata or air element.

2018 CANCER RISING: LUNAR ECLIPSE GUIDE and GUIDE TO FULL and NEW MOONS

The moon moves too quickly to write about but pay attention to the Lunar Eclipses during the year and to planets moving through Capricorn and Cancer on that axis for major influences on your life during the year.

Eclipses are good for meditation and that is the best way to spend time during an eclipse, as the meditations can be deeper. Outwardly the emotions and mind get a bit frazzled so never a good time to make major decisions during an eclipse. I usually do laundry or clean or meditate to pass the time.

Both of my Gurus have advocated meditation during eclipses over the years. Sri Sri recently commented on this one: *"The mind is connected with the moon, the body is connected with the Earth and the Sun is connected with both. The time when all three come in alignment is good for spiritual practices. It is not a good time to eat or indulge in pleasures. It is a good time to conserve energy. So, from the ancient times it is said that you should not eat during the eclipse, and you should meditate. Eclipse is a very good time for mantra chanting and meditation. Chanting mantras at the time of eclipse is much more powerful. This is the ancient saying.*

One or two hours before an eclipse, stop eating so that the food gets digested well and during the eclipse time you have an empty stomach, and on empty stomach chanting and mantras are done for maximum result.

Eclipse is a very auspicious time for saadhaks; it is not a bad time. It is a bad time for enjoyment and for pleasures. And when you chant 108 times during this period it is equivalent to 10,000 times or more! So, meditation and chanting are highly recommended during this period.

When we are in activity, our mind is always focused in the front of the body. Close your eyes now, you'll feel your mind is in front because the mind goes through the eyes to look at the world, and through the ears. During activity the mind is mostly focused in the frontal part of the body."

"For relaxing, we take our mind to the background. You will see suddenly there is something different happening. This is necessary, from time to time." (SSRS)

The day of an eclipse or even a few days afterwards do not have to produce dramatic fall. On an emotional level, lunar eclipse feels a bit unnerving. Do not act on any thoughts that come up during an eclipse, as they are often fear-based and irrational. Best to be in meditation and do sacred chanting - Shiva Rudram may be a particularly powerful experience. I always avoid doing anything important within 3 days before and after an eclipse. I tend to do laundry and clean the house to keep busy if I am not meditating and it is recommended to fast 2 hours before and 3 hours after as food is harder to digest and can lead to indigestion.

In the end, eclipses reveal deep secrets and bring out deep unconscious patterns that need to be healed and are a good thing and should not be feared. Some people are actually empowered by eclipses but still it is thought not to watch them as they may manifest innate or hidden health problems that have the potential to emerge. Still remember that fear is a big illusion. We are taken care of by the Divine and sometimes a little emotional drama is needed to shake things up and move us out of our rut.

Eckhart Tolle is fond of telling us that that 98% of the stuff going through our heads is rubbish. On eclipse days, it is more. Relax, rejuvenate and avoid important decisions. God is with you in the storms and sometimes storms are very powerful and make us stronger.

So, steer through the storm with God's grace, eat lightly today, meditate, and chant. Focus on the Divine and the eclipse will enlarge all of those qualities.

This can be a very spiritual time. Enjoy the eclipse!

2018 New and Full Moon Chart

JANUARY

FULL MOON ON MONDAY, JANUARY 1, 2018 21:24

NEW MOON ON WEDNESDAY, JANUARY 16, 2018 21:17

FULL MOON ON WEDNESDAY, JANUARY 31, 2018 08:27

FEBRUARY

NEW MOON ON THURSDAY, FEBRUARY 15, 2018 16:05

MARCH

FULL MOON ON THURSDAY, MARCH 1, 2018 19:51

NEW MOON ON SATURDAY, MARCH 17, 2018 09:12

FULL MOON ON SATURDAY, MARCH 31, 2018 08:37

APRIL

NEW MOON ON SUNDAY, APRIL 15, 2018 21:57

FULL MOON ON SUNDAY, APRIL 29, 2018 20:58

***DAYLIGHT SAVING TIME BEGINS AT 02:00 AM ON SUNDAY, MARCH 11, 2018 IN THE UNITED STATES

MAY

NEW MOON ON TUESDAY, MAY 15, 2018 07:48

FULL MOON ON TUESDAY, MAY 29, 2015 10:19

JUNE

NEW MOON ON WEDNESDAY, JUNE 13, 2018 15:43

FULL MOON ON THURSDAY, JUNE, 28, 2018 00:53

JULY

NEW MOON ON THURSDAY, JULY 12, 2018 22:48

FULL MOON ON FRIDAY, JULY, 27, 2018 16:20

AUGUST

NEW MOON ON SATURDAY, AUGUST 11, 2018 05:58

FULL MOON ON SUNDAY, AUGUST 26, 2018 07:56

SEPTEMBER

NEW MOON ON SUNDAY, SEPTEMBER 9, 2018 14:01

FULL MOON ON MONDAY, SEPTEMBER, 24, 2018 22:52

OCTOBER

NEW MOON ON MONDAY, OCTOBER 8, 2018 23:46

FULL MOON ON WEDNESDAY, OCTOBER 24, 2018 12:45

NOVEMBER

NEW MOON ON WEDNESDAY, NOVEMBER 7, 2018 11:02

FULL MOON ON FRIDAY, NOVEMBER 23, 2018 00:39

DECEMBER

NEW MOON ON FRIDAY, DECEMBER 07, 2017 02:20

FULL MOON ON SUNDAY, AUGUST 26, 2018 07:56

FULL MOON ON SATURDAY, DECEMBER 22, 2017 12:49

JANUARY 2019

NEW MOON ON SATURDAY, JANUARY 5TH, 2019

***DAYLIGHT SAVING TIME ENDS AT 02:00 ON SUNDAY, NOVEMBER 4, 2018 IN THE UNITED STATES.

2018 ECLIPSE GUIDE: ASPECTS AND ECLIPSES

Venus in Capricorn aspecting Cancer:
The combination of Venus being in Saturn's sign during the eclipse will create instability in relationships, weaken technical abilities in business, support oils, iron, steel and antiques and older people. Love will feel restricted and there will be a lack of pleasure. So the key is to take care of your health, and women and elders in your life, as they may be vulnerable today.

Mercury in Capricorn aspecting Cancer:
The combination of Mercury being in Saturn's sign Capricorn during the eclipse will create deception and an obscuring of facts in the workplace. Compulsions and obsessions may be forced to the front in the mind and actions where you feel subject to mental disturbances and distractions, disruptions and depressions. In some cases, you may feel that your ability to learn is sluggish and find it hard to recall details. During the eclipse, Mercury may lose sight of the big picture. It's best to retreat today and spend the time in quiet contemplation, gentle rest and meditation to ease any agitation or discord.

Mars in Capricorn aspecting Cancer:
The combination of Mars being in Saturn's sign of Capricorn during the eclipse will create an added boost of energy with Mars being in his sign of exaltation so tackle your projects with the courage of a warrior and by taking some calculated risks and applying focused energy, you could come out a winner today! Still this eclipse brings moodiness, aggressiveness and impulsive action so feelings are strong and angry outbursts likely. People may be more expressive and opinionated so be careful not to fly off the handle.

Ketu in Capricorn and Rahu in Cancer until March 2019
The combination of Ketu being in Saturn's sign of Capricorn during got eclipse will create a fanatical pursuit of ideas and projects or an obsessive one-tracked mind that is disarray and losing the big picture, one's projects may fall apart at the seams. Career activities could be on a positive rise but then go belly up. This is a good day to stay away from business related activities, as they are unstable due to the sudden fluctuating energies of success and failure.

Lunar Eclipse: July 27, 2018 16:20 EST 11.45 Degrees Capricorn

Venus in Cancer aspecting Capricorn:
The combination of Venus being in Moon's sign of Cancer during the eclipse is feeling overly emotional and high on expectations that lead to disillusionment and dissatisfaction or being lazy. Venus, during the eclipse in Cancer, doesn't know when to quit and may be overly sexual and jazzed up on love and pleasures or full of the sorrows of the world. Today it would be best to rephrase any negatives into positives and realize that we all have a great capacity to love and be loved. There is an inability to

express emotions and affections causing strain in relationships. People will be moody and overly sensitive. It's not a good time to plan parties or social event.

Mercury in Cancer aspecting Capricorn:
The combination of Mercury being in Moon's sign of Cancer during the eclipse is the inability to act and feeling scattered and fragmented with too many thoughts running through the mind and being prone to an overactive imagination. To get out of feeling restless and nervous, get creative in writing activities or listening to music. Mercury likes to move and be active so today is a good day to take a walk in the park and breathe in some fresh air or aerobic activity to get the breath moving and air flowing so it's not clogged up in the 'mental mind.'

Rahu in Cancer aspecting Capricorn:
The combination of Rahu being in Moon's sign of Cancer during the eclipse is a feeling of confusion and insecurity. One may feel apprehensive and uncertain which may lead to feelings of vulnerability and seeking comfort in food, drugs, and alcohol. Instead, find some way to rid yourself of any "*shadowed*" emotional toxins that come up. One of the best ways to get out of the muck of self-pity is to rise up in service of others so go out and help the community or care for the 'underdog' and those that are in need. It's a good day to help women, mothers and clean the house.

ECLIPSE GUIDE FOR 2018

TOTAL ECLIPSE OF THE MOON
JANUARY 31, 2017
18 DEGREES CANCER
US 08:27 EST
Begins 10:51 GMT; Ends 16:08 GMT

Visible in Northwestern South America, Western USA, Asia, Australia, the Middle East, Eastern Africa, Eastern Europe.

This is probably the most significant eclipse of the year as it is total and widely visible. It is said to have an impact within 20 days of where it is seen.

It is thought that when Venus aspects the eclipse, then the standing crops are destroyed, and the commerce becomes bullish. Towns impacted by eclipses may face difficult times and inflationary trends. With this eclipse hitting South America where wheat, corn and beans are grown, there could be an impact.

Still it is said that eclipses happening during the month of Magha, starting **January 21st** brings timely rains. Traders are known to hoard commodities and buy a great deal and food grain prices expand.

The eclipse is on a Wednesday and it is thought to support the rise in cotton, copper, gold, and wheat up to two months before the eclipse.

Cancer is a moveable sign, so it is thought that this eclipse could disrupt national trade, functioning of government, impact crops negatively, and create upheavals in political affairs. In Cancer, it could lead to the destruction of marine products and create labor distress. Excessive rain could lead to floods.

It would seem that Australia, Northwestern, and South America are most likely to be impacted along with Venezuela, which is a mess, and about to explode.

If you have planets within 3 degrees of 18 degrees Cancer, are Cancer rising or Capricorn rising or are in a Moon/Rahu or Rahu/Moon period, it will have the most impact on your life.

The Moon is very close to the North node, Rahu, showing a total eclipse, which involves Mercury and Venus, while the Sun in Capricorn transits alongside the South node, Ketu. Lunar eclipses show an immediate trigger, more obviously observable in those experiencing a cycle of the nodes, or with planets close to the eclipse degree. So the impact will be felt over the next two weeks through February 15th at the solar eclipse.

The Moon is eclipsed in the lunar sign Ashlesha that is represented by a serpent and is connected with poisons and toxins. Emotionally, this is an intense eclipse and I never recommend watching them, particularly if you are Cancer rising. This would be a good time to be deep in meditation.

PARTIAL ECLIPSE OF THE SUN
February 15, 2018
4 DEGREES AQUARIUS
US 16:06 EST
Begins 18:55 GMT; Ends 22:47 GMT

It is visible in Chile, Argentina, southern Brazil, Uruguay, Falkland Islands, and Antarctica.

This eclipse is also occurring in the month of Magha, on a Thursday, in an air sign and a fixed sign. With this eclipse hitting South America where wheat and corn and beans are grown, there could be an impact.

The eclipse is thought to impact oil seeds, so soybean oil is likely to show an increase within 1.5 months of the eclipse.

Aquarius is a fixed sign, so this eclipse could disrupt national trade, functioning of government, have a negative impact on crops, and create upheavals in political affairs. Eclipses taking place in air signs cause disturbances in weather patterns, sickness, famine and strained relationships with nations and political disruption.

Although, the nodes are in Cancer and Capricorn, a partial eclipse is possible in an adjacent sign.

Aquarius also represents humanitarian issues, technology, biomedicine and healing. Mercury transits this eclipse degree the day after the eclipse occurs so Mercury related affairs such as writing, and the media might be largely impacted.

The solar eclipse occurs in the Nakshatra or lunar mansion of Dhanistha ruled by Mars.

PARTIAL ECLIPSE OF THE SUN
July 12, 2018
27.41 DEGREES GEMINI
US 22:38 EST
Begins 1:48 GMT; Ends 4:13 GMT

It is visible in Tasmania, extreme southern Australia, islands south of New Zealand, the edge of Antarctica below Australia

The second solar eclipse of 2018 occurs on **July 12** and is a partial eclipse in Gemini.

This eclipse occurs opposite Saturn, as well as Pluto - almost by exact degree. When Saturn aspects an eclipse, it tends to create conditions of famine, scanty rain and resources. This will mostly impact Australia, which was on the troubled annual chart list anyway. This can also impact mining.

Pluto aspecting the eclipse can produce devastating results creating ethnic disturbances where share markets can be hurt.

Again, Australia is impacted and they are already thinking about anti-Islamic laws.

The eclipse is occurring in the month of Asahda on **June 22 - July 22** and can impact China, Afghanistan and the central regions of India. This should lead to political disturbance and problems with crops leading to steep rises in grains.

The eclipse is on a Thursday, so it can cause a price rise in edible oil for 1.5 months.

The lunar mansion involved is Punarvasu, which is represented by goddess Aditi.

TOTAL ECLIPSE OF THE MOON
July 27, 2018
11.45 DEGREES CAPRICORN
US 16:20 EST
Begins 17:14 GMT; Ends 23:28 GMT

It is visible in Australia, Africa, Middle East, South American, Eastern Caribbean, most of Europe,

The second total lunar eclipse of **2018** is on **Friday, July 27th**. The Moon is at the same degree at the start of the eclipse as Mars, in close conjunction to the South node, Ketu. This is highly volatile for the planet and our personal lives. With the Sun and Rahu in the opposite sign, and Mercury retrograde at the sensitive juncture between Cancer and Leo, there is ample opportunity for big shake-ups and events that trigger immediate changes.

The eclipse is taking place in the month of Sravana and will impact China, Afghanistan and Kashmir. Winter crops get destroyed extending into a 6 months period. Rainfall is plenty and food grain is abundant and prices fall.

Mars causes problems again when it goes direct over the eclipse point on October 1st and could trigger violence and fires again. It is occurring in an earth sign so it can create agricultural and natural produce droughts on areas that are impacted. It also can create earthquakes and mining disasters connected with Capricorn.

Governments open to misadventures and problems with trade and financial problems will be affected: Europe, Australia, the Middle East and South America.

The eclipse is in the lunar mansion of Shravana for the 2nd time this year. Shravana, much like the following sign, Dhanistha, is represented by our ability to listen. Hidden secrets are likely to be unearthed with this eclipse as that is a theme for the year.

PARTIAL ECLIPSE OF THE SUN
August 11, 2018
25 DEGREES CANCER
US 05:58 EST
Begins 5:02 GMT; Ends 11:30 GMT

It is visible in parts of Northeastern Canada, Greenland, Iceland, Scotland, Scandinavia, Russia, and Mongolia, other and mid-China, Korea
Best seen in northern Russia with 68% coverage

The last partial solar eclipse of **2018** occurs in Cancer. Mars is retrograde and close to Ketu for the eclipses, while Mercury is retrograde and close to the Sun. Mars aspects to eclipses create war, fire and accidents and theft. Mercury in the sign of the eclipse creates troubled communications and media problems for the ruling party.

The eclipse is on a Saturday and can affect oil prices.

2018 Partial Solar Eclipse

February 15 16:06
4 Degrees Aquarius

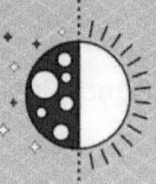

July 12 22:38
27.41 Degrees Gemini

August 11 05:58
25 Degrees Cancer

2018 Total Lunar Eclipse

January 31, 2018 08:27 EST
18 Degrees Cancer

July 27, 2018 16:20 EST
11.45 Degrees Capricorn

2018 LIBRA AND TAURUS RISING: TRANSITS OF VENUS

Venus transits are considered auspicious through all signs from the Natal Moon or ascendant except the 6th, 7th and 10th places.

For Libra rising that means Venus in Pisces, Aries and Cancer.

For Taurus rising that means Venus in Libra, Scorpio or Aquarius will bring up more challenges.

VENUS IN CAPRICORN: JANUARY 13 - FEBRUARY 6

Venus enters Capricorn: **January 13th at 04:14**

Venus moves into Capricorn on **Saturday, January 13th** and enters the friends' sign of Saturn. Capricorn is a complex sign and is the natural 10th sign of the zodiac and connected to business and the natural need of Saturn for security. Capricorns often have great organizing power, desires success, fame and is a bit of reclusive energy. Ketu afflicts Venus during this transit, so it is a bit more difficult and the **January 31st** eclipse will be close to it.

In general, Venus in Capricorn showers material pleasure on its friend Saturn. If you have this position in your natal chart (like I do) it can create loyal and mature love, conventional marriage and supports the underdog and the poor. When it is afflicted it may create sexual coldness, fascination with death or reproductive problems or emotional flatness.

The combination of Venus being in Saturn's sign creates stability in relationships, strong technical abilities in business, support oils, iron, steel and antiques and older people. I often think the Venus/Saturn connection is one of creating beautiful infrastructure to support our aesthetic sense and I think of the murals and mosaics that were engineered into the new highway walls in Phoenix that add beauty to the concrete commute.

On a physical level, this transit supports attention to the body, to having the discipline to start that diet and supports activity like massage, which combines the sensuous nature of Venus with the solid grounding of the needs of the body. This is a good month to find a good massage therapist, take an exercise class that sculpts your body or to shop for new clothes. Building a beautiful new business, website or publishing a book seems like a perfect activity this month for this transit as Venus there will be support from superiors and authorities.

Venus in Capricorn should be quite successful with adjusting fortunes coming from the influence of Ketu that could lead to conceptual breakthroughs in the areas of work and business, especially religion, ethics and higher education. Relationships with father, bosses and superiors could also take a turn for the better and foreign travel could be enlightening with innovative learning opportunities.

There could also be unique forms of communication and self-expression that bring fortune. This could help one with the ability to accumulate merit in life, and with patience on the Cazimi path, the power to achieve the fruits of life through the use of one's own efforts. This is in contrast to the upcoming move into Aquarius **February 6 - 28th.**

So time to get that massage, go for sculpting your beautiful body and go for the riches of material success and enjoy great shopping but do not lose sight of your spiritual balance. Venus is one of the two Guru planets, along with Jupiter and it gets out of balance if too lost in the material realm and the transit of Capricorn can easily do that.

The dancer pose in Yoga embodies Venus in Capricorn with balance and beauty and is always a great pose to do balance out beauty and structure in our life.

Venus conjunct Ketu in Capricorn January 29th

When Venus is afflicted in Aquarius, it can create delays or setbacks in relationships, love for lost causes, unconventional relationships, reproductive complications, sexual imbalances and dysfunctional partners. If you have this in your natal chart or have Venus conjunct Ketu or Mars in your natal chart or are running a Venus/Rahu or Venus/Ketu or Venus/Mars period or some combination like that you might feel this transit more intensely.

Venus will transit within 3 degrees of Ketu the South node, the fiery and spiritual monkish planet, **January 27 - February 1st**. If you were born with this combination, it can create unresolved past life relationships that are unhappy or painful. You may attract spiritual or emotional partners with a lot of baggage and you may change partners frequently or may reject partners for fear of being rejected yourself.

If you are male, you may choose women are unconventional and that society may reject from another class, race or religion or gender orientation-causing problems. In any case if you have this signature in your natal chart it may bring up unorthodox and complicated relationships and with Mars in Aquarius often, there may be a lot of passion or quarrels. If you are a revolving door relationship person, use this month to go deeper and hang in there instead of rejecting.

VENUS IN SAGITTARIUS TIL JANUARY 14, 2018

During the start of this **January** transit, Venus' energy is conjunct the Sun on **January 8th** in Sagittarius. In Medieval astrology and by experience, by this creates what is called, Cazimi, or being "*in the heart*" of the Sun. Instead of burning up the planet and preventing it from producing its significations, Cazimi gives the combust planet a spiritualizing boost that adds strength to the planet rather than weakening it so the planet is actually not harmed or overpowered by the Sun's fiery light. This can lead to an enhanced state where the planet becomes inseparable with our spirit. Cazimi Venus may be become more sexually addicted, have a supernatural charm, an enhanced radiance, and more insight to feelings. Venus, being warmed by the Sun, could also be infused with inner light and sit on the fringes becoming ethereal, alluring, unusual and dreamy.

Taurus and Libra rising will benefit most from this transit, bring out more happiness or joy at home and beauty of art and nature in foreign travel. Aries and Scorpio rising will have more difficulty with women during short trips, with siblings, or with women in the workplace. Cancer and Leo risings will have the most difficulty with the transit, which can lead to loss of money, or problems with female enemies. Capricorns will enjoy this transit greatly as Venus will activate love of beauty, art and may bring a new relationship into one's life. Pisces and Sagittarius rising may find monetary benefit from this transit and Virgos could find new romance and spiritual adventure.

Venus in Capricorn should be quite successful with adjusting fortunes coming from the influence of Ketu that could lead to conceptual breakthroughs in the areas of work and business, especially religion, ethics and higher education. Relationships with father, bosses and superiors could also take a turn for the better and foreign travel could be enlightening with innovative learning opportunities.

There could also be unique forms of communication and self-expression that bring fortune. This could help one with the ability to accumulate merit in life, and with patience on the Cazimi path, the power to achieve the fruits of life through the use of one's own efforts. This is in contrast to the upcoming move into Aquarius **February 6 - 28th**.

So, time to get that massage, go for sculpting your beautiful body and go for the riches of material success and enjoy great shopping but do not lose sight of your spiritual balance.

Venus is one of the two Guru planets, along with Jupiter and it gets out of balance if too lost in the material realm and the transit of Capricorn can easily do that.

The dancer pose in Yoga embodies Venus in Capricorn with balance and beauty and is always a great pose to do balance out beauty and structure in our life.

Venus conjunct Ketu in Capricorn **January 29th**
When Venus is afflicted in Capricorn, it can create delays or setbacks in relationships, love for lost causes, unconventional relationships, reproductive complications, sexual imbalances and dysfunctional partners. If you have this in your natal chart or have Venus conjunct Ketu or Mars in your natal chart or are running a Venus/Rahu or Venus/Ketu or Venus/Mars period or some combination like that you might feel this transit more intensely.

Venus will transit within 3 degrees of Ketu the South node, the fiery and spiritual monkish planet, **January 27 - February 1st**. If you were born with this combination, it can create unresolved past life relationships that are unhappy or painful. You may attract spiritual or emotional partners with a lot of baggage and you may change partners frequently or may reject partners for fear of being rejected yourself.

If you are male, you may choose women are unconventional and that society may reject from another class, race or religion or gender orientation-causing problems. In any case if you have this signature in your natal chart it may bring up unorthodox and complicated relationships and with Mars in Aquarius often, there may be a lot of passion or quarrels.

If you are a revolving door relationship person, use this month to go deeper and hang in there instead of rejecting.

For Libra rising, the Ketu transit conjunct Venus will upset family life and create difficulties with mother or create unexpected problems with vehicles or problems in the home as a 4th house transit of the chart lord. For Taurus rising, it will bring up unexpected problems with 9th house matters like trips to foreign countries, problems with one's father, Guru, or religious leaders. Those running a Venus maha dasha will feel it more strongly.

VENUS IN AQUARIUS: FEBRUARY 6 - FEBRUARY 28

Venus enters Aquarius: February 6th
End Venus Combustion February 19th
Venus moves into Aquarius **February 6th** but is afflicted in transit by a 60-degree aspect from Saturn into **February 16th** and this will be felt most **February 14 -18**. Saturn and Venus are friends so this may bring up older more mature relationships or a love of old books and spending time with elderly women.

Aquarius is the 2nd most difficult sign to have anywhere prominent in ones' chart, as it is ruled by the Shakti of suffering Saturn and Rahu, which is the seat of desire. Rahu gives and then takes away so we are reminded that we are here to find the Divine. Aquarius is on the opposite side of the zodiac from Leo, the giver of light and it tends to take away the material, creating great pain and suffering from the losses that arise. Aquarius is a bitter enemy with the moon and mother so issues around maternal care, nurturing and food become prominent. Whenever the rising sign in any Varga chart has planets in Aquarius this creates suffering and loss in this area.

Still there are bright sides to this transit as it is friends with Saturn and Rahu, the owners of Aquarius. Venus this month will foster a love of poetry and creative writing so for creative writers, this is your time to get that pen out and get that novel started or that book of poetry edited. Venus in Aquarius may lend innovation to your ideas, which will be sure to be full and overflowing! If you were born with an unafflicted Venus in Aquarius, then you are friendly charming and fun loving, logical, enjoy learning, popular and good in relationship with others.

Still the earlier part of the transit through the Saturn sextile into **February 16th** will create delays and setbacks in relationships. When Venus is afflicted in Aquarius, it can create delays or setbacks in relationships, love for lost causes, unconventional relationships, reproductive complications, sexual imbalances and dysfunctional partners.

Aquarius is a vata or air sign so the earthy solidity of Capricorn will be dislodged. The good news is that Venus will be exalted in Pisces in March. This will be a sweet time for romance and relationship in general but will treat different signs in different ways.

Venus will be in the constellation of Shatabashak (Aquarius 6.40-20.00) **February 11 - 22nd**, known for its independent nature. This group of stars represents a love for travel and adventure, so it may be time to pack your bags and plan a road trip! It is also connected with healing and technology so time to work on self-healing or creating those new gadgets.

This is a 10th house transit of Venus for Taurus rising and 10th house transits of Venus are not considered good because Venus want to have fun on the 10th house is about work and status. Still some status elevation is possible in the later part of the transit between **February 17 - 28th**.

For Libra rising, this is a 5th house transit and can bring deep love with your children, a new romance or deep spiritual initiations and success in the theatre.

Aries rising will benefit from income and Scorpio rising may have expenditures around the home and vehicles and more domestic quarrels. Pisces rising may have passionate sexual experiences while Cancer rising may have big problems with deep karmic issues from the past. Aquarius rising will feel a bit lighter for having the transit of a good friend visiting and creating deeper connections and may increase the desire for new and unconventional clothes. Geminis will have deep spiritual experiences or go on luxury trips to foreign lands and Virgos will have to watch illness related to the reproductive area, kidneys or bladder or pancreas. Again all of this is very individual to the larger cycles that you are running.

VENUS IN PISCES: MARCH 1 - MARCH 26

Venus enters Pisces: March 1st
Conjunct Mercury March 4th
Venus moves into her sign of exaltation on **March 1st** until **March 26th**. In Pisces, Venus, the ruler of women and relationships, brings out love, harmony, creativity, beauty and artistry. Mercury, the ruler of communication and the link between mind and spirit, brings out deep intelligence, learning, and ingenuity. This conjunction will blend the mind with pleasures. We can expect a more imaginative or creative side of business with fresh, original ideas. This is also a good time for writers and musicians to feel their creativity expand and they could also receive more public recognition.

Venus is a Guru planet in its own right and has an important role in materializing the spiritual essence of the human being and brings spirituality into the material world and in esoteric astrology it allows men to aspire after spiritual immortality and learn graceful manners, calmness, endurance, sociability and love of the arts. It is connected to wealth and Lakshmi, poetry, beautiful clothes, fine arts and music.

Venus is the teacher of the demons and in modern a term that means those stuck in material existence. Still Venus is the best of the benefics and seeks to bring spirituality to us after creating material abundance. While often connected to beauty and the senses, it is also a great teacher and like Jupiter has its own depth of wisdom. Looking forward to this conjunction with the high energy and teaching capabilities to soothe troubled souls and seething angers and maybe Venus will bring more peace to the planet the next few months. Let's hope so!

The communicative support of Mercury will assist Venus and women during this transit to be more prominent in the spotlight spreading their messages. So, write and publish that book! If you are working on a course, get out in front of an audience and start teaching! Now is the time to be heard and seen!

If you are Taurus rising, this is a really great time for you with an 11th house transit of your ascendant lord as it brings great new friends, fulfillment of desires and strong income.

If you are Libra rising, you will feel good but have to watch challenges from enemies and with health issues. Dual signs, Pisces, Gemini, Virgo and Sagittarius benefit from a Malava Yoga in transit with Venus exalted in an angular house supporting home, happiness, career.

Aries rising will have to watch overspending and expenditures and Scorpios may have challenges with children and investments. Results for other rising signs are not as spectacular.

As always, every chart is so unique and if you are running a Venus period or sub-period or have Venus in Pisces already, the energies will be more activated.

VENUS IN ARIES: MARCH 26 - APRIL 19

Venus in Aries March 26th - April 19, 2018
Venus in Aries is aspected by Jupiter in transit with Jupiter in Libra and the exact opposition on **April 18th**. This aspect creates too much expansiveness and you have to watch overspending. Because this opposition is happening between the Aries and Libra, it is on the core level 1st and 7th natural zodiacal signs so it will bring up core level relationship issues and possible fights about money if one partner is spending too much.

Still Aries is a bitter enemy of Venus and the darker side of Venus is Aries is felt where one can get intimate too quickly looking for the thrill of romance and being strongly sexed and attracted to lose or unreliable people. It can generate reproductive problems. As it moves away from the early degrees of Aries, it does get better and develops a sense of fiery play and becomes seductive, fun to be with, playful, adventurous, spontaneous and generous and a bit passionate and very creative.

Venus will first be in the constellation of Ashwini (Aries 0-13.20) **March 26-April** 6th. Prash Trivedi reminds us that Ashwini is known in modern astronomy as Alpha-Arietes and Beta-Arietes near the bright star of Andromeda between **March 2-April 1st.** The symbol for Ashwini is a horse's head representing a dauntless spirit of adventure and a headstrong nature. This transit usually fosters self-starters and energy to complete projects. It is also a very healing constellation and so there will be more energy for healing. The ruling deities are the Ashwin twins who ride in a golden chariot and shower healing energy down to the earth plane. They are the *"Physicians of the Gods."* This is a nakshatra of initiation, revitalization and transformational healing. The ruling planet is Ketu (South Node of the Moon), which gives a mystical and mysterious bent to their life journey. Ketu is channeling the moon's energy from Shravana (Capricorn 10-23.20) and Mars is the constellation of Purva Ashadha, which is owned by Venus. This transit can bring a lot of sexual passion in the first part of transit. At the same time, it can create a push pull toward austerity and celibacy if one is recovering from a broken relationship or regrets a hasty affair. In the end, slow down before jumping in and out of relationships or moving too quickly as thing may suddenly seem like they are moving too fast

Venus will conjunct Uranus during this transit on **March 28th** in Aries. This conjunction can create unexpected events and excitement and the quest for new experiences through love and artistic expression.

You might suddenly meet someone out of the blue who seems radically different and exciting. Enjoy the change and excitement for a few days. Venus/Uranus energy creates a lot of excitement and deep energy and usually is great for artistic adventure. Venus conjunct Uranus usually is positive for movement in the US stock market and can create a lot of movement contextual to what is happening.

Venus moves into the constellation of Bharani (Aries 13.20-26.40) **April 6 -15th** where its most creative energies unfold for artistic projects and heightened creativity. Venus will be more unafflicted creating more courage to get things done quickly.

So, the party is over for Venus who enjoyed a nice *"staycation"* in Pisces where the height of its relationship skills and artistic expression were able to come out.

Libra rising will definitely have more of the sudden and quick relationship energy that we have discussed above with a 7th house transit of the ascendent lord. Taurus rising, owned by Venus can also have a lot of sexual energy but may experience more expenditures over the next month so watch your shopping addiction if romance gets too complicated and difficult over the next month. Geminis will benefit from more female friendships with an 11th house transit and woman's groups. Scorpio and Virgo and Cancer rising, and moons could have the most difficult with this transit as they are 6 and 8th and 10th from the ascendent.

VENUS IN TAURUS: APRIL 19 - MAY 14

Venus enters Taurus: April 19th

Venus will be very strong in the sky in Taurus for a month and totally unafflicted, so Venus's strong qualities come out. If you are Taurus or Libra rising or have a strong Venus in your chart, its a good time for feeling expansive, refined, pleasant, comfortable, kind, generous, artistic, strong in relationship skills.

Taurus brings the blessings of Krishna and Shiva and is one of the more material signs of abundance. This transit with Venus in its own sign creates a Malavya Yoga for Taurus rising and indicates the highest manifestation of Venus's qualities so it is a good time to enjoy good food, the arts, and home while pursuing partnerships and romance.

Finances will be good. It is a time to feel at home and to move forward solidly in your life with lots of Grace.

Libra rising will experience an 8th house transit of Venus in its own sign and this is a time for personal transformation and unexpected money coming from lotteries, insurance or other unexpected sources. Meditation and spiritual experience could be powerful and so a good time to take a spiritual retreat and withdraw from the senses.

VENUS IN GEMINI: MAY 14 - JUNE 8

Venus enters Gemini: May 14th

Venus moves into Gemini on **May 14th** and stays there until **June 8th**. It is a mixed transit with an expansive Jupiter aspect into **June 1st** and a Saturn opposition into **May 26th**. Overall it is positive with some affliction from Saturn around **May 30th-June 3rd** but will still foster a love of poetry and creative writing so for creative writers, this is your time to get that pen out and get that novel started or that book of poetry edited.

If you were born with an unafflicted Venus in Gemini, then you are friendly charming and fun loving, logical, enjoy learning, popular and good in relationship with others. The natural 3rd sign of the zodiac Gemini is very creative as is Venus so there is a lot of flow this month for creative ideas and inventions and creative computer programming. I often find that computer programmers have a lot of Venus/Mercury connections in their charts.

Venus in Gemini can bring out sexuality, as Gemini is the natural 3rd house of the zodiac is connected to Kama and sexual expression and relationship energy and love of pleasure, good food and the arts.

This transit benefits Taurus and Libra rising the most with a 2nd house transit of Taurus bringing gains from family, finance and love and appreciation of good food. For Libras, it can bring love of foreign travel, deep love and appreciation of Guru or spiritual wisdom or great love in attending church or synagogue.

Aquarius and Gemini and Leo rising will also do well with this transit whereas Cancer rising may get caught up in too many expenditures or sensual indulgences. Aries has to also watch for an increase in sexual energy and turn it into creative expression.

Venus continues in the constellation of Mrigashira (Orion, Taurus 26.40-Gemini 6.40) **May 15 - 19th** where intellectual searching and deep spiritual wisdom is supported. Venus in Ardra nakshatra **May 20 - 31st** (Betelguese, Gemini 6.40-19.59) is a bit more tumultuous for relationships and thoughts of breaking up a relationship could come up in order to foster the soul's growth.

Venus in the constellation of Purnavasu **June 1 - June 12th** (Gemini 20-Cancer 3.20) will connect it with Jupiter and maybe the two Gurus energy together can soothe any turmoil from the first Mars/Ketu conjunction on **June 3rd**.

Still Venus's transit here may still create desire to change partners or create uncertainty in relationship. But the universal mothering and nurturing qualities of Purnavasu will bleed into Venus's maternal energy well.

VENUS IN CANCER: JUNE 8 – JULY 3

Venus is in Cancer June 8, 2018
So, a bright spot in the sky, Venus moves into Cancer on Friday, **June 8th - July 3rd** and pretty much being unafflicted except when it gets conjunct Rahu on **June 19th** which may create some confusion around emotions and unhappiness in love affairs with deceit, and disillusionment. Venus with Rahu may act a little taboo or unconventional. Venus and the Moon are good friends in being the two most feminine planets and Venus in Cancer brings out artistic creativity, comfort, elegance, deep compassion and caring, emotional openness, sensitivity, and a deep capacity to love.

Venus goes into the constellation of Pushya on **June 22 - July 3rd** where it gets connected to a strong Saturn that is stationary. While the two are friends, Saturn and Venus combinations can create love with restrictions, emotional dryness, detachment or love of older people and strong business abilities. Still Venus can get frustrated with love and passion because it has too many responsibilities. The lesson with this transit is to be less selfish and less indulgent in the senses. The constellation of Pushya is one of the more auspicious ones for deep spirituality and wisdom to come out. Pushya is connected to the deity Brihaspati who has the wisdom to advise the gods and is a rival to the devata, Shukracharya, the advisor to the material world.

Venus goes into the constellation of Ashlesha **July 4 -16th** where it is connected Mercury. Venus gets debilitated in Virgo, so it is not happy to be in Mercury's star where ugly and jealous gossip and sharp tongues can lead angry battles between women.

Relationships suffer here and can be angry or vicious or filled with controlling energies. Still Venus can deal with the poisons of Ashlesha better than any other planet with its nurturing and healing qualities but has to move into selfless service in order to do so.

VENUS IN LEO: JULY 4 - JULY 31

Venus in Leo July 4, 2018
Venus moves into Leo on **Saturday, July 4th**. Venus will be in the star constellation of Ashlesha (Hydra, Cancer 16.40-29.59), ruled by Mercury. Of the 27 constellations in the zodiac, Ashlesha can stir up more emotional turmoil than many others so watch out for vicious communication arguments and speaking out and lashing out at people without thinking so hold your tongue and wait before your bust forth in anger. The darker side of this constellation is that it can make Mercury and planets connected to the constellation impolite, tactless, unpopular, lacking in social skills, dismissive rules, lacking gratitude, depressed, reckless, isolated and lacking grace

Prash Trivedi reminds us that the symbol for this intense nakshatra is the coiled serpent at the base of the spine, reflecting the potent kundalini energy that resides here. Ashlesha means the tangled one and denotes the challenges of our addictions. The main deities are the Nagas, the Serpent Kings. The Shakti revealed here is the "*power to inflict poisonous venom*". Great mystical talents and enlightenment can be experienced if the primordial energy of this lunar asterism is harnessed.

Serpents have two connotations being connected to poison and spirituality. When the constellation is operating strongly, it can bring deep mystical experience and spiritual inquiry and on the dark side it can lead to poisonous gossiping so watch your tongue as the planets transit through here. It can tend toward gluttony and debauchery and drug use and addictive patterns. The constellation may increase the desire for unquenchable sensual gratification so remember moderation in all things.

For Taurus and Libra Rising this will be a beneficial transit as Venus goes though the 3rd and 10th house of artistic expression and how one is seen in the world.

VENUS IN LEO: JULY 4 - JULY 31

Venus in Leo July 4, 2018
Venus moves into Leo on **Saturday, July 4th**. Venus in Leo can amplify feelings and passion and support the business of art and getting acclaim in shows or being more successful with art sales. It also supports actors and actresses and our love of luxuries, beauty and will promote strong affections.

Venus ends her visit in Cancer in the constellation of Purva Phalguni, a star she rules where she has the brilliant skills in fine arts and a love pleasure. This is a great time to start working on creative projects!

Taurus and Libra rising will need to be cautious not to stir up harsh conversations at home or within the family during this transit as Venus goes through their 4th and 11th house of home and social groups of affluence.

In the end, Venus always has fun in Leo and women love fun but watch the dark side of the ego coming out in Leo where the need for too much attention can lead to disappointments.

VENUS IN VIRGO: AUGUST 1 – AUGUST 31

Venus in Virgo August 1,2018
Venus transits into Virgo on **Wednesday, August 1st** and it is a time for her to rest and meditate. Technically it is debilitated here but that just means that it has to work 3 times as hard to get results.

It is a particularly difficult time for relationships as Venus tends to be too critical and picky in Virgo and this can lead to picking poor partners, being a victim in relationships, broken romances, problems with reproductive organs and bladder problems and sugar imbalances

Venus in Virgo can bring out the "*lusty*" energy of Venus rather than the higher energies of artistic expression. If you give into this energy, you may find your creative juices drained further and this can be a challenge for artists or designer or professional dancers and singers who count on Venus. Moderation is always the key with Venus in Virgo.

Saturn will be giving an aspect to Venus on **August 9th**, so this is a time to either focus on love or restrict it.

Relationship skills really will need a deep tweaking. The key will be to accept your partner in his/her imperfections and to avoid being too critical about things that bother you.
Relationship is always about compromise and acceptance. Trying to change your partner usually does not work but use your skills to communicate your needs in a non-

aggressive manner and find a way to compromise and you will get through.

Venus governs business expansion and the desire to buy and in Virgo, these energies may be lessened. I often find the stock market will fall when Venus is in Virgo or that sales may drop so you have to work 3 times as hard with your creative marketing efforts during this time. Venus governs peace and diplomacy and given the fragile state of the world with the US and North Korea, this is a troubling transit.

The lion pose is connected to Venus and the 2nd chakra of creativity and pro-creativity so you can do that pose if your creative juices seem at a low point.

Taurus and Libra Rising Sign people running Venus periods will have the most problems with this transit while Virgos and Capricorns may do best with it. Libra rising in particular will need to rest more, conserve energy, take more time for meditation and go on spiritual retreats in order to balance out the yearly imbalance.

VENUS IN LIBRA: SEPTEMBER 1 – DECEMBER 31

Venus in Libra September 1, 2018
Venus moves into Libra on **Saturday, September 1st** giving us a welcome breath of fresh air around relationships and supporting comfort. It's a life saver and kicks in all kinds of wonderful energies including elegance, being well-respected, artistic creativity, balance in thought and deep, good intuition, passion, enthusiasm, comfort, luxury and humanitarian enterprises.

Venus will be in conjunction with Mercury on **October 15th**. A few times a year Mercury and Venus come together and while there is an official planetary war today until tonight with Venus winning as the brighter star, they are good friends and can handle their tight quarters together.

The conjunction supports artistic creation of art music and poetry and may allow one to express their feelings in relationship in a very detailed way so this may be a day to "*talk about the relationship*" and take it deeper for greater understanding.

The Venus and Moon conjunction on **November 6th** offering good imagination, love of refinement and comfort, artistic sensibilities, and brings comfort to others to enrich their lives.

Venus will be in the star constellation Chitra at first **September 2-10** and this will be a very successful time for artists to propel themselves forward with the ability to accumulate recognition for their work. The constellation of Swati, (Libra 6.40-20.00) **September 10 - October 30th**, offers the energy to scatter creativity like the wind so your power to spread your talent far during this transit so use your excellent communication skills and creativity in all enterprises and they are bound to bring success!

Libra rising will feel this most as it is a Malavya Yoga but Capricorns and Aquarians will benefit greatly from it as will Geminis and Virgos. Enemies of Venus, like Mars and Jupiter and the Sun may have challenges with the transit. Scorpios have to watch expenditures and sexual indulgences. Leo and Taurus and Aries rising get 3rd, 6th and 7th house transits of Venus, which are more challenging. Still a deeper sense of ease and comfort will come as it such a contrast for Libra rising going from the deep debilitation of Virgo to the comfort of being home. More harmony in relationships should be felt unless you have any natal malefics in Aries or Libra causing problems. Ah, the break that refreshes.

VENUS (R) CONJUNCT MERCURY: OCTOBER 15

Mercury conjunct Retrograde Venus in Libra: October 15th

A few times a year Mercury and Venus come together and while there is an official planetary war, they are good friends and can handle their tight quarters together. The conjunction supports an unusual interest in love when Venus is retrograde, supporting relationships that don't go along with mainstream society. Some may practice celibacy or be sexual "celebrants!" This transit can put one's love life into a spin, causing disinterest, or increased interest — usually the opposite of whatever is the normal state and with Mercury sharing space with Venus, partnerships may not be serious.

The transit normally supports scientific discovery and appreciation for the beautiful symmetry of the way the universe works. Mercury and Venus are also the two business planets so Libra and Taurus, but with Venus retrograde and reflective, wins during this transit will most likely be delayed or come in unusual ways that might not support closing a good deal or making new contacts.

For Libra rising, the 9th house and 12th house owner Mercury will support spiritual development and potential pilgrimages and visits to ashrams.

For Taurus rising it is a 6th house transit which is more difficult and may curtail sexual enjoyment. Use the time to work on diet, exercise and other health issues that will strength your system.

2018 ARIES AND SCORPIO RISING: TRANSITS OF MARS

The transits of Mars are considered auspicious when they are 3rd, 6th and 11th from the rising sign or natal Moon.

MARS IN SCORPIO: JANUARY 16 - MARCH 7

Mars enters Scorpio: January 16th
Mars goes into Scorpio **January 16th - March 7th** and will be unafflicted except by Rahu from **February 14 - 28th** but still this transit will be a good time for deep

transformation and energy and will particularly support Scorpio rising and a return to better health after the 12th house transit through Libra.

Mars is strong in its own sign of Scorpio, the ruler of the natural 8th house of transformation and intense desires. This increased fire energy will bring a "*try anything*" attitude to the transit. Mars will have a sharp mind and be very passionate, making quick decisions, solving problems, and enjoying a strong warrior spirit that gets results and excels in short duration tasks. On the downside, this can create arrogance, problems in partnerships, and impatience.

Scorpio is true to conviction and set in its ways. Ketu is the co-ruler of the sign which lends some instability but yields a vast amount of spirituality and this is symbolic of the Scorpio's need to regenerate itself through suffering and perhaps some self-destructive behaviors. Yet, the beauty here is that Scorpio can experience full vastness of life at levels with great depth and intensity just like the Phoenix, it often dies to the ashes and is reborn into the mythical bird, soaring in transformative freedom.

All in all, it's a good transit if you want to work hard but just make sure that you don't leave the job undone. This would be a great time to work on transforming habits and patterns that no longer serve you or diving deep into spiritual, mystical and occult studies.

Mars entry into Scorpio on **Wednesday, January 17th** points to a dynamic dance in Scorpio and the constellation of Vishaka, Pada 4. Vishakha (20.00 Libra-3.20 Scorpio) **January 17 - 22nd** is ruled by Agni and Indra and is a constellation of four stars forming the left half of the scales of Libra. Prash Trivedi notes that it is connected to the deities of Agni and Indra. Agni has the ability to do Herculean talks to achieve its goals with great fiery energy and courage. Indra provides leadership but may create danger for those around one but may act cowardly at the first sign of danger. People born with this constellation are often seeking a bit of power and status and position. Prash Trivedi notes that the English word 'fixation' can best describe the essence of Vishakha, which is marked by concentration and single mindedness, although it can be affected by the nature of the goal it pursues. With the frequency of unwholesome goals, it is a concern for handling vices and people born in this constellation could easily fall prey to alcohol, drugs and sex. Mars is debilitated in this Pada so take time to rest and not overdo it **January 17 - 22nd**.

My friend Edith Hathaway describes the nature of Scorpio best: "*Scorpio is a fixed sign, and the Sanskrit word sthira means also stationary or still — an oxymoron for Scorpio – often characterized by a seething, volcanic kind of energy when prominent. This energy can erupt suddenly, having been in the molten lava stage for some time; and in human terms such an eruption may not necessarily lead to clarity and enlightenment but to further confusion and real damage on many levels. More of the difficult part of the transit will come starting* **February 13 - 28th** *when Mars is getting aspecting by Rahu which may lead to dubious or unethical schemes so be careful with characters across the tracks or hare-brained ideas.*

As Edith Hathaway notes, with Scorpio, we should pay close attention to what lies hidden or unacknowledged. So just like molten lava threatening to unleash itself, this planetary and real-life scenario reflects a seething cauldron."

Aries rising will have an 8th house transit happening so unless you are able to do transformational work, this transit can bring up feeling worried or vulnerable or irritable so be careful not to overwork. Avoid risk-taking and hold firm if falsely accused or if legal issues arise. The more difficult part of the transit for Aries will be **February 14 - March 7th**.

During the first part of the transit for Aries rising during the **January 16th to February 14th**, which is more favorable, unexpected money could manifest, desire for research could develop. Attention to health is always advised with 8th house transit.

Scorpio rising will have as strong sense of being home and grounded in the self between **January 16 - February 13th** but may have more challenges in the constellation of Jyestha, **February 14 - March 7th** since Mars and Mercury are enemies and this can lead to disputes but also strong business development with new partners.

Mars goes into the gandanta (Scorpio 27-30) **March 1 - 7th** where deep emotional churning arises so be prepared to do deep transformational work here or find a way to ground your uneasy emotional upheavals. Be prepared to she material attachments and move toward spiritual development as Mars goes into the Sagittarius gandanta (Sagittarius 0-3) **March 8 -12th**.

MARS IN SAGITTARIUS: MARCH 7 - MAY 3

Mars enters Sagittarius: March 7th
The first part of this transit, **March 8 - 30th** can bring out the darker side of

MARS IN MULA: MARCH 8 - MARCH 30TH

Mars with first connect to Ketu in Mula Nakshatra, **March 8-30th**. On a personal level, the connection between Mars and Ketu means that you cannot let anger be repressed or it will explode in a verbal or physical attack. Exercise is a good way to work of this energy but also just let it out by screaming in your empty house. Continue to be 100% focused when doing physical activity and driving as unexpressed anger can rear its ugly head.

Stay alert, let the energy out and use to help others in need. The warrior pose in yoga is a good balance pose for activating the third eye nakshatra and alertness in activity.

For Aries rising and Scorpio rising, you will be most affected by this transit and it can increase intuition and for Aries rising, it can increase spirituality and a desire to go inward and withdraw from the world. If you do not have the luxury for long meditation courses or being a recluse, then you will have to get your active button in gear.

Prash Trivedi notes that Mula consists of nine stars at the end of Scorpio and is the place of the center of the galaxy, which Western Astrologers are fond of calling the Galactic Center as that wonderful part of the sky that looks like a white river in the night sky.

He goes onto to note that Mula means "*root*" or "*the center*" and people who have a sun, moon or ascendant lord in this constellation are very direct and do not like to beat around the bush. This is the core of the galaxy and it is ruled by Ketu who wants to get to the core of everything: hidden motives, events, core roots. Ketu is connected to past lives and Mula wants to tie up all the talents from one's past lives and bring them together. It seeks deeply for the truth of existence.

The deity of Mula is Nritti, the Goddess of calamity and yet she resides in the lucky sign of Sagittarius which mythical means she may destroy ignorance to reveal deep truths.

Ironically, Nritti is connected to the peak of material achievement and yet the nature of this nakshatra is very spiritual in her quest to go beyond the domain of ego and self-centeredness.

I will be interested to see if our politicians change with this transit. This star can give power and influence and great material accomplishment and can confer magical powers but often it releases its energy in an explosive manner--which is so true of Ketu.

The 9/11 disasters occurred during the Ketu/Mars conjunction in this constellation. Hence it has a dreadful nature in bringing out the most explosive and darkest side of Ketu, which means blowing up the material can point and force one to the spiritual. Adolf Hitler had Jupiter conjunct Ketu in this nakshatra without any balancing influence from Saturn and he was the embodiment of destruction. Lets hope the terrorists are not emboldened in their quest during this transit but this was exactly what happened during 9/11.

Mula combines the energy of Jupiter and Ketu and hence it initiates spiritual transformations for the better. With Jupiter's grace it can confer magical powers to help those in need with Grace.

Mars is favorable placed in Sagittarius and this can lead to jumping on opportunities, expanded knowledge, wealth, leadership, and becoming a spiritual warrior for charitable causes.

MARS IN SAGITTARIUS CONJUCT SATURN: APRIL 2ND

Mars conjunct Saturn in Sagittarius: April 2nd

The problem with this transit is that Mars is afflicted with fellow malefic planet, Saturn here with an exact conjunction on **April 2nd**. This transit brings out the darker psychological qualities in one may want to do things too quickly and may drive others away with their high intensity, hurting others feelings, manipulation and rabble rousing. On a positive note, Mars and Saturn can do well here with a lot of activity and physical activity, which makes them good at jobs involving aggression, risks, danger, courage and stamina. Their directness and energy gives them and edge in skills that make them in demand because they get results!

The highest aspect of this transit is moving into ones' spiritual warrior energy and doing service for humanity without ego. It can foster pride and strength and speaking the truth. There some dangers from fire or electricity or surgery if you are running a Mars/Ketu or Ketu/Mars cycle and your ascendant is Taurus rising or Capricorn rising.

FOR SCORPIO AND ARIES RISING

Scorpio rising has a 2nd house afflicted transit of Mars which means one has to avoid risky financial undertakings and get rich quick schemes. Avoid vices like tobacco or alcohol or recreational drugs to drown any emotional pain.

Aries rising has a 9th house transit that is afflicted so avoid unethical short-cuts and be cautious with foreign journeys and say away from dangerous circumstances.

The transit improves **April 11 - May 2nd** when Mars moves 5 degrees away from Saturn but the period of unrest is strong **March 27 - April 11th** so plan ahead carefully.

MARS IN CAPRICORN: MAY 2 - NOVEMBER 5

Mars enters Capricorn: May 2nd
Mars moves into Capricorn on **May 2nd** and because it goes retrograde there **June 26-August 27th**, it spends six months in its sign of exaltation. **May** is the best month for this transit because of the connection with the exalted Sun through the Nakshatra Uttarashadha (Sagittarius 26.40-Capricorn 10). Action is quick and effective; stamina and higher energy are there for major tasks. Hard work will bring fruits and Martian charm can lead to landing key deals. Technical savy will prosper. For moveable signs, Aries, Cancer, Libra and Capricorn, this creates a Ruchaka Yoga and brings out Mars highest qualities.

The problem is **June, July and early August** and **September** where Mars stays within 3 degrees of Ketu the entire month. Ketu will engulf Mars' fiery spirit and become further engorged with passion. Ketu and Mars are deeply at odds in Capricorn, a business sign. Ketu wants to leave the world and discover the Divine and in the business sign of Capricorn and is uncomfortable with Capricorn's need to face reality and be in the material world and wants to reject discipline and hard work.
The positive side of the transit is that Mars/Ketu can bring a strong quest for meditation,

spiritual development and bring up wanderlust. It also supports intuition. Still facing the realities of living in the material world will continue to be forced upon one but Mars is determined to manifest his desires. So, take the passion of both Mars and Ketu into the meditation room or the boardroom and use that fire to move forward towards your victory!

August 13 - September 11th, Mars has moved at least 5 degrees away from Ketu and that will give Mars a bit of breathing room from the seething anger. Still much of the transit between **June 1 - September 13th**, the darker side of Mars will come out with impatience, rashness, deception, and incompletion of tasks, arrogance, accidents and dangers from machinery and fevers and knee problems.

Finally, **October 10 - November 5th**, Mars is far enough away from Ketu to bring back its stronger qualities discussed above which manifest in May.

For Aries rising this is a strong 10th house transit of Mars so use **May and October** for strong career advancement and elevation of status. Ok to take out a home loan or car loan during those months. During the afflicted months **June-September**, work hard to gain the favor of your boss by working on being a better employee and avoid seething anger from being passed over. Avoid putting yourself at risk with the government.

For Scorpio rising this is a 3rd house transit. The **May and October** periods are a time to use your extra physical strength and courage to do great things. Take time for athletics, music dance and art and writing and spend more time with your younger siblings. Take seminars to advance your career and sales and marketing abilities.

During the more difficult time **June - Septe**mber, get extra exercise to have a channel to release the seething anger. Avoid aggression and try not to get caught up being the center of attention and let others share it. Watch out for accidents with machinery and be cautious with your hands and neck and arms and ears. Avoid getting into fights with younger siblings and neighbors although you will be tempted.

MARS IN AQUARIUS: NOVEMBER 6 - DECEMBER 23

Mars enters Aquarius: November 6th
Mars moves into the sign of Aquarius **November 6th**. Aquarius is an idealistic sign connected with humanitarian ideals, scientific discovery and is also a very spiritual sign and also one where the demons of the past come up to be healed.

The first few days of Mars in Aquarius (**November 6-9**), may require us to take more rest. After the extra energy of Capricorn and the exact exaltation of Mars, there is a sudden chasm as Mars is not sure exactly where he is as he enters a new sign and is bit more tired and getting his bearings. Do the frog pose and rest more to get through the transition.

Aquarius is an air sign dominated by the Vata or air element and it can activate Mars to solve problems quickly, but it also can create quick waves of anger that are quickly forgotten and create love of adventure and promote solutions with engineering.

So, use this energy to create great positive social change, invent new technological wonders but go slowly as to not activate too much reckless energy.

The transit is not without affliction as Mars gets a 60-degree aspect from Saturn into **November 28th** with a few weeks degree if influence **November 23 - December 3rd**. If you did not have enough of the Mars/Saturn conjunction from early **April** and its frustration and pent up anger, then you get a revisit with this transit. The better part of the transit is from **December 8 - 23rd** when Mars transits into Jupiter's constellation of Purva Bhadrapada (Aquarius 20-Pisces 3.20).

For Scorpio rising, this is a 4th house transit so family matters could be test, which also includes your relationship with hour partner. Be patient. Stay on top of your insurance policies and make sure they are up-to-date. Frustration will be high and patience low so find a way to release pent up anger. The second part of the transit in **December** may be a good time to work on your house, refinance, spend more quality time with your family and consider a new car.

For Aries rising, this is an 11th house transit. The first part of the transit until December 8th may create problems with older siblings and avoid giving loans to friends or family members during this time. Watch out for get-rich-quick schemes and avoid overspending, as you will need to save money for expenditures when Mars goes into the 12th house of Pisces. December is better and cash flow should pick and it is a good time to make new friends and fulfill some desire that you have had for a while. Your older sibling may surprise you in a helpful and unexpected way.

MARS IN PISCES: DECEMBER 23 - JANUARY 14 - FEBRUARY 5

Mars enters Pisces: December 23rd

Mars goes into its friend's house, Pisces, through **December 23rd** and can create overspending, living too big and too fast, problems with children, staggered expansion, broken promises, zealousness. Later, its brighter side will come out with this transit with its braver outlook, generosity, devoted to ideals, and being an activist for legal causes. Scorpio and Aries rising will be most affected Aries being more troubled by expenses and trips to foreign countries and Scorpio rising probably getting enriched by spiritual knowledge and new spiritual initiations.

Capricorn, Libra and Taurus rising actually may benefit most, as it is a 3rd, 6th and 11th house transit from their rising signs.

Pisces and Virgos will also be affected most by relationship and sexual tensions issues. As this is a 12th house transit for Aries, it is a good time for spiritual pilgrimages and trips to foreign counties and a visit to the Ashram.

Watch expenditures if you are Aries rising during this time and be prepared for setbacks.

Saturn casts a 75% aspect (square) onto Mars **January 19 - 22, 201**9 within 2 degrees and even though it is only a 75% aspect in Vedic astrology it may be felt strongly in terms of increasing anger and frustration and delays so be patient. Overall since planets in Sagittarius aspect Pisces, there is a larger influence for this during the transit in Pisces.

GEMINI AND VIRGO RISING: TRANSITS OF MERCURY

The transits of Mercury are considered auspicious 2nd, 4th, 6th, 8th, and 10th and 11th from the ascendant or the natal moon.

MERCURY IN SAGITTARIUS: JANUARY 6 - JANUARY 25

Mercury enters Sagittarius: January 6th
Mercury goes back into Sagittarius on **January 6th** and because Mercury and Jupiter are not friends, it is a mixed transit. There can be some trouble with concentration, higher education, misunderstandings with superiors, teachers or your father that may leave one feeling conflicted and doubtful. There could also be legal issues, so this is not a good time to sign contracts. When Mercury is in Sagittarius, he acts unreliable and superior. So be mindful your Mercurial manners and soften your blunt speech, don't be a know-it-all, exaggerate or think too much of your own viewpoint. Instead be respectful and lead by a respectable example. Being imprudent and living a lavish lifestyle at this time could lead to health problems related to the hips, thighs, breathing and nervous disorders.

We get a double whammy with this transit with Mercury in the star constellation, Mula, (Sagittarius 0-13.20) **January 6-16th** ruled by karmic Ketu. Prash Trivedi tells us that Mula consists of nine stars at the end of Scorpio and is the place of the center of the galaxy, which Western Astrologers are fond of calling the Galactic Center as that wonderful part of the sky that looks like a white river in the night sky. Mula means "*root*" or "*the center*" and people who have a sun, moon or ascendant lord in this constellation are very direct and do not like to beat around the bush.

This is the core of the galaxy and it is ruled by Ketu who wants to get to the core of everything: hidden motives, events, core roots. Ketu is connected to past lives and Mula wants to tie up all the talents from one's past lives and bring them together. It seeks deeply for the truth of existence. Because Ketu is so close to Mars and Neptune, Mercury will be channeling some of the afflicted and complex energy.

Mula combines the energy of Jupiter and Ketu and hence it initiates spiritual transformations for the better. With Jupiter's grace, it can confer magical powers to help those in need with Grace. Mercury's entrance into Mula can bring deep intellectual insight and wisdom but can lead to a feeling of not being supported.

Remember to do your spiritual practices and yoga to stay on top of your game and when communications just do not happen, rest, let it go and be patient. Energy may not be there to push the envelope the next few days. The cobra pose is good for balancing Mercury and the shoulder stand can sort out a confused mind so those may help the next few days.

This is a positive 4th house transit for Virgos and as Mercury moves away from Saturn and out of Ketu's constellation and reach after **January 16th**, it will bring more benefits. Gemini rising will experience a difficult 7th house transit so karmic relationships that need closure could come up for healing particularly during **January 6 - 16th**.

MERCURY IN CAPRICORN: JANUARY 28 - FEBRUARY 14

Mercury enters Capricorn: January 28th
Mercury has been in Sagittarius and that has been uplifting writing, teaching, deep wisdom and we have a shift on **Sunday, January 28th**. Mercury in Capricorn is afflicted with an aspect from Rahu in Cancer in the constellation of Ashlesha with the power to inflict poisonous venom. This star's constellations is ruled by Mercury so caution is advised in watching your words in the workplace and avoid gossiping at the water cooler and getting caught up in a dreary routine.

Mercury moves toward conjunction with Ketu exactly into **February 9th** in the true node system. Mercury, a benefic, will uplift the disturbing eclipse energies but the affliction to itself will disturb communication and probably create a new hornet's nest around the media. Chances are a scandal involving the media will erupt as fake news is proved to really be fake news. This energy will continue as Mercury moves toward conjunct with Neptune into **February 25th** and this will unveil the illusion of the media and their quest for ratings and sensationalism rather than the truth.

Mercury conjunct Ketu into **February 9t**h can create mental chaos, confusion anger, mental imbalance, a mind filled with surprises and a desire to change everything.

Mercury and Saturn, the ruler of Capricorn, are friends and it is a 5th house transit for Virgos bringing more joy with children, romance and spiritual initiations and sports and given Mercury's nature, game nights and word games and crosswords might flourish. Gemini rising has more problem with this 8th house transit and Libras and Taurus rising probably benefit more than Leos, Cancers or Scorpio rising.

The affliction is that Saturn, the owner of Capricorn, is gaining strength in transit and this could create good and shrewd business transaction, especially for those in the technological field and can also create deep analytic thinking, strong mathematical abilities if you use the time to focus. It could lead to more restricted thinking and belief structures, which is something we do not need given political unrest. It is also a good time for service work.

The first part of the transit is in the constellation of Uttara Ashadaha, ruled by the Sun between **January 25 - February 2nd**. The next constellation of Shravana (Capricorn 10-23.20) **February 2nd — 10th** is more problematic as Mercury is more uncomfortable with the Moon's more feeling nature of connection with others, even though this will bring material success. Thankfully, Mercury flourishes in this satvic constellation when Mercury is particularly strong and understands using the intellect for the good of others and to develop spiritual wisdom.

MERCURY IN AQUARIUS: FEBRUARY 14 - MARCH 2

Mercury enters Aquarius: February 7th
Mercury moves into Aquarius on **Thursday, February 7th**, and is weak in degrees for a day creating more nervousness, worry, out-of-step thinking or being stuck in small details. The transit this month is a bit afflicted as Mercury gets hit by Saturn in aspect on **February 21th** and a partial eclipse of the Sun on **February 15th**. As Mercury moves farther away from Saturn, it will increase in power.

The Saturn aspect on Mercury creates loss of the big picture, obsessive behavior, being too detailed, being stubborn, distracted and minor depression. The Cobra pose helps balance Mercury and the plank pose can energize Mercury and help it though this energy the next few days. Meditation will help focus and keep you from being scattered or negative thinking. Even a shoulder stand may help get you out of a troubled head but of course do these poses with the care and aid of a good yoga instructor if you do not know them. Definitely a month to stay on top of your meditation routine.

Geminis and Virgos will be most affected by this transit because it is a 6th house transit for Virgos, which can bring up illness or problems with enemies or debt. Geminis fare a bit better with it being a 9th house transit of the ascendant lord spurring them on to spiritual journeys, issues with their fathers or Gurus or religious activity but the first part of the transit is more afflicted.

Taurus and Libras will do best with this transit. Again, charts are very individual, and we do not ever want to stereotype people by sign but sometimes it's a way of putting one's finger right away on a core problem for the person's entire life.

MERCURY IN PISCES: MARCH 3 - MAY 8

Mercury enters Pisces: March 3rd
Mercury moves into Pisces on **Saturday, March 3rd** and because of retrograde motion stays there until **May 8th**.

Mercury is debilitated in Pisces which bring out nervousness, being spacey, depression, too many thoughts and being too talkative and during the start of this transit he is involved in a planetary war with Venus until **March 6th** when he can get ahead of the mind verses pleasure energy so this will be good for bringing out a more fun-loving disposition where Mercury will enjoy a more creative and imaginative side of business or trade with fresh and original ideas. This is a good time for writers and musicians that may have see the fruits of their efforts produce a fine harvest later.

Mercury's debilitation is cancelled by the Venus conjunction **March 2-26th** so this lightens this difficult transit in **March** but not in **April**. James Braha is fond of saying that cancellation of debilitation is like losing a limb and getting a prosthetic. It helps but it is not like it is normal.

Mercury goes retrograde **March 22-April 15th,** and this may be a particularly difficult one once Venus leaves Pisces so stay on top of backing up computers and being redundant about communications.

Mercury is the trickster, in Pisces he delights in frustrating us with things not working so learn to be patient. Still it can bring out miscommunication and computer issues.

If you have a lot of writing projects to do, get them done before March.

Mercury is debilitated in Pisces because he can get lost in spiritual dreaminess and not pay attention to the logic that runs him. Make sure that your pipe dreams are run through the filter of logic and practicality.

Virgo rising will experience a 7th house transit making relationships difficult particularly if you are known to have communications issues anyway.

Gemini rising can do better with this transit as it supports status and career development and March will be better with the exalted Venus conjunction.

MERCURY IN ARIES: MAY 9 - MAY 26

Mercury enters Aries: May 9th

On **May 9th** Mercury will enter Aries and will be in the constellation of Ashwini (Aries 0-13.20) until **mid-May 18th**. Prash Trivedi notes that Ashwini is known in modern astronomy as Alpha-Arietes and Beta-Arietes near the bright star of Andromeda. The symbol for Ashwini is a horse's head representing a dauntless spirit of adventure and a headstrong nature. This transit usually fosters self-starters and energy to complete projects. It is also a very healing constellation and so there will be more energy for healing. The ruling deities are the Ashwin twins who ride in a golden chariot and shower healing energy down to the earth plane. They are the "*Physicians of the Gods*." This is a nakshatra of initiation, revitalization and transformational healing The ruling planet is Ketu (South Node of the Moon), which gives a mystical and mysterious bent to their life journey.

The first part of the transit is through the gandanta Aries 0-3 degrees (**May 9-11**). There is underlying strength to work out new beginnings in a new cycle of growth initiated by moving into the start of the zodiac. The energy is there to untie deep karmic knots, but frustrations will still come up strongly and given all the changes going on in the sky.

The ruling constellation of Ashwini is Ketu spurring you into new spiritual growth and development, but Ketu is still pretty afflicted in transit from its connection to Saturn and Capricorn. This may create an interest in new projects but the inability or weakness to finish them so make sure you only take on what you can handle. It can also bring on stubbornness or racing around wildly with too much "wild horse" energy so make sure to slow down and stay balanced.

Mercury in Ashwini brings a strong and fiery intellect than can be impulsive, independent and aggressive. Mercury in Aries creates a mind that wants to accomplish things too fast and this can lead to frustration, an angry mind poor planning, deceit, too much debt or risk-taking, abuse of drugs and alcohol and nervous strain.

Mercury and Mars are bitter enemies, so this is not a happy transit and can bring up more disputes and arguments and fighting. Drive carefully and do not fight in the car.

This is an 8th house transit for Virgos, which requires transformation, or unexpected illness or accidents can arise if your dasha period is so indicating. It is an 11th house transit for Geminis suggesting more fun with friends and fulfillment of desires and increases in income and a chance to engage in competitive sports.

MERCURY IN TAURUS: MAY 26 - JUNE 9

Mercury enters Taurus: May 26th
Mercury finally gets out of Aries on **May 26t**h and Virgos and Geminis can finally get major relief going into a friend's sign. If you were born with Mercury in Taurus, you have good creative writing and reasoning abilities are clear happy, love reading and writing and speaking and love being with deep thinkers. This placement creates good humor, generosity and lover of the arts.

The Shakti of Taurus is that it gives power to bring wealth, social success, prosperity and enjoyment. For Vedic lovers, it is connected to Krishna. Keyword to remember here is Blessings and it is easy to remember the blessings of Venus who brings material prosperity to us. Planets placed in Taurus in any part of the chart bring blessings.

Taurus is a sign, which is very stubborn, but planets going through there benefit from wealth, social status and prosperity and this is of course dependent on your larger cycles. Mercury does better with transit through the 2nd, 4th, 6th, 8th and 10th and 11th houses from the natal moon or ascendant. Still I think Virgos will do well with this transit through 9th house of foreign travel and spirituality and good luck and good fortune while Geminis will have to watch expenditures but need to focus on service and donations and commitment in marriage to bring out the highest energies.

MERCURY IN GEMINI: JUNE 9 - JUNE 25

Mercury enters Gemini: June 9th
Mercury moves into the star constellation of Mrigashira know by the West as Orion (Taurus 23.20-Gemini 6.40) known as the constellation of Orion on **June 7th** and stays there until **June 12th** and will channel Mars and this can lead to disputes so do not get into arguments while you are driving.

Mercury moves into Gemini, its own sign on **June 10th** until **June 24th** and generally this is a very good transit. Retrograde Jupiter is sending an unfriendly aspect glance, but Mercury doesn't seem to mind as he is getting a boost from an aspect glance from his friend Retrograde Saturn on **June 2nd**. So even though there may be times when Mercury is spending time lost in detail, reading and thinking too much instead of acting, he is happy in his own sign of Gemini where he is the intellectual adventure where he likes to have fun. This is a good time to write and spend some time journaling if your mind is full of chatter and work through any inner disruptive thoughts. So, move away from Saturn-like thinking, avoid being idle and get the creative juices flowing!

Virgos and Geminis will delight in this transit as Mercury is home and will feel optimistic from the Jupiter aspect that peaks into **June 5th**. Good support for health and advancement. The 10th house transit of Mercury for Virgos will support career development and status. The better part of the transit is **June 5-25th.**

MERCURY IN CANCER: JUNE 16 - SEPTEMBER 2

Mercury enters Cancer: June 25th
Mercury spends almost 69 days in the sign of Cancer this year due to its retrograde action **July 25 - August 27th** that is more than its typical retrograde movement of about 21 days. It gets a full Mars aspect on **July 5th** causing disputes and potential accidents so watch **July 2-10th** as being a vulnerable period.

It is also is conjunct Rahu in the true node system **July 3rd** and while they are friends this can increase mental disturbance. By **July 6th** is past Rahu enough to not be impacted. Mercury is also in Cancer during the **August** eclipses further creating mental disturbances and poor judgment.

Mercury stays in the gandanta area **July 18 - August 3rd** and then again **September 1 - 2nd** in the constellation of Ashlesha where one has to watch out for one's sharp tongue or one will make many enemies. It is time to be careful with poisons and toxins. This is a troubled emotional area where people need to encounter their karmic past and unravel difficult knots and problems from past lives.

Mercury is debilitated at the end of Cancer in the D-9 chart, so it cannot use its intellectual superiority to unravel the past and most find solace in spiritual faith, which it does not do well as Mercury likes to use his mind and intellect.

Gemini rising, and Virgo rising are likely experience deep emotional and troubling psychological turmoil in August but may find enough spiritual energy to work through the mental fray of issues connected to home, family, security, nurturing that are likely to come up in Cancer.

The good news is that this is a 2nd and 11th house transit of Mercury for Virgos and Geminis so there will be gains once you sift through delays and blockages and arguments.

MERCURY IN LEO: SEPTEMBER 2 - SEPTEMBER 18
Mercury enters Leo: September 2nd

Mercury will transit Leo **Sunday, September 2nd** and will have an afflicted transit with an 8th house aspect of Mars from Capricorn exactly into **September 5th** and will be combust from **September 5 - October 11th**.

The difficult 3-degree orb of the Mars aspect is between **September 3 - 7th** and can bring arguments and disputes to the forefront, which will impact Virgos and Gemini rising signs strongly.

If you were born with Mercury in Leo, you are bright-minded, have good memory, are inspiring speaker or writer, are confident and are a good planner and organizer, may be well-known in business, are ambitious, travel frequently and have a keen intellect.

The first part of the transit is through Magha (Leo 0-13.20) until **September 9th**, which is known as Regulus by Western astrology and is owned by Ketu. Mercury in Ketu's constellation can create a strong vision, but the ambitious nature of Leo/Magha may force them to cut corners or rush through projects and be a bit impulsive. Slow down and do not be too hasty with big projects. Ketu is mystical and intuitive so be sure to seek divine guidance within and to get the answers to difficult decisions.

The second part of the transit is in the constellation of Purva Phalguni (Leo 13.20-26.40) **September 10-16th**. This will connect Mercury to Venus who will be transiting through Mercury's sign of Libra in **September** and set up a nice symbiotic relationship supporting harmony, and balancing opposites. It is a highly charged constellation and Mercury, the prince, likes to play in the bed in this constellation symbolized by the front legs of a bed.

This constellation is considered fierce and is not considered a good time for major new events unless you're scheming. It does support construction but stay on top of accidents and health.

Mercury will be combust on **September 5th** in the sign of Leo and this actually has a spiritualizing impact on Mercury as the material and rajasic desires of Mercury for money and success in business are turning to the Divine so a good time to take a meditation retreat. Mercury is considered combust until **October 11th** when he is away from the Sun's heat and in the sign of Virgo.

Mercury transits from the moon or the ascendant are best in the 2nd, 4th, 6th, 8th, 10th and 11th positions so if you have your moon or rising sign of Libra, Scorpio, Capricorn, Pisces, Taurus or Cancer, this transit will be beneficial for you. For Gemini and Virgo rising, ruled by Mercury it is more difficult with Geminis particularly needing to curb their sexual dalliances and Virgos being inclined to foreign travel, meditation retreats or deep inward and psychological introspection.

Mercury governs plant life and gardening so take time to enjoy the outdoors and the beauty and greenery of nature, Mercury's color. Good month for writing poetry or songs or creative writing, for a meditation retreat.

MERCURY IN VIRGO: SEPTEMBER 19 - OCTOBER 6

Mercury enters Virgo: September 19th
Virgo is one of the more fascinating signs representing the World mother. Virgo ascendants sometimes feel cut out of material prosperity and sensual pleasures and feel unhappy taking on the sins of the world embodying the German word, Weltscmertz. The sign is endowed with great intelligence, Shakti, physicality, Universal life, the gift of poetry and speech and music and great psychic and intuitive powers. And yet despite all these gifts, there is often great dissatisfaction with life.

Whenever a planet appears in Virgo in any sign of the zodiac it means where we need to be better, improve or be pure. Being the natural 6th house of the zodiac, it means that we need discipline around regular work, health and diet to prevent illness and we also need to develop skills to work with people so that we do not develop enmity with co-workers at work. The challenge is Saturn and wanting too much perfection in the world and being too hard oneself and one's weaknesses.

There can be too much self-deprecation and continual beating oneself up on the dark side or a continual focus on always wanting to do it better, which can also become a good quality. Key words to remember are purity and improvement.

Mercury transits into Virgo, its sign of exaltation **September 19th - October 5th** and this enhances Mercury's powers as described above and is a great time for deep thought and creative expression in music and writing and is a great time for a clear intellect and coherent thinking. Geminis and Virgo rising particularly do well with the transit for health and career. It is a 4th house transit for Geminis bringing up richness in family life and a chance for real estate development and remodeling projects.

For Virgos, it can bring good health and status and the self-confidence with a strong ability to achieve their goals.

Saturn does aspect Virgo and hits Mercury exactly on **September 23rd,** but Mercury moves so quickly that any temporary depression or stress will be quickly relieved.

Good month in general for writing, computer programming and communications so start that book or get it published.

MERCURY IN LIBRA: OCTOBER 6 - OCTOBER 26

Mercury enters Libra: October 6th
Mercury enters the sign of Libra on **Saturday, October 6th** and is unafflicted in transit until **October 10th** when he opposes Uranus which may lead to reform and sudden change by destroying the old in preparation for the new, so this is a transit that will be about displacements that force us to let go.

Mercury in Libra wants a balance between opposites and harmony so its positive qualities of fun loving, love of philosophy, musical and artistic interests and humanitarian energies are enlivened. It also can foster comedic sensibilities, persuasive speaking, love of clubs and spiritual performances.

Mercury stays in Libra until **October 26th** and will benefit Virgos and Gemini rising will do best 2nd and 5th house transits from the ascendant bringing love of family for Virgos and artistic expression, romance and theatrical expression for Virgos.

With Uranus in Aries, Mercury may be spurred to act with a mind that wants to accomplish things too fast, so the ends may not justify the means. Want out for deceit, taking risks, gambling or overly speculative ventures. It's better to be clever, adaptable and dance your way over the map and keep a steady step, rather than burn your way through it.

This is one of the better transits of Mercury for the year as it is unafflicted and supported by its friend Venus so a good time for artistic enterprises, romance and literary pursuits.

MERCURY IN SCORPIO: OCTOBER 26 - DECEMBER 31

Mercury enters Scorpio: October 26th

Mercury will be transiting the sign of Scorpio for 65 days as it completes its retrograde transits in the water signs this year stirring up old emotional grunge to heal. What does it mean? Mars, the ruler of Scorpio and Mercury are the bitterest enemies. At best, it may create quick-witted speaking, strength in technical and mechanical and medical work and being quick to solve problems. I often find in finance it may lead to deals and corporate takeovers.

Mercury is relatively unafflicted in Scorpio but still in an enemy's sign. For a few days it is channeling the Jupiter's energy in Vishaka Nakshatra (Libra 20-Scorpio 3.20) but will move into and then channel's Saturn's darker energy in Anaradha (Scorpio 3.21-16.40) **October 27 - December 26th**.

The dark side of Mars/Mercury associations is that it creates angry moods, slow deliberate thinking, strong achievement and ambition, aggressive confrontations and arguments, self-centeredness and ruthlessness around achieving ones' goals. Also, you have to be very careful to not get into heated arguments while driving as this can lead to reckless behavior and potential accidents. I often find that accidents are a pinnacle of rage that bubbles up in arguments. So, if this happens to you, pullover, and fight it out — but not while driving. You may need to be most careful here particularly if you have a Mars/Mercury association in your natal chart.

Mercury in the natural 8th house of Scorpio is about transcendental thinking. People with Mercury in their 8th houses are quick minded, have good research abilities and mystical interests, deep meditations and philosophical insights.

Stuttering may be a problem because the mind is so fast that it's difficult for people to keep their speech flowing with their thoughts.

Mercury goes retrograde **November 16 - December 6th** here so plan ahead for this during the first few week of November and expect a lot of deep chances for transformation in this intense sign.

CAPRICORN AND AQUARIUS RISING: TRANSITS OF SATURN

Saturn's transits are considered auspicious 3rd, 6th and 11th from the ascendant or Natal Moon.

SATURN IN SAGITTARIUS: UNTIL JANUARY 23, 2020
Saturn in Sagittarius: Part 1

As my colleague Sam Geppi puts it, Saturn is about doing the hard work to get our goals done: "*Saturn shows the willingness to face the hardships of life and persevere through the difficulty because some things are worth the trouble — worth the TIME – and we do not have unlimited time. As we gain experience-facing problems, we become less reactive and develop grace under pressure. This eventually brings a level of calm and cool when stressed, which allows us to keep going and staying focused on what is important.*"

The key to Saturn is hard work, being responsible and focused. Venus can balance Saturn out so when it gets intense, relationship time, massage, the arts, intimate connection can soothe out the tension of Saturn.

Saturn will be transiting into Mula nakshatra (Sagittarius 0-13.20) most of 2018 but it is a place where Saturn cannot escape from the past and must take responsibility for karma. This is a time to heal old wounds, redress and forgive, cleaning out and apologizing for our mistakes and releasing. Good time for a healing therapy and releasing the old, otherwise, it will gnaw at you.

Sagittarius is about beliefs. If we move toward being too dogmatic, then we can face our deepest insecurities. One would have to think that fundamental religion will go through a huge transformation and revival during the next 2.5 years as Saturn clashes with Jupiter's energy in the rather belief-orientated sign of Sagittarius. Luckily, Saturn and Jupiter are neutral toward each other and not intense enemies as was the case with Saturn in Scorpio, a sign owned by Mars. This is a time to shed our dogmatic belief structures and see beyond them and look into our own self for the answers. The hit Hulu Series, The Path, is an eye-opening series about cults, belief structures and moving out of the box, which takes great courage. A must-watch for Saturn in Sagittarius and obvious Muslim and Christian fundamentalism will again move strongly onto the world stage during the next 2.5 years.

Remember forecasts are general and their impact will depend on your specific rising sign, period and key factors in your chart.

Saturn in Sagittarius Part 2:
Impact on Health and The Physical Body

Saturn into Sagittarius is impacting new areas of the cosmic body. When Saturn is strong, it is like a mountain and creates calmness of mind and self-control.

The problem with much of the rest of 2018 is that Saturn is weak with the Sun combustion into January 7th, and it can create more problems. Still in the constellation of Mula (Sagittarius 0-13.20) until **March 2nd**, it is a bit of a problem.

Saturn when weak can be lazier and more fearful and the fire energy will be disturbed by Saturn's air Vata energy. The tendency will be toward rushing through obstructions with carelessness and this may create problems.

Basically, we have to stay on top of our health, diet and exercise routines this year, otherwise Saturn is going to do its job and kick us into a disciplined program to take care of our body.

We have to be more alert and focused in everything to avoid careless activities that can lead to accidents or wounds. Activating Mars and focusing in the third eye by doing the warrior pose in yoga will be helpful every day and we will have to stay rested so that we do not make mistakes.

Handling mental energy, worry and anxiety will require another article and I have discussed this previously in my series on Saturn in Transition.

Saturn in Sagittarius will be aspecting Aquarius, its own sign, Virgo and Gemini and of course impacting Sagittarius mostly.

It rules Capricorn and will be 12 houses from its own sign, which is a difficult transit for Capricorns. Saturn is weak all year being in the juncture point between the water sign of Scorpio and the fire sign of Sagittarius so Capricorn rising will be impacted.

Virgos and Geminis will be affected greatly from the aspects and more directly in 2018 if your rising signs are located at 0-6 degrees Virgo or Gemini and to a lesser degree 0-6 Aquarius.

So how will all of these signs be impacting in terms of health? This is not to scare you but to make you aware of how the planets interact with your body and impact it. There is always something to do.

If you are in a malefic Saturn period and are over 60 or 70 when Saturn is more dominant, then the impact of health problems will be greater. Basically, you have to take better care of your body next year with a disciplined diet, regular exercise and yoga, and taking advantage of Ayurvedic oil massages to lubricate dry areas of your body. Pick up Dr. Lad's classic book *Ayurveda: Science of Life*, if you do not own a copy.

The natural signs of the zodiac govern the different parts of the body for everyone so there are some general things to be said about Saturn in Sagittarius and are aspecting Aquarius, Gemini and Virgo.

Sagittarius, the 9th sign of the zodiac governs arteries, lower back, hips and thighs so these are particularly impacted for everyone. Diseases connected to Sagittarius include obesity, hip injuries and arthritis in the hips. There are yoga postures you can do to keep your hips flexible and there are Ayurvedic treatments to bring oil to your hip areas to lubricate them more and prevent arthritis, which is a disease of dryness. We have to take care of our hips during the next few years.

The Pigeon pose in yoga can help pop hip joints back in but make sure you have proper instruction on how to do it.

Virgo governs the lower abdomen, colon, digestive, and large intestine. Jupiter in Virgo is supporting this area until September when it moves into Libra. More attention will be required in the fall.

When Virgo is afflicted it creates poor digestion, gas, constipation, ulcers, food allergies, hypoglycemia, diabetes, appendicitis and problems with the immune systems. The secret in Ayurveda is to keep the colon clean. Taking a pro-biotic (Natren is best and is the one most alive and is kept refrigerated) at night and first thing in the morning will keep your elimination healthy. Doing regular colon cleans or Panchakarma or more simply doing regular laxative and cleanings programs are good to keep things moving as many health problems are tied to accumulation of toxins in the body.

Drink lots of warm water during the day to flush out toxins regularly and stay off of GMO's and move to organics to keep your immune system strong and prevent food allergies. Obviously watch your sugar and carb intake if there is a history of diabetes in your family. This is something to watch as diabetics is becoming a global epidemic.

Gemini governs the shoulders, upper arms and upper chest. When it is afflicted, it creates lung disorders, shoulder injuries, and nervous disorders. There are all kinds of yoga postures you can do for the shoulders to keep them limber. The Cobra pose is important.

People with lung problems have to cut down on dairy and wheat products, which increase mucus. A product called Clear Lung has saved my life many times by eliminating difficult coughing and breathing problems.

Capricorn governs the bones and joints and the basic 10th house area of the zodiac or the knees. Afflictions to Saturn, the ruler of Capricorn, can create arthritis of the knees and weakness of the bones in general. There are therapies for this. Regular light walking is a good start and oil massages on the knees can be helpful. Get a brace or ace bandage for stability if you need more knee support or if you are prone to knee problems. Ayurveda has a practice of placing warm, oil soaked, bread-like donuts on the knee to lubricate the knee joints. Talk with your health care practitioner about holistic therapies that support joint and cartilage health such as Ayurveda treatments, MSM and Chondroitin supplements.

Finally, Aquarius governs the skin and the calves. Even if Saturn is aspecting its own sign, it can still create some mild health disorders and cause some problems including skin disorders, poor circulation and weakness in the lower legs.

Walking is great and I have resorted to my rebounder/trampoline to get my circulation going.

Staying hydrated and drinking lots of water is essential to flush out toxins and prevent skin irritations while staying off of white non-organic flour and GMO can support the body and prevent skin irritations.

When afflicted, Saturn signifies old age, chronic and wasting diseases, weak digestion and poor resistance to disease. It contributes to depression, diseases of dryness like constipation, arthritis, rheumatism, broken bones, osteoporosis, premature aging, cancer, tremors and infertility.

Be more vigilant about taking care of your body with exercise, diet, yoga, and meditation and not to become lazy around these things. Saturn responds to discipline and is always inspiring you to a higher calling if you listen to its messages.

There are emotional components to each part of the body connected to Saturn's influence. For example, if you have lower back problems, you are probably manifesting that issue because you do not feel supported in life. We can always see the connections between the physical, emotional and mental body as physical problems manifest when we do not address them in the mental and emotional bodies. If you are interested in this kind of material, you can schedule readings with Gary O'Toole and me for more insights into all of this and to taking better care of your body. See Applied Vedic Astrological Consultations or visit the link: http://www.appliedvedicastrology.com/transformational-counseling-2-ayurvedic-astrologyyoga/

Vedic astrology is like reading strands of DNA and people are so different. Do not get caught up in negative thinking. Articles bring awareness to what could be triggered, and the goal is to inspire you to be more aware of your body and taking care of it over the next year.

Not to worry. Find a good health practitioner. Stay rested and do not run around like a rabbit. If you are in a good period for your rising sign and are young, you might have minor problems but if you are in a Saturn period or sub-period and older, then more pronounced events can happen. Diet, exercise and proper care can prevent problems and lead to minor glitches rather than major problems.

Still Saturn will do its job. It creates suffering to point us toward the Divine and ultimately spirituality will help us get through anything. Of course, consult your doctor and a trained professional, as an astrological advisor is no replacement for expert medical attention. So focus on health, don't worry and Saturn will richly reward you!

Saturn Changes by Sign:
A Guide to Prosper with Saturn's New Transit into Sagittarius and A Change of Sign

Saturn stays in Sagittarius until **January 23, 2020**. Usually transits from the rising sign affect our material world most while transits from the Moon affect our emotional or mental state. We also have to look at transits from the Sun as a third factor particularly, if our Sun is stronger than our rising sign or Moon.

Eventually in **2018**, Saturn will mature more, and its transits will soften as it goes into Venus's constellation, which will happen in **March 3 - June 4, 2018**, and we will see the more favorable impact. I will write about it later on my blog.

Below is a guide. I am not into sugar coating but giving you an early warning system about what areas of your life need more attention. Saturn requires discipline, awareness, patience and hard work. Then it will reward you but if you are careless, lazy or lacking focus, then challenges will come up.

Your individual profile will depend on how many Ashtakavarga points you have in Sagittarius for Saturn, what dashas you are running and what natal planets are being impacted in your natal chart.

If your rising sign or your Moon is the following and to a lesser degree your Sun, use the following guide to understand what your focus should be during the next 6 months and next few years.

*Note: All transits are from the Sidereal zodiac in Eastern Standard Time

Aries - This is a 9th house transit from your Moon in Aries or rising sign and will bring up issues around father and spiritual teachers where setbacks might arise. The tendency will be to be critical, so lighten up and accept the situation. If you are publishing a book, there might be delays in finding a publisher or in your writing. Spiritual pilgrimages or trips to foreign countries might meet with more problems, anxiety and travel fatigue than usual. For heath, watch hips and make sure you keep them flexible by doing the right exercises. Sagittarius governs hips for everyone so there is a double chance of hip problems. Another potential problem is the lungs if you have an aspect into Gemini and the 3rd house. If you have grief to release, this is a time to let go and not keep it bottled up.

Taurus - This is an 8th house transit of Saturn, which means that you need to get more support over the next 2.5 years. Make sure to choose supportive people to work with who are committed, like yourself, to service. Attend to your health. As the transit improves in **late 2018**, new research projects should be profitable. For the next year, you may feel very reclusive and want to escape to an ashram. Use these next six months to get more rest, take spiritual retreats and go inward. Focus on health and education to prevent problems from coming up. Take care of your immune system by taking products that boost it like Colostrum. Make sure your retirement, annuities and pension plans are in order. If there is any cause for concern, handle it before it becomes a big problem. Pension plans around the country are suffering from problems, as is the case in Chicago and in Dallas with their police department programs. Make sure your plan is solid or do something before it becomes a bigger problem. Use the transit to solve long-term problems that have been plaguing you for many years.

Gemini - This is a 7th house transit for Gemini rising for people with Gemini moon. This may bring up a desire to get married or take on a new business partner. It may create a desire to work in a foreign country. Until Saturn strengthens in **late 2018**, you may want to delay these ideas or evaluate them very carefully. Your own current relationship may feel confined or restricted or empty and you will have to work hard now on healing this dissatisfaction. Saturn always wants to complain but are you willing to do the hard work to make the necessary changes? Can you find ways to increase your friendship with your partner and make it work better? Your partners may be more depressed so work on cheering them up and supporting them with their health. If your business partner relationships are not working, it is time to re-evaluate or get real and create meaningful change for profit. Take care of your health.

Cancer - This is a 6th house transit for Cancer rising and Cancer moons, so the focus will be on service for the next 2.5 years. Focus on fitness and health. The first few years of this transit are rockier, and you will need to foster more on compassion and avoid feeling righteous. Avoid getting attached to small things. Avoid risks and disputes. This is a great time to focus and improve organization skills. If you work hard, you will be rewarded steadily, particularly as Saturn gets stronger after **November 2018**. Take care of regular exercise, be disciplined about it and eat properly, as better health habits will support vigor. If you get into battles with co-workers or in legal disputes, you will have the support to win but the next year may be a challenge with such matters. Avoid strains in relationships and being too critical about partners. Try to accept, appreciate and praise. If you need help understanding your own personal life, chart and transits at this difficult juncture, sign up for a reading by hitting the request button at http://www.appliedvedicastrology.com/reading-information-submission/

Or consider our new class on timing for your personal life with Module 1 available on transits and module 2 starting live February 12th at:
http://www.appliedvedicastrology.com/products.../timing-your-life/

Leo - This is a 5th house transit for Leos. This is a time not to fight the government around taxes. Also, be very conservative around investments. Problems with your children may arise. Delays with romance or frustration may arise even if there are cravings to make something happen. Balance your life out but socializing so that you do not seem too reclusive and make sure too find more time for recreational fun and amusement even though it will seem this is not possible. Watch out for intellectual fatigue if you are engaged in a lot of research. This may be a good time to work on degree or certification programs.

Virgo - This is a 4th house transit for Virgo rising or moons. Happiness is impacted so balance this by getting out more even if you feel gloomy or depressed. This transit may create additional problems with home reconstruction, remodeling or repairs, making you weary. Spend more time with your mother and be patient with her if she suffers from stress or health issues. Take care of your heart by getting regular aerobic exercise and see your physician if anything comes up. Hard work for career and status is supported but make sure to stay balanced to avoid burn out.

Libra - This is a 3rd house transit for Libra rising and Libra moons. Saturn is a friend, so you may do better with Saturn in Sagittarius. Still, communications may be difficult so practice being clear, concise and to the point. Artistic expression may seem frustrated at times but just work hard and do not be so critical of the process. Be light and have fun with it. Be easy on sibling relationships and not critical. Be careful with your hands, wrists and shoulders so if you do a lot of typing, make sure you have a wrist elevation to avoid carpal tunnel syndrome. Find a way to empower and praise yourself as you move forward in your goals.

Scorpio - If this is a 2nd house transit from your moon or rising sign, your Sade Sati period is wanting to come to an end but there is still some karma to complete. Make sure that your words are sweet like Venus and not harsh like Saturn, as the 2nd house of speech will be impacted. Hold your tongue on bashing others. Avoid vices like junk food, drugs and alcohol as the 2nd house governs food and it will be important to be disciplined about what you put in your body. If you are not on top of this you could suffer from food allergies. Becoming disciplined about your finances means saving 10% of your income for those emergencies that will come up. Make this a priority! Avoid over spending and become disciplined about budgeting, as Saturn aspecting your 11th house may crimp your income, so you will have to be creative in generating new sources.

The 2nd house governs family and Saturn may bring out gloomy and oppressive family relationships so practice kindness, acceptance and tolerance no matter what they throw at you. No matter what others do to us, if we give love to them, we are always a winner!

Sagittarius - Particularly if your moon is in Sagittarius, there is a feeling of formlessness or uncertainty as you try to shape a new life for yourself. Low confidence or self-esteem may come up. If your rising sign is Sagittarius, it will be a time to educate yourself about your physical body. Exercise, diet and nutritional counseling will be necessary to stay on top of your health but if you rise to the occasion, Saturn will reward you. With Saturn in the first, a diet may finally succeed. Learn to keep your agreements and honor your commitments or you may face serious relationship challenges. Stay on top of exercise to avoid feeling too sluggish. Be patient with setbacks and realize that you are going to have to work harder to make things happen. There could be a tendency to isolate yourself so remember the remedy for Saturn is Venus so stay in relationships, get massages, sing, dance and throw off the heaviness - it is not who you are. Use this time for transformation as Saturn is pushing you to become mature and take responsibility for your spiritual growth. Stay more rested and be patient before jumping into a new marriage with Saturn's aspect on the 7th house or realize that starting a new business with Saturn's aspect on the 10th house may require hard work and patience. This may be frustrating depending on the dasha you are running.

Capricorn - If your moon or even your Sun is in Capricorn, your Sade Sati is beginning. The 12th house transit of Saturn can bring up issues of abandonment or betrayal and can bring up great emotional and mental distress. Be careful with expenses because debts can mount during this transit so watch those credit card purchases! Freeze your cards in an ice cube in your refrigerator to only use them for emergencies. Forgive those people who took advantage of you or resentment will give rise to disease. Avoid risk so this not a time to take up a dangerous sport. Be around pleasant people and pursue spiritual knowledge to uplift your energy. If you are Capricorn rising or Sun, this is a time for self-sacrifice and doing volunteer work. Do quiet, spiritual reading before you go to bed to avoid sleep problems. This is a time for closure, finishing long projects, contemplating a change of residence and healing unconscious patterns that block you from fulfilling your purpose.

Aquarius - This is an 11th house transit from the ascendant and an Aquarius natal moon. Many Aquarians are ruled by Saturn but also Rahu. This transit particularly the last few months of the year will continue to create edginess, fatigue, excessive fear and potential laziness. It will be important to be focused but not run around and create too much craziness in your life or nervous health problems could develop. Make sure to get enough sleep, do yoga and use meditation to calm overactive energy.

Ketu - will still be in Aquarius until September and is not helping the situation. Manage your cash flow as income may be slow at times and profits may be delayed particularly when Saturn goes retrograde in **April**. Align yourself with inspiring friends with high moral and ethical values and be clear in communicating to them to avoid misunderstandings. Over the upcoming years into **late 2018 and 2019**, this transit will bear more fruits for fulfillment of desires and income, but this year will be slower so be patient, save money and practice the Saturnian love of economy and being frugal.

Pisces - This is a 10th house transit for Pisces ascendants and 10th from a Pisces moon. Time to increase knowledge to support career development so take that extra class or webinar. There will be a tendency to want to change jobs and this can be a good thing during the 2.5-year transit but this first year with Saturn weak and then going retrograde may bring delays and obstacles so make sure you have something better lined up before switching or making changes. Pay attention to challenges at work to avoid setbacks, and delays. Make sure that you find a way to be noticed at work but be patient if you are not appreciated and do not beat yourself up around this. Take care of regular automobile and home maintenance over the next year to avoid costly expenses.

Take care of knees if they pose a problem and get a supportive bandage while doing exercise to keep them stabilized. Be patient with family challenges, as Saturn will want to complain.

Saturn in Sagittarius and Mula Nakshatra:
Spiritual, Intellectual Awakenings and Material Discord

Saturn is fully in Sagittarius now in the constellation of Mula (Sagittarius 0-13.20). Saturn is very slow here and it will remain in this constellation until March 3rd but then retrogrades back in **June 5 - November 28, 2018**, so most of next year will have that influence.

Saturn in Mula will not let you escape from the past, symbolized by Ketu. It requires that you take responsibility for past karma and do something to make it right. Similar to one of the 12 steps from the Alcoholics Anonymous (AA) program, one has to make amends for past actions where we may have caused hurt or injury. This will be a theme for the coming years. Best advice is to extend your hand out first in a gesture of offering to say that you are sorry and do something to address your mistakes.

This transit can make us face and recognize the often hidden, shadowy, ugly parts of our personality. This gives us the opportunity to bear witness to our flaws, accept them with compassion, purify them and become a better person. It is never an easy process, but Saturn will not let up on us until we work through the process. Draw on your wisdom and insights from the past and from past lives to make the transformations now. Let go of the past and stop beating yourself up for what you did wrong. If you make amends in the present, then all is healed.

The first pada of Sagittarius (0-3.20) owned by Aries and Mars is the most difficult part of the transit, as it requires more suffering and forbearance. Saturn is here until **November 28th, 2018**. Anxiety levels are higher and if you rush around recklessly or are careless, mistakes are made, so slow down, drink your calming teas and take care of your health. Avoid the heavy self-deprecating energy that Saturn can create here and praise yourself instead. Be kind to yourself and accept your imperfections. This is a repeat of territory that we went through **January 26 - March 15, 2017** and you may continue to feel heavy so do your meditation and yoga to get balance energy from fun loving Venus and it will lighten.

Mula consists of nine stars at the end of Scorpio and is the place of the center of the galaxy, which Western Astrologers are fond of calling the Galactic Center, a wonderful part of the night sky that looks like a white river.

Mula means "*root*" or "*the center*" and people who have a sun, moon or ascendant lord in this constellation are very direct and do not like to beat around the bush. This is the core of the galaxy and it is ruled by Ketu who wants to get to the core of everything: hidden motives, events, core roots.

Ketu is connected to past lives and Mula wants to tie up all the talents from one's past lives and bring them together. It seeks deeply for the truth of existence. Ketu is not really happy in Capricorn where its deep spiritual striving is at odds with Saturn's hard work ethic.

Prash Trivedi notes that the deity of Mula is Nirrtti, the Goddess of Calamity and yet she resides in the lucky sign of Sagittarius, which in mythology means she may destroy ignorance to reveal deep truths. Ironically, Nirrtti, is connected to the peak of material achievement and yet the nature of this nakshatra is very spiritual in her quest to go beyond the domain of ego and self-centeredness. I will be interested to see if our politicians change with this transit. This star can give power and influence and great material accomplishment and can confer magical powers but often it releases its energy in an explosive manner, which is so true of Ketu!

Still with Ketu in Shravana, the need is to do spiritual service work and seva (selfless service) to transform the past. This is a time to help those in need and to give to charity as a way of purging past mistakes. There is a saying that it is easy to a saint on a mountaintop, but the real proof is when you return to the marketplace and with so many in need of help and services from the recent disasters. Through the practice of seva, one can definitely work with others in a tangible way to give back to the planet.

Mula combines the energy of Jupiter and Ketu, hence, it initiates spiritual transformations for the better. With Jupiter's grace it can confer magical powers to help those in need with Grace.

Understanding the 7.5 Years of Saturn in Connection with Transits Through the Constellation: Sade Sati

Most people that know a little Vedic astrology get caught up in a huge amount of fear around Sade Sati, the 7.5 years that Saturn goes through the 12th, 1st and 2nd house from your moon. Actually, Sade Sati can also be applied to your rising sign and your sun sign. If you really want to get all bent out of shape, depending on your chart, you could have some level of Sade Sati happening much of your life. Is it all bad? Of course not. It depends on when Saturn is transiting the 1st, 3rd, 5th and 25th stars from your birth moon constellation.

Saturn has a purpose to teach responsibility, discipline and focus. This is something that people may feel lazy about because Saturn is not necessarily a fun planet. With Saturn in Sagittarius until **January 2020**, we have a whole new group coming into play.

If your Moon is in Capricorn or your Ascendant is Capricorn, or your Sun is in Capricorn being born **January 14 - February 12th**, you may be going through the more difficult 12th house transit of Saturn. Specifically, if you have moon in Shravana Nakshatra the impact will be felt most. This is particularly triggered when Saturn goes through the 25th nakshatra from your natal moon or ascendant called the Mananas nakshatra, which governs the mind. Saturn can disturb this area and create a huge desire for change because of unsettled feelings.

You might feel abandoned, betrayed, unfocused or experience changes around jobs or relationships. Remember that change is good. Stay rational and use judgment if it is time to make a change. God has a plan.

Sometimes we think that by forcing change through moving or leaving partnerships, we will get rid of the inner unsettledness but there is a famous saying, "*wherever you go, there you are.*" Start by creating a shift within by practicing meditation, yoga, exercise, getting more quality sleep, drinking more water and herbal teas, feeding the body a clean, healthy non-processed diet. You may be surprised to discover that these inner changes will create subtle, yet powerful shifts in your outward reality that create positive, natural shifts in your environment that are gentle and easy. Don't forget to unplug from electronic devices, social media and engage with pets, people and community!

The key to understanding Sade Sati is through the Nakshatra predictive system known as Navatara and Tara Bala where transits through key nakshatras from the natal moon trigger events.

During the 7.5 years of Saturn, the key triggers are when Saturn goes through the 25th nakshatra from the moon but the 26th and 27th nakshatras are ok. Then the 1st, 3rd and 5th Nakshatras from the moon are difficult and known as Janma, Vipat and Pratyak and even the 7th is considered difficult and called Naidana. The 2nd, 4th and

6th are okay. So, the Divine does give you a rest. However, because Saturn moves slowly and retrogrades, it may spend 9-12 months in a nakashatra that may be challenging.

Andrew Foss, in his seminal book, *Yoga of the Planets*, discusses some of the deeper meanings of Tara Bala and below I have noted and explained why the Saturn transits through 1st, 5th, and 7th positions are most challenging for Saturn. Below is a summary of his wonderful discussion of these key stars (Reference *Yoga of the Planets*, pp. 511-12)

"The Janma Nakshatra (constellation that your natal moon is in now as position 1) is connected to the fruit or one who grants us the fulfillment of our desires according to what we deserve. Mercury and Ketu are lords and Mercury wants to preserve what we have gained from birth in terms of our physical existence and Ketu wants to take away everything and create liberation." When Saturn transits this star, it really shakes things up because Saturn is naturally an enemy with Ketu and Mercury and our health may be challenged to remind us of our deeper call for liberation in this lifetime.

The Vipat Nakshatra (3rd constellation from your natal moon) means to strike down or kill or fly away like arrows. As Andrew notes, it has the power of the king to destroy those who violate dharma and is ruled by the Sun connected to wealth. Hence this position is critical for acquiring or taking away wealth. Given that Saturn and the Sun are bitter enemies, it is no wonder that Saturn transiting this position can be so difficult for finances during Sade Sati. If your natal moon is Jyestha (Scorpio 16.20-29.59) then when Saturn transits into Uttara Phalguni (Sagittarius 13.20-26.40) **March 3, 2018 - June 4, 2018** this year, or later in the year, and again **November 28, 2018 - December 2019** this energy will get triggered.

The Pratyak nakshatara (5th constellation from your natal moon) is ruled by Mars and it is worried about you violating your dharma or movement toward right action. As Andrew notes, its represents obstacles because no one wants to face an angry warrior waving weapons in the air. The transit of Saturn here is natural enemies with Mars and creates frustration and indecision if we hesitate to do battle. The key to the 5th position transit is fight or competes for what is right. Mars has a purpose in fighting for just causes and standing up for ourselves, so this transit should force us rise to the occasion. If your moon is in Swati Nakshatra (Libra 6.40-20.00) then Saturn now in Mula is in the 5th position and while you may think your Sade Sati is over because it is 3 signs away it is not, and it will ask you to rise up and fight new Dharmic battles.

So, the key to Sade Sati is not just the signs that Saturn is going through but also the sequence of the nakshatras and key numbers that Saturn is transiting.

So, if your Moon is in Shravana, then in Mula, it is going through the 25th nakshatra and that is the most difficult time but if your moon is in Uttara Ashadha (Sagittarius 26.40-Capricorn 9.59) or Purva Ashadha (Sagittarius 13.20-26.59) then the transit is not that difficult. So timing the most difficult part of Sade Sati is really connected to counting the distance from the moon's nakshatra.

Saturn governs work and it responds to getting the work done. Get the work done and Saturn will not cause you any problems. And you can change your chart by changing your life-style. Saturn responds well to meditation and calms the mind. Saturn likes yoga and exercise, which grounds the body. Saturn increases the Vata or air element, so you can do Ayurvedic treatment and diets to calm those influences. Saturn likes rules and disciple and inspires you to move in that direction. If you do not, then it feels stressful and you may feel victimized. You do not have to be - do the work!

Some people buy an iron ring and wear it on their middle finger during Sade Sati. It may help a little but giving your power to gems and thinking all your problems will go away is not learning the lessons of Saturn. Take action to focus, meditate, and be disciplined then Saturn will reward you with the calm strength of Capricorn. Be the mountain, unshakable and steady. If you are lazy and unfocused, Saturn will seem like an earthquake in your life. You do have a choice. There are mantras, chants and pujas that will help calm the mind so that you can move forward out of fear.

There are mitigating factors in chart, which will make Saturn less problematic. If your 12th house or moon has high Bindu points or Jupiter or Venus is favorable and impacting your 12th house, and supporting Saturn, then it may not be as bad. Saturn, after the age of 36, matures and ripens. This means that the 2nd or 3rd Sade Sati may not be as problematic because we are more mature. So, remember, there is nothing to fear. Saturn is your friend, but he is the type of friend that kicks your butt because he loves you.

The Divine is always taking care of us if we understand its message. Listen, act, be disciplined, focus, work hard and you will be fully supported. Venus always supports Saturn so use that energy to lighten Saturn up with more fun, relationship type activities such as massage, art, dance, painting, and fashion design.

You are safe! You are infinitely safe, my loved ones! If you only knew how much the Divine loves, cares and cherishes you at every moment of your life and how much you are protected, there would never be another moment of fear in your life! You ARE love and you are LOVED!

Special thanks and honor to some of my Jyotish Gurus: Komilla Sutton, Andrew Foss and James Braha for their insights into some of this material.

Saturn in Purva Ashadha Nakshatra:

March - June 4th and November 28 - April 2019

Saturn enters the constellation of Purva Ashadha nakshatra (13.20 Sagittarius-26.40) on **March 3rd, 2018** and stays there for 3 months and then returns there in late **November until April 2019**. This constellation is connected to Venus, a friend, and finally gives some relief from the intensity of Mula nakshatra, which has been going on much too long.

Saturn will now channel the sweet energy of Venus supporting mature relationships and the creation of material art and has more wisdom from the energy of Sagittarius. When Venus is strong in transit, exalted in Pisces **March 2 - 26th, 2018**, and in Taurus, **April 20 - May 14th**, there will be a lot of positive synergy between Venus and Saturn.

Saturn and Venus are friends and when Venus spends much of the spring in positive signs like Pisces, Taurus and Gemini, the connection with the nakshatra relationship can create durability in relationships, business and technical abilities, hard work, benefits from agriculture and technology, love of older things and people and care of the poor. It can support beauty in the body, love of massage and exercise and mature artistic creativity that will come through labored-hard work, so it will be a good time to start that sculpture or get back into ceramics or making beautiful jewelry.

When afflicted in transit with the Venus is in Aries **March 26 - April 18**, the darker side of the connection may come out with a desire to shun sensual experience, delays in marriage, dismissal of the joys of luxury, feeling unworthy of luxury and wealth or finding difficult relationships with older partners.

Saturn, even though friends with Venus, still afflicts the constellation in transit and may bring out the more challenging qualities of not being open to advise, taking low-paying jobs that require hard-work, attracting incompetent managers, creating aloofness from people and at the same time being coarser in one's personality.

When Venus is strong in transit the constellation as when it is exalted in Pisces and in Taurus in the spring, it may support devotion to friends, popularity, courage, wealth, love of good food, intelligence and steadiness with some happiness at work. Overall the transit of Saturn in this constellation will allow one to develop one's talents and draw on Saturn's wisdom and life experience in times of challenge. This transit will offer an opportunity to connect with elders in a loving way so a good time to visit elderly parents and mentors and enjoy their company.

Prash Trivedi tells us that astronomers know this constellation as Epsilon, Delta and Sagittarii, which are three stars close to the Milky Way. The Sanskrit name translates into meaning "*the former Invincible One*" or the "*undefeated.*" It symbol is a fan which is a mask to hide oneself, or something to cool the fire or to fan the flames. This nakshatra is ruled by Venus and as a decorative fan, it shows the glitzy and glamorous side of

Venus. It has inspiring energy to keep the fires of enthusiasm burning. It also is good at concealing facts, information, and feelings and has a shy and sensitive nature.

He goes on to note that the deity of this constellation is Apah, a little-known water goddess sometimes associated with the ocean goddess like Aphrodite. She is the mythical mermaid who is sensitive, alluring, mysterious and exciting. She is the feminine counterpart of the Ocean god, Varuna. Her positive side is a procreative fecundity and on the negative side is the poison that she can generate which reminds us of the dangers of gossip. Still she embodies the higher qualities of Venus and real love and compassion.

Trivedi notes that the one personality quality that this constellation has is that it feels it cannot lose and is invincible. She embodies the traditional qualities of Sagittarius of wild, ambitious spirit, wanderlust and it can most easily deal with setbacks. With the strong Jupiter association, people with Moon, Sun or Ascendant in this constellation are able to hold onto the key to joy and happiness and the joy of living.

The Sagittarius quality that comes out most strongly is loyalty and giving great support to those they admire and fighting injustice with heroic valor and this certainly will continue to support women's speaking out against their perpetrators and not being victimized.

Saturn: Enough Doom and Gloom Already!
Focus on Saturn in Mula Nakshatra and Mars and Saturn connections:
March and April

The media makes money by spinning fear and if you turn on your TV you will be ready to run from the next major blizzard, build a bomb shelter before North Korea or Russia attacks us or stay in your house concerned about the latest serial killer. Yes, evil in the world exists but there are also a lot of good things happening that the media never tells us about.

Saturn forces us to be more real with everything in our life and particular, finances, as it transits through Mula nakshatra where sometimes the material is challenged so we can find our spiritual life. Instead of fearing the collapse of the stock market, now is the time to talk to a financial planner and get your retirement situation in order so that you feel more secure. Be aware that these underlying feelings of dread about financial implosions are just a wake-up call to get you to look at your budget, income and savings plans so that you have a strong infrastructure behind you to support your spiritual growth. And yes, the world is going through the same thing as Central Bankers have created huge debts for the world, inflated the stock market and not created real economic development and throw smoke and mirrors statistics at us to make us think that everything is great.

Saturn governs the base chakra and often-spiritual folks work more on their upper chakras because they spend so much time in meditation. As a result, often, their root chakra is not developed, and Saturn is weak in their chart, their financial planning and infrastructure and connection to the earth is a bit out of balance. This can create a lot of instability and fear. It's like a pyramid. If the base of the pyramid is strongly supported, the energies can move higher to the peak. If we have a solid bank account and savings plans, then we have the freedom to pursue our spiritual development and not be thrown off balance. If the pyramid is inverted and there is low energy at the base and all the energy is very strong at the top, then there is no stability to support all the spiritual growth. The current transits are challenging our systems.

Capricorn, the main home for Saturn, requires security and safety to move forward. As it is 12 houses from its home in the sign of Sagittarius, it is a bit uneasy on a subconscious level. Capricorn rising in particular, with a 12th house transit from its home, may feel insecure. China, which is a Capricorn rising country is likely to go through huge changes the next few years with this transit and their growth and debt structuring scheme has been a mess on many levels and Trump wanting to pull out support. I suspect that our relationship with China will be the biggest challenge as Saturn moves into Sagittarius and is 12 signs from Capricorn.

MARS IN SATURN: APRIL 2

Mars and Saturn Conjunction: April 2, 2018
We are also moving toward a Mars /Saturn conjunction in which peaks into **April 2nd** but will be felt on Tuesdays and Saturdays particularly strongly from **March 27 - April 8th**.

Afflicted Saturn requires us to look deeply at unconscious fear and dread and requires looking deeply into those fears and realizing that most of the time that which we fear does not happen. 99% of the time, the things we fear do not manifest and it are the surprises that get us.

Remember that with Saturn is afflicted most of the year by Ketu in Capricorn and that fear is all in the mind. We are getting a lot of end of the world prophecies and this is just Saturn doing its thing. Even if it were true, can we do anything about it other than meditate, create inner peace and spread it throughout the world?

Do more meditation and yoga and breath work to transform the energy. The chair pose in yoga, grounds us to the earth chakra as does the Mountain pose so that we feel our feet grasping the earth and this creates more security in our life. Use the fear as a wake-up call to handle your finances, get into your body and take care of your health. Look up the magicians "*fear sleeve*" and expose him for the fraud that he is. You are infinitely safe in this universe. (If you want to connect astrology to hatha yoga and chakra analysis, see our workshop at: http://www.appliedvedicastrology.com/products-2/yoga/)

Afflicted Saturn requires us to go more slowly, to not rush around like a rabbit and not to do too much; otherwise, our anxiety level increases and we are more likely to get sick from hypertension or anxiety-related illness. With winter in the Northern Hemisphere, the vata or air element increases. Drink more hot water and calming herbal teas, slow down, do slower exercise, get oil massages and eat more hot meals and you can keep this aspect at bay.

If you are running a Saturn period or are ruled by Capricorn or Aquarius or are Aries Scorpio or Sagittarius rising, you may feel the impact more over the coming year. It can get handled. The planets are your friends if you heed their advice and do your work.

The world will not end you will not die in an apocalyptic ball of flame. Yes, there are people doing stupid things like the leader of North Korea and the weather damage is very real. Continue to pour your heart out to those suffering, so service work, raise money, donate but do not feel that installing a bomb shelter or bunker will be the answer to Saturn's fear. So, take it easy and slow down and calm the fears of Saturn.

Saturn/Ketu Connections 2018: Cleaning Up the Past
Ketu in Capricorn until March 2019
Saturn in Ketu's Nakshatra until March 3
Retrograde June 4 - November 28

Saturn is in Mula nakshatra owned by Ketu until **March 3rd** and again retrograde starting **June 4th** until **November 28th**. Ketu is in Saturn's sign of Capricorn so that is a strong association and connection between the two planets most of the year.

Ketu, that funny headless mystical guy know in Western astrology as the South node of the moon, tends to take away the material world to point us toward liberation and enlighten us. He is continuing his journey retrograde in Capricorn the planet of responsibility and hard work.

What does it all mean? Since Ketu is like Mars, Saturn is one of its greatest enemies. They both are there to guide you toward your spiritual path but can create hard lessons. Saturn separates, and Ketu renounces and Ketu forces us to revisit the past and the Saturn's transit through Ketu's nakshatra of Mula is forcing us to take responsibility for our past karma and do the right thing. In the 12 Step Programs, they are fond of saying, "*clean up your own messes.*" This is a time to re-address people that you have hurt in the past and clean up your karma, to repay debts and to learn the hard lessons of responsibility.

Sometimes there is someone that we had an argument 20 years ago and we have not talked to since then and it festers in our mind like an old wound and blocks our joy from being expressed. This is time to clean up those messes and reach out your hand first and say you are story. Get over the Aries stubbornness of wanting to be right and reach out and say you are sorry.

I have done this, and it is very powerful. Chances are the other person has forgotten or is just as stubborn and will be happy to clear the air. It is particularly powerful with parents and siblings. Why hold onto the past hurts? Even if you are right, clearing the air will free your mind and allow you not to be haunted with regrets. If you owe some old debt, this is a time to work hard and pay it back.

Saturn keeps us anchored in the material world and being responsible, so we are going to have to bear down and learn those lessons. Saturn and Ketu are both wanderers so there may be a tendency to want to run away to an ashram or live abroad to flee the pain of the past, but this transit is beckoning us to clean it up.

Ketu is happy to live simply and not face up to the responsibility of the material world. He would rather refrain from doing the hard work to succeed and would rather hide away in the ashram and meditate all day and not deal with the world. With Saturn in Mula nakshatra there can be intense anger directed at others for the past but Jupiter, the owner of Sagittarius can provide the wisdom to move through the challenges of the subconscious and transform the old energy.

In Mula (Sagittarius 0-13.20) at the galactic center, the goddess Nittriti is there to destroy material desire and move us toward spiritual development. Sometimes the material is taken away from us so that we are forced to move beyond the changing world and create a new spiritual beginning to discover our real purpose on the planet to achieve Union with the Divine and not to acquire the biggest bank account ever. If you have not found your spiritual path and or started your spiritual journey, the transit of Saturn in Mula nakshatra (Sagittarius 0-13.20) will awaken that energy.

The aspect fosters Viragya or disillusionment and detachment. This is often misunderstood and in its highest understanding it is not about escaping the material world for meditation but learning not to be upset and thrown by the winds of change when material existence throws you a curve. It means staying centered in Being and recognizing the ever-changing nature of the physical world when the winds of change hit. One has to find spiritual equanimity or feel suffering. The stronger part of the transit in **2018** will foster more mystical awakenings as Saturn in Mula can cause deep spiritual awakenings.

Still, I remember 1973-1974 when the stock market fell 50% and people came to our meditation centers to find peace because the material world was changing so much. I am not looking for stock market crash in **2018 - 2019** but even a 10-15% pullback this summer and fall will shake people up and turn them to the spiritual.

The Saturn/Ketu combination can be seen as one of the toughest combinations and if you have association in your chart (Saturn in Mula, Magha or Ashwini) a Saturn/Ketu or are in a Ketu/Saturn period or have key planets at 0-13 degrees Sagittarius, you may feel the intensity of this transit most. The US ascendant is 5 degrees Sagittarius in my rectification and the US moon is 7 Aquarius and I think the craziness in the US will continue for a while with these transits.

As my friend Juliana Swanson noted, the last time we had Saturn in Sagittarius aspecting Ketu in Aquarius was **July - November** 1960 when it led to the Kennedy election and there was a lot of civil unrest going on around Afro-American rights. Wikipedia notes that we also had more of the Cuban revolution with Castro nationalizing American interests in Cuba and Belgium threatening to leave the United Nations. Also, during that aspect, Soviet premier Nikita Khrushchev pounded his shoe on a table at a meeting of the United Nations General Assembly, his way of protesting the discussion of the Soviet Union's policies toward Eastern Europe.

The energy of Saturn/Ketu can sometimes create pessimism and lethargy and it forces us to work hard and be mindful of depressive tendencies in order to move through. Again, initiation onto a spiritual path will lighten this transit, as without a spiritual path, you may find yourself suffering or mired in tragedy or if staying stuck in gloominess, selfishness or fundamentalism. The trick is to let go of the old and the old ways and to accept change and the new of way of doing things. I was going through this now in finally accepting social media marketing and letting go of all the ways that I use to promote my financial businesses. Accept the new generation and their wisdom and adapt to the changes that are happening in the world or be miserable. With Ketu moving into Capricorn in **September** for 1.5 years, we will continue to have to deal with Saturn/Ketu issues and letting go of the old and embracing the new.

As we noted yesterday, we do get an upliftment for Saturn **March 3 - June 4th** when it gets into Purva Ashada Nakshatra (Sagittarius 13.20-26.40). With Ketu in Capricorn until **March 2019**, we will continue dealing with Saturn/Ketu issues and the need for letting go of the "*old*" and embracing the "*new.*"

On the positive side, Ketu/Saturn can give a mastery of precision and detailed work, so craftsmen may benefit from this influence. It also promotes deep philosophical thinking particularly as Ketu continues through Aquarius until September and Jupiter is lightening the influence with Saturn at least transiting in

Virgo and throwing an aspect by sign (Rashi drishtri) onto Sagittarius. There is also a mystical side to Saturn in Mula nakshatra, which will come out more when Saturn is out of the 1st pada of the constellation into 3.20-13.20 Sagittarius **March 15th - April 27th**. My friend Juliana Swanson notes that it is" a *higher more evolved expression can be about awakening sacred power and accessing those mysterious past-life and otherworldly gifts."* More of that mystical part will unfold in **2018**.

So, this influence will be there for a while for a few years and Saturn in Ketu's nakshatra of Mula for so much time until **late November 2018** will continue this desire to clean up the past and free yourself. There is also a nadi nakshatra influence with Saturn in Mula, Ketu's nakshatra aspecting its despositor Ketu in Capricorn, a sign owned by Saturn.

Find the courage now with Mars in Scorpio, **January 16 - March 4th**, to apologize to those who you have hurt or injured or apologize to them even if you think you are right. Let it go and find the freedom that Ketu so wants you to find.

Special thanks to my teacher Komilla Sutton and all my Jyotish Gurus and spiritual gurus for their wisdom and continual inspiration.

Saturn Retrograde:
April 18 - September 6 Revisiting Regret
Purva Ashada Nakshatra April 18 - June 4
Mula Nakshatra: June 4 - September 6

Saturn goes retrograde on **April 18th** this year and teaches being patient with overcoming the lessons of the past and the pain and suffering that we are feeling. There is a need to avoid being scattered and to focus deeply to accomplish work and yet the tendency is to rush around too much and do things carelessly and then pay the price. Much of the Saturn retrograde this year will be in Mula nakshatra (Sagittarius 0-13.20) where we tend to regret the past and wanting to make amends for things we have done.

The key with Saturn will be to shut yourself away from distraction and focus and not let every issue and distraction get in the way of your responsibilities. This will be hard, and this energy will manifest most on Saturdays, ruled by Saturn or when the Moon is transiting Saturn's constellation of Pushya (Cancer 3.20-16.40), Anuradha (Scorpio 3.20-16.40) and Uttara Bhadrapada (Pisces 3.20-16.40) or the signs of Capricorn or Aquarius and particularly when Mars is conjunct Saturn within a few weeks around **April 6, 2018**. If you are Capricorn or Aquarius rising, running a Saturn period or have Saturn as the Atmakaraka (planet with the highest degrees in your chart), then the Saturn issues will be most pronounced the rest of the year.

Saturn is often misunderstood. If you have a strong Saturn in your natal chart in its own signs of Capricorn or Aquarius or exalted in Libra or connected to Taurus, you may have learned the messages of Saturn. Saturn does well in the 3rd, 6th and 11th houses and is particularly challenging in the 12th and 1st house. Saturn in Aries or Cancer or Leo may be particularly difficult in many charts in the wrong houses.

Saturn is both the good and bad parent. The good parent is responsible, provides security for his children is disciplined and provides for our material infrastructure so that we can play in the life and move through our work. The good parent Saturn turns up in the chart when Saturn is well placed and in association with benefics like Jupiter and Venus and is connected to the better houses like the 3rd and 6th and 11th house and has other strengths.

Saturn as the bad parent has too much excessive fear and is prone to being too restrictive with his kids and saying no: you cannot go outside and play alone; you cannot have the ice cream and candy because it will be bad for your health. You cannot watch TV because you have to study for your exam. Over time as we grow up these restrictive messages run our lives and create too much fear around living life. Having a very restrictive Victorian nanny when I was growing up, I can attest to how these messages continue to run my life. When Saturn is weak in transit as it will be into Thanksgiving, the "*bad parent*" Saturn comes out and too much fear gets exaggerated into creating restrictions that block us from living life. The media pounds us with fears that the world is going to blow up every day and activates Saturn's lowest energy of survival, but this gets so exaggerated and ignores Saturn the good parent who is connected to the Divinity that guides the planet and who is really in charge.

Saturn also gets us caught up in the past and particularly now with its transit through Mula nakshatra connected to Ketu which is about cleaning up the past karma and creating regrets: "*I should not have done this*." It brings up guilt and remorse that keeps us swimming in a sewer pit which is not of much use. Catch the guilt and remorse thoughts that are coming up and dismiss them. There is no point living in the past and swimming in the sewer water. You are a new and different person now. We have written about Saturn/Ketu and the need to use this time to address those we have hurt and make reparations and apologize and do something to change the way we have operated before.

When Saturn is too afflicted it creates too much fear and if we made a mistake and its retrograde motion will revisit the past, but it may create too much blocking energy about moving forward. The past is really a dream and there are new and fresh circumstances to create a new life now and make new choices.

It's like the Bill Murray movie, Ground Hog Day (1993). If you are not familiar with the movie, Bill Murray plays a weatherman who goes to Pennsylvania every February to see if the groundhog will see his shadow. Bill is boorish and rude and insults his staff and gets trapped in a nightmare where he cannot leave the town and every day, wakes up at the same time to the same silly tune on the clock radio and has to relive the same day. Since he cannot die, he keeps making bad choices at first like overeating or driving a car off of a cliff, but as the movie goes on he takes up piano, saves people's lives, becomes an incredible romantic and the whole town suddenly looks up to him as a model citizen.

The movie is like a seminar in learning to be kind, artistic, creative and a humanitarian. It becomes a metaphor for reincarnation and overcoming our negative qualities of selfishness, addiction, and rudeness.

When we have a poorly placed planet or afflicted planet in our chart, it is as if we had not learned the lessons of that school. If it is Jupiter, it may be around children, respect of Gurus, judgment or wisdom. When the planet goes weak in transit, it brings up lessons for that school. Are we going to do it differently this time? Are we going to bring out the higher values?

Rather than blame the planet, learn what lessons you did not master in the past and get it right this time. Get out of your nightmare by being kinder and help others and then you will not suffer. The planets just want us to get it right this time so we do not have to wake up in the same nightmare every morning.

We can change our karma through awareness, self-reflection, service, giving to charities and doing things to bring out the highest qualities of those planets. Our strong planets are gifts, which we are here to share with others so be sure to use them. Our weak planets are the ones that we are here for and need our attention, but they do not make our job easy. We tend to gravitate toward things we are good at to get praise rather than face potential failure at the things that we are not good at. If you are not good at relationships because your Venus is weak, then that is the planet to work on so go for the relationship seminars, the painting and the singing even if you may fall on your face. Like Bill Murray, after repeated efforts you will get it right.

Focus on Saturn at Work: Grumbling and Complaining

Saturn is still weak much of the rest of the year in the constellation of Mula nakshatra and its darker side comes up with a tendency to complain. So often it is about work because Saturn governs work and it is such a larger part of our life. The nature of work, ruled by Saturn, is naturally ruled by problems. Chances are if there were no problems at work, you would not have a job. Be grateful the ever-constant series of problems at work.

There is a whirlpool of emotional churning going on as deep emotional patterns come up to be purified so that can move into a higher spiritual realm. I have noticed more complaining on my part and hearing it from many others. When Saturn is out of balance it sees everything wrong with the world. Pity-party.

No one enjoys listening to someone complain for hours and in fact it is exhausting for your own energy and leads to hopelessness and frustration. It is very unconscious, and we have to become conscious of it otherwise we will wear-out our friends and family members.

Grumbling is replaced easily by gratitude as an anecdote. When you go to bed at night, write down or reflect on 5 good things that happened to you that day. Maybe someone smiled at you or your child told you they loved you or your dog licked your face. There is always something wonderful. The mind however, finds one bad thing and blows it up 100-fold and exaggerates it into a typhoon. Yes, there are problems and they are real, but we neglect basic things in our life. Do we have a nice home that keeps us warm? The homeless do not. Do we have two eyes that can see the beauty of this world? Some people are less fortunate. Do we have a loving partner? Many do not. Focus on what works in your life and be happy and grateful. Catch yourself before you pour out your problems on some undeserving friend for an hour.

Saturn is hard at work trying to make you miserable and focusing on the lack. Turn the energy to the Divine and Jupiter and replace lack with gratitude, replace faultfinding with praise. Do this exercise and you will get through this intense transit of Saturn.

Saturn and Fear of The Future: Trust In The Divine

When Saturn is weak in transit, and much of this year it is not happy in the constellation of Mula nakshatra (Sagittarius 0-13.20) we are going to have master fear of the future or be miserable. The mind cannot have an emotion on an abstract level, so it attaches to something in the environment. Whatever is up in the news feeds our fear weather it is volcanoes, North Korea, global warming.

Most of the things we fear never happen and it's that 1% surprise element that knocks us out of the park. Fear is a survival mechanism to keep us out of danger. If we stick our hand into the fire when we are small, we learn not to do it again but then maybe we are inordinately afraid of fire our entire life. Just remember that most of what we fear does not happen and dismiss it.

Capricorn, the main home for Saturn, requires security and safety to move forward. As it goes into transitional zone this year changing signs and staying in the weaker and more vulnerable areas of the zodiac, its security and safety issues are up. Capricorn rising in particular, with a 12th house transit from its home, may feel insecure.

Ketu in Capricorn continues to stir up unconscious fear and dread and requires looking deeply into those fears and realizing that most of the time that which we fear does not happen. 99% of the time, the things we fear do not manifest and it are the surprises that get us. Remember that with, that fear is all in the mind. Do more meditation and yoga and breath work to transform the energy. The chair pose in yoga, grounds us to the earth chakra as does the Mountain pose so that we feel our feet grasping the earth and this creates more security in our life. Use the fear as a wake-up call to handle your finances, get into your body and take care of your health. Look up the magicians "*fear sleeve*" and expose him for the fraud that he is. You are infinitely safe in this universe. (If you want to connect astrology to Hatha yoga and chakra analysis, see our workshop at: http://www.appliedvedicastrology.com/products-2/yoga/)

Afflicted Saturn requires us to go more slowly, to not rush around like a rabbit and not to do too much; otherwise, our anxiety level increases and we are more likely to get sick from hypertension or anxiety-related illness. The cold winter increases the air element and fear. Drink more hot water and calming herbal teas, slow down, do slower exercise, get oil massages and eat more hot meals and you can keep this aspect at bay. If you are running a Saturn period or are ruled by Capricorn or Aquarius or are Sagittarius rising, you may feel the impact more over the coming year. It can get handled. The planets are your friends if you heed their advice and do your work.

On a personal level, use the transits to transform your deep unconscious fears, which is what is coming up heal. What are you afraid of? What are you avoiding dealing with? What can you do to get in unstuck?

Again, charts are very individual, and we do not ever want to stereotype people by sign but sometimes it's a way of putting one's finger right away on a core problem for the person's entire life.

2018 AQUARIUS RISING: MORE TRANSITS OF SATURN URANUS INTO ARIES: THE FIRE OF SURPRISE
Uranus Stationary Direct, January 2, 2018 - August 7, 2018
Uranus Retrograde: August 7, 2018 - January 6, 2019

Watch the beginning of the New Year as Uranus stations can increase earthquake activity and create unexpected events particularly fires and military action with the planet in the sign of Aries.

For Mundane astrology, the outer planets are very significant and in thirty years of charting them, Vedic astrologers cannot ignore them. Uranus moved into the fire sign of Aries on **April 7th, 2017**. It will stay in Aries for 7 years.

As a Neo-Vedic astrologer, I pay attention to Uranus. Dennis Harness, in his article "*Pluto: A Neo-Vedic View*," discusses the importance of the outer planets and Uranus stating:

"*In comparing the Hindu mythology of these three planetary deities with the Uranus, Neptune and Pluto myths; there are many common themes and metaphors. For example, Prajapati is the lord of progeny and creativity. He "exerts his heat and duplicates himself" and his "divine voice sounds like thunder". 3 One of the translations of Prajapati is Indra, the lord of thunder and lightning. A similarity to the planet Uranus can easily be seen. Uranus represents the Prometheus myth of bringing fire to earth, the bringer of change and innovation. Uranus is often associated with heat, lightning and thunder. He was also the father of Venus, the goddess of creativity. Narendra Desai felt that Uranus was a higher octave of Mercury, the god of creative intellect. He said that a prominent Uranus was often seen in the chart of a good astrologer.*"

Uranus is a planet that embodies the Chinese curse: "*May you live an interesting life.*" Uranus brings genius, but its "standard bearers" (Edison, Watts, etc.) seldom succeed at higher learning — often, Uranus-ruled people have a hard time in University, though the IQ is 200 or 300! Uranus rules revolutionary actions and humanitarian work and given that the transit is happening going into the presidential conventions, one would expect even more eruptions. Its placement may promise great social change but, in the war, -like sign of Aries, that may mean even more violence.

Uranus signals unpredictable, sudden occurrences, such as **May 2010s** "*flash crash*," when the Dow dropped 1,000 points in 5 minutes, wiping out many small investors. This planet rules electricity, shock, the nervous system (sometimes heart attacks) computers, inventiveness, social activism, revolt, friendship, humanitarian motives, eccentric behavior, alertness, genius and divergent thinking, gentle kindness and dictatorial tyranny. The last time Uranus entered Aries was 1933.

Aries rules war, assertiveness, new growth, exploration, armies, fire, explosions, machinery and engines and so it would seem that military technology will get a huge boost over the next 7 years. That is not something we need. Clearly with Trumps $54 billion increase in the military budget, Defense stocks are a good place to park money and the military industrial complex makes sure they get used. With the US in a Rahu, the North shadow node related to technology, and the US major dasha period, it is clear that Nasdaq, which is leading the market higher, is still a long-term investment even if it has a correction **June - October** of this year. I wonder if the car that drives itself, that is currently going through massive testing, will become a part of all our lives with this transit?

Last June's shock with Brexit came just after Uranus went into Aries. The transits in Mars during the vote were messy and very weak, making people angry. Venus was combust and too close to the Sun. Jupiter was conjunct Rahu within a degree and Uranus was a few days from going into Aries. These planetary transits created great emotional impacts, supporting a trend where I find that people are more emotionally charged when many planets are whacked.

We do have a bunch of key European votes coming in France with an election decision on **May 7th** and Italy is on the back-burner making decisions about new elections and Uranus, the planet of revolution is more likely to swing voters into action against the norm.

On October 19, 1987, when the US stock market had a huge crash, Uranus was in the Gandanta, the karmic junction between the water sign of Scorpio and the fire sign of Sagittarius. On October 19th, 1987 when the DOW crashed over 500 points, a huge percentage for that era, it was at 0.0 Sagittarius. On **June 27th**, Uranus will be at 0.00 Aries again in another karmic junction point. I am not predicting an **April** crash but a surprise correction after the NQ cash hits 5500 or 5550 would make sense with Mercury conjunct Uranus on March 6th as it gets ready to go into Aries, a more bearish air sign.

The EU is a total failure. This federalization of Europe is a deliberate Utopia for politicians with high paying jobs and tax exemptions. The people have no possible ability to ever vote for a policy change. This is the most anti-democratic structure ever thought of in Western culture.

If the oligarchy continues to get away with their power games, the Saturn/Pluto/Ketu/Jupiter conjunction into **2020** is going definitely force a major confrontation between democracy, government and power mongers who are out of control. For this year and a bit more, it would seem the shadow government will stay in control. Maybe, finally, Uranus fully in Aries, will allow larger change as we saw in 1933 - 1940 but it may only ultimately rebalance with another war. Lets hope consciousness can rise enough so that suffering does not have to repeat itself in history.

2018 GUIDE TO THE NODAL TRANSITS: RAHU AND KETU

Rahu is in Cancer until **March 2019** and Ketu is in Capricorn until **March 2019**

Rahu will impact Aquarius Rising most and Ketu will impact Scorpio Rising most

Here is a guide to Rahu and Ketu in Cancer and Capricorn by Rising Sign and Moon Sign:

RAHU IN CANCER/KETU IN CAPRICORN

The North and South Nodes, Rahu and Ketu, create eclipses, and govern our desire nature in the material world and the desire to leave the world and discover the Divine.

In the true node system, Rahu transited into Cancer on **September 9th, 2017** and Ketu into Capricorn on **September 9th**. I prefer true nodes for transits, but it is still a big transition and will have a huge impact until **March 2019**.

Rahu and the Moon are enemies as Rahu is friends with Mercury and exalted in Gemini and would rather work on the intellectual realm. In the sign of Cancer, it will bring up phobias, fears and have more discomfort with feelings. Cancer wants security and the safety of the home and Rahu will throw a wrench into the works by creating toxic problems there to force us to face our issues around safety and comfort. With huge displacements going on in Florida, Texas and the Caribbean, with the onset of mold and toxins from the hurricane, you can see how this issue around home, safety and security are going to be stirred up during the next 18 months.

The problem will be trying to rationalize your feelings rather than just experience them and this will be particularly true in the constellation of Ashlesha, which will be present until **April 29th** in the true node transit. Rahu in Cancer will create a strong drive for home, family life, maternal affection and will increase intuitive energies. The transit will force a need for more nurturing and caring. The first part of the transit is more afflicted until late **October** when Rahu gets out of the Gandanta area (Cancer 27-30).

So, watch out for toxins in the home. This is a good time to check for Radon, get a carbon monoxide detector, and a dehumidifier for mold or other household pollutants. Prevent bug and rodent infestations, which could rear up. That will be one way to stay on top of the transit.

Make sure your vehicle is in good shape and inspected and that you are on top of maintenance. If you have lung problems, now is the time to stay on top of them as moon/Cancer is very connected to lungs and Rahu may create problems from toxins or pollution so now may be a good time to invest in an air purifier if you are having those kinds of problems.

On a mundane level, later in the transit, more compassion for the homeless and immigrants is likely to manifest. Given the plight of migrants in the world this will be a good thing but not without its challenges given what has happened in Europe and countries like Sweden. We can only imagine the effects of all the destroyed homes in Florida, Texas and the Caribbean and its impact on migration and rebuilding. Rahu in Cancer will probably increase the problem and bring a better solution by **spring 2019** but a crisis around it will develop first.

Ketu wants to leave the world and discover the Divine and in the business sign of Capricorn, he is uncomfortable with Capricorn's need to face reality and be in the material world but wants to reject discipline and hard work. During **September/October** with the Saturn aspect tight within 3 degrees, there may be more ups and downs with work as one is unclear about whether to be in business or run off to a meditation retreat.

Capricorn, governing the knees and joints, will be afflicted. If you have knee problems, be careful and take care of your knees by doing exercises to keep them healthy. This may also be true for the joints so stay limber with your yoga!

Both nodes are uncomfortable. Rahu, in the natural 4th sign of the zodiac of Cancer, wants happiness but fears the consequences of material happiness. Ketu gets stuck in the material world of Capricorn and goes into self-denial and rejection. The key to the next 1.5-year will be to not deny your needs for love and happiness but rather to find a way to meet your obligations on a spiritual level and while not denying the need for love.

Ketu in Capricorn may increase religious fundamentalism, but it may also force you into lessons of austerity and duty. Ketu and Saturn are great enemies like Mars and Saturn, although, they both want to guide you toward your spiritual path. The key will be to go deeper with spiritual practices.

Saturn/Capricorn was a reality checks in the material world and Ketu wants to run to the ashram and meditate or travel around the world wandering on spiritual pilgrimages in search of God. Still, facing the realities of living in the material world will continue to be forced upon one by Saturn. The exact aspect of Saturn onto Ketu from Scorpio to Capricorn will emphasize this conflict into the exact aspect in the true node system during **October 7 - 8th** but the 3rd degree of influence will be felt much of **September and October**.

RAHU IN CANCER/ASHLESHA: EMBRACE LIFE WITH MODERATION

In the mean node system, Rahu moves into the constellation of Ashlesha (Hydra, Cancer 16.40-29.59) on **August 17th** and in the true node system on **September 10th** and journeys through there until **April 29th** in the true node system. Of the 27 constellations in the zodiac, Ashlesha (and Ardra) can stir up more emotional turmoil than many others and it's a long transit so we have a bit of an emotional storm brewing for a while.

Ashlesha is a constellation which grounds us to the earthy suffering of life, death and unhappiness, while Rahu loves to fully embrace life and live every moment in sensual gratification, causing him to stay frustrated and psychologically imbalanced.

The first part of the transit is in the Gandanta or karmic knot (Cancer 27-29.59) at least until **October 25th** in the true node system. Here difficult problems are knotted and hard to unravel and the soul must confront deep karma. Ashlesha can make you a visionary but can also get you very caught up in being isolated. If you have not come to the spiritual path, you could be caught up in difficult additive patterns.

The symbol for this intense Nakshatra is the coiled serpent at the base of the spine, reflecting the potent kundalini energy that resides here. Ashlesha means the tangled one and denotes the challenges of our addictions. The main deities are the Nagas, the Serpent Kings. The Shakti revealed here is the *"power to inflict poisonous venom."* Great mystical talents and enlightenment can be experienced if the primordial energy of this lunar asterism is harnessed.

Serpents have two connotations connected to poison and spirituality. When the constellation is operating strongly, it can bring deep mystical experiences and spiritual inquiry. On the dark side, it can lead to poisonous gossiping so watch your tongue as the planets transit through here as Rahu has no control. This combination of Rahu in Ashlesha, owned by Mercury, puts the media on hyper-drive so make sure to turn off your television or be subjected to angry tirades.
Rahu here could tend toward gluttony, debauchery, drug use and addictive patterns. The constellation may increase the desire for unquenchable sensual gratification so remember moderation in all things.

The key through getting through this long transit is to remember that all mental blocks that come up are created from your own mind and you need to transform the frustration into spiritual energy as Rahu ultimately seeks liberation from the cyclic ups and downs of the material world.

The problem with shifting Nodes is a great increase for desired changes: new relationships, moving, jobs. Rahu will never be satisfied. Make sure you are changing for really good reasons and enjoy!

If you have a natal malefic like Saturn, Mars, Sun or Rahu placed in Cancer/Capricorn or aspecting it in your natal chart, it Ketu may bring out the darker side of the transit while an aspect or association with a benefic like Mercury, Venus or Jupiter may bring good results.

RAHU IN PUSHYA APRIL 29 - DECEMBER 7, 2018

RAHU IN PUSHYA NAKSHATRA (CANCER 16.40-3.20)

In the true node system, Rahu moves into Pushya **April 29th** for 7.5 months and gets connected with Saturn. Pushya is one of the most auspicious constellations in the zodiac being connected to the chief deity, Brahaspati, the high priest of the gods.

For Western astronomers, Pushya is formed by North and South Aselli, the two donkeys, which reflect the manger and the birth of the Christ child, which occurs under the spiritual energy of this benefic lunar mansion. This transit is a big relief from the poisonous Ashlesha. Rahu settles down here and can accept the restrictions of this auspicious constellation and this allows it to control phobias and fears. For one of the rare transits of Rahu, he is able to take on the responsibility of Saturn and move more toward the light. If you are Cancer rising, this transit can be powerful on a spiritual level unless your subconscious resists the urge to grow.

The problem is that much of the transit between **March 7 and November 5th**, Cancer has aspects from Mars from Sagittarius and mostly Cancer. The darker energy of this constellation can come out in being too talkative, too interested in too many things, overly sensitive and emotional, moving toward martyrdom rather than true service, and being defrauded by fake Gurus. The Mars energy can bring up fighting and conflict with rebels and we have to sense that the far right or left may want to take on their opponents and oppress liberal and radical values, which Rahu fights for.

The Mars aspect to Rahu is peaking much of **June** within 3 degrees but with retrograde motion, the aspect stays pretty tight until **mid-August** and then returns again in **late September**. Mars/Rahu aspects promote violent rebellion. The aspect will be tense and test your courage and power. Too much impetuous temper, adventurism, ambition and courage can also lead to reckless violence if not controlled. The energy has to be channeled in rebellion toward just causes in a peaceful way or will lead to major unrest and violence. I am concerned about US rioting this summer and while the trigger is unclear, the energy is in place.

In the end, if we are to have a Mars/Rahu aspect, we would rather have it in Pushya the most benevolent nakshatra and nourishing influence and I suspect when it is all complete, something good and transformational will happen.

RAHU AND KETU IN CAPRICORN/CANCER: YOUR GUIDE FOR THE NEXT 18 MONTHS

Vedic astrology pays most attention to transits from the Moon Chart since the mind is most impacted but the transits from the Ascendant Lord and sometimes the Sun Chart and the Arudha Lagna may reveal more material manifestations.

The Arudha Lagna is how others see you and I call it the perception chart. If you know your Arudha lagna rising sign (I can't teach you how to calculate it here) then Rahu, trining the Arudha Lagna will create Raj Yogas particularly if interacting with a natal benefic. Hence if your Arudha Lagna is a water sign (Cancer, Pisces, Scorpio) then Rahu in Cancer will set up a trinal relation and be a positive.

Rahu creates our central desire in this lifetime based on where it is in our natal chart and Ketu creates detachment and takes things away in order to move us toward our goal of Moksha or liberation from the earthly plane. Rahu is like a carrot on a string as it keeps taunting us for more and more and when we finally attain it, we are not satisfied.

Rahu in the 1st house is common for actors and rock stars. While they want ruble recognition and attention, in the end when they get it, they lose all their privacy as they are often the subject of tabloid exposures and tattle but then they realize they want nothing but privacy and freedom from the gossip columnists and flashing camera lenses of the paparazzi!

Rahu and Ketu in transit will open up new desires in our life bringing with them new levels of attachment. Rahu transits are good in the 3rd, 6th, 10th and 11th from the natal moon or rising sign and Ketu is beneficial in the 3rd, 6th and 11th from the natal moon or rising sign. So, if you have moon in Taurus, Aquarius, Libra or Virgo then the Rahu transit may be beneficial. If you are Scorpio, Leo, or Pisces rising or moon sign, then the Ketu transit will be beneficial.

Any transit can be good or bad. If you have a natal malefic like Saturn, Mars, Sun or Rahu placed in Cancer/Capricorn or aspecting it in your natal chart, it may bring out the darker side of the transit while an aspect or association with a benefic like Mercury, Venus or Jupiter may bring good results.

Planets in transit and aspecting Cancer and Capricorn will impact Rahu and Ketu also. For example, Saturn is now in Scorpio aspecting Rahu in Cancer within a few degrees and has a negative impact until it moves into Sagittarius on **October 26th** and then it will negatively impact your houses connected to Gemini, Aquarius, and Virgo. This is how to gauge your afflicted and unafflicted guide below.

If your Moon or Sun is in Cancer or Capricorn, then the nodes will eclipse it at some point over the next 18 months and the critical part of that transit may be when Rahu or Ketu are 3 degrees on either side of your natal Sun or Moon. Hence, if you were born **August 13 - 16**, Rahu is eclipsing your natal Sun in transit now and can either lead to a sudden rise in fame, attention or the loss of status based on the houses involved.

If your moon is in Cancer then Rahu is transiting your moon and can cause deep mental unrest and instability, especially if your natal moon is already weak in the 6th, 8th or 12th houses or afflicted by other malefics. The mental unrest may be difficult to handle, and you may cope with the added stress by turning to addictive substances if you are not into yoga and meditation.

Each chart is very unique and if you are running a Rahu or Ketu dasha or sub-period, then these transits will be more impactful.

RAHU AND KETU IN CAPRICORN/CANCER: YOUR GUIDE FOR THE NEXT 18 MONTHS

I discussed Rahu and Ketu in Cancer and Capricorn, which moved there in the mean node system **August 17th, 2017** and moved in the true node system on **September 9 - 10, 2017** depending where in the world you live. This is a long and dominant transit that will impact you for 18 months.

Vedic astrology pays most attention to transits from the Moon Chart since the mind is most impacted but the transits from the Ascendant Lord and sometimes the Sun Chart and the Arudha Lagna may reveal more material manifestations.

The Arudha Lagna is how others see you and I call it the perception chart. If you know your Arudha lagna rising sign (I can't teach you how to calculate it here) then Rahu, trining the Arudha Lagna will create Raj Yogas particularly if interacting with a natal benefic. Hence if your Arudha Lagna is a water sign (Cancer, Pisces, Scorpio) then Rahu in Cancer will set up a trinal relation and be a positive.

Rahu creates our central desire in this lifetime based on where it is in our natal chart and Ketu creates detachment and takes things away in order to move us toward our goal of Moksha or liberation from the earthly plane. Rahu is like a carrot on a string as it keeps taunting us for more and more and when we finally attain it, we are not satisfied.

Rahu in the 1st house is common for actors and rock stars. While they want ruble recognition and attention, in the end when they get it, they lose all their privacy as they are often the subject of tabloid exposures and tattle but then they realize they want nothing but privacy and freedom from the gossip columnists and flashing camera lenses of the paparazzi!

Rahu and Ketu in transit will open up new desires in our life bringing with them new levels of attachment. Rahu transits are good in the 3rd, 6th, 10th and 11th from the natal moon or rising sign and Ketu is beneficial in the 3rd, 6th and 11th from the natal moon or rising sign. So, if you have moon in Taurus, Aquarius, Libra or Virgo then the Rahu transit may be beneficial. If you are Scorpio, Leo, or Pisces rising or moon sign, then the Ketu transit will be beneficial.

Any transit can be good or bad. If you have a natal malefic like Saturn, Mars, Sun or Rahu placed in Cancer/Capricorn or aspecting it in your natal chart, it may bring out the darker side of the transit while an aspect or association with a benefic like Mercury, Venus or Jupiter may bring good results.

Planets in transit and aspecting Cancer and Capricorn will impact Rahu and Ketu also. For example, Saturn is now in Scorpio aspecting Rahu in Cancer within a few degrees and has a negative impact until it moves into Sagittarius on October 26th and then it will negatively impact your houses connected to Gemini, Aquarius, and Virgo. This is how to gauge your afflicted and unafflicted guide below.

If your Moon or Sun is in Cancer or Capricorn, then the nodes will eclipse it at some point over the next 18 months and the critical part of that transit may be when Rahu or Ketu are 3 degrees on either side of your natal Sun or Moon. Hence, if you were born **August 13 - 16**, Rahu is eclipsing your natal Sun in transit now and can either lead to a sudden rise in fame, attention or the loss of status based on the houses involved.

If your moon is in Cancer then Rahu is transiting your moon and can cause deep mental unrest and instability, especially if your natal moon is already weak in the 6th, 8th or 12th houses or afflicted by other malefics. The mental unrest may be difficult to handle, and you may cope with the added stress by turning to addictive substances if you are not into yoga and meditation.

Each chart is very unique and if you are running a Rahu or Ketu dasha or sub-period, then these transits will be more impactful.

A GUIDE TO RAHU/KETU: GOING THROUGH THE HOUSES

ARIES RISING OR MOON:
Rahu Transiting: 4th House
Ketu Transiting: 10th House

If you have no malefics like Saturn, Rahu, Ketu or Mars in Cancer or aspecting Cancer, then the Rahu transit will be a time to learn about foreign people and customs, travel to the Southwest, or engage in buying a new home or residence or vehicle. You may suddenly feel unhappy in your course of work with Ketu transiting your 10th and desire a change at work or take up non-traditional "*out of the box*" work.

Ketu transiting the 10th house could positively spur you to do good reorganization at work but if there are afflictions to Ketu, you could feel fragmented and disconnected at work and your reputation could diminish.

If you have malefics afflicting Cancer or Capricorn, you may feel more weighed down by responsibilities. Relationships might seem boring or you might want to bolt from a committed relationship. You may have to deal with toxins in your home like mold, insects infestation, or you may have emotional challenges with your mother or she may be prone to illness.

TAURUS RISING OR MOON:
Rahu Transiting: 3rd House
Ketu Transiting: 9th House

If your 3rd house is not afflicted by malefics in transit or in your natal chart, then the 3rd house transits of Rahu will support you physically, make you feel stronger and create more determination and courage to make changes in your life. It will foster creativity for writing projects or artistic development. You might take up Toastmasters and do more public speaking and be drawn to spiritual journeys and short-trips.

If your 9th house is unafflicted in transit or in your natal chart, then Ketu transiting there might lead to a deep spiritual, philosophical or religious breakthrough and foreign travel could be beneficial. It is a good time to write the big philosophical and spiritual tome and get it published!

If Cancer is afflicted in your natal chart or transit, then Rahu might create a misunderstanding with younger siblings, or develop moodiness, which could be alleviated by writing or creative activities.

Ketu transiting through your 9th if afflicted may lead you to question your Gurus or teachers and consider leaving them. You might be drawn into switching your beliefs at this time and take a different spiritual path. Foreign travel might be fraught with challenges so have a back up plan and make sure someone has copies of your passports and that you have the flexibility to change airline tickets if something unexpected comes up. If you are working on book, be prepared for major rewrites and that the process will take much longer than expected.

GEMINI RISING OR MOON:
Rahu Transiting: 2rd House
Ketu Transiting: 8th House

If Rahu is unafflicted in transit or in your natal chart with no malefic associations from Saturn, Ketu or Mars, then this is a time to clean up your family relationships and possibly profit from foreign investments. Focus on speaking the truth and being cordial and pleasant. You might get a promotion, raise or earn extra money if you can start a side business or venture.

If Ketu is unafflicted in transit because of no natal or malefic associations from Saturn, Mars or the Sun, then your intuition may blossom during this transit. Research, self-discovery and psychological insights could be keen. This is a good time for seminars, courses or sessions with your therapist. Your partner may come into some unexpected money and you may become interested in esoteric subjects or metaphysics, as Ketu in the 8th house could make you much more sensitive to other dimensions.

If Rahu is afflicted in transit because of malefic associations from Saturn or Mars, then finances might be challenged. Money might dry up at times and come in spurts. You have to watch diet and eat pure foods as you might be prone to binge eating to cover up emotions. If you have not overcome addictive patterns than stay away from alcohol and recreational chemicals and do not use sexual activity to cover up emotional distress. Watch your speech to avoid cursing or rough language so you do not hurt others.

If Ketu is afflicted in transit because of malefic associations with Mars, Saturn or the Sun, watch your health and your hypersensitivity. This may require being more grounded and doing regular yoga and exercise. You may develop hidden and undiagnosable health issues so keep looking for answers with alternative practitioners. There is always an answer out there even if traditional medicine cannot find one.

(**Note:** Saturn into Sagittarius **October 26th** will be there for 2.5 years so it will be afflicting Gemini during the entire transit)

CANCER RISING OR MOON:
Rahu Transiting: 1st House
Ketu Transiting: 7th House

If Rahu is unafflicted in transit or in your natal chart with no malefic associations from Saturn, Ketu or Mars then this is a time to purify your system, get your affairs in order and get clearer about your life. Use this time for self-improvement, business relationships with foreign companies and get rid of toxic relationships.

Rahu in transit could make you more charismatic, allowing you to be a leader and attract followers, which might grant some temporary fame.

(**Note:** Saturn moving out of Scorpio **October 26th** for 2.5 years will leave Cancer unafflicted by Saturn)

If Rahu is afflicted in transits by malefic associations with natal planets like Saturn, Mars and Ketu then you might be subject to toxins, pollutants, chemical or hormonal changes and it will be important to do regular detox diets. You will have to defend your status and position from others who might snipe at you and try to bring you down. The air element or Vata will dominate so you will need to eat hot, calming foods and drink calming herbal teas to ground you. Exercise, meditation and yoga will be necessary.

If Ketu is unafflicted in transit or in your natal chart with no malefic associations from Saturn, Mars or the Sun, this will be a good time to reevaluate business related actives such as relationships, conditions and contracts. Your romantic partner may need support and your challenge will be to be there with devotion.

If Ketu is afflicted in transits by malefic associations with natal planets like Saturn and Mars and the Sun, then you will be wanting to change business relationships and consider breaking up with your partner if you are dissatisfied. Avoid flying off the handle and throwing out the baby with the bathwater. You will be prone to want to do more travel in search of deep spirituality and truth but if it is not planned carefully, it could lead to aimless wandering with no direction.

LEO RISING OR MOON:
Rahu Transiting: 12th House
Ketu Transiting: 6th House

If Rahu is unafflicted in transit or in your natal chart with no malefic associations from Saturn, Ketu or Mars, then this a good time for a foreign trip or spiritual pilgrimage or an outing in the mountains. Donate to charity, good causes and do service work but avoid over-working.

If Rahu is afflicted in transit or in your natal chart with no malefic associations from Saturn, Ketu or Mars, then you may develop sleep problems because the Vata or air element will be over activated so be quiet in the evening and don't do heavy aerobic exercise or watch violent action movies before you go to sleep. Avoid eating late. You may develop difficult-to-diagnose ailments and you will have to seek alternative practitioners to find an answer. You may have trouble being grounded or develop foot problems and feel psychologically unsettled. It will be an important time to turn to spirituality, meditation and yoga. Avoid sexual addiction as Rahu transiting through the twelfth house can unearth psychological complexes related to fear, worry and paranoia. Remember that the things that you are worrying about are illusionary and 99% of the things we worry about do not happen.

If Ketu is unafflicted in transit or your natal chart or associated with benefics, then there will be a desire to reorganize your life for the better and move toward self-improvement. Medical and healing work may be aided, and spiritual remedies will be strong.

If Ketu is afflicted in transit or by malefic natal chart associations, there may be a desire for liberation and letting go of what is routine and normal in your life. You may become very unhappy with work (6th house) and want to change or just not show up, so find a way to modify your situation for the better.

VIRGO RISING OR MOON:
Rahu Transiting: 11th House
Ketu Transiting: 5th House

If Rahu is unafflicted in transit or in your natal chart or positively impacted by benefics like Jupiter, Mercury and Venus, then this transit could bring in powerful new friends and new group associations. There could be monetary windfalls or bonuses but be careful how you invest money at this time with Ketu transiting through the 5th house of speculation and investment. Use this transit to support groups and humanitarian organizations. You could have beneficial relationships with older siblings or unexpected money could come from the Southwest direction. Find new mentors to lead you to positive growth.

If Rahu is afflicted in transit or in your natal chart or positively impacted by malefics like Saturn, Mars, Ketu and the Sun, then this transit could lead to connections with swindler or con-artists that present things that are too good to be true. Evaluate them in the light of common sense and do your due diligence. You may have problems with older siblings or develop ear infections. Make sure to save carefully to avoid negative cash flow if income gets hit by irregular ups and downs.

If Ketu is unafflicted in transit or your natal chart or associated with benefics like Jupiter, Mercury and Venus, then there will be a desire to shift spiritual affiliations and spend more time in meditation and reading holy works about theology. Romance may be impacted, and you will need to be more demonstrative about affection rather than withdrawing. Work with your children to make unexpected adjustments and there may be unexpected gains from investments.

If Ketu is afflicted in transit or by malefic natal chart associations, you may be overprotective of children and that may lead to rebellion if you smother them too much. You may attract needy or difficult people in romance or you main receive surprise losses in investments. You may have trouble sitting to meditate and your mind may feel restless and ungrounded.

LIBRA RISING OR MOON:
Rahu Transiting: 10th House
Ketu Transiting: 4th House

If Rahu is unaffected in transit or in your natal chart or positively impacted by benefits like Jupiter, Mercury and Venus, then this transit could bring in promotions in career, being seen more, more status, learning unusual skills, success with foreign countries. You may even expect some gain from cordial relationship with people of distinction. You are also likely to get new opportunities in your work front, which would give you higher responsibilities and more freedom. Rahu in the tenth house can produce major changes in your career. You may change jobs, receive a promotion or decide to do something entirely different. Your company could be bought out and an entire new management team could be put into place. This area of life will be a major focus for this entire time. You may not spend much time at home as a result.

If Rahu is afflicted in transit or in your natal chart or positively impacted by malefic like Saturn, Mars, Ketu and the Sun, then this transit could lead to having problems with decision making and are not clear what to do. Make sure to take only credit for your achievements. You might be exposed to scandals so be careful before you get into shady undertakings. Finances would require your focused attention or else you may lose some of them. Health could be a matter of concern during this particular time. You are likely to develop sleep disorders, which could also be a result of your constant worries.

If Ketu is unaffected in transit or your natal chart or associated with benefits like Jupiter, Mercury and Venus, then there will be a desire to reorganize your home and rearrange furniture or your garage. Find a way to make your home more spiritual, get a Vastu or Feng Shui reading. This is a time for spiritual education and a chance to upgrade your job skills.

If Ketu is afflicted in transit or by malefic natal chart associations such as Saturn or Mars, your home may need costly repairs. It is recommended not to buy or sell real estate during this transit. Your emotions may be more sensitive and less stable so be patient and avoid making decisions when your mood is too strong. Make sure your car is in good repair. Attend to your mother and work on healing past challenges. Watch out for undiagnosable problems in the heart and chest area and work on finding a good doctor to get through it.

During this period, Rahu will move through your tenth house from the Moon. This brings in mixed results for you. Hence, if you see a great time during the first half of this period you may have to experience some negative results in the second half of this phase.

Finances should be in a good shape as you are likely to gain in your field of work.

You may expect a cooperative atmosphere at work, as you are likely to establish cordial relations with your superiors. You may even expect some gain from your cordial relationship with people of distinction. You are also likely to get new opportunities in your work front, which would give you higher responsibilities and more rights.

Finances would require your focused attention or else you may lose some of them. Health could be a matter of concern during this particular time. You are likely to develop sleep disorders, which could also be a result of your constant worries. Rahu in the tenth house can produce major changes in your career. You may change jobs, receive a promotion or decide to do something entirely different. Your company could be bought out and an entire new management team could be put into place. This area of life will be a major focus for this entire time. You may not spend much time at home as a result.

With Ketu in the 4th house of home and family you may have some major repairs to your residence that will be costly. It is recommended not to buy or sell real estate during this transit.

SCORPIO RISING OR MOON:
Rahu Transiting: 9th House
Ketu Transiting: 3rd House

If Rahu is unaffected in transit or in your natal chart or positively impacted by benefits like Jupiter, Mercury and Venus, then use this transit as a time to support higher learning. Continue your growth as a perpetual student. If you already know your spiritual path, then go deeper with it. If you have not found your path, then you will be on a definite quest. Overall, this is a time to revamp and solidifying your whole belief system.

This is an opportunity to examine your beliefs and either reject worn out ones or come into a stage of wisdom and knowing. Pay attention to your father and taking care of him and also to your spiritual teacher. Benefits could come from publishing at this time. You could have beneficial visits to foreign countries for business, unexpected good luck may arise.

If Rahu is afflicted in transit or in your natal chart or positively impacted by malefic like Saturn, Mars, Ketu and the Sun, then beware of false teachers and make sure you do not get caught up in spiritual grumbling. Keep your ethics intact and avoid unscrupulous dealings. Be careful with foreign travel and spiritual pilgrimages. Health would also require your attention as you may suffer from a few minor ailments at this time

If Ketu is unaffected in transit or your natal chart or associated with benefits like Jupiter, Mercury and Venus, then there will be a desire to go on an adventure trip and have more fun and this good lead to major transformations. Time for you to take up dancing writing and acting and playing an instrument. Work on your relationships with your younger siblings and neighbors.

If Ketu is afflicted in transit or by malefic natal chart associations, you may have trouble with younger siblings that surprise you with their behavior. Watch communications with others as they may end up confusing. Realize that writing may lead to major re-writing and allow plenty of extra time to get your publications done on time.

If you have been pondering going back to school or obtaining a higher degree or certification then this is the time to do it. The ninth house is about higher learning, spiritual studies and higher learning. People with this natal placement can become perpetual students. It's like they never know enough and try to absorb every bit of knowledge and wisdom that they can. If you already know your spiritual path and then go deeper with it. If you have not found your path, then you will be on a definite quest. Be careful of false teachers. If something does not resonate with you on a soul level, then reject it and move on.

For those of you that are in a position to travel, you will have more opportunities and may hop from one place to another. Overall, you are revamping and solidifying your whole belief system during this transit. This is an opportunity to examine your beliefs and either reject worn out ones or come into a stage of wisdom and knowing. Avoid any kind of arguments with your siblings. Handle your friends and acquaintances carefully to avoid being forsaken by them. Moreover, due to your cosmic graph, this could be a trying time for your parents and siblings. Avoid bad company to keep yourself away from more trouble particularly during this time. Health would also require your attention as you may suffer from a few minor ailments at this time.

SAGITTARIUS RISING OR MOON:
Rahu Transiting: 8th House
Ketu Transiting: 2nd House

If Rahu is unaffected in transit or in your natal chart or positively impacted by benefits like Jupiter, Mercury and Venus, then this transit could bring in luck through lotteries or insurance money or income coming out of the blue. Use this time to work on your health and trust your intuition, as it will be strong. It is time to get your finances in order in general. Sit down with a financial advisor and review your current portfolio and make adjustments.

If Rahu is afflicted in transit or in your natal chart or positively impacted by malefic like Saturn, Mars, Ketu and the Sun, then this transit could lead to health issues and diseases of the reproductive organs, or other sexually transmitted diseases. Do not take any health-related complications for granted as it might prove to be life risking for you. You may also suffer from mental anxiety and unnecessary fear from everything. Keep away from corruption and malpractices as you may end up with the judiciary. You may also have to face humiliation and defamation during this particular phase. People may take credit for work you have done so be kind around that one. Get second opinions on chronic ailments.

If Ketu is unaffected in transit or your natal chart or associated with benefits like Jupiter, Mercury and Venus, then there will be a desire to study scripture, engage in kirtan or spiritual chanting. Watch finances and expenditures and keep them in order. Time for you to modify your diet and get creative with speech to take up Toastmasters or attend a poetry or creative writing class.

If Ketu is afflicted in transit or by malefic natal chart associations, you may want to be careful with the money that you receive from other sources could go out just as quickly as it came if you are not careful with your spending. There could be a tendency to find happiness through spending money on material possessions so be aware. Disruptions in your home life could cause you to seek counseling. Breaking family patterns and cycles is very hard work, but it is important that you change it for you and the coming generations.

You may need some dental work as the second house deals with teeth. Make sure that you are getting enough nutrition as you may have a loss of appetite. Make sure you eat fresh foods and avoid vices like smoking, drinking and drug use.

As with the sign of Cancer, this axis is all about money and resources, earned and unearned. Rahu transiting the eighth house could bring in money or settlements related to inheritance, divorce or an insurance payout. It is time to get your finances in order in general. Sit down with a financial advisor and review your current portfolio and make adjustments. With Ketu transiting the second house, the money that you receive from other sources could go out just as quickly as it came if you are not careful with your spending. There could be a tendency to find happiness through spending money on material possessions so be aware. Disruptions in your home life could cause you to seek counseling. Breaking family patterns and cycles is very hard work, but it is important that you change it for you and the coming generations. You may need some dental work as the second house deals with teeth. Make sure that you are getting enough nutrition as you may have a loss of appetite. The Serenity prayer is your mantra — *"God grant me the serenity to accept the things I cannot change, Courage to change the things I can, and Wisdom to know the difference."*

This period may make you suffer from diseases of the reproductive organs, small pox, and various sexually transmitted diseases. Do not take any health-related complications for granted as it might prove to be life risking for you. You may also suffer from mental anxiety and unnecessary fear from everything. Those who are also going through the maraka period in your Janma Rashi must avoid taking risks with their lives. Keep away from corruption and malpractices as you may end up with the judiciary. You may also have to face humiliation and defamation during this particular phase.

CAPRICORN RISING OR MOON:
Rahu Transiting: 7th House
Ketu Transiting: 1st House

If Rahu is unaffected in transit or in your natal chart or positively impacted by benefits like Jupiter, Mercury and Venus, then this transit could bring in a chance to support your partner. Profits in business with business partners may happen and there may be new opportunities for foreign travel for business overseas. You could meet someone new or decide to put more energy into a current relationship. If you do meet someone new, then they will be very different from the people that you are usually attracted to. They could be from a foreign country or a different culture from yours.

During this period, Rahu will move through your seventh house from the Moon. This brings in fatigue and worry for you. This is the time when you need to keep away from any kind of property related litigations and trade, as you are likely to lose your property at this time. However, some of you may even gain profit or suddenly progress in your field of trade.

If Rahu is afflicted in transit or in your natal chart or positively impacted by malefic like Saturn, Mars, Ketu and the Sun, then this transit could lead to problems with relationships at home, avoid any kind of argument with your spouse as this might lead to quarrels. Try and maintain a cordial relationship with your friends and relatives to avoid being deserted by them. You are susceptible to getting involved in an illicit affair with a person of the opposite sex. Avoid this kind of relationship during this time as this might end up ruining your name in the society. Pay attention to your health as you may catch some venereal diseases. You may also develop some bile and wind related diseases. The health of your spouse may also cause worry during this particular time. Keep an eye on your behavior and avoid any kind of arguments with your enemies.

If Ketu is unaffected in transit or your natal chart or associated with benefits like Jupiter, Mercury and Venus, then there will be a desire to increase your spiritual growth. Your intuition may flourish. People will have trouble knowing who you are. You may find yourself having some pleasant surprises. Time for a personal makeover, changing jobs but do focus on adding more spiritual content to your life.

If Ketu is afflicted in transit or by malefic natal chart associations, you may have trouble staying grounded and living in the real world. Unexpected changes may hit you and force moving, changing jobs. Be proactive and stay ahead of the curve to prevent excess anxiety. Energy could be wild and high at times and make you erratic so make sure you ground yourself at the gym with weights or hiking.

Ketu, the planet of spiritual enlightenment will be in your first house and this will be causing you to be even more spiritually inclined than before. You will be more intuitive and sensitive to many other realms of existence. In fact, sometimes you may feel that you are not even connected to this world or like you have one foot in and one foot out. People may perceive you as evasive or hard to get to know. This transit can definitely make you more detached in general. Rahu is in your seventh house of partnership. You could meet someone new or decide to put more energy into a current relationship. If you do meet someone new, then they will be very different from the people that you are usually attracted to. They could be from a foreign country or a different culture from yours.

During this period, Rahu will move through your seventh house from the Moon. This brings in fatigue and worry for you. This is the time when you need to keep away from any kind of property related litigations and trade, as you are likely to lose your property at this time. However, some of you may even gain profit or suddenly progress in your field of trade. At home, avoid any kind of argument with your spouse as this might lead to quarrels. Try and maintain a cordial relationship with your friends and relatives to avoid being deserted by them. You are susceptible to getting involved in an illicit affair with a person of the opposite sex. Avoid this kind of relationship during this time as this might end up ruining your name in the society. Pay attention to your health as you may catch some venereal diseases. You may also develop some bile and wind related diseases. The health of your spouse may also cause worry during this particular time. Keep an eye on your behavior and avoid any kind of arguments with your enemies.

AQUARIUS RISING OR MOON:
Rahu Transiting: 6th House
Ketu Transiting: 12th House

If Rahu is unaffected in transit or in your natal chart or positively impacted by benefits like Jupiter, Mercury and Venus, then this transit could bring in advancement in your life despite minor obstructions. Time for you to be proactive and disciplined around health, which means joining a gym, getting a nutritionist or getting an Ayurvedic treatment. There could be a lot of energy and enthusiasm. Engage in service work particularly with foreign organizations. If you have any legal issues that arise then you have more of a chance of coming out victorious with Rahu transiting your sixth house.

If Rahu is afflicted in transit or in your natal chart or positively impacted by malefic like Saturn, Mars, Ketu and the Sun, then this transit could lead to service work where there is confusion. Avoid not being too toxic with others by spilling your emotional guts out too much. Stay out of debt and avoid legal complications and avoid getting burned out. Rahu in or transiting the sixth house can increase the chance of Vata related illness. You have the power to overcome them if you change your lifestyle. This is the time to face any addictions head on and conquer them for good. If you are in a position to hire new employees, then make sure that you conduct a thorough background check. There is a possibility that you could attract dishonest individuals to your company

If Ketu is unaffected in transit or your natal chart or associated with benefits like Jupiter, Mercury and Venus, then there will be a desire to disconnect from the world, visit an ashram, or engage in long meditation. Good time to take a retreat, visit India. Work on creating a new life for yourself as this a time to let go of the past. Through regular meditation and your sadhana practice you can make a lot of spiritual progress in this time period. You may have profound flashes of insight or past life memories. Your dreams will be more vivid and spiritual in content.

If Ketu is afflicted in transit or by malefic natal chart associations, you have to be careful with finances and expenditures, which could be irregular. Travel in foreign countries could be filled with challenges and ups and downs.

This is the best placement for the nodes in terms of house placement. Ketu the planet of spiritual enlightenment and moksha is transiting the twelfth house of spiritual enlightenment and moksha. Through regular meditation and your sadhana practice you can make a LOT of spiritual progress in this time period. You may have profound flashes of insight or past life memories. Your dreams will be more vivid and spiritual in content. If you have any legal issues that arise then you have more of a chance of coming out victorious with Rahu transiting your sixth house. More health issues may arise that you have to deal with. Rahu in or transiting the sixth house can increase the chance of Vata related illness. You have the power to overcome them if you change your lifestyle. This is the time to face any addictions head on and conquer them for good. If you are in a position to hire new employees, then make sure that you conduct a thorough background check. There is a possibility that you could attract dishonest individuals to your company.

During this period, Rahu will move through your sixth house from the Moon. This brings in wealth from various sources for you. You may expect smooth sailing on your work front during this time. If you are into trade or business, agriculture or poultry farming you may expect a considerable profit in your respective fields of work. You may even expect some monetary gain from your opponents during this time. Chances are that you may also be benefited by your maternal uncle. Health would require your attention as you may develop some chronic diseases. However, if attended on time, you can be cured of all your ailments and regain your sound health. Socially you would be in a great shape. Your respect and honor in the society would see an upward move during this time.

PISCES RISING OR MOON:
Rahu Transiting: 5th House
Ketu Transiting: 11th House

If Rahu is unaffected in transit or in your natal chart or positively impacted by benefits like Jupiter, Mercury and Venus, then this transit could bring in new romance particularly from a foreign partner. You may be drawn to foreign entertainment and foreign movies.

Investments may be up but be careful as Rahu can take them away quickly. Good time for spiritual reading. If you desire children or new pets, consider planning this carefully. This is the time to put your creative stamp on the world. If you have let some creative hobbies fall by the wayside, then take them back up. They could generate an extra source of income for you.

If Rahu is afflicted in transit or in your natal chart or positively impacted by malefic like Saturn, Mars, Ketu and the Sun, then this transit could lead to difficulties with romance and family planning. Problems with investment might arise or children may become rebellious. You mind may seem clouded by shadow and doubts about your spiritual practices may arise. You will have many ideas and can even become obsessed with. You may feel rebellious against others and their expectations of you as a result of this transit. Mentally you may suffer from increased agony and confusion. Your decision-making skill may go haywire making you get carried away to make the wrong decision.

If Ketu is unaffected in transit or your natal chart or associated with benefits like Jupiter, Mercury and Venus, then there will be a desire to consider new money ventures that increase your income. This is a time to meet new people and make new friends.

If Ketu is afflicted in transit or by malefic natal chart associations, you may have friends that suddenly leave or for whom you find that you no longer have anything in common. Beware of friends that drain your energy or are too needy. In general, friends can disappoint you during this transit. Make sure to save money, as cash flow could be erratic. There could be disappointments with elder siblings or they are under stress and strain. Find a routine, as activity could be erratic and random. Stay on top of checking out new ventures.

You will have many ideas and can even become obsessed with them as Rahu is transiting the fifth house. This house is the house of the mind and one of the Dharma houses. It is also the house of Poorvapunya (previous good deeds from past lives) and this transit could unlock the rewards depending on whether you have been naughty or nice…This is the time to put your creative stamp on the world. If you have let some creative hobbies fall by the wayside, then take them back up. They could generate an extra source of income for you. You may feel rebellious against others and their expectations of you as a result of this transit. Friends may fall away because you no longer have anything in common. Beware of friends that drain your energy or are too needy. In general, friends can disappoint you during this transit. Single Aries will have more opportunities for meeting new dating prospects. There will be more passion and romance during this transit. The fifth house is a house that rules over love affairs and courtship. There could be the birth of a new baby.

During this period, Rahu will move through your fifth house from the natal Moon. This signifies grief, especially due to matters related to your children. Financially this may not be regarded as a good time for you. Hold tight to your finances, as it is likely to be spent on unnecessary purchases. Health of your parents and spouse may become a cause of concern, as they are susceptible to developing diseases.

Matters related to your children may worry you more during this particular phase which is termed as the period of Putra Dosha meaning sorrow related to your son. Attend to any health problem of your children that may come up during this time. Some of you may even find your children going astray or developing some serious ailments. Mentally you may suffer from increased agony and confusion. Your decision-making skill may go haywire making you get carried away to make the wrong decision.

Special thanks to Komilla Sutton and Bill Levacy for their insights with these transits.

2018 RAHU ASPECTS

Rahu, the North node, and planet of desire and ambition and shady dealings cast trinal aspects to other planets and also have a sneak 30-degree aspect that it casts onto Leo this year. Below are some of the major Rahu aspects this year but this list is far from complete. The degree of influence is 3-5 degrees for these energies so watch 2-3 days before and after the exact true node conjunctions listed below. (Special thanks to Komilla Sutton, Prash Trivedi and Manik Jain for their insights on nodal aspects)

Rahu exact aspect to Mars in Scorpio at 20.45 degrees February 19
Rahu will aspect Mars in Scorpio on **February 19th** at 20.45 degrees at 18:25 EDT from his house in Cancer. Generally, there will be a lot of energy to accomplish actions by taking an unusual approach, but you will need to be watchful of angry, vindictive and possibly antagonistic people, especially family members. Quick outbursts could lead to feverish fights and cause angry feelings.

One a positive note, look for real estate or take out loans if you need them as the energies are up and continue with your education pursuits and family responsibilities. This is a good time to buy new clothes, accessorize your home or buy a new car.

Family issues or problems with your mother could cause stress at this time and test your patience. Diplomacy could be low and cause overall agitation and worry so be careful not to get into family spats.

This would be good time to update insurance policies on your home and car.

With Rahu, the toxic planet, spending time in Cancer, the natural 4th house of home and family, it's a good idea to be extra careful about being "*Spic and Span*" clean as mold, bacteria, insects and other rodent infestations is Rahu's specialty and with Mars, as a malefic adding energy to this conjunction transit — be prepared, otherwise, impurities in the body can build up (skin afflictions, allergies and other inflammatory conditions). So, take precautions and be mindful of your health.

Be careful when driving and check the electricity, chemical, and other toxic build up in your home. It's a good time to fix anything that's broken and be sure to check your fire alarms, carbon monoxide and fire extinguishers. Might be a good idea to add floodwater alarms in your basement too! If you have water filters on your faucets or hooked up to your refrigerators be sure to change those as well as, the filters in your vacuum cleaners and heating and cooling systems.

If you have air purifiers or filtration systems, now is the time to clean them. It's amazing what a carpet can hold — debris from regular foot traffic, pets, kids...it's a good time to call in the professionals for a cleaning!

Rahu trine Venus in Pisces at 20.19 degrees on March 18

Rahu sends a friendly aspect wave to Venus on **March 18th** as she sits in the liberation house of Pisces. This is a transit of fullness of love and prosperity.

Venus is very happy in her place of exaltation and this transit brings with it the promotion of all-good in one's affairs, expanded pleasures, and a focus on women's issues. These heightened and expanded feelings, albeit with a shadowy tint from Rahu, will entice one towards unique and unconventional practices in the areas of spirituality and healing. This is a good time for self-care and seeking out unique ways to recover from stress. You might look into learning alternate or holistic therapies such as Reiki, energy and chakra healing, acupuncture treatments, or Chinese needling or discovering a different spiritual path.

Now is a great time to be selfless, carefree and to offer your services to others by volunteering your time in spiritual havens, educational institutes, and other charitable organizations.

Rahu trine Sun in Pisces at 11.46 degrees on April 2nd
Rahu will exactly trine the Sun in Cancer on **April 2nd** and block the energy of the Sun. The expanded focus will be centered on feeling gloomy as Rahu sends his dark cloud over the Sun's house. This transit is about expansive, just action and feelings of frustration.

There may be job and residence changes, and the rebel may come out if there isn't a good explanation for the changes which may spark arguments, getting into debt, lack of regard and fear of losing one's freedom.

The health dangers with this expanded energy include leg ailments, liver complaints, nervousness, lung problems, and hip trouble. So, try to remain calm and practice meditation and other forms of stress relief.

It's best to try to find activities to cheer your mood and do things that you enjoy. Seek out the company of good friends or lay low and keep your head down until the transit passes. Keep a positive attitude and be fair, knowing that this storm will pass, and the Sun will shine again!

Rahu exact conjunction Mercury in Cancer at 11.54 degrees July 3
Rahu and friend Mercury will be in exact conjunction on **July 3rd** thinking unusual thoughts, so the mind may be drawn to connections with foreign lands or could get cloudy when the pressure is on and starts to feel anxious and confused. At worst this could lead to criminal tendencies.

A mostly positive transit, it is a great time to focus on knowledge oriented towards spiritual pursuits and enlightenment. It's possible that you may find yourself interested in spiritual, charitable, or other service and health-oriented organizations that involve some self-sacrifice.

The mind is unbounded in this transit and it would be a good time to learn about philosophy or visit a faraway place or pursue education.

Rahu (30°) aspect Mercury in Leo at 11.13 degrees **September** Rahu will be sending his friend Mercury, in the sign of Aries, a small aspect wave during this **September** transit and will be a bit challenging as the mind will be more critical and worried over little things and it will be hard to please people.

There are too many details to attend to and you may find that you get into arguments and disagreements with micromanagers if tasks take too long. This is a 'mentally overworked' transit where the mind goes into hyper-drive and it's just too fast for Mercury to contain so be careful of anxiety and nervous disorders such as panic attacks and problems with respiration.

Try to stay calm and remember that Mercury transits are fairly quick, and this too shall pass. You are not your thoughts, or your emotions and you have the ability to step back, breathe and simply be a 'witness' to the events that are happening around you. Be in the eye of the storm and not the storm itself.

Spiritual practices such as prana breathing, and meditation will be very beneficial during this transit. Be sure to get plenty of rest and stay away from depressive news media and spicy foods because they will be more 'active' and stimulating.

Think about ways to focus on relaxation such a reading a good book, getting a massage, exercise such as stretching or yoga, or visiting with a positive, uplifting friend. Go take your dog or a neighbor's dog for a walk. Pet your cat. Studies have shown that spending time with animals reduces stress and blood pressure.

Or go volunteer to reduce your stress as a way of being in selfless service of someone else can alleviate the thoughts running in the 'monkey mind' and lifts not only your spirits but of the people that you're helping. It's a WIN-WIN!

Rahu (120° trine) aspect Mercury in Scorpio at 6.30 degrees **October 31**
Rahu (120° trine) aspect Mercury (R) in Scorpio at 3.36 degrees **December 4**
Rahu (120° trine) aspect Mercury in Scorpio at 3.12 degrees **December 7**
Rahu is sending Mercury a friendly wave in aspect during these transit points over the last quarter of **2018** and will bring imaginative feelings to the forefront as we become more inspired to learn through books and lectures.

Mercury is interested in knowledge and education in philosophical pursuits by using creative imagination and being cheerfully devoted to family and loved ones, especially the Mother and that will be the focus here.

It's a good time to focus on agriculture, research, teaching, music, science, languages and intellectual pursuits with humor, kindness and consideration. People that work from home will also do well during this time.

If you are considering or would like to start a home-based business, now is a great time to get started! Network marketing or Multi-level (MLM) marketing businesses should flourish at this time and we are entering the holiday season of merriment and socializing, which both Mercury and Rahu loves - so be like them and go out, be seen! 'Warm chatter' people and make new friends! You never know whom you may connect with and what new ventures may grow from that connection.

Jupiter's conjunct and expansive influence will be with Mercury on **October 31st** and is a good time for learning and sight. It's favorable for publishing, hosting seminars, classes, children's education, music, dance, art and general wisdom in business.

One caveat is that Mercury will be Retrograde on **December 4th** and that means more inward reflection, so this would be a good time to dream. Even though there will be some disruption in thoughts with depressed feelings and shadowed emotions, this is a great time to get out those journals and write!

Put disjointed thoughts down on paper and start thinking about what you would like to learn about or pursue focus on in business and communication. Write down your sad thoughts, happy thoughts, and foreign or unusual thoughts. These is a 'mind-dump' for you so you can get clear on goals or clean out the spaces of your mind.

Some ideas to spark your journaling: What's your value statement? What's your mission? Reflect on the last 3 quarters of **2018**. What went well? Where could you have improved? What did you learn? Are there insights that you can carry forward into the last quarter of **2018** to help propel you into a stunning **2019**?

Start thinking about what has worked for you during the past year and what has not worked. Know that you're still a winner with the knowledge you've gained from your experiences and take that gain into your new adventures and pursuits when Mercury goes direct.

Don't be afraid to try new things or pursue new, innovative ideas in usual ways as you have Rahu and Mercury spurring you on with the forthcoming aspect transits.

Great things can happen when one imagines and steps outside of the box. It may be a bit disorienting at first but sometimes it takes innovation and making great changes to lead to the breakthroughs that Rahu promises!

Rahu exact conjunction Venus in Cancer at 12.25 on June 19

Rahu is conjunct to Venus in Cancer during this transit and it's all about love out of the ordinary for these two planets! This is a great time of disposition in beauty and love where there will be a lot of skill in relation to others in a charming and artistic way.

People will be drawn to the comforts of wealth and enjoying pleasures from good finances so naturally; this good fortune (a welcome event!) will be an expansion in seductive and persuasive sensuality. It's all about pleasing, devotion and being friendly. Sounds like a great time to plan a party so get together with your friends and loved ones — enjoy some good food and fine wine! Laugh, love and be joyful!

Venus will be over-beaming with joy, so this would be a great time to throw that graduation, bridal shower, baby shower, or wedding party. Have Rahu join the fun and throw an unconventional Alice-in-Wonderland Summer Un-Birthday party for yourself or your friends! It's a great time to socialize and enjoy life!

Rahu aspect Venus in Leo at 11.46 degrees on July 15

Rahu sends a brief and friendly aspect wave to Venus on **July 15th** as she sits in the royal house of Leo. This is a transit that promotes business acuity, companionship, fun-loving connections, games, entertainment, athletics and amusements as well as romance, loves and children.

Earnings through art and works before the public should do well.

With the expansion of Rahu's wave and Venus's natural conflict with Leo's lord, the Sun, passions could turn to arguments, one could fall in love too fast, and poor business activities and decisions could be made during this transit. So be careful not to act too quickly.

Be mindful of becoming complacent, self-absorbed, and conceited.

This should be a good time for women and all things related to the feminine.

Rahu conjunction Sun in Cancer at 11.46 degrees on July 28

Rahu will exactly conjunct Sun in Cancer on **July 28th** and block the energy of the Sun. The expanded focus will be on personal issues related to the family, home and mother. You may find yourself at cross-purposes between your wants and those of your family in this push-pull dynamic. The energy levels are higher now and the impulse to take action will be aggressive to get things done so go ahead and tackle those things that take more effort to get done but know that this is not be a great time for diplomacy, so sparks may fly while you're rushing around marking tasks off your to-do list.

Feelings of anger coupled with selfish impulses is the highlight here so be careful of rushing ahead with too much steam and landing into an accident, especially if you're out driving, biking or walking on or near the streets.

The danger with this expanded energy of the Sun is headaches and heartaches so be careful and if you get overheated try to cool down or better yet, keep a cool head and you'll make it through this difficult transit just fine!

Rahu aspect Sun in Leo at 11.30 degrees on August 28
Rahu sends a small wave aspect to his enemy the Sun, who is in his own sign of Leo on **August 28th**. Sun is very happy in the realm of his kingdom, the royal house and only receiving a small, venomous aspect from shadowy Rahu so the push-pull dynamic on relationships will not be as prominent as felt on **July 28th**.

The Sun king is back on his throne and holding court and has the courage and focus of the Lion to handle any issues such health, career or individual with authority and conscious dignity. So be bold, have grace and use your wise intellect to handle anything that comes at you during this transit and you'll come out shining!

Rahu aspect Sun in Scorpio in at degrees on November 20
Rahu aspects Sun in the sign of Scorpio on **November 20th** and this transit will lead to an expansion of liberation. So now is a good time to take a long trip to a foreign place or go on a spiritual meditation retreat, as anything you dive deep into should be more effective for healing and emotional release. Jupiter's' conjunct energy with Sun helps to uplift here and gives added expansive energy to this transit.

Now is also a good time to enjoy intimate pleasures with your mate or go for a health check. Be charitable and pay off some of your debts.

Some old emotional feelings may start to surface from the depths and bring with them feelings of loss. These old issues are coming to the surface for healing and release. Allow them to come and see them for what they are — simply "*old stuff*" that needs to be felt and acknowledged.

Once these shadowy illusions of the past rise up in the air like wisps of smoke, just let them fade away. Bid them farewell by being a good witness to them and with humility, thank them for their lessons, acknowledge them and know that they will pass to the ethers and leave you in peace.

You are not your ego or your emotions. You can choose to release, let go and allow room for light to flow in and take up residence in the space that the shadows vacated.

Sleep and sexual activities might be disrupted at this time so be prepared to shake off any gloominess by engaging in positive activities. Eating good, quality foods and exercise such as gentle stretches, yoga and breath work should help alleviate any anxiety. Gentle, herbal sleep aid teas (Celestial Seasonings, Traditional Medicinal Tea and Yogi Tea are nice brands) may help if you have trouble falling asleep.

Don't isolate yourself. Resist the urge to spend too much on new activities that will be less fruitful if you start them at this time, as it's best to wait until this transit passes.

Rahu exact trine Jupiter in Scorpio at 5.41 degrees on November 7
Rahu will exactly aspect Jupiter in Scorpio on **November 7** and bring with it the expansive disposition to know the wise thing to do to find opportunities for growth. This is a good time to learn and take comfort in knowing that you will be able to stay up to date with any changes.

There is a strong sense of self-purpose with an interest in transcendental knowledge. It's a good time to travel to exotic places as you may discover something knew that leads to higher, spiritual knowledge.

There may be new and unusual approaches to the practices of law, education and philosophy that are expansive. It's a good time to publish esoteric works.

Special thanks to Jamie Bateman for compiling this list and to Komilla Sutton for her excellent insights into nodal aspects.

KETU IN SHRAVANA: SPIRITUAL AWAKENING AND MATERIAL CONFLICTS

December 2nd, 2017 - September 24, 2018

In the true node system, Ketu went into the Shravana (Capricorn 10-23.20) on **December 2nd, 2017** and stays there until **September 24th**. Modern astronomers say this constellation consists of 3 stars, Altair, Alshain and Tarazed and that myth logically correspond to the three steps taken by Vishnu. Prash Trivedi notes that the translation of Shravana is "*hearing*" or "*the one who limps.*" It is sometimes connected to the Pipal tree and the sacred tree where Buddha received enlightenment. This constellation is often connected to a trident or an ear and its symbol is to listen and if planets are strong in this constellation it means that one has to learn to be a good listener or to listen to one's inner voice.

Ketu is a very spiritual planet and Shravana is a very spiritual constellation. Any of the nodes in Shravana means the snake deity has obtained the blessings from God Vishnu and since it is the snake, which Vishnu is reclining on, the snake is carrying spiritual power on top of its body. Ketu in Shravana supports intuition and silence and meditation and one has to listen carefully to follow one's intuition. This constellation is very much connected to Vishnu and one who crosses the heights and supports moving beyond ones' capabilities. In a sense, this supports the business and ambitious side of Capricorn, which is at odds with Ketu's very spiritual desire to leave the world. So, a good time to tap in and develop your spiritual energies with this transit and to learn to trust your intuition and not get caught up in the intellect with Rahu on the opposite side in Ashlesha which is governed by the logical Mercury.

With Saturn in Ketu's nakshatra of Mula (Sagittarius 0-13.20) there is a deep connect between Saturn and Ketu until **March 3** and again between **June 3rd** and **September 24th**. These connections can bring up a search to crystallize past life issues and bring up challenges so that you can grow and move beyond them. There is a conflict here as Ketu brings past knowledge, but Saturn wants to deal with it in the present in a very practical and concrete way. Ketu wants to leave the material world, but Saturn wants you to live practically in the materially world. Ketu may want you to leave your job or your work place or rebel against the government and Saturn will hold your feet to the coals and live in the everyday work world. There is a great conflict and it is like balancing oneself on a bicycle to live in both worlds but ultimately it can be done with regularly spiritual practice and turning your work-life into a discipline and realizing that it supports your spiritual life. Meditation gives the ability to be dynamic in action and our paycheck supports going on spiritual retreats to advances our spiritual knowledge.

Since the owner of Shravana, the moon, moves so quickly every 2.5 days, the impact on Ketu can vary greatly. When the moon is weak in Scorpio and Saturn ruled signs or badly afflicted, this transit could lead to excessive generosity leading to debts or being unable to move out of poverty. One might get too caught up in ethical dogma and create enemies. When the moon is strong like in Taurus or Leo or Libra, it can create cordial business relationships, success with foreign countries, and love of the scriptures, being drawn to humanitarian causes. Still with Saturn being the underlying ruler and being placed 12 houses from Capricorn, the darker and more challenging energies of this constellation will come up more.

According to Prash Trivedi, people born with this constellation tend to be peaceful and persevering even if sometimes stubborn, but they like to complete their tasks. They are gentle, kind, amicable and liberal-minded and reasonable. Its darker side can lead to naïveté in falling prey to deception and bad advice. Still this group of stars is a wonderful combination of business skills and at the same time a softness that puts people at ease.

Special thanks to Komilla Sutton and Prash Trivedi for their guidance on this constellation. I always stand humbly on the shoulders of my great teachers.

2018 PLANETS CONJUNCT KETU

Sun conjunct Ketu in Capricorn: February 3rd
The Sun is conjunct Ketu on **Saturday, February 3rd** using the true node system. Sun and Ketu are both fiery planets and their conjunct will increase that element. This transit brings up a lot of rajasic energy, which creates a lot of fiery energy to want to change everything. There is not enough calming satvic energy to keep one balanced. One may want to fly off the handle in all directions or lash out at a boss, supervisor or loved one if you cannot reign in this energy.

Drink coconut water or coconut milk to calm the fire. Channel the energy into exercise, drink calming herbal teas and stay away from spicy food, which will fan the flames. Find ways to ground yourself with gentle yoga, long walks in cool woods or being near more water.

Leo, Pisces and Cancer rising, or moon signs may be more vulnerable because the transit is happening in the Leo (5th), Cancer (4th) and Pisces (10th) houses.

Again, charts are very individual, and I do not ever want to stereotype people by sign but sometimes it's a way of putting one's finger right away on a core problem for the person's entire life.

Mars conjunct Ketu in Capricorn: **June 8th**
Mars conjunct Ketu in Capricorn: **July 20th**
Mars conjunct Ketu in Capricorn: **September 26th**

If you watch small kids in a playground, they get angry, fully express it and then go back to being normal. Anger is a natural emotion that is often an expression of an unfulfilled desire. Kids are great about it but we tend to repress our anger until it explodes and that is dangerous. Mars will approach Ketu in Capricorn and they will be conjunct on three occasions in **2018**.

On the highest level, the Mars/Ketu conjunctions encourage us to express the multifaceted spiritual warrior in career when in the sign of Capricorn and when they are frustrated or blocked, it can lead to anger and vindictiveness. As I have said before, use the anger to do charity work and channel the energy into positive, social service rather than raging at things that you cannot control.

This conjunction challenges us to use cleverness and skills of flexibility to adapt to changing and challenging circumstances. This transit supports being an active leader who is not afraid to innovate and pursue goals. Self-sufficiency is key here, as this transit supports mathematics and engineering so time to go deep into invention mode.

For Scorpio and Aries rising, it will foster spiritual experience and intuition, as Ketu is the most spiritual planet. It's time for a meditation retreat or extra spiritual practice. Other activities may be frustrating.

Overall, this conjunction is very difficult for the planet and is a signature for violence and terrorism. The race riots in St. Louis and in Milwaukee a few years ago were recent examples of Mars/Ketu aspects. 9/11 also happened during a Mars/Ketu conjunction in Sagittarius.

Find another way to express your feelings. Write letters, do posts on Facebook or call your Congressperson. In the extreme, this aspect can lead to accidents, fires, burns and explosions if the energy is not released. Be careful around your home and when driving.

The bright side of the conjunction of Mars is that it forces us to face our unconscious fears and repressed angers, so we can look at and transform them. Capricorns and Cancers need to find an outlook to unlock pent-up anger or it will explode. Exercise and healthy competition is one way to let it out.

Usually yoga and exercise are good to get things moving but be gentle on yourself as too much activity will increase the air element or vata and create more anxiety. Also, just use the Nike slogan, "*Just Do It*," to get moving as Mars/Ketu can create very sluggish and lazy energy, making it hard to get started.

Capricorns, Cancers, Scorpios, Aries, Pisces and Leos will probably be most affected by the transit and people having key planets at Cancer 07-18/Capricorn 07-18 will be affected most as will people running Mars/Ketu periods or Ketu/Mars periods. If you are running those periods and they are connected to difficult houses in the 4th, 5th, or 8th, houses then be particularly careful driving. Otherwise, nothing will get triggered. I am not here to frighten you, but rather suggesting that you be alert.

Anyway, like Forrest Gump reminds us, life is a box of chocolates: there are some with sweet cream fillings and some with hard nuts that you have to chew carefully. Express your emotions in a healthy manner and do not let anyone steal your joy. Help others and donate to your favorite charities.

Mercury conjunct Ketu Capricorn: February 9th
Mercury is conjunct Ketu on **Friday, February 9th** using the true node system. Mercury and Ketu are planets with fire and air elemental combinations and their conjunction will increase the energy of fire, making thoughts either sublime or erratic. This transit brings up a lot of quick shifts in thinking with spiritual undertones.

Thoughts may be subtle and highly intuitive during this transit so pay attention to those little hints and 'ah-ha' moments! This will be a good time to focus on spiritual and philosophical pursuits in career, hobbies and writing. It's also a good time to go on a pilgrimage or meditation retreat.

Be thoughtful, discriminating and seek first to understand any new occupation that you undertake in order to avoid losing your mental stability.

Venus conjunct Ketu in Capricorn January 27 - February 1
When Venus is afflicted in Capricorn, it can create delays or setbacks in relationships, love for lost causes, unconventional relationships, reproductive complications, sexual imbalances and dysfunctional partners. If you have this in your natal chart or have Venus conjunct Ketu or Mars in your natal chart or are running a Venus/Rahu or Venus/Ketu or Venus/Mars period or some combination like that you might feel this transit more intensely.

Venus will transit within 3 degrees of Ketu the South node, the fiery and spiritual monkish planet, **January 27 - February 1st**. If you were born with this combination, it can create unresolved past life relationships that are unhappy or painful.

You may attract spiritual or emotional partners with a lot of baggage and you may change partners frequently or may reject partners for fear of being rejected yourself.

If you are male, you may choose women are unconventional and that society may reject from another class, race or religion or gender orientation-causing problems. In any case if you have this signature in your natal chart it may bring up unorthodox and complicated relationships and with Mars in Scorpio often, there may be a lot of passion or quarrels.

If you are a revolving door relationship person, use this month to go deeper and hang in there instead of rejecting.

For Virgo rising, the Ketu transit conjunct Venus may foster deep spiritual experiences or romances or adventures as it is a 5th house transit of the chart lord.

For Aries rising, it will bring up unexpected problems in the workplace. Those running a Venus maha dasha will feel it more strongly.

Pisces rising will benefit from income and Libra rising may have expenditures around the home and vehicles and more domestic quarrels. Aquarius rising may have passionate sexual experiences while Gemini rising may have big problems with deep karmic issues from the past. Capricorn rising will feel a bit lighter for having the transit of a good friend visiting and creating deeper connections and may increase the desire for new and unconventional clothes. Taurus will have deep spiritual experiences or go on luxury trips to foreign lands and Leos will have to watch illness related to the reproductive area, kidneys or bladder or pancreas. Again, all of this is very individual to the larger cycles that you are running.

THE SNAKE IN TIME: KALA SARPA YOGA IN TRANSIT 2018

January 4, 2018 - January 16, 2018
August 10, 2018 - August 24, 2018
September 7, 2018 - September 20, 2018
October 4, 2018 - October 19, 2018

Kala Sarpa yoga is when Rahu and Ketu contain all the planets between them inclusively in the zodiac and when Rahu and Ketu are in moveable signs like Cancer, Capricorn, Aries and Libra. But a single planet going out of the axis negates it. So, until **February 3rd**, whenever the moon is between Cancer and Capricorn all the planets are hemmed in between Rahu in Cancer and Ketu in Capricorn. The yoga is broken when the moon goes into Aquarius and until it gets to Rahu in Cancer every two weeks.

This yoga will continue until the Sun transits past Ketu after **February 3rd**. While not normally included, Pluto and Neptune are also part of this combination and only Uranus in Aries is out of the snake "*biting its own tail*" configuration. It will happen again in **2018** and probably 1 or 2 times in **2019** before Saturn transits past Ketu in Sagittarius.

Kala Sarpa Yoga is controversial because it is not included in the traditional Vedic literature. Raman thinks it is very important in mundane astrology but that it does not impact people as much. My experience is that it can create great intensity in people and in the world with too much solar energy. Prash Trivedi thinks there is a messy imbalance of solar and lunar energies that create either aggressiveness or passivity.

The energies during **September 2018** and **December 2018** seemed rather hostile and intense. People I know with this configuration tend to be aggressive.

Kal means time and Sarpa means snake. The yoga or special planetary combination refers to the subconscious caught in its rope of karma, unable to pull free. This creates a psychological impact of being caught in destiny — kind of like wanting to desperately wake up from a nightmare. This analogy falls short but suffice it to say that a lot of intense events keep happening and it's hard to prevent them from manifesting.

If you have this combination in your natal chart, it could be felt strongly through the early **February** transit and particularly if you are running Rahu or Ketu periods on the first few levels of your dashas. Some people may not notice it at all. The impact of this yoga is not felt as much once Rahu matures around the age of 44.

The karmic access involved depends on what houses Cancer and Capricorn represent in your life. For example, if you are Libra rising, then the 4th house of mother and home is impacted, as well as, the 10th house of career and status. If you are Cancer rising, then marriage may be impacted with the 1st and 7th nodal axis. There are mitigating factors impacting the natal chart if the house lords are strong and well placed.

The bright side of this yoga is that it can make people industrious, hardworking and aware of one's talents despite continual restlessness. Still with the wrong placement it can lead to betrayals from friends and relatives if the 2nd and 11th houses are impacted, which would be the case for Gemini rising or Virgo rising. Again, the transits will trigger the yoga particularly if you are born with this combination in your natal chart and you are running a Rahu or Ketu period.

Many will not notice it but it is still an intense time for the world. Most mundane astrologers note that major events happen during this transit and now we have the Middle East war tensions bubbling up with the Jerusalem capital issue. This yoga will fuel violence with the snake likely intensifying the situation.

The Rahu/Ketu emphasis from Cancer/Capricorn will also favor rises in mundane matters and will greatly affect the political scene. The Capricorn urge to get out in the world and work hard to gain status will be a huge focal point for everyone challenging the natural 4th house of Cancer, where home and security are strained by the natural disasters and most recently, the California fires where so many have been displaced and are facing insecurities around housing security and safety. Continue to open your pocket books to help those impacted by these natural disasters in the spirit of seva.

The bright side of this yoga is discussed by my friend, Juliana Swanson of Astral-Harmony when she writes about it:

"This combination can tend to remind us of what is missing in our lives, that which is needed to find more harmony and balance. This dynamic can have an all or nothing flavor to it. Key words are 'intense, sensitive, extreme, fixated or obsessive'."

Again, donate and help people in need, do your spiritual practices and turn to spirituality during this time. This yoga can be a wake-up call that all the material success or frustration cannot satisfy the intense longing for the Divine and it could propel you deeper in your search and that is ultimately a good thing. For consultations on the impact of this on your chart, sign up on the request form at Applied Vedic Astrology or visit: http://www.appliedvedicastrology.com/

Special thanks to Komilla Sutton and B. V. Raman and Juliana Swanson for their discourses on this subject

2018 SAGITTARIUS AND PISCES: TRANSITS OF JUPITER BY RISING SIGN OR MOON SIGN

In Vedic astrology transits are often counted from the Moon because they impact the mind and emotions the most, but I find that transits from the ascendant are better at predicting material existence and even transits from the Sun should not be ignored for their impact on career and the material world.

When malefics like Saturn, Mars, Rahu and Ketu reside in Libra or aspect Libra in your natal chart or when they impact Libra in transit, as Mars will do so **November 30 - January 17th**, then the darker side of the transit may manifest.

Uranus continues to aspect Libra all year and exactly into **September 27th**. Uranus gaze at Jupiter is a bit annoying and disruptive but it may prevent your life from becoming too static and if you go with it, it will help you be truly alive!

This transit will force you to release yourself from obligations that have limited you in the past. It could create a sudden break from a job or relationship that might generate a great sense of freedom! Release yourself from obligatory relationships that are no longer serving you and move on!

Of course, all transits are subsumed by the dasha period that we are running and other natal chart influences, but this is a general guide and may be helpful.

Aries Rising or Moon
This could be a favorable year for new business partnerships, the call for a marriage, or some good work travel that will benefit you. Rely on diplomacy to be successful. With the Uranus aspect, you might explode and release a bad or obligatory relationship and bring new freedom to your life.

When afflicted, there is a lot of waffling back and forth before big decisions are made in connection with partnership. Finish your business transactions and do not leave a lot of loose ends. Don't delay in making trips and find a way to be decisive about mates so get good advice from a professional.

Taurus Rising or Moon
This year could create a lot of wisdom about being of service and get your health together if you are disciplined. If there are legal messes in progress, they may finally go your way. Focus on getting your health together with good diets and exercise and routines.

Libra governs kidneys, hips, ovaries, and lower back, and if afflicted, problems with diabetes and STD's may occur so you'll want to be watchful of your health in those areas. If you are lucky, a great doctor may appear to finally help you with any health-related issues. Be frugal with financial matters and watch your children's health and make sure they are disciplined with diet.

Gemini Rising or Moon
Jupiter is transiting your 5th house enhancing romance, children, creativity and spiritual initiations so go on that spiritual retreat and get on match.com if you are looking a romantic partner. Classically, Jupiter transiting the 5th house can also bring children so if you want to get pregnant, the gods may offer support this year. It's a good time to grow investments.

If Libra is afflicted by malefics in your natal chart, be careful with investments, and make sure you are not neglecting your children. Be discriminating while getting into a new romance to prevent a broken heart as over-optimism could lead to making bad decisions.

Cancer Rising or Moon
This is a good year to continue your education, buy a new home or remodel it, get a new car or mend relationships with your mother. Good time to heal family wounds.

If Libra is afflicted by malefics in your natal chart, then be careful with home repairs, make sure you get a good contractor and do not delay doing something needed. Be mindful of maintenance of your car. Work on your family relationships and be particularly kind to your mother.

Leo Rising or Moon
This is a good year for writing, self-expression, and acting, speaking and taking up a new musical instrument. It's a good time for marketing and enjoying new neighbors or spending time with your younger siblings.

Ideally, Jupiter in Libra transiting the 3rd House would enable you to undertake beautiful new projects involving communication — a new blog, book, or album.

If Libra is afflicted in your natal chart, you might be lazy about starting new projects. Younger siblings might have problems and may require financial assistance but make sure you have a clear plan to get repaid.

Virgo Rising or Moon
This year is a time to focus on increasing money, wealth and assets. It may be a good time to buy gems and jewelry. It's a good year for expanding and healing family and doing consulting work. Remember that Jupiter represents increases as well as excesses.

If afflicted than do not be careless with money or over-spending on luxuries or over-eating. Does something here need to be re-balanced?

Libra Rising or Moon
This transit deals with expansion of the Self. If you do not have any malefic planets like Mars/Rahu or Saturn in the 1st, this transit creates optimism, comfort, and confidence. Your energy will be on the upswing! Good opportunities in business partnership and relationships should come your way and your health should be stronger. You may be attracted to personal philosophies and new wisdom as well as being drawn to doing teaching, coaching or consulting.

If you have malefics in Libra or aspecting Libra, then be careful of being falsely optimistic without checking out the facts. Do not neglect responsibilities and avoid being lazy or over-extravagant. You may have problems with weight gain if you eat too much so cut down on the sweets.

Scorpio Rising or Moon
This is a 12th transit of Jupiter and if there are no afflictions to Libra by malefics, you may reexamine a quest for enlightenment or desire to go on a spiritual pilgrimage to India, Peru or a spiritual country. This is a good time to take a spiritual retreat, perform sea or service work, donate to charities and engage in work that is a surrendering-like sacrificial activity such as devotion to your children.

It's a good year to spend at the ashram if you are drawn to such work. Jupiter may support you in overcoming secret enemies, seeing your blind spots or overcoming debts and enemies. It's a good time for counseling and unwrapping deep layers of the psyche.

If Libra is afflicted by natal malefics aspecting or in your 12th house, you may be worried about doing too much service work and getting exhausted. You may be subject to unexpected expenses, or fines. Deep subconscious patterns may be coming up to heal but if you are not able to deal with them, avoid your addictions or sexual obsessions.

Sagittarius Rising or Moon
This is a good year for Jupiter if it is not afflicted, as support from friends and groups will prosper. Cash flow should be better and it's a good year for fulfilling your desires and developing consciousness. This is a good time for networking as the support will be there. Jupiter owns Sagittarius, so an 11th house transit of the ascendant lord is particularly potent.

If Libra is afflicted by malefics, this is not a good time to lend money to elder siblings or friends unless it is a gift and you are not in a hurry to get it back. Malefic aspects to the 5th could lead to bad investments in get-rich-quick schemes so do your due-diligence and check things out carefully. Avoid overindulging and overspending.

Capricorn Rising or Moon
This is a 10th house transit of Jupiter and if unafflicted it will increase status in your life and be an opportunity to network with successful people and expand your position at

work. You may find an increased appreciation for your work and it will be a good time to take up teaching, coaching and consulting. Take time to evaluate your work/life, home/work balance to make sure it does not get out of control.

If Libra is afflicted, your reputation may take a downward slide if you are not on top of your responsibilities. Do not get lazy or overly cautious — jump at opportunities or they might pass you buy! Stay busy to avoid boredom.

Aquarius Rising or Moon
This transit brings knowledge, fortune, spiritual knowledge and love of travel. It's a good time to visit your father or Guru, or to teach and work on that book you want to publish. You are victorious in legal matters. It may be time to join a new spiritual group, a meditation circle or group at church.

Take time to make new spiritual connections that enrich your life.

If Libra is afflicted, watch your finances and avoid getting too lazy about spiritual practice. Pay more attention to your children and don't let opportunities to spend time in spiritual knowledge pass you by!

Pisces Rising or Moon
This could be a year where an unexpected positive windfall could come your way through inheritance, lottery or insurance. It is a great year for doing research and there is support to get through difficult health problems.

If Libra is afflicted in your natal chart by malefics, then there may be problems with financial support, particularly if you are not disciplined around these issues. Watch your children and keep them healthy to prevent illness. Stop being so hard on yourself and on your progress in life. Mental afflictions could be increased. If you get caught up in people pleasing and not expressing your truth, you might end up in limbo in the Never-never land of *"everything is FINE."*

JUPITER IN SWATI NAKSHATRA: LIBRA 6.40-19.59

RETROGRADE: JUNE 18 - JULY 10
DIRECT: JULY 10 - AUGUST 2

Jupiter retrogrades into the constellation of Arcturus on **June 18th**, which in the Vedic system is called Swati. That means it channels Rahus' energy from Cancer. Rahu and Jupiter associations are expansive and can bring great material gains, but it spoils Jupiter's' purist form and gets Jupiter too involved in material accumulation and happiness can be denied. It can also move one toward foreign philosophies and religion, create scandals with corrupt Gurus or teachers or put one in a religious fundamentalist environment. Given the problems with fundamentalism, we do not need more of this stirred up.

Jupiter is not at home in Swati in the enemy side of Libra and that means its profound wisdom can get lost in the commercialization of wisdom. Since Jupiter and Venus are enemies, too much emphasis for Libra and Aries rising signs may be on successful and material relationships at the cost of deep spiritual knowledge.

People born in Swati nakshatra have a very material pursuit in life ad Venus luxuriates in comfort and Rahu amplifies the desire for materialism. Swati's presiding deity is Vayu the God of wind. People born in this nakshatra are very loyal, intelligent, and fair and have the ability to serve. They have a very balanced personality. There are many rich people born in this nakshatra but after attaining wealth and comfort the person is not satisfied in life. They eventually get tired being pursuing materialistic pleasure.

2018 SAGITTARIUS AND PISCES RISING: JUPITER IN LIBRA

JUPITER IN LIBRA: SEPTEMBER 11 - OCTOBER 11
Jupiter in Libra: September 11th

Jupiter transits into Libra September 11th for 13 months until October 11, 2018.
Jupiter transits usually bring a shift in luck and grace to new areas of our life.
Jupiter always expands our experiences, our wisdom, and our understanding.
It represents optimism, growth, generosity, joy, and abundance. By moving into the air signs now, it will be trining and blessing Libra, Aquarius and Gemini in our life and whatever houses those signs are connected to.

What is the sign of Libra about? Wherever Libra falls in your chart in any rising or Varga chart, it brings blessings of prosperity and Lakshmi, the grace to end conflicts.

The Shakti of Venus is that if it can end conflict, bring prosperity, growth and fulfill desires by helping to distribute resources. Still the dark side is intense psychological brooding, particularly in Chitra (Libra 0-6.40) or Swati Nakshatras (Libra 6.40-19.59) where there is never happiness. Artistic creativity has to replace sexual energy for balance to prevail here. Libra always wants to do everything together, so cooperation is needed now to say "*Yes!*" to being in a relationship rather than going it alone.

Libra is the natural 7th sign of the zodiac so it supports all types of partnerships, romantic relationships and business partnerships. This gives us added skills to be diplomatic by working together with others and finding ways to harmonize towards peace. Let us hope this transit supports and melts international relationships with North Korea and other troubled areas of the world.

Libra supports business development and the scales of Libra are connected to the merchant scales of the Middle Ages when transactions were weighed before we had cash registers. Jupiter in Libra should support business expansion by bringing optimism. The downside of Jupiter/Venus associations is that we can be too optimistic and expansive and buy too much so you have to "*weigh*" your purchases carefully and leave your credit cards at home as the desire to shop will increase. This is generally good for economic expansion and for the United States, it is an 11th house transit of the ascendant lord so it should bring economic expansion for the United States this year. Rahu in Cancer also supports this, as **1999 - 2000** was an expansive time for the United States when the stock market first peaked.

Jupiter in Libra increases our desire to value people and relationships more. If your relationship is rocky, it may be time for counseling and going deeper into making things work. The wisdom of a good counselor will be particularly supportive over the next year. This is the time to be more compromising with your partner. The key to relationships is always saying, "*yes*" first, even if you disagree and then diplomatically backing out if you feel the ideas are not good. Go the extra mile with compromise and you will be rewarded. It's a good time to go to a counselor, as Libra is a very deep and psychologically intense. This sign loves delving into the depths of the psyche, particularly in the first two constellations. Still certain rising signs may experience more breakups while the energy for others will support more reconciliations and new pairings. The trick in achieving balance in relationships is always compromise, meeting people "*at their level*" and communication. Jupiter in Libra will support bringing out new depths in your relationships.

This is the time to take up painting, jewelry-making, fashion design, poetry or graphic design. Jupiter in Libra loves to create and enhance Jupiter's natural artistic abilities. Libra is connected to massage so if you have a desire to take up this art, go for it or just enjoy deep massages all year and they will seem extra powerful this year.

Jupiter in Libra is a time for business partnering so get into marketing and reach out to expand your business by developing new relationships. The energy will be there to provide synergy if you can find a way to mutually benefit each other. Get creative in thinking about how you can help the other business and it will come back to you.

Jupiter and Venus are the two Guru planets and they are enemies. Jupiter-ruled signs like Sagittarius and Pisces have to watch health issues with 6th and 11th house transits of the ascendant lord as over-indulgence in sensual pleasures can lead to getting out of balance.

That means avoid the extra piece of cheesecake at the party or undertaking too many one-night stands in any given week as energy could get depleted leading to health imbalances.

If you have Sun, Moon or your rising sign is an air sign, i.e., Gemini, Libra or Aquarius, you will feel an increase in optimism, joy and expansion! This is always welcome, particularly for the gloomy Aquarius. Still, the air signs will have to work on moderation, as too much over-eating could lead to gaining weight over the next year but with Saturn-like discipline, exercise will come to the rescue!

Find a way to partner harmoniously and diplomatically with Saturn. Avoid excessive spending and over-indulgence in the senses and explore the depths of your psyche to receive the blessings of Jupiter over the next year.
Of course, these articles are general and written for everyone. Jupiter in Libra will be different for every chart.

JUPITER IN VISHAKHA (Libra 20-Scorpio 3.20)
December 17, 2017 - June 17, 2018
August 3, 2018 - October 28, 2018

Jupiter transited into the constellation of Vishaka on **December 17th, 2017** and will stay there until **June 17, 2018**. Vishakha (20.00 Libra-3.20 Scorpio) is ruled by the deities Agni and Indra and is a constellation of four stars forming the left half of the scales of Libra. Agni has the ability to do Herculean talks to achieve its goals with great fiery energy and courage. Indra provides leadership but may create danger for those around one but may act cowardly at the first sign of danger. People born with this constellation are often seeking a bit of power, status and position.

Jupiter placed in this constellation in your natal chart will bring out counselors and advisors and makes them wise in worldly and spiritual matters. Jupiter will spend a long time in this constellation — almost 10 months — except when it retrogrades back into Swati for a few months, so it should be supportive for Vedic astrologers and advisors.

Prash Trivedi notes that the English word 'fixation' can best describe the essence of Vishakha, which is marked by concentration and single mindedness, although it can be affected by the nature of the goal it pursues. With the frequency of unwholesome goals, it is a concern for handling vices and people born in this constellation call easily fall prey to alcohol, drugs and sex. In essence, the Jupiter/Venus combination can bring in Vishakha natives that have an urge to throng the local bar and to engage in the sensual and material energies of life. There may be love parties, but this may lead to a sense of emptiness in their lives, which ideally should lead to searching for deeper spiritual meaning.

Vishaka is connected to outcasts, outsiders and rebels who do not follow traditional religious norms as one might think that Jupiter would. Hence, they often become artists, and unconventional people who want to change society.

Venus and Jupiter combinations are the best way to describe the mixed energy in Libra but because of the 3:20 degrees of the constellation overlap into Scorpio, it also brings in the Mars, Pluto and Ketu energies of higher spirituality. Jupiter transiting through the 1st Pada of Scorpio **October 11 - 26, 2019** will bring out a deeper spiritual energy as the excesses of partying, socializing and sensual gratification may become exhausting.

I suspect that this transit in **2018** will continue the rampant material excess that has overtaken the world with the stock market bubble and the Bitcoin craze. More sobering energy and spiritual awakening will come when Jupiter goes into Scorpio. For now, enjoy the party and your holiday gatherings that Jupiter in Vishaka will promote.

JUPITER IN SCORPIO: OCTOBER 11 - NOVEMBER 4, 2019

Jupiter enters Scorpio: October 11
Jupiter moves into Scorpio, **October 11, 2017**, and stays there about 13 months. Jupiter and Mars are friends with Ketu the secondary ruler of Scorpio, also doing well with Jupiter. Except for a trinal aspect from Rahu in Cancer to Scorpio between **late October** and **late November** within 3-5 degrees, and combustion by the Sun from **November 12 - December 9th**, Jupiter is relatively unafflicted except by a Mars opposition in **early May 2019**.

When Jupiter is unafflicted it brings out active, competent, articulate energies and finds opportunities for growth. It supports positive self-esteem, strong feelings and passions and interest in spiritual life. It's a good time for transforming your life and developing new patterns by diving deep into your soul.

When afflicted, which is mainly in the **late fall of 2018**, Jupiter may have trouble with debts, overindulgence, and being subject to criticism and legal problems. Problems with children may occur as well as losses in speculation. Attached to mistakes, Jupiter can be self-absorbed or may have trouble with doing the right and ethical thing. The Rahu aspect in **November 2018** is the most troubling for it.

Jupiter can have an expansive effect on Scorpio, the natural 8th sign of the zodiac and this can stir up a deeper interest in the occult and astrology but also may help support issues around abortion, Planned Parenthood and sexual freedom.

Jupiter in Scorpio can bring out more self-absorption as it may over-support Mars to be more sexual and career orientated. We cannot help but think of male film stars generating even more charisma when they walk into a party or pose in front of the cameras allowing the paparazzi to worship them. Thank of Leonardo DiCaprio in The Great Gatsby attracting incredible magnetic energy wherever he arrived. Scorpio rising may benefit from this mix and may create deep success for leading public meetings or teaching occult knowledge.

Scorpio can bring out scandals and Jupiter transiting through Scorpio may support more truth and ethical behavior. Even more scandals surrounding male dominated sexual predatory behaviors are likely to emerge. Corruption can be exposed. With Pluto, also being connected to Scorpio, when Jupiter is afflicted, it may create more cravings for power but when it is stronger, it will create a positive balance in this area. Jupiter can bring ethical action into the forum.

Jupiter is one of the expansive planets connected to speculation and with Jupiter in Libra, this area has gone out of control with Bitcoin and buying stocks. Probably even more risk-taking will develop with this transit until Jupiter and Saturn move toward conjunction in **2020**.

As the natural 8th house ruler, Scorpio rules joint ventures, shared assets and *"other people's money"* — loans, inheritances, royalties, commissions, debt and property ownership could all become hot issues.

Jupiter in Scorpio is also a great time to do retirement and estate planning, to build up your savings or to get a living will in order. You might consolidate your debt, cut up your credit cards or look for ways to get tax breaks through charitable giving. Mars is also connected to landed property, so we wonder if Jupiter going through Scorpio will not increase desire for more land during this transit.

Jupiter will help expose scandals around finances so maybe this transit will be the start of really exposing the mess that our bankers and politicians have gotten us into and this will certainly unravel in **2020**.

Still Jupiter's transit could bring legitimate ways of earning passive income through affiliate programs, commissions, royalties and other *"shared economy"* innovations.

The global pairing of Jupiter here with Scorpio, the natural 8th sign of the zodiac, is connected to certain infectious and contagious diseases and could create pressing world health issues. Since sexuality, blood work and reproductive health fall under Scorpio's domain, the Zika virus might become a more widespread health concern — or magnanimous Jupiter could illuminate breakthrough cures and vaccines!

Interestingly, Jupiter was also in Scorpio in late 1982 into 1983 when the AIDS crisis took hold. If we are fortunate, we may see inspiring advances in stem cell research or new cures for cancer, particularly lymphoma, leukemia, ovarian and prostate cancer.

Scorpio can be a bit adventurous by living on the edge and Jupiter will support daredevil events, mountain climbing, bungie jumping and wild things that guys like to do. If you do not have a strong Mars or are prone to accidents, then avoid those urges.

Still the natural 8th sign of the zodiac can lead to addiction if we cannot deal with the powerful psychological and sexual energy that it brings up. Be careful with addictive substances and obsessive pursuits, as you could be drawn to danger now. Jupiter can give us the Divine guidance to move through our addictive nature and vices so use this transit to build spiritual fortitude.

This is a great time to join a 12 Step Program if that is coming up for you. The drug crisis may also get some support.

Scorpio is also an intensely psychological sign and can bring up mental health issues at times for vulnerable people. Mental health issues might gain more attention and understanding during this cycle. Hopefully high-minded Jupiter will bring more education and awareness to these widespread struggles.

The highest aspect of Scorpio is spiritual development and transcendence. Jupiter in Scorpio will support mystical experience so it's a good time to take up more practice and dive deep! It can also lead to an intense interest the occult and life after death. Now would be a good time to pick up books by Elizabeth Kubler-Ross. In any case a time to dive deeply into all aspects of the natural 8th house and to transform your life.

NEPTUNE TRANSITS THE CONSTELLATION OF PEGASUS/PURVA BHADRAPADA
MARCH 18, 2018

I do not get to write about Neptune very often because it moves so slowly staying 14 years in a sign but it will go into the constellation of Purva Bhadrapada (Aquarius 20-Pisces 3.20) known by Western astronomers as Pegasus **March 18th, 2018**. The last time we had this transit was **March 1853 - April 1859**.

While the outer planets are not a traditional part of Vedic astrology, I find them important for understanding collective behavior and if they impact sensitive points in your chart within 2 degrees by transit or in your natal chart, they can be rather impactful.

As Dennis Harness has discussed, Narendra Desai saw an ancient Vasistha Nadi palm leaf in a museum in Madras, India, which predicted that three important grahas or planets would be discovered by the jyotishis of the Kali Yuga. The middle one, Varuna is known today as Neptune. "*Varuna is the lord of the cosmic waters and is associated with the mysterious laws of fate. He is a powerful, mystical healer and is the lord of Maya or illusion. Varuna is the bestower of spiritual wisdom and the god of cosmic medicines. This sounds strikingly similar to the role and meaning of Neptune, god of the mystical seas, in modern tropical astrology.*"

Neptune is now connected to Jupiter in this constellation in transit and is going to increase psychic and intuitive energies and spiritual idealism. With the positive connection to Jupiter through the nakshatra, it will promote idealism, universality, compassion and spiritual bypassing where we shirk reality and use religion and spirituality to escape our personal problems.

On the level of mundane astrology, Neptune is connected to schemes, inflation, conspiracies, grand governmental plans so everything will get bigger in scope for growth ideals in this constellation. Neptune can deflate these bubbles, but the high hopes of Neptune/Jupiter connections can inflate bubbles. We only have a small window for this until **July 11th** but then it returns with a bang between **March 2018 and January 2025**. It is also supportive for the film industry, raw cotton, medicine, surgical goods, tobacco, drugs, chemicals and perfumes.

Neptune also rules socialism, so the Bernie movement will probably come back strongly from **2018** onward but it also contributes to political instability as if we do not have enough of that!

Depending on the strength of Jupiter in transit over the coming years, it will negatively or positively impact. Jupiter in Virgo now seems relatively strong and is moving toward station on **June 9th** and its strength will probably create more of the intense optimism and bubble energy in the markets.

The darker side of the constellation of Pegasus is secret societies and conspiracies and we have to be concerned that the" Deep *State*" will be emboldened with this transit to create more Neptunian fog. Will it take Saturn aspects Neptune exactly in a sextile (sixty degrees) in **January 2019** to burst the "*Deep State*" bubble? For now, they will probably get more powerful.

The symbols for this unique nakshatra are a sword, the first two legs of a funeral cot, and a two-faced man. The sword represents the ability to cut through negativity to get to the truth. The two-faced man indicates the ability to see both sides of an issue but also may be symbolic in Western psychology of our dark side or shadow.

The benefic Jupiter, which reflects the high idealism of this asterism, rules this nakshatra but for a star ruled by Jupiter, it has an unusual dark quality to it. On the positive side, this constellation teaches us to lead a life of personal sacrifice with no expectation of glory. On the dark side, it can bring out sexual obsessions and greedy power struggles. Luckily in transit, it will be channeling a strong Jupiter in Hasta nakshatra (ruled by the Moon) in Virgo and bringing out the higher qualities.

The Deity of this constellation obscure and is called Aja-Ekapada or the one-footed goat that is part of the entourage of Shiva and in Tarot it is connected to the devil card. It is troubling that secret societies like the Illuminati consider the goat god their main deity and this constellation is connected with black magic.

On a symbolic level this is a constellation where the fires of Shiva can destroy those aspects of a decaying society. Given the power struggles going on between George Soros, the CIA and our new President, I wonder what fireworks will develop?

We have to watch out for more sexual scandal for the coming years as this constellation brings out the darker side. For a constellation ruled by Jupiter, this star is connected with negative human traits including paranoia, pessimism, debauchery, violence, cruelty and erratic sexual behavior. It is by far the most intense constellation in the zodiac. If you were born with the Sun here during the dates **March 5 - 17th** or have the ascendant or moon here, the major lessons are learning humility and not getting caught in the ego. If you are born under this star, it is important to get devoted to the light right away. Still people in this constellation are sincere, hardworking and will do anything to achieve their goals. I still people born with this star and they will have extremes in sexual behavior that may be viewed by society as abnormal or out of the box.

On the bright side, if Jupiter is unafflicted, the dark side of this constellation will be controlled. They can lead us to penance, detachment and generosity and purification. It is the most Jekyll and Hyde constellation in the zodiac. People born under this constellation may look well-mannered and acceptable on the outside but are they using their wealth and resources to benefit society? We need to surrender our ego and find our highest calling for more service and philanthropic action.

Historically, we saw this the last time this cycle happened, in 1853. For example, in October 1853, on the East coast of the United States, Donald McKay launches the Great Republic, the world's biggest sailing ship, which at 4,500 tons is too large to be successful. It sank. The recent launch of the world's largest plane is a modern comparison.

This cycle can inflate but, in the end,, it deflates as high hopes crumble. Uber is putting cabbies out of business but losing millions on paper, as are many other Silicon Valley startups. This new Neptune cycle that began in mid-June 2017 will also support the film industry, raw cotton, medicine, surgical goods, tobacco, drugs, chemicals and perfumes.

The darker side of this cycle is secret societies and conspiracies and we have to be concerned that the "*Deep State*" will be emboldened to create more smoke and mirror deception until maybe **January 2019** when that bubble will break. For now, they will probably get more powerful. The current war with the CIA, the "*Deep State*", the FBI and government is probably going to get more ominous.

Most of you know that the Federal Reserve Bank is privately owned with shareholders in foreign countries such as the Rothchilds. The United States has been under economic tyranny ever since 1913 when the Federal Reserve was signed into law by then president Woodrow Wilson. In its 104-year history, any independent government or private agency has never once audited the Federal Reserve. There is a total lack of transparency where the Federal Reserve is concerned.

The Federal Reserve acts as a law unto itself. It creates fiat currency out of nothing and charges the US government and therefore the taxpayer interest on it. This is something for nothing usury at the highest level — the ultimate Ponzi scheme. The Federal Reserve does whatever it wants with regard to foreign banks with no accountability to congress or the general public. If established political, economic, and industrial social and physical infrastructures potentially fail, it's very possible that the US will break into regions and people are forced to survive in their local community's human society will be forced to reinvent itself.

There is some kind of climax around **2019 - 2020** for this. Exactly what will happen is unclear, but I think we have another year to focus on self-sufficient agricultural in our homes with hydroponic pod gardens where you can grow vegetables in the corner of your apartment.

Special thanks to my friend Juliana Swanson for a discussion on this material and to Komilla Sutton and Prash Trivedi for their deep insights into this constellation.

FOCUS OF FESTIVALS: VEDIC HOLIDAYS

Vedic Holiday: Makara Sankranti - A New Beginning
January 14th, 2018 and 2019

Sun enters Capricorn

Sun moves into Capricorn on **Saturday, January 14th** and it is a larger event than you might imagine. In the Vedic calendar, it is the real beginning of the New Year where the days start lengthening, and more light descends on the planet.

Surya, the Sun God, is regarded as the symbol of divinity and wisdom, and is one of the most important planets (heavenly bodies) of the zodiac and our daily lives. It represents a new kind of New Year — a "*new beginning*" for which we want to strengthen the Sun within in our lives.

Surya actually means self, representing in our Jyotishis (Vedic Astrology) charts both the big Self, and our little individual egos. As the Self, or Atman, Surya stands for and represents that Divine quality that all of us have within us. Thus, it is good to give some attention to this element within us. So, it represents a day to celebrate our individuality and the Divinity within.

The equivalent for Westerners would be for us to clean a closet out on **Friday, January 13th** and take stuff to the dump or give stuff to the 2nd hand store which becomes symbolic of discarding the old and then on **January 14th** to celebrate our own individuality as well as, the Divine within and revisiting our New Year's resolutions or making a list of intentions if we did not get to it on **January 1st** when the Western culture tends to do so.

Apart from a harvest festival, Makara Sankranti is also regarded as the beginning of an auspicious phase in Indian culture. It is said as the 'holy phase of transition.' It marks the end of an inauspicious phase, which according to the Hindu calendar begins around **mid - December**. It is believed that any auspicious and sacred ritual can be sanctified this day onwards.

It represents realization, transformation and purification of the soul by imbibing and inculcating Divine virtues. So, think of Friday and Saturday as a time to release the old, to release the past and move forward.

Enjoy the rich symbolism and ritual of the Makara Sankrati, the Sun moving into Capricorn.

Vedic Holiday: Maha Shivaratri - Overcoming Darkness and Ignorance

February 14th

The Maha Mrityunjaya Mantra
"Om Tryambhakam Yajamahe
Sugandhim Pushtivardhanam
Urvarukamiva Bandhanan
Mrityor Mukshiya Maamritat"

- Sukla Yajurveda Samhita III. 60.

Maha Shivaratri is the most auspicious day of the entire year to worship Lord Shiva and receive his most compassionate grace. On this day, Lord Shiva's complete grace showers down upon the entire Earth. While the Western communities may have difficulty relating to Vedic deities, they are largely symbolic.

Shiva, always painted blue, represents the unbounded transcendental value of the Divine that is experienced in the deepest point of meditation when there is only unbounded awareness. Hence, this holiday is embraced with the notion of merging into the Divine in total Unity. It is a major festival in Vedic culture and is a very solemn holiday that marks a remembrance of "*overcoming darkness and ignorance*" in life and the world.

The planets most connected to Shiva are the Sun and Jupiter. If you have those planets in your 5th house you may have a strong inclination to Shiva. In the Karakamsha Navamsha chart (rotated D-9 chart around the Atma Karaka), if you have Sun or Jupiter in the 12th house or aspecting it by Rashi Drishtri, then Shiva is your Ishtadevata and this is a special day for you.

For thousands of years, spiritual seekers have sought Lord Shiva's blessings on this day by engaging in various practices dedicated to him. Meditation, maintaining silence, repeating Shiva mantras, singing Shiva stotras and bhajans, or performing worship (puja) are all excellent forms of practice (sadhana) during Maha Shivaratri.

It is said that those who worship Lord Shiva, especially on Maha Shivaratri, will receive his grace in the form of true wealth, wisdom, peace, inner healing, spiritual virtues, and divine courage.

There is also a special practice, or vow (vrata), that many devotees of Lord Shiva undertake at the time of Maha Shivaratri. This practice involves fasting and staying awake for the entire night, making sure to worship Lord Shiva during every quarter of the night until dawn breaks. This practice is very powerful for inner purification and makes it possible to absorb the abundant divine energy that is available to all on this night.

The Shiva Mantra is a prayer for rejuvenation that bestows wealth, health, long life, peace, prosperity and contentment. The spoken chant is a vibration that when spoken, wards off all negative and evil forces, creating a shield of protection against accidents and misfortune and ignites a fire within every cell and molecule of the body to energetically consume all negativity, thus, the mantra is very purifying.

The power of the mantra is in connecting us with our own inner divinity. You can use the mantra anytime during your meditation or spiritual practices to discover or enhance the happiness that is already within you.

Vedic Holiday: Holi - Festival of Love and Colors
By Jamie Bateman
March 2 - 9

Holi, the Festival of Love and Colors, is the Hindu annual celebration of the return of spring. This year the national holiday begins on **Friday, March 2nd**, lasting for one day and one night and starts on the eve of the Full Moon. This is this the day that Hindus meet others and end conflicts, forgive or pay debts and enjoy the start of a new year and welcome spring and the return of the God of Love, Kama.

The merriment begins with an evening bonfire prayer ritual, followed by the day festival of smearing each other with colors made from water and colored powders and drenching each other with water using water guns and water filled balloons. Parties, dancing, eating Holi delicacies and drinking bhang (marijuana) makes the Holi Festival of Love and Colors a day of joy, laughter and play.

Celebrated in India and Nepal, the festivities begin on the evening of the Full Moon Day with a prayer-led ritual invoking the flames of a lit bonfire to destroy the 'internal evils' within the soul, a symbolic rendition of the mythological fire that killed sinister Holika, the sister of the demon king Hiranyakashipu. The ritual and symbolic burning of pyres represents spiritual devotion and faith triumphing over evil.

The following morning is Rangwali Holi, the Festival of Colors begins. Colored powders are thrown or mixed with water and sprayed or smeared on people. Groups of people play drums and instruments down the streets, walking from place to place, singing and dancing to celebrate victory of good over evil, the end of winter, and thanksgiving on this day of riding past errors.

Historically, the festival commemorated a good spring harvest and fertile land. It was a time to say farewell to winter and welcome the abundant colors of spring! Today, the Hindu religious holiday is not only celebrated in India and Nepal. The Sikhs celebrate Holi as a 3-day martial arts festival and the thanksgiving holiday has even become popular in Europe and North America.

Here's a simple Holi ritual for burning your 'inner evils:' Take a piece of paper or prayer paper and write down all of the conflicts and issues that you would like to burn away, purify and release. It can be a situation that is stagnant or perhaps a relationship that you are holding onto, or deep hurt that needs to be forgiven. The forgiveness is for you. It doesn't excuse the hurt or the feelings associated with the situation but will help you release it so you're not carrying the weight with you as you move forward into the new spring. Set a positive intention to release, that which holds you back and allow the flame to consume the paper.

Your ritual can be as simple as writing one word on a piece of paper and lighting it with a match, placing it in a flame proof bowl or container and allowing the paper and your issue to be consumed by the flame. As the smoke rises in the air, imagine the smoke carrying your issue or situation to the heavens where the Divine will receive it with loving hands and transmute the energy into something more fertile and loving. Lovingly release it and let it go in devotion, love and faith.

Celebrate your "*Holi-Day*" by eating, drinking, dancing, singing and having a good time! Today is a good day to play with colors of all sorts — so go paint, grab a coloring book and crayons or redecorate a room in your house with fresh spring colors! Get creative, love, laugh, play and have fun!

Resource:
Holi. (n.d.) In Wikipedia. Retrieved January 3, 2018, from
https://en.wikipedia.org/wiki/Holi

Vedic Holiday: Spring Navaratri - Chaitra
Navatri: Beginning of The Journey of the Soul
March 18 - March 26

This new moon day in Pisces is very special in the Vedic calendar and starts the nine days of Mother Divine. We liken this period from **March 18th until March 26th** as a rebirth period where the soul is gestating in the womb of the Mother Divine and about to be reborn to a new life after 9 days rather than 9 months.

This period can be an intense time during the first three days ruled by Durga as deep purification of your subconscious energies are brought up to be healed and transformed. If you are receptive and open to transformation, this is a time for fasting, deep meditation, prayer and faith that the Divine Mother, with her immense love, is ready to pour her blessings upon you. Use this time to go deep within and transform.

Each day of the nine days is part of the journey of moon from the new moon towards its fullness. This Year it is from **March 18th - March 26th** with the new moon in the US being late at night on **Sunday, March 18th** as well as in Europe and India on the **Sunday, March 18th**. During these nine days of activity, the sap of our energy rises chakra by chakra to reach the crown.

Throughout the nine days of Chaitra Navaratri, there are dedications to one aspect of Mother Divine with the first 3 to Durga. One of my teachers, Indu Aurora has written beautifully about the first day and Durga:

'Durga' means someone who has accomplished the impossible and the impossibility. That is the power hidden-sleeping — inert, as well as, innate in each of us. On the first day, we invoke Durga as "*Ma Shailaputri*". She is the daughter of the great Himalayas. She has made up her mind to rise from the great earth below to the heavens above. She is invincible and immovable like the great Himalayas itself.

Once we become grounded and determined with 100% conviction of what we deserve, we are ready to break through the earth upon which we stand but we remain still like Ma Shailaputri.

In order to move, we have to be stirred but Ma Shailaputri motivates us to be stirred and yet maintain still. She holds a trident on the right hand, which symbolizes the victory over three kinds of sufferings (karmic, cosmic and manasic), over three Gunas (sattva, Rajas and tamas) and in the left hand she holds a lotus. In order to be strong, we don't have to lose our grace, gentleness and kindness. When you invoke Shailaputri within, no one can take your kindness as your weakness and your silence as your ignorance.

Sunday will be a good day for silence, meditation, fasting, prayer and inner transformation. You can sponsor into pujas for the nine days at www.puja.net or visit your local temple. It is a very beautiful time for deep transformation so enjoy. I find the Durga days always a bit intense so use the time to go within and heal.

The Divine loves you so much during this time. Just embrace and let it in to cleanse the darkness into light. Savor and delight in the process!

Vedic Holiday: Navaratri - Journey toward Enlightenment
October 9 - October 17

A special time of year begins **Tuesday, October 9th** with the new moon in Virgo, Navaratri. These 9 days and nights begin from the first day of the journey of new moon towards its fullness. Each day the sap of our energy rises chakra by chakra to reach the crown.

On the first day, **November 7th**, we invoke Durga as "*Ma Shailaputri*." She is the daughter of the great Himalayas. She has made up her mind to rise from the great earth below to the heavens above. She is invincible and immovable like the great Himalayas itself.

Below is a beautiful description of the Navaratri Holiday by one of my teachers, Komilla Sutton:

"According to the Puranas, Durga also fought the demon Mahishaasura in her form as Goddess Chamundeshwari and on the 10th day she emerged victorious. These wars, for a spiritual aspirant are the wars we fight with our inner demons so that we can progress on the path of self-realization. The nine days are nine steps to moksha and the goddesses give our power to find our higher self.

Rahu represents the demon in our chart. Those who want to pacify Rahu; this is the best time. Although this festival is celebrated in a big way, people forget the spiritual aspect of it and its connection to our spiritual development. To fight the fears of Rahu, the rejections of Ketu, it is important to fast during the day during these nine days with the mind set to overcome our inner fears and the resolve to confront and overcome our weaknesses.

The divine mothers are representation of Shakti and they alone give the power to their devotee to conquer all. These divine mothers are known as the Nava Durga (9 Names of Durga). Each of the days honors an aspect of Divine Mother and step by step the aspirant."

The days are also subdivided into 3 sets of three days:
Kali: The first three days are devoted to Kali, the Goddess of Destruction and Restoration. She is the wife of Shiva. It is a time of purification, a time to let go of all that is not right for your life so that the heart is clear to accept the new energy from the divine. This is also a time to control the demon of Rahu: the desires, the needs, and the fears that keep us tied to the world and give rise to more and more desires and therefore, disappointments in life.

Lakshmi: The second three days are devoted to Lakshmi, the Goddess of Prosperity and Wealth. She is the wife of Vishnu. It is a time of preservation of your good nature and what is good in your life and acquiring new things — ethically — that make your life wealthy and prosperous. Think about preserving and acquiring spiritual wealth.

Saraswati: The last three days are devoted to Saraswati, the Goddess of Wisdom, Knowledge and the Arts. She is the wife of Brahma. This is the time of receiving Divine Guidance on how to properly use all resources.

With each set of three days, you move closer to your spiritual goals. Goddess Kali helps to purify your mind and free it up for new possibilities. The mind has to be free of its old obsessions and desires, only then it is ready to take on new information.

In the second set, Goddess Lakshmi helps you to preserve what is good already and take positive steps towards making yourself wealthy, both materially and spiritually.

Finally, Goddess Saraswati gives the knowledge and wisdom to embrace the path of Brahman and overcome any obstacles on the path to moksha. If we do this ritual annually then we will slowly but surely find the path to realization.

This holiday is about Durga, who rides on her lion and has the courage to fight fear and overcome Rahu, the demon of fear, addiction and sensual obsession as she heads on her 10-day journey of victory over ignorance to the higher crown chakra.

For us, this is a time to curb our fears and addictions and go for the highest knowledge of the Self, which Goddess Saraswati starts bringing on Day 7.

It's a good day for silence, meditation, fasting, prayer and inner transformation. You can sponsor pujas for the nine days at www.puja.net or visit your local temple. It's a very beautiful time for deep transformation so enjoy!

I find that the Durga days are always a bit intense so use the time to go within and heal as this is the perfect time for a deep inward journey and a lot of healing.

In a discussion of this important holiday, themes can be seen in the celebratory festivities and rituals. One such example is seen in the symbolic activities that take place on Day 4, known as Kusmanda, She Who Brings Happiness and Warmth, and the connection with the value of a soft smile in relation to the heart chakra and how Durga inspires us to remain in our hearts as we interact with each other. My yoga teacher, Indu Auroa:

"Kushmanda Ma-"Kushm-anda" means the Creator of the "Brahma-anda"-the Universe. "Ku" means little. "Ushma" means warmth and "anda" means cosmic egg. Devi Kushmanda resides in the heart of the sun and creates the Universe merely with a Divine smile (Ku-ushma). We often underestimate the power of a smile, softness and gentleness...Devi Ku-ushma-anda resides in our hearts as Anahata Chakra, (heart chakra) which receives its energy from Heart Chakra, (solar plexus) also called as the Surya (sun) Chakra. Sun is not just de-termination, courage, fierceness, aggression but also light, brilliance, warmth and life. We often have fear to be established in the heart… we often fear to be taken for granted by being gentle, humble and kind…but there is the presence of Sun-like strength in this softness...Today the Devi inspires us to be nourished by this Sun, to be like the Sun, to stay in our heart. Reside in the Sun and yet be smiling with light and not burning with the heat of it. She rides a lion, which symbolizes "Dharma." As we ride on our righteous paths, may the rays of the warmth and gentleness of smile allow us to touch millions of hearts and establish a spiritual family wherever we go...world as one family!"

So, start coming out of your deep descent and bring your solar smile to the world to bless it with Divine love and a strong heart to heal the world!

Another example comes from Skandamata, Mother of Skanda, The Destroyer of Tamas and Materialism, celebrated on day 5 and associated with the Shakti Skanda Mata, a fifth form of Durga, the wife of Shiva and mother of Skanda.

The Devi on the 5th day rises from the Manipura Chakra, the solar plexus, with a fierce light and clarity, residing in the Vishuddhi Chakra, the throat chakra, the undiluted force of mind, to warn us to be mindful of what we ask for in life when we invoke the power of our spoken word.

The Vak-Shakti, power of speech, that made the Demon Tarakasura ask for a boon to be slaughtered by the son of Shiva and Parvati, rose as Devi Skanda Mata residing in Vishudshi Chakra and gave birth to Skanda who became the destiny of Tarakasura.

This also symbolizes that the undiluted Shakti of mind in each one of us gives birth to that powerful spirit, Kartikeya, that can put an end to our own malicious, tamasic, desires or Tarkasura.

Skanda has 6 heads that symbolize the 5 senses (eyes, nose, ears, tongue and skin) and mind. Once we give a re-birth to our senses by internalizing them, their powers combine like a laser beam and become Skanda, the chief of strongest army against negativity.

The symbolic growth continues with the Devi Katyayani, the Nurturing Mother aspect of the Divine Mother. She embodies the values of sharing and caring. Young girls pray to Devi Kathyayini for a good husband. Marriage comes with a sense of security, commitment, togetherness, team spirit and belongingness. She signifies the finer qualities of being in a relationship. The ultimate relationship is the union with Oneness with the soul.

The Shakti focus on the 6th day that is associated with Devi Katyayani travels from the Vishuddhi to Ajna Chakra, the third eye. This Shakti was born from the anger radiated from the eyes of Brahma, Vishnu and Shiva to slay the demon Mahisha-asur, a buffalo headed demon. The demon symbolizes tamas or inertia, laziness, dormancy and slothfulness. The fire out of which Goddess Katyanai was born is sattva-rajas: the fire of pure intent and right action.

The moment this Shakti awakens, we are ready to face the demon of tamas within and this moment of birth of Devi Katyayani within us is insight. The moments we allow ourselves to be fed by tamas, is the very same moment we allow the nourishing of the demon Mahishasura within us.

It is always a choice to feed the Devi or the Demon within. This is a constant dance between the Gunas of sattva, rajas and tamas within. It is according to our Viveka-khyati, discernment, that we choose one over the other!

Let your practice lead you from tamas to sattva from moment to moment. The battle is not going to be easy but rewarding for sure!

The 7th day is celebrated in recognition of the goddess Kalratri, a powerful avatar of the goddess Shakti, in the form of the Goddess Kali, the fiercest form of Maa Durga. The symbolic message of the day is one of peace.

As you join Durga on her journey, you may find yourself struggling during the last few days. I have to go back to the metaphor of the challenges of rebirth and the difficult process of moving out of the womb. I have been discussing the nine days as a process of the child being reborn from the womb of the mother and we are getting closer to our new rebirth.

The 8th day is connected to Maha-Gauri, the White Pearl and Mother of Full Grace and Beauty and Serenity, radiant like the moon. It's a day where we look into the darkness, examine our challenges and seek to muscle the energy and power to transform and move beyond our limits. Like the moon in the darkness, Maha-Gauri is always providing light and nurturing us in the darkest of times, but she beckons us to grow beyond our limits and that requires looking deep into the darkness and making changes.

This day is continued movement into the darkness and marking difficult choices and changes. We must muster additional courage and know that the Blessings of Mother will support us with her light even in the darkest of times before we are going to emerge from the womb. Everything is possible if we are ready with unblemished intention and strong will to transform our deepest problems. We have to muster the self-esteem and confidence to know that we are worthy of our highest good!

It is a time to reflect on our darkest situations and let the light of Divine Mother's moonlight shine within us. It's a great day for healing, inner reflection and transformation. Divine Mother will be there if you are willing to let her light shine into your darkest crevices and to realize that the darkness is only an illusion. Once the light is there, you wonder why you agonized and analyzed and gave so much power to the darkness. Blessings for a wondrous day! Rebirth shortly at hand!

The 9th and final day is reserved for the goddess Navaratri, The Gift of Centeredness Amidst Change. Ma Siddhi Datri is the ninth goddess and an embodiment of Goddess Saraswati.

Her name means the "*giver of Boons/accomplishments*." She blesses those who practice their yoga and meditation regularly due to discipline. She reminds us that if we are regular in our spiritual practices, then nature will support us with the fulfillment of our desires. She teaches us that hard, discipline and dedication are necessary to create enough clarity of mind in order to fulfill our desires.

Ma Siddhi Datri is an embodiment of the highest quality of Venus, healthy relationships and her deep friendship with Saturn and the blessings of elders. She bestows intelligence and health. She is a reminder if we learned from Lakshmi, that wealth is not just physical cash, but good health, wonderful relationships and a quest for the Divine.

While her name, Siddhi reminds us of Patanjai and the perfections of walking on water or flying through the air, she actually teaches us to remain balanced and grounded in the most difficult situations. The value of meditation and yoga is that it centers us in our Self and so no matter what problems arise, we have the poise and invincible strength to deal with it. There will always be problems with the changing nature of the physical body and ups and downs with the material world, but can we have the fortitude and centeredness like Ma Siddhi Datri to be 100% secure amidst change? This is grace and is one of the greatest gifts of Mother Divine.

Be kind to yourself, keep the Divine spark warm for growth — toward something higher and be patient. This process happens one, small step, at a time.

The call to action is to be regular with your spiritual practice so that you can have the strength and courage like all the goddesses riding tigers to conquer your deepest fears and move forward through the darkness into the light and rebirth!

The celebration ends with Victory Day on **October 19th**.

You can sponsor into ceremonies at www.puja.net or visit your local temple. This is a very special time for deep purification and a chance to increase all aspects of wealth in your life.

Vedic Holiday: Diwali - Festival of Light
November 6 - November 10

> Light the lamp of love in your heart.
> Light the flame of wisdom in your mind.
> Light the steady candle of faith in your resolve.
> Light the fire of strength that exists within you waiting.
> It is Divali time.
> - Divya Prabha

The festival is known to be mentioned in Sanskrit scriptures such as Skanda Purana and Padma Purana. The former text has a mention of diyas or tiny lamps and are said to be symbolic of parts of the sun — the light and energy giver to all. According to popular mythology, Diwali is associated with Yama and Nachiketa on Karthik Amavasya or the new moon night of Diwali. The story is revered from ages as that about right versus wrong, true wealth and knowledge. Probably this is why, people celebrate Diwali as the Festival of Light, which also signifies knowledge, prosperity and wisdom.

In a seventh century Sanskrit play, King Harsha mentions "*Deepapratipadutsava*," when lamps are lit and newly married couples are given gifts, in remembrance of the god Vishnu and goddess Lakshmi's marriage.

In the ninth century, Kayvamimamsa Rajasekhara referred to "*Deepavali*" as "*Dipamalika*", which sees the tradition of homes being cleaned and streets and markets being decorated with lights in the night.

Many celebrate Diwali in remembrance of the return of Rama and Sita after 14 years of exile, while others celebrate it as the return of Pandavas after 12 years of vanvas and a year of agyatavas.

How is Diwali celebrated?
From the onset of the autumn, people start gearing up to celebrate the festival. People buy gold, silver and utensils for home, clean and furnish their houses and decorate them with colorful rangolis and bright diyas.

People worship Lakshmi — the goddess of wealth and prosperity, and Ganesha, the remover of all obstacles, on Diwali.

The Diwali Five-Day Celebrations

Day 1: Dhanteras: the Festival of Wealth - lamps are ritually kept burning all through the nights in honor of Lakshmi and Dhanvantar.

Day 2: Naraka Chaturdashi: Early morning religious rituals and festivities take place: house decorations and colorful floor patterns called rangoli are created and women decorate their hands with henna designs.

Day 3: Deepavali: relatives, family and friends acknowledge important relationships and friendships by exchanging gifts and sweets.

Day 4: Diwali Padva: Celebrating the mutual love and devotion between a husband-wife bond.

Day 5: Bhai Dooj: The major festivities end with a dedication to the sister-brother relationship on the fifth day.

Pujas may be performed throughout the 5 days of festivities.

Before the night of Diwali, people clean, renovate, and decorate their homes and offices. They dress up in new clothes, light up lamps and candles and participate in pujas worshipping Lakshmi. After puja, fireworks follow, and a family feast that includes the exchange of sweets and gifts between family members, friends and loved ones.

For many businessmen, this is also the day when they start a new financial year with the adoption of a fresh 'bahi khata' or accounts book, after offering it to goddess Lakshmi. They believe that with her blessings, it will be a profitable year for them. (Indian Post)

Special note of thanks to Komilla Sutton, Jamie Bateman, and other sources, including Wikipedia, for assistance in gathering information on special Hindu holidays.

Final Note

I hope that this Almanac will be a useful guide for you for **2018 - 2019** and bring you much knowledge and freedom.

The Ocean of Knowledge is unbounded, and one can study it all of one's life. I hope that you will consider my classes, which are my biggest joy to teach, or readings if you need very specific information on your life.

Special thanks again to Jamie Bateman for her exhaustive work in compiling and editing this extensive work.

We do plan on continuing with a **2019 - 2020** edition. We hope to publish the **2019 - 2020** edition in **October 2018**.

Have a Great Year!

Barry Rosen

ABOUT BARRY ROSEN:
CONFESSIONS OF A JYOTISH ENTHUSIAST:
THE WIZARD BEHIND THE CURTAIN IN THE LAND OF OZ

I often wake up at 4 am in the morning with these ideas floating through my mind that demand that they be written down in the wee hours of the morning. In that tender twilight, when my emotions are a bit raw coming out of sleep, I often feel the planetary energies and their challenges, and they demand to be written about. Often, they flow out from the vast void of my 8th house, ruled by Gemini that has a stationary Jupiter in Purnavasu nakshatra aspecting Mercury in Aquarius.

I have been blessed with automatic writing at times and stuff just flows out and I am not sure where it comes from. Luckily, I can produce good material in 20-40 minutes due to 30 years of daily writing for my financial columns. Lately my astrological writings have replaced my self-deprecating poetical musings and become my poetry.

I have Vena yoga with 7 planets in 7 houses and so I have been blessed with the ability to write and stuff just wants to pour out. Jyotish is such an abstract and difficult subject and I have been frustrated by years of reading difficult books and trying to understand the English of the Indian masters that I have studied with and my mission has been to simplify and clarify this material and put into English, so people can understand and benefit from its great wealth. I feel an urgent need to clarify and verbalize complex relationships that never should be labeled "*good*" or "*bad*." They just are our coaches and our teachers trying to support us to become better people and their message has to be understood.

The last year I have been compelled to teach, which is my truest dharma. My stationary Jupiter in Gemini shows up in the first house in my Karakamsha Rashi chart and life purpose chart from Jaimini astrology. Nothing makes me happier. I am unhappy with many of the books that I read, and my mission is to modernize and clarify and re-spiritualize Jyotish for a new generation. I am drawn to developing new and innovative classes, or "*boutique classes*" that find new ways of looking at things and my classes force me to bring out and express new knowledge as has been the case with my just completed Money Karma class. In developing my new class on Secrets of the House, I realized that there is hardly a good book out there that offers the depth of the secrets of the houses. My new course will probably become a book someday.

I am in a Rahu period now with Rahu in natal Mula nakshatra owned by Ketu so there is an obsession about spiritual knowledge and Jyotish. I like to explain Rahu as enthusiasm and passion and creativity to create something new and fresh and change traditional ways of doing things and continue to look for new ways to express and modernize and spiritualize this knowledge. I rarely quote Parashara but always honor him as his light.

I feel that that is knowledge belongs to everyone and I try to generously share it. And like most modern Brahmans, I face a dilemma. The village no longer supports the village priest and so I have to charge for readings and classes, but they are just a small portion of my income and the classes are just something that I have to do to bring out deeper knowledge. If I am always promoting a class or a service, it is just the plight of the in the modern age.

I am blessed with my financial business that supports me but no longer holds the passion it once did and my 3rd Saturn return has moved me into Jyotish education and writing and it makes my heart sing. At some point, I need to move totally into Jyotish education and spiritual teaching and I see that as the next major phase of my life. My passion does come out at cost as I do not get enough exercise or spend enough time with my wife or have time for fun things but there is always a price for passion.

Rahu always craves a bit of attention, so I hope I do not offend anyone with the volume of writing that pours out of me. It is passion and enthusiasm more than desire for fame. My mission is just to share my talents and what is most precious to me and translate it into plain English so that the puppet strings of the planets, that pull our emotions and psychology, can be cut and we can be free to live a liberated life and not be gripped by the drama and Maya of our thoughts.

This piece is not meant to be about self-absorption but unveiling my mystery. I often find people wandering to my personal Facebook page to find out who I really am and that personality has continued to fade but Rahu never quite lets it go. (To read more about me if you are really curious, read my interview with Christina Collins at http://www.appliedvedicastrology.com/interview-with-barry/)

All gratitude to all my spiritual Gurus and Jyotish Gurus for their blessing. I am particularly grateful to Komilla Sutton for her maternal guidance and clarity in creating coherent courses, which has been my inspiration, and to Sanjay Rath for his deep insights from Jaimini Astrology. I am particularly grateful to Juliana Swanson who has become a wonderful mentor and dear friend and who is there to support me in my troubled times. Every Jyotishi needs someone to turn to also.

A true Jyotishi need to be in service and devoted to removing suffering. That is what I strive to do. My spiritual Guru has been found of saying that we start off wanting to be a somebody (Mars in our teens) and have to become a nobody (moksha and transcending the ego) in order to become an Everybody (Brahman conscious and enlightened with the universe). Lets hope that I can continue to transcend Rahu and become my truest Ketu nature.

Jyotish Star of The Month

Jyotish Star Copyright 2016 C. C. Collins - All Rights Reserved
http://www.jyotishstar.com/jyotish-star-barry-rosen-february-2016.html

Barry Rosen
By Vachaspati Christina Collins
Interview Date: 01/15/2016

Christina Collins: Hi Barry thank you for being our February Jyotish Star. Let's begin by talking about how you got your start in Astrology and especially Jyotish?

Barry Rosen: I had my first reading with Chakrapani Ullal in 1985 during a very difficult part of my life. It filled me with light and hope for a shift in my life that happened when my malefic Venus period ended and was followed by a great Sun period in 1986. My Sun is lord of the 10th in the 5th in Pisces in Jupiter's nakshatra and Jupiter is stationary in the 8th house with Ketu in Gemini. I suddenly started studying astrology with my friends in the TM movment and reading every book I could get my hands on. At that time, the TM community in Fairfield, IA had a great new age bookstore and they were getting in all of B.V. Raman's books and I was studying and memorizing Pundit Ojha's book, Predictive Astrology of the Hindus. . Then the Western Vedic authors starting publishing and Tom Hopke and James Braha had an early influence on me. At the same time I was fascinated by investments and commodity trading. I was fascinated watching the Financial New Network (the predecessor to CNBC) and was wondering why different markets went up and down every day and knew there had to be an astrological component. My Dad has 5 planets in his 5th house in Virgo and his only obsession was the stock market and he got me involved when I was 13 year also buying me stocks for my college fund and I would watch the prices go up and down every day in the paper.

Christina What got you started in your financial research some 29 years ago? How did you begin to merge that with astrology?

Barry: I had a good friend who was a mathematician and trader and he was W.D. Gann scholar and he knew that Gann used astrology and went to India. He taught me Gann and trading and I started teaching him astrology. I began by watching the daily transits of the markets and seeing how the stock market reacted every day. My sense is that if you get attuned to the planets and they start talking to you and that is what happened. One's intuition starts to grow.

I learned a lot from the Western Financial Astrologers and went to early Financial Astrology conferences in Chicago in 1988 and later spoke at them. J.P. Morgan, the founder of the Morgan Bank, was fond of saying that millionaires do not use astrology, billionaires do. He had a private astrologer, Evangeline Adams, who helped him tremendously. I got to purchase rare books in Financial Astrology from the Evageline

Adams library that was purchased by an early colleague of mine Norman Winski. One of the local investment companies had a Vedic astrologer who would call the markets for them and in 1990-1, I was hired to do research for them and was given a research budget and was able to collect a lot of rare books on Financial Astrology.

I knew Muhurtha and in 1992, I incorporated a Leo rising chart with Sun in Aries and Jupiter in the 1st and Leo and when my Sun period hit in 1993, my company took off. I have since used Muhurtha to support people in starting companies and using Vedic Astrology for marketing and supporting business growth. My company is still here 29 years later, www.fortucast.com.

Christina: Do you follow a specific spiritual path or guru? And how did that come about?

Barry: I began Transcendental Meditation when I was 18 at the University of Illinois and became obsessed with enlightenment, the Bhagavad Gita and went on to become a meditation teacher and work for the university and was able to study the Vedas as part of a graduate program at Maharishi International University. It was a golden time of my life. I have been fascinated by Vedic literature since I was 19 and studied the Bhagavad Gita in detail. Eventually after 1979, the politics of the TM movement turned down and while I taught at the university in 1983-4 and 1987, I started to get disenchanted and was feeling the need for something of greater depth for my spiritual development.

I met my current Guru, Sri Sri Ravi Shankar in 1990 in California and have been teaching his breath-work program through the Art of Living the last 26 years and have been to India 4-5 times with him. Last year, he invited me to get initiated into the Gayatri mantra in India and learn the Sandyavadanam practice and now I do a fire homa ever morning after going deeply into a Shiva Rudram meditation. As I have been studying the D-20 chart, I am fascinated that my Guru knew exactly what I needed for my spiritual life without ever looking at my chart. While I was in India, I got to teach introductory Jyotish to 160 students from 59 countries and got a directive from my Guru to develop an on-line Jyotish curriculum. I subsequently have tried to create a marriage between the Art of Living and ACVA which is still work in progress.

Christina: Now, here is a question from Willie, one of my Jyotish students. *"Astrologically, when is a good time to press your luck, and what is a good time to be more reserved with financial investments?"*

Barry: I think you have to trade from your chart or at least know the pitfalls of your psychology. If you are running a Rahu period or sub-period, you have to watch for gambling tendencies if Rahu is poorly placed. If you are running periods connected to the lords of the 8 and 12th, then you are also going to have to careful or if you have a lot of major 8th and 12th house transits going on. The challenge is that even when you know the pitfalls of your chart, you may be swayed by impulsive tendencies and make mistakes. It takes a lot of spiritual practice, tithing and discipline to overcome bad investment karma in your chart.

Christina You are currently presenting a series of very well received, live webinars on Financial Astrology. Could you tell us a little about these and how people can get involved?

Barry: I turned 60 this year and my Saturn return is pushing me to recreate my life. My Guru told me to retire from Financial Astrology in a few years and in preparation for more spiritual teaching and Jyotish teaching. To pass the baton, I founded the London Institute for Global Economic Forecasting last year to support fund managers and do long-term forecasting and started training a group of people to do Financial Astrology and become a father figure to the Institute. I also started an executive astrological coaching program to support corporate executives and professional traders. As a result, I have been teaching advanced classes to students around the world over Go to Meeting and videotaping them and now have 3 completed modules of about 12 weeks each and am starting a 4th module in a few weeks. I met a lot of these people when I was lecturing at BAVA in London and will be going back there in April for their Financial Astrology track this year. People can contact me at swfort@gmail.com to get information on my seminars and there is some of the older information is on my website at ww.fortuast.com/tools_astr.aspx. People with a lot of Vedic Astrology background and move through the material quickly and get to the more advanced material quickly.

Christina Tell us Barry, do you have other family members involved with finance or astrology or both? Children who are taking an interest in the field?
Barry: My Dad began investing in the stock market in the 1950's when he ran a small grocery store in Chicago. He was a buy and hold trader and very savvy and would spend all his time reading stock analysis reports and still does at age 93. He took nothing and built it into an immense portfolio. My brother studied Western astrology in his early 20's but when he shared it with me when I was 21, I told him it was nonsense. Ironically, I then became a great astrologer. My wife and I have no children but I have done the charts of my dogs when I knew their birth charts and times from the breeders. I predicted that my first Australian shepherd would have 3 boys, which she did.

Christina What is your opinion on the price of Gold with the Jupiter/Rahu conjunction now in Leo, and receiving the aspect of Saturn from Scorpio? Which do you think will be stronger the Rahu or the Saturn influence?

Barry: I used to be the number 1 gold trader in the world according to Timer Digest in January of 2011 and sold my gold when it was at 1880.00 close to the top of 1900 around 4-5 years ago. I researched this question carefully and decided that the Saturn's aspect on Leo is enough of a negative that we will have to wait for it to end. In 1979, when Saturn went out of Leo into Virgo, gold started taking off. It was Mars/Rahu/Jupiter in Leo in the Nakshatra of Purva Phalguni that caused that huge move in 1979-80 that nakshatra is very key for gold. I think gold can rally this year $200-250.00 but still may hit 800.00 the first 6 months of 2017. I think it will take off thereafter. The Central Bankers are manipulating and they do want competition with their worthless paper money and bonds but China and Russia are hoarding to have gold-backed currencies when the US debt level implodes.

Christina: And what do you think the price of crude oil (liquid gold) will be similar to metallic gold, or do you think it will now continue to go back up in price as Saturn the karaka is still in a water sign and influencing Leo, the sign for gold, or do you think it's going down? It does appear to be changing, for just at the last Friday of the year a 40 year ban on oil export was lifted (just as Rahu reached zero degrees on its transit into 29 degrees of Leo. Would you like to comment on that?

Barry: I think that the Neptune Square to Saturn has been rather deflationary and is still a big influence and will continue to be so into next year. Crude seasonally goes up in January but then usually goes down into March. Last time we had Rahu in Leo, crude was up the first few months of the transit but down the rest of the transit and may not be a factor. I do think the Sun is an important planet for timing oil. Saturn in Scorpio is not helping and it is a 12th house transit to the natal chart for heating oil that I use which goes back to Nov. 14, 1979 and it is a Sagittarius rising chart. The Saudi Arabia natal chart is not promising for a rise in crude and I suspect that crude will continue to be in trouble when Saudi Arabia goes into a Saturn major period in 2020. The world is waking up to alternative energy and I think the politics of oil will continue to crumble. Look how all the wars that the oligarchy have been stirring up have not been able to really budge the price of crude. I suspect we will be between $20-42 a barrel for a while and probably fall to $22-26.00 this year.

Christina As a CTA (Commodity Trading Advisor), do you focus on a particular area of interest, and how do you apply astrology to your trading? What general advice can you give our readers?

Barry: I cover 20 commodity markets have daily and monthly newsletters for forecasting and have a newsletter for ETF's which are a popular trading vehicle for people who do not want to open a commodity trading account. You can buy a stock called SGOL and when you buy it, a Swiss firm takes that money and buys gold bullion.

The best advice I can give your readers is that you need to learn how to be a good trader, to manage your money well and to trade when your dashas are providing a tail wind. Astrology can give you a hidden edge but you have to know as much as the other traders also.

Christina: Do you have any books you have written or are you planning on a series?

Barry: With my Saturn return, I am going back to my spiritual roots and I have developed a class which combines Ayurveda, Hatha Yoga and Jyotish. I think they will were intimately connected 1000's of years ago and have become separated. I studied with Ed Tarabilda, a radical astrologer, who worked with Dr. Vasant Lad and developed a class on prescribing yoga postures for emotional and psychological and physical problems. I have developed his work and am writing a book on Astro-Yoga. Today, young people will do yoga but many will not get involved in Vedic mantras and yagyas if their cultural heritage is different. I think that we can prescribe cures for afflicted planets using specific postures and having them done in the direction of the planet involved. It is fascinating that there are 108 core yoga poses and 108 padas and now Andrew Foss in his new book has a 108 mantras for each pada. Astro-Yoga has become my new passion and am writing a book on it with Gary O'Toole an astrologer from Ireland of Timeline Astrology.

Christina: What other projects are you involved in?

Barry: The last few years I have become obsessed with Jaimini astrology and spiritual astrology and spend all my spare time studying and going more deeply.
I have been attracting more spiritual people for readings and I like to focus my readings around the Karakamsha Rashi and Navmasha charts to support people in their life purpose and soul's journeys and also the D-20 for supporting their specific spiritual path. I wish I had learned this material 20 years ago as figuring out the nuances is taking more time and experience. Robert has been a big help on my journey here.

Christina: Does Jaimini astrology have any potential influence for Financial Astrology?

Barry: I am just starting to explore this but I think that Rashi based dashas are more materially and concretely based and thus Jaimini Chara Dasha and a few others may be better for predicting material gains and losses than Vimshottari Dasha which may deal more with our subjective reactions to the material.
Christina: Any final thoughts?

Barry: The abundance of the universe is open to all that pursue it. You have to have good karma or create good karma by tithing and service work and helping others. I think we all have to dedicate our lives to more service and helping to make the planet a better place. I am very concerned that our new generation is losing its spiritual focus that we were blessed with growing up in the 60's and 70's. With the US entering a Rahu major period, we all have to do our best to bring spirituality and astrology to the new generations.

BIBLIOGRAPHY

The following books have deeply shaped my writing and interpretations of Transits and have directly impacted my book. I am indebted to the following authors and books and highly recommend you purchase them for your library:

William Levacy, Beneath a Vedic Sky. Hay House, 1999.

Komilla Sutton, The Nakshatras: The Stars Beyond the Zodiac. Wessex Astrologer, 2014.

Komilla Sutton, The Lunar Nodes: Crisis and Redemption, Wessex Astrologer, 2001.

Zoran Radosavljevic, Brush Up: On the Vedic Astrology Basics, vol. 1. D.O.O Siva Sentar, 2015.

Robert Hand, Planets in Transit. Schiffer Publishing. 2001. 2nd edition.

Prash Trivedi, The 27 Celestial Portals: The Real Secret Behind 12 Start-Signs Revealed. Lotus Press. 2004.

Bepin Behari. The Timing of Events. Motilal Banarsidass Publishers, 2014.

Andrew Foss, Yoga of the Planets, Their Mantras and Philosophy. ShriSource Publications. 2016.

Dennis Harness, The Nakshatras. The Lunar Mansions of Vedic Astrology. Lotus Press, 1999.

Supplemental: Vedic Astrology Material

2018 Total Lunar Eclipse
January 31, 2017 08:27 EST 18 Degrees Cancer
July 27, 2018 16:20 EST 11.45 Degrees Capricorn

2018 Partial Solar Eclipse
February 15, 2018 16:06 EDT 4 Degrees Aquarius
July 12, 2018 22:38 EDT 27.41 Degrees Gemini
August 11, 2018 05:58 EDT 25 Degrees Cancer

Fortucast Applied Vedic Astrology Course Listings
See Page 339

For More About Barry Rosen and Applied Vedic Astrology:

Barry Rosen
www.appliedvedicastrology.com
support@fortucast.com
Office: 928-284-5740 ext. 5000 or 5983

Sign up!

http://www.appliedvedicastrology.com/financial-and-investment-counseling-readings

For questions, email barry2@fortucast.com

Readings and Courses are available.

Basic knowledge of Vedic Astrology is required.

Credit cards accepted by phone at Fortucast at 800-788-2796.

PayPal also accepted

Transits, Aspects and Sign Ingresses: 2018 – 2019
New York for United States EST

1st column is the Transiting planets, the third is the Natal planets

Note: Convert to your time zone using www.timeanddate.com and note beginning of Daylight Saving Time March 11, 2018 and the return to Standard Time, November 4th for the United States and Canada.

Transits and Aspects 2018 - 2019

Planet	Aspect	Planet	Date and Degree
Mo [2]	7H (180°)	Su [8]	exact at 1/1/2018 Monday 21:24
Ra [3]	conjunction	Mo [3]	exact at 1/4/2018 Thursday 02:47
Jp [6]	conjunction	Ma [6]	exact at 1/6/2018 Saturday 19:38
Ve [8]	conjunction	Su [8]	exact at 1/9/2018 Tuesday 02:01
Jp [6]	conjunction	Mo [6]	exact at 1/11/2018 Thursday 03:21
Sa [8]	conjunction	Me [8]	exact at 1/13/2018 Saturday 02:03
Me [8]	conjunction	Mo [8]	exact at 1/15/2018 Monday 02:02

Mo [8]	conjunction	Su [9]	exact at 1/16/2018 Tuesday 21:17
Ve [9]	conjunction	Mo [9]	exact at 1/17/2018 Wednesday 01:29
Ke [9]	conjunction	Ve [9]	exact at 1/29/2018 Monday 18:06
Ke [9]	conjunction	Su [9]	exact at 2/3/2018 Saturday 15:00
Sa [8]	10H (270°)	Mo [5]	exact at 2/4/2018 Sunday 01:49
Ma [7]	conjunction	Mo [7]	exact at 2/9/2018 Friday 01:39
Ke [9]	conjunction	Me [9]	exact at 2/9/2018 Friday 10:29
Mo [9]	conjunction	Su [10]	exact at 2/15/2018 Thursday 16:05
Sa [8]	3H (60°)	Ve [10]	exact at 2/15/2018 Thursday 18:19
Me [10]	conjunction	Su [10]	exact at 2/17/2018 Saturday 07:27
Ke [9]	2H (30°)	Mo [10]	exact at 2/17/2018 Saturday 02:35
Ra [3]	5H (120°)	Ma [7]	exact at 2/19/2018 Monday 18:25
Sa [8]	3H (60°)	Me [10]	exact at 2/21/2018 Wednesday 15:23
Ke [9]	2H (30°)	Ve [10]	exact at 2/22/2018 Thursday 14:04
Ma [7]	7H (180°)	Mo [1]	exact at 2/24/2018 Saturday 00:56
Sa [8]	3H (60°)	Su [10]	exact at 2/25/2018 Sunday 12:45
Ke [9]	2H (30°)	Me [10]	exact at 2/25/2018 Sunday 22:16
Ra [3]	conjunction	Mo [3]	exact at 2/28/2018 Wednesday 00:03
Mo [4]	7H (180°)	Su [10]	exact at 3/1/2018 Thursday 19:51
Ra [3]	2H (30°)	Mo [4]	exact at 3/2/2018 Friday 01:36
Jp [6]	5H (120°)	Me [10]	exact at 3/2/2018 Friday 08:04
Ve [11]	conjunction	Me [11]	exact at 3/4/2018 Sunday 13:04
Ke [9]	2H (30°)	Su [10]	exact at 3/5/2018 Monday 01:10
Jp [6]	5H (120°)	Su [10]	exact at 3/13/2018 Tuesday 16:05
Ra [3]	9H (240°)	Me [11]	exact at 3/16/2018 Friday 17:34
Mo [10]	conjunction	Su [11]	exact at 3/17/2018 Saturday 09:11
Jp [6]	5H (120°)	Mo [10]	exact at 3/17/2018 Saturday 02:10
Ra [3]	9H (240°)	Ve [11]	exact at 3/18/2018 Sunday 06:38

Ve [11]	conjunction	Me [11]	exact at 3/19/2018 Monday 00:02+
Ke [9]	5H (120°)	Mo [1]	exact at 3/23/2018 Friday 01:04
Ma [8]	4H (90°)	Su [11]	exact at 3/24/2018 Saturday 12:07
Ra [3]	9H (240°)	Me [11]	exact at 3/30/2018 Friday 14:22
Mo [5]	7H (180°)	Su [11]	exact at 3/31/2018 Saturday 08:36
Me [11]	conjunction	Su [11]	exact at 4/1/2018 Sunday 13:52
Ra [3]	9H (240°)	Su [11]	exact at 4/2/2018 Monday 16:15
Sa [8]	conjunction	Ma [8]	exact at 4/2/2018 Monday 11:44
Ra [3]	5H (120°)	Mo [7]	exact at 4/5/2018 Thursday 03:33
Ke [9]	conjunction	Mo [9]	exact at 4/10/2018 Tuesday 04:09
Mo [11]	conjunction	Su [12]	exact at 4/15/2018 Sunday 21:56
Ma [8]	4H (90°)	Mo [11]	exact at 4/15/2018 Sunday 03:45
Ve [12]	7H (180°)	Jp [6]	exact at 4/17/2018 Tuesday 02:59
Ke [9]	5H (120°)	Mo [1]	exact at 4/19/2018 Thursday 03:14
Sa [8]	7H (180°)	Mo [2]	exact at 4/21/2018 Saturday 01:49
Ra [3]	9H (240°)	Me [11]	exact at 4/27/2018 Friday 21:36
Mo [6]	7H (180°)	Su [12]	exact at 4/29/2018 Sunday 20:58
Ke [9]	5H (120°)	Ve [1]	exact at 5/2/2018 Wednesday 17:12
Ma [9]	conjunction	Mo [9]	exact at 5/6/2018 Sunday 02:19
Jp [6]	7H (180°)	Su [12]	exact at 5/8/2018 Tuesday 20:38
Ra [3]	9H (240°)	Mo [11]	exact at 5/12/2018 Saturday 01:54
Mo [12]	conjunction	Su [1]	exact at 5/15/2018 Tuesday 07:47
Ma [9]	8H (210°)	Mo [4]	exact at 5/22/2018 Tuesday 01:56
Jp [6]	7H (180°)	Me [12]	exact at 5/23/2018 Wednesday 01:53
Sa [8]	7H (180°)	Ve [2]	exact at 5/26/2018 Saturday 02:39
Ke [9]	5H (120°)	Su [1]	exact at 5/28/2018 Monday 21:17
Mo [7]	7H (180°)	Su [1]	exact at 5/29/2018 Tuesday 10:19
Ke [9]	5H (120°)	Me [1]	exact at 6/2/2018 Saturday 04:20

Me [1]	conjunction	Su [1]	exact at 6/5/2018 Tuesday 22:01
Ke [9]	conjunction	Ma [9]	exact at 6/8/2018 Friday 01:09
Jp [6]	7H (180°)	Mo [12]	exact at 6/11/2018 Monday 01:14
Mo [1]	conjunction	Su [1]	exact at 6/13/2018 Wednesday 15:43
Jp [6]	9H (240°)	Mo [2]	exact at 6/15/2018 Friday 02:09
Sa [8]	7H (180°)	Me [2]	exact at 6/15/2018 Friday 21:46
Jp [6]	9H (240°)	Me [2]	exact at 6/19/2018 Tuesday 15:42
Ra [3]	conjunction	Ve [3]	exact at 6/19/2018 Tuesday 08:38
Ve [3]	7H (180°)	Ma [9]	exact at 6/21/2018 Thursday 12:53
Mo [8]	7H (180°)	Su [2]	exact at 6/27/2018 Wednesday 00:52+
Me [3]	7H (180°)	Mo [9]	exact at 6/30/2018 Saturday 04:00
Ke [9]	2H (30°)	Mo [10]	exact at 7/3/2018 Tuesday 01:35
Ra [3]	conjunction	Me [3]	exact at 7/3/2018 Tuesday 05:42
Jp [6]	9H (240°)	Su [2]	exact at 7/5/2018 Thursday 07:04
Me [3]	7H (180°)	Ma [9]	exact at 7/5/2018 Thursday 07:48
Mo [2]	conjunction	Su [2]	exact at 7/12/2018 Thursday 22:47
Ma [9]	7H (180°)	Mo [3]	exact at 7/14/2018 Saturday 01:11
Ra [3]	2H (30°)	Ve [4]	exact at 7/15/2018 Sunday 05:39
Ke [9]	9H (240°)	Mo [5]	exact at 7/18/2018 Wednesday 01:59
Ke [9]	conjunction	Ma [9]	exact at 7/20/2018 Friday 06:29
Sa [8]	conjunction	Mo [8]	exact at 7/25/2018 Wednesday 01:46
Mo [9]	7H (180°)	Su [3]	exact at 7/27/2018 Friday 16:20
Ra [3]	conjunction	Su [3]	exact at 7/28/2018 Saturday 20:58
Sa [8]	3H (60°)	Mo [10]	exact at 7/30/2018 Monday 02:47
Me [3]	conjunction	Su [3]	exact at 8/8/2018 Wednesday 22:05
Sa [8]	10H (270°)	Ve [5]	exact at 8/9/2018 Thursday 21:33
Ma [9]	7H (180°)	Mo [3]	exact at 8/10/2018 Friday 01:12
Mo [3]	conjunction	Su [3]	exact at 8/11/2018 Saturday 05:57

Ke [9]	9H (240°)	Ve [5]	exact at 8/12/2018 Sunday 15:41
Ma [9]	8H (210°)	Su [4]	exact at 8/21/2018 Tuesday 18:51
Mo [10]	7H (180°)	Su [4]	exact at 8/26/2018 Sunday 07:55
Ra [3]	2H (30°)	Su [4]	exact at 8/28/2018 Tuesday 20:00
Ra [3]	2H (30°)	Me [4]	exact at 9/8/2018 Saturday 20:29
Mo [4]	conjunction	Su [4]	exact at 9/9/2018 Sunday 14:01
Me [5]	conjunction	Su [5]	exact at 9/20/2018 Thursday 21:51
Sa [8]	10H (270°)	Me [5]	exact at 9/23/2018 Sunday 12:45
Mo [10]	7H (180°)	Su [5]	exact at 9/24/2018 Monday 22:52
Jp [6]	5H (120°)	Mo [10]	exact at 9/24/2018 Monday 01:25
Ke [9]	9H (240°)	Me [5]	exact at 9/24/2018 Monday 11:01
Sa [8]	10H (270°)	Su [5]	exact at 9/25/2018 Tuesday 19:50
Ra [3]	9H (240°)	Mo [11]	exact at 9/25/2018 Tuesday 03:18
Ke [9]	9H (240°)	Su [5]	exact at 9/26/2018 Wednesday 24:00
Ke [9]	conjunction	Ma [9]	exact at 9/26/2018 Wednesday 01:16
Ra [3]	2H (30°)	Mo [4]	exact at 10/6/2018 Saturday 01:04
Mo [5]	conjunction	Su [5]	exact at 10/8/2018 Monday 23:46
Sa [8]	10H (270°)	Mo [5]	exact at 10/8/2018 Monday 02:46
Ve [6]	conjunction	Me [6]	exact at 10/15/2018 Monday 16:20
Mo [12]	7H (180°)	Su [6]	exact at 10/24/2018 Wednesday 12:44
Ve [6]	conjunction	Su [6]	exact at 10/26/2018 Friday 10:15
Me [6]	7H (180°)	Mo [12]	exact at 10/26/2018 Friday 04:45
Sa [8]	7H (180°)	Mo [2]	exact at 10/29/2018 Monday 03:32
Jp [7]	conjunction	Me [7]	exact at 10/29/2018 Monday 07:04
Ra [3]	5H (120°)	Me [7]	exact at 10/31/2018 Wednesday 12:51
Ra [3]	2H (30°)	Mo [4]	exact at 11/2/2018 Friday 02:49
Ve [6]	conjunction	Mo [6]	exact at 11/6/2018 Tuesday 03:18
Mo [6]	conjunction	Su [6]	exact at 11/7/2018 Wednesday 11:01

Ra [3]	5H (120°)	Jp [7]	exact at 11/7/2018 Wednesday 10:47
Ke [9]	2H (30°)	Ma [10]	exact at 11/14/2018 Wednesday 08:53
Ma [10]	conjunction	Mo [10]	exact at 11/16/2018 Friday 00:01
Ra [3]	5H (120°)	Su [7]	exact at 11/20/2018 Tuesday 20:52
Mo [1]	7H (180°)	Su [7]	exact at 11/23/2018 Friday 00:38
Jp [7]	conjunction	Su [7]	exact at 11/26/2018 Monday 01:32
Me [7]	conjunction	Su [7]	exact at 11/27/2018 Tuesday 04:14
Ra [3]	conjunction	Mo [3]	exact at 11/27/2018 Tuesday 00:17
Sa [8]	3H (60°)	Ma [10]	exact at 11/27/2018 Tuesday 16:30
Jp [7]	conjunction	Me [7]	exact at 11/27/2018 Tuesday 17:27
Ra [3]	2H (30°)	Mo [4]	exact at 11/29/2018 Thursday 02:48
Ra [3]	5H (120°)	Me [7]	exact at 12/4/2018 Tuesday 11:38
Mo [7]	conjunction	Su [7]	exact at 12/7/2018 Friday 02:20
Ra [3]	5H (120°)	Me [7]	exact at 12/7/2018 Friday 11:28
Sa [8]	conjunction	Mo [8]	exact at 12/9/2018 Sunday 00:08
Ke [9]	2H (30°)	Mo [10]	exact at 12/13/2018 Thursday 02:01
Sa [8]	3H (60°)	Mo [10]	exact at 12/14/2018 Friday 02:31
Ve [6]	7H (180°)	Mo [12]	exact at 12/19/2018 Wednesday 01:53
Me [7]	7H (180°)	Mo [1]	exact at 12/21/2018 Friday 00:41
Jp [7]	7H (180°)	Mo [1]	exact at 12/21/2018 Friday 00:58
Jp [7]	conjunction	Me [7]	exact at 12/21/2018 Friday 12:36
Mo [1]	7H (180°)	Su [8]	exact at 12/22/2018 Saturday 12:48
Ma [10]	4H (90°)	Mo [1]	exact at 12/22/2018 Saturday 00:40
Ra [3]	9H (240°)	Ma [11]	exact at 12/27/2018 Thursday 06:19
Sa [8]	conjunction	Su [8]	exact at 1/2/2019 Wednesday 00:49
Jp [7]	conjunction	Mo [7]	exact at 1/3/2019 Thursday 03:23
Ra [3]	5H (120°)	Ve [7]	exact at 1/4/2019 Friday 01:41
Mo [8]	conjunction	Su [8]	exact at 1/5/2019 Saturday 20:27

Sa [8]	conjunction	Me [8]	exact at 1/13/2019 Sunday 08:30
Ke [9]	conjunction	Su [9]	exact at 1/16/2019 Wednesday 23:54
Mo [3]	7H (180°)	Su [9]	exact at 1/21/2019 Monday 00:15
Jp [7]	9H (240°)	Mo [3]	exact at 1/22/2019 Tuesday 00:11
Ke [9]	conjunction	Me [9]	exact at 1/22/2019 Tuesday 01:47
Ve [7]	conjunction	Jp [7]	exact at 1/22/2019 Tuesday 07:25
Jp [7]	5H (120°)	Ma [11]	exact at 1/25/2019 Friday 12:52
Me [9]	conjunction	Su [9]	exact at 1/29/2019 Tuesday 21:51
Ra [3]	5H (120°)	Mo [7]	exact at 1/29/2019 Tuesday 03:21
Sa [8]	conjunction	Mo [8]	exact at 2/2/2019 Saturday 01:56
Ke [9]	conjunction	Mo [9]	exact at 2/3/2019 Sunday 01:35
Mo [9]	conjunction	Su [9]	exact at 2/4/2019 Monday 16:03
Me [9]	conjunction	Mo [9]	exact at 2/5/2019 Tuesday 02:10
Ra [3]	9H (240°)	Mo [11]	exact at 2/8/2019 Friday 02:46
Ke [9]	2H (30°)	Me [10]	exact at 2/8/2019 Friday 08:36
Ke [9]	2H (30°)	Su [10]	exact at 2/15/2019 Friday 05:51
Sa [8]	conjunction	Ve [8]	exact at 2/18/2019 Monday 05:51
Mo [3]	7H (180°)	Su [10]	exact at 2/19/2019 Tuesday 10:53
Sa [8]	3H (60°)	Me [10]	exact at 2/19/2019 Tuesday 21:39
Ra [3]	9H (240°)	Me [11]	exact at 2/26/2019 Tuesday 14:11
Ke [9]	conjunction	Ve [9]	exact at 2/26/2019 Tuesday 01:53
Mo [10]	conjunction	Su [10]	exact at 3/6/2019 Wednesday 11:03
Sa [8]	3H (60°)	Su [10]	exact at 3/9/2019 Saturday 02:09
Ke [9]	5H (120°)	Mo [1]	exact at 3/12/2019 Tuesday 02:21
Me [11]	conjunction	Su [10]	exact at 3/14/2019 Thursday 21:47
Ra [3]	9H (240°)	Me [11]	exact at 3/14/2019 Thursday 05:18
Ra [3]	9H (240°)	Su [11]	exact at 3/15/2019 Friday 13:40
Sa [8]	7H (180°)	Mo [2]	exact at 3/16/2019 Saturday 02:23

Mo [4]	7H (180°)	Su [11]	exact at 3/20/2019 Wednesday 21:42
Sa [8]	3H (60°)	Me [10]	exact at 3/20/2019 Wednesday 10:26
Ke [9]	2H (30°)	Ve [9]	exact at 3/21/2019 Thursday 22:20
Ke [9]	5H (120°)	Ma [12]	exact at 3/22/2019 Friday 09:55
Ve [10]	conjunction	Mo [10]	exact at 4/2/2019 Tuesday 02:31
Sa [8]	3H (60°)	Mo [10]	exact at 4/3/2019 Wednesday 02:57
Mo [11]	conjunction	Su [11]	exact at 4/5/2019 Friday 04:50
Sa [8]	3H (60°)	Me [10]	exact at 4/7/2019 Sunday 05:16
Ke [8]	5H (120°)	Mo [12]	exact at 4/8/2019 Monday 03:02
Ma [1]	conjunction	Mo [1]	exact at 4/9/2019 Tuesday 04:15
Ra [2]	9H (240°)	Me [10]	exact at 4/9/2019 Tuesday 16:04
Sa [8]	3H (60°)	Ve [10]	exact at 4/12/2019 Friday 11:07
Ra [2]	9H (240°)	Ve [10]	exact at 4/13/2019 Saturday 21:58
Jp [8]	5H (120°)	Su [11]	exact at 4/14/2019 Sunday 09:40
Mo [6]	7H (180°)	Su [12]	exact at 4/19/2019 Friday 07:11
Ma [1]	8H (210°)	Mo [8]	exact at 4/25/2019 Thursday 02:34
Ke [8]	conjunction	Sa [8]	exact at 4/30/2019 Tuesday 16:24
Jp [7]	5H (120°)	Me [11]	exact at 5/2/2019 Thursday 23:58
Me [11]	conjunction	Mo [11]	exact at 5/3/2019 Friday 04:46
Mo [12]	conjunction	Su [12]	exact at 5/4/2019 Saturday 18:45
Jp [7]	7H (180°)	Ma [1]	exact at 5/5/2019 Sunday 17:56
Ke [8]	5H (120°)	Su [12]	exact at 5/10/2019 Friday 02:41
Ke [8]	5H (120°)	Me [12]	exact at 5/16/2019 Thursday 05:13
Mo [6]	7H (180°)	Su [1]	exact at 5/18/2019 Saturday 17:11
Ra [2]	5H (120°)	Mo [6]	exact at 5/18/2019 Saturday 01:42
Me [1]	conjunction	Su [1]	exact at 5/21/2019 Tuesday 09:06
Ke [8]	2H (30°)	Mo [9]	exact at 5/25/2019 Saturday 02:52
Ke [8]	5H (120°)	Ve [12]	exact at 5/30/2019 Thursday 07:50

Mo [1]	conjunction	Su [1]	exact at 6/3/2019 Monday 06:01
Jp [7]	7H (180°)	Su [1]	exact at 6/10/2019 Monday 11:27
Ma [2]	4H (90°)	Mo [5]	exact at 6/12/2019 Wednesday 02:18
Sa [8]	10H (270°)	Mo [5]	exact at 6/12/2019 Wednesday 04:21
Ra [2]	conjunction	Ma [2]	exact at 6/12/2019 Wednesday 18:46
Sa [8]	7H (180°)	Ma [2]	exact at 6/14/2019 Friday 11:49
Ra [2]	conjunction	Me [2]	exact at 6/15/2019 Saturday 13:57
Sa [8]	7H (180°)	Me [2]	exact at 6/16/2019 Sunday 10:00
Mo [7]	7H (180°)	Su [2]	exact at 6/17/2019 Monday 04:30
Me [2]	conjunction	Ma [2]	exact at 6/18/2019 Tuesday 12:04
Ve [1]	7H (180°)	Jp [7]	exact at 6/23/2019 Sunday 12:44
Mo [2]	conjunction	Su [2]	exact at 7/2/2019 Tuesday 15:16
Sa [8]	7H (180°)	Mo [2]	exact at 7/3/2019 Wednesday 03:00
Ma [3]	conjunction	Mo [3]	exact at 7/4/2019 Thursday 01:40
Ke [8]	conjunction	Sa [8]	exact at 7/4/2019 Thursday 03:27
Jp [7]	9H (240°)	Mo [3]	exact at 7/5/2019 Friday 02:24
Ra [2]	2H (30°)	Mo [3]	exact at 7/5/2019 Friday 03:04
Me [3]	conjunction	Ma [3]	exact at 7/8/2019 Monday 18:27
Sa [8]	7H (180°)	Su [2]	exact at 7/9/2019 Tuesday 13:06
Mo [8]	7H (180°)	Su [2]	exact at 7/16/2019 Tuesday 17:37
Sa [8]	conjunction	Mo [8]	exact at 7/16/2019 Tuesday 03:17
Ke [8]	conjunction	Mo [8]	exact at 7/16/2019 Tuesday 03:22
Sa [8]	7H (180°)	Ve [2]	exact at 7/17/2019 Wednesday 01:33
Ra [2]	conjunction	Ve [2]	exact at 7/17/2019 Wednesday 20:49
Ma [3]	7H (180°)	Mo [9]	exact at 7/18/2019 Thursday 01:49
Me [3]	conjunction	Su [3]	exact at 7/21/2019 Sunday 08:33
Sa [8]	3H (60°)	Mo [10]	exact at 7/21/2019 Sunday 02:27
Ra [2]	9H (240°)	Mo [10]	exact at 7/21/2019 Sunday 03:55

Ve [3]	conjunction	Me [3]	exact at 7/24/2019 Wednesday 20:26
Jp [7]	9H (240°)	Ma [3]	exact at 7/25/2019 Thursday 08:22
Ke [8]	5H (120°)	Mo [12]	exact at 7/26/2019 Friday 03:19
Ra [2]	2H (30°)	Ma [3]	exact at 7/29/2019 Monday 12:17
Mo [3]	conjunction	Su [3]	exact at 7/31/2019 Wednesday 23:11
Jp [7]	9H (240°)	Su [3]	exact at 8/7/2019 Wednesday 03:31
Ra [2]	2H (30°)	Su [3]	exact at 8/10/2019 Saturday 03:04
Ra [2]	2H (30°)	Ve [3]	exact at 8/10/2019 Saturday 00:46+
Ve [3]	conjunction	Su [3]	exact at 8/14/2019 Wednesday 02:07
Mo [9]	7H (180°)	Su [3]	exact at 8/15/2019 Thursday 08:29
Jp [7]	9H (240°)	Me [3]	exact at 8/21/2019 Wednesday 06:04
Ra [2]	2H (30°)	Me [3]	exact at 8/22/2019 Thursday 08:13
Ve [4]	conjunction	Ma [4]	exact at 8/24/2019 Saturday 13:04
Mo [4]	conjunction	Su [4]	exact at 8/30/2019 Friday 06:36
Ma [4]	conjunction	Su [4]	exact at 9/2/2019 Monday 06:42
Me [4]	conjunction	Su [4]	exact at 9/3/2019 Tuesday 21:39
Me [4]	conjunction	Ma [4]	exact at 9/3/2019 Tuesday 11:39
Ke [8]	9H (240°)	Ve [4]	exact at 9/3/2019 Tuesday 04:13
Jp [7]	conjunction	Mo [7]	exact at 9/6/2019 Friday 03:19
Ke [8]	9H (240°)	Me [4]	exact at 9/6/2019 Friday 08:50
Ke [8]	9H (240°)	Su [4]	exact at 9/8/2019 Sunday 18:20
Ke [8]	2H (30°)	Mo [9]	exact at 9/11/2019 Wednesday 01:17
Ke [8]	9H (240°)	Ma [4]	exact at 9/11/2019 Wednesday 20:20
Mo [10]	7H (180°)	Su [4]	exact at 9/13/2019 Friday 00:32+
Ve [5]	conjunction	Me [5]	exact at 9/13/2019 Friday 11:10
Jp [7]	5H (120°)	Mo [11]	exact at 9/16/2019 Monday 03:28
Sa [8]	10H (270°)	Me [5]	exact at 9/22/2019 Sunday 12:18
Sa [8]	7H (180°)	Mo [2]	exact at 9/23/2019 Monday 01:38

Ra [2]	conjunction	Mo [2]	exact at 9/23/2019 Monday 01:55
Sa [8]	10H (270°)	Ve [5]	exact at 9/25/2019 Wednesday 15:19
Mo [5]	conjunction	Su [5]	exact at 9/28/2019 Saturday 14:26
Ke [8]	conjunction	Sa [8]	exact at 9/28/2019 Saturday 02:20
Sa [8]	10H (270°)	Mo [5]	exact at 9/29/2019 Sunday 04:07
Ra [2]	5H (120°)	Mo [6]	exact at 10/1/2019 Tuesday 03:42
Sa [8]	10H (270°)	Su [5]	exact at 10/7/2019 Monday 15:06
Ke [8]	2H (30°)	Mo [9]	exact at 10/8/2019 Tuesday 02:01
Ra [2]	5H (120°)	Me [6]	exact at 10/12/2019 Saturday 11:48
Mo [11]	7H (180°)	Su [5]	exact at 10/13/2019 Sunday 17:07
Ma [5]	8H (210°)	Mo [12]	exact at 10/15/2019 Tuesday 02:23
Ve [6]	7H (180°)	Mo [12]	exact at 10/15/2019 Tuesday 03:25
Ra [2]	5H (120°)	Ve [6]	exact at 10/17/2019 Thursday 18:50
Ra [2]	conjunction	Mo [2]	exact at 10/20/2019 Sunday 03:28
Jp [7]	9H (240°)	Mo [3]	exact at 10/23/2019 Wednesday 01:40
Mo [5]	conjunction	Su [6]	exact at 10/27/2019 Sunday 23:38
Sa [8]	10H (270°)	Ma [5]	exact at 10/27/2019 Sunday 10:30
Ve [7]	conjunction	Me [7]	exact at 10/30/2019 Wednesday 18:05
Ra [2]	5H (120°)	Su [6]	exact at 11/2/2019 Saturday 21:09
Sa [8]	conjunction	Mo [8]	exact at 11/2/2019 Saturday 03:28
Ke [8]	2H (30°)	Mo [9]	exact at 11/4/2019 Monday 02:39
Sa [8]	3H (60°)	Mo [10]	exact at 11/7/2019 Thursday 02:18
Me [6]	conjunction	Su [6]	exact at 11/11/2019 Monday 10:21
Mo [12]	7H (180°)	Su [6]	exact at 11/12/2019 Tuesday 08:34
Ve [8]	conjunction	Jp [8]	exact at 11/24/2019 Sunday 08:33
Mo [7]	conjunction	Su [7]	exact at 11/26/2019 Tuesday 10:05
Ra [2]	5H (120°)	Ma [6]	exact at 12/2/2019 Monday 07:38
Ke [8]	conjunction	Ve [8]	exact at 12/2/2019 Monday 20:30

Sa [8]	conjunction	Ve [8]	exact at 12/11/2019 Wednesday 05:04
Mo [1]	7H (180°)	Su [7]	exact at 12/12/2019 Thursday 00:12
Mo [8]	conjunction	Su [8]	exact at 12/26/2019 Thursday 00:12
Jp [8]	conjunction	Mo [8]	exact at 12/26/2019 Thursday 02:28
Ke [8]	2H (30°)	Ve [9]	exact at 12/26/2019 Thursday 21:09
Jp [8]	conjunction	Su [8]	exact at 12/27/2019 Friday 13:25
Ke [8]	conjunction	Su [8]	exact at 12/30/2019 Monday 04:52
Ra [2]	9H (240°)	Mo [10]	exact at 12/31/2019 Tuesday 03:25

Retrogression Report for United States 2018 EST

Date	Time	Days	Degrees	Sign	Planet	Retrograde Action
1/4/2018	5:50	3	21° 5'	Ca	Rah	goes Direct
1/ 8/2018	6:10	7	21° 10'	Ca	Rah	goes Retrograde
1/18/2018	6:09	17	20° 47'	Ca	Rah	goes Direct
1/24/2018	6:10	23	20° 52'	Ca	Rah	goes Retrograde
1/31/2018	6:09	30	20° 49'	Ca	Rah	goes Direct
2/ 3/2018	6:10	33	20° 49'	Ca	Rah	goes Retrograde
2/ 7/2018	6:09	37	20° 49'	Ca	Rah	goes Direct
2/14/2018	6:10	44	20° 53'	Ca	Rah	goes Retrograde
2/23/2018	5:50	53	20° 41'	Ca	Rah	goes Direct
2/28/2018	5:50	58	20° 45'	Ca	Rah	goes Retrograde
3/ 9/2018	0:17	67	29° 6'	Li	Jup	goes Retrograde
3/ 9/2018	6:09	67	20° 18'	Ca	Rah	goes Direct
3/13/2018	6:10	71	20° 23'	Ca	Rah	goes Retrograde
3/22/2018	20:07	80	22° 48'	Pi	Mer	goes Retrograde
3/24/2018	6:09	82	19° 35'	Ca	Rah	goes Direct
3/27/2018	6:55	85	19° 36'	Ca	Rah	goes Retrograde

4/8/2018	5:50	97	18° 26'	Ca	Rah	goes Direct
4/10/2018	5:50	99	18° 27'	Ca	Rah	goes Retrograde
4/15/2018	5:10	104	10° 40'	Pi	Mer	goes Direct
4/17/2018	21:04	106	15° 2'	Sg	Sat	goes Retrograde
4/22/2018	6:09	111	17° 7'	Ca	Rah	goes Direct
4/23/2018	6:10	112	17° 7'	Ca	Rah	goes Retrograde
5/20/2018	6:09	139	14° 17'	Ca	Rah	goes Direct
5/21/2018	6:10	140	14° 17'	Ca	Rah	goes Retrograde
6/3/2018	6:09	153	13° 1'	Ca	Rah	goes Direct
6/6/2018	6:10	156	13° 3'	Ca	Rah	goes Retrograde
6/16/2018	6:09	166	12° 22'	Ca	Rah	goes Direct
6/20/2018	5:50	170	12° 25'	Ca	Rah	goes Retrograde
6/26/2018	16:46	176	15° 6'	Cp	Mar	goes Retrograde
6/30/2018	6:09	180	11° 51'	Ca	Rah	goes Direct
7/6/2018	5:50	186	11° 57'	Ca	Rah	goes Retrograde
7/10/2018	13:26	190	19° 13'	Li	Jup	goes Direct
7/13/2018	6:09	193	11° 46'	Ca	Rah	goes Direct
7/19/2018	6:10	199	11° 49'	Ca	Rah	goes Retrograde
7/26/2018	0:51	206	29° 20'	Ca	Mer	goes Retrograde
7/27/2018	6:09	207	11° 46'	Ca	Rah	goes Direct
7/28/2018	5:50	208	11° 46'	Ca	Rah	goes Retrograde
8/4/2018	6:09	215	11° 44'	Ca	Rah	goes Direct
8/10/2018	6:10	221	11° 47'	Ca	Rah	goes Retrograde
8/18/2018	5:50	229	11° 37'	Ca	Rah	goes Direct
8/19/2018	0:17	230	17° 24'	Ca	Mer	goes Direct
8/24/2018	5:50	235	11° 44'	Ca	Rah	goes Retrograde
8/27/2018	9:54	238	4° 29'	Cp	Mar	goes Direct

Date	Time	Deg	Pos	Sign	Planet	Status
9/ 2/2018	6:09	244	11° 14'	Ca	Rah	goes Direct
9/ 6/2018	7:42	248	8° 25'	Sg	Sat	goes Direct
9/ 6/2018	6:10	248	11° 16'	Ca	Rah	goes Retrograde
9/16/2018	6:09	258	10° 35'	Ca	Rah	goes Direct
9/20/2018	5:50	262	10° 37'	Ca	Rah	goes Retrograde
10/2/2018	5:50	274	9° 25'	Ca	Rah	goes Direct
10/3/2018	6:10	275	9° 25'	Ca	Rah	goes Retrograde
10/5/2018	14:52	277	16° 43'	Li	Ven	goes Retrograde
10/16/2018	6:09	288	8° 5'	Ca	Rah	goes Direct
10/17/2018	6:10	289	8° 5'	Ca	Rah	goes Retrograde
10/30/2018	6:09	302	6° 31'	Ca	Rah	goes Direct
10/31/2018	6:10	303	6° 30'	Ca	Rah	goes Retrograde
11/13/2018	6:09	316	5° 3'	Ca	Rah	goes Direct
11/15/2018	6:10	318	5° 3'	Ca	Rah	goes Retrograde
11/16/2018	21:26	319	19° 22'	Sc	Mer	goes Retrograde
11/16/2018	5:51	319	1° 7'	Li	Ven	goes Direct
11/27/2018	5:50	330	3° 54'	Ca	Rah	goes Direct
11/29/2018	6:10	332	3° 56'	Ca	Rah	goes Retrograde
12/6/2018	17:13	339	3° 9'	Sc	Mer	goes Direct
12/10/2018	6:09	343	3° 3'	Ca	Rah	goes Direct
12/15/2018	6:10	348	3° 9'	Ca	Rah	goes Retrograde
12/24/2018	6:09	357	2° 43'	Ca	Rah	goes Direct
12/29/2018	5:50	-3	2° 48'	Ca	Rah	goes Retrograde
1/ 6/2019	6:09	5	2° 35'	Ca	Rah	goes Direct
1/14/2019	5:50	13	2° 39'	Ca	Rah	goes Retrograde
1/16/2019	6:09	15	2° 39'	Ca	Rah	goes Direct
1/20/2019	6:10	19	2° 39'	Ca	Rah	goes Retrograde

1/27/2019	6:09	26	2° 35'	Ca	Rah	goes Direct
2/ 3/2019	5:50	33	2° 41'	Ca	Rah	goes Retrograde
2/12/2019	6:09	42	2° 17'	Ca	Rah	goes Direct
2/17/2019	5:50	47	2° 22'	Ca	Rah	goes Retrograde
2/26/2019	6:09	56	1° 50'	Ca	Rah	goes Direct
3/ 2/2019	6:02	60	1° 55'	Ca	Rah	goes Retrograde
3/ 5/2019	14:08	63	5° 31'	Pi	Mer	goes Retrograde
3/14/2019	5:50	72	0° 42'	Ca	Rah	goes Direct
3/16/2019	6:10	74	0° 43'	Ca	Rah	goes Retrograde
3/28/2019	9:50	86	21° 58'	Aq	Mer	goes Direct
3/28/2019	5:50	86	29° 37'	Ge	Rah	goes Direct
3/29/2019	6:10	87	29° 37'	Ge	Rah	goes Retrograde
4/10/2019	12:24	99	0° 13'	Sg	Jup	goes Retrograde
4/25/2019	6:09	114	26° 37'	Ge	Rah	goes Direct
4/26/2019	6:10	115	26° 37'	Ge	Rah	goes Retrograde
4/29/2019	20:32	118	26° 23'	Sg	Sat	goes Retrograde
5/ 9/2019	6:09	128	25° 13'	Ge	Rah	goes Direct
5/11/2019	6:10	130	25° 13'	Ge	Rah	goes Retrograde
5/22/2019	6:09	141	24° 21'	Ge	Rah	goes Direct
5/26/2019	6:10	145	24° 24'	Ge	Rah	goes Retrograde
6/ 5/2019	6:09	155	23° 45'	Ge	Rah	goes Direct
6/10/2019	5:50	160	23° 49'	Ge	Rah	goes Retrograde
6/18/2019	6:09	168	23° 30'	Ge	Rah	goes Direct
6/25/2019	5:50	175	23° 35'	Ge	Rah	goes Retrograde
7/ 3/2019	5:50	183	23° 29'	Ge	Rah	goes Direct
7/ 7/2019	19:03	187	10° 20'	Ca	Mer	goes Retrograde
7/16/2019	5:50	196	23° 31'	Ge	Rah	goes Retrograde

Date	Time			Sign	Planet	Motion
7/24/2019	6:09	204	23° 24'	Ge	Rah	goes Direct
7/30/2019	6:10	210	23° 28'	Ge	Rah	goes Retrograde
7/31/2019	23:59	211	29° 50'	Ge	Mer	goes Direct
8/ 7/2019	6:09	218	23° 13'	Ge	Rah	goes Direct
8/11/2019	9:54	222	20° 22'	Sc	Jup	goes Direct
8/12/2019	6:10	223	23° 18'	Ge	Rah	goes Retrograde
8/23/2019	6:09	234	22° 32'	Ge	Rah	goes Direct
8/26/2019	6:10	237	22° 34'	Ge	Rah	goes Retrograde
9/ 5/2019	6:09	247	21° 50'	Ge	Rah	goes Direct
9/ 8/2019	6:10	250	21° 50'	Ge	Rah	goes Retrograde
9/18/2019	4:48	260	19° 46'	Sg	Sat	goes Direct
9/21/2019	6:09	263	20° 17'	Ge	Rah	goes Direct
9/23/2019	5:50	265	20° 17'	Ge	Rah	goes Retrograde
10/20/2019	5:50	292	17° 16'	Ge	Rah	goes Direct
10/21/2019	6:10	293	17° 16'	Ge	Rah	goes Retrograde
10/31/2019	11:25	303	3° 30'	Sc	Mer	goes Retrograde
11/1/2019	6:09	304	16° 10'	Ge	Rah	goes Direct
11/4/2019	5:50	307	16° 11'	Ge	Rah	goes Retrograde
11/16/2019	5:50	319	15° 1'	Ge	Rah	goes Direct
11/19/2019	6:10	322	15° 4'	Ge	Rah	goes Retrograde
11/20/2019	15:03	323	17° 27'	Li	Mer	goes Direct
11/29/2019	5:50	332	14° 30'	Ge	Rah	goes Direct
12/4/2019	5:50	337	14° 36'	Ge	Rah	goes Retrograde
12/13/2019	6:09	346	14° 15'	Ge	Rah	goes Direct
12/19/2019	5:50	352	14° 19'	Ge	Rah	goes Retrograde
12/26/2019	6:09	359	14° 15'	Ge	Rah	goes Direct

Sign Ingresses

2019 Jan. 1 Rashi: Venus enters Scorpio at 10:12 Tuesday
2019 Jan. 14 Rashi: Sun enters Capricorn at 09:21 Monday
2019 Jan. 20 Rashi: Mercury enters Capricorn at 10:36 Sunday
2019 Jan. 29 Rashi: Venus enters Sagittarius at 12:58 Tuesday
2019 Feb. 5 Rashi: Mars enters Aries at 13:17 Tuesday
2019 Feb. 6 Rashi: Mercury enters Aquarius at 23:40 Wednesday
2019 Feb. 12 Rashi: Sun enters Aquarius at 22:18 Tuesday
2019 Feb. 24 Rashi: Mercury enters Pisces at 22:22 Sunday
2019 Feb. 24 Rashi: Venus enters Capricorn at 12:14 Sunday
2019 Mar. 14 Rashi: Sun enters Pisces at 20:09 Thursday
2019 Mar. 14 Rashi: Mercury enters Aquarius at 23:29 Thursday
2019 Mar. 21 Rashi: Venus enters Aquarius at 18:14 Thursday
2019 Mar. 22 Rashi: Mars enters Taurus at 05:34 Friday
2019 Mar. 23 Rashi: Rahu enters Gemini at 03:07 Saturday
2019 Mar. 23 Rashi: Ketu enters Sagittarius at 03:07 Saturday
2019 Mar. 29 Rashi: Jupiter enters Sagittarius at 10:32 Friday
2019 Apr. 11 Rashi: Mercury enters Pisces at 18:53 Thursday
2019 Apr. 14 Rashi: Sun enters Aries at 04:38 Sunday
2019 Apr. 15 Rashi: Venus enters Pisces at 15:34 Monday
2019 Apr. 22 Rashi: Jupiter enters Scorpio at 15:45 Monday
2019 May 3 Rashi: Mercury enters Aries at 07:32 Friday
2019 May 6 Rashi: Mars enters Gemini at 21:22 Monday
2019 May 10 Rashi: Venus enters Aries at 09:35 Friday
2019 May 15 Rashi: Sun enters Taurus at 01:30 Wednesday
2019 May 18 Rashi: Mercury enters Taurus at 14:04 Saturday

2019 June 1 Rashi: Mercury enters Gemini at 14:46 Saturday
2019 June 4 Rashi: Venus enters Taurus at 01:49 Tuesday
2019 June 15 Rashi: Sun enters Gemini at 08:07 Saturday
2019 June 20 Rashi: Mercury enters Cancer at 16:56 Thursday
2019 June 22 Rashi: Mars enters Cancer at 13:52 Saturday
2019 June 28 Rashi: Venus enters Gemini at 16:03 Friday
2019 July 16 Rashi: Sun enters Cancer at 19:03 Tuesday
2019 July 23 Rashi: Venus enters Cancer at 03:18 Tuesday
2019 July 30 Rashi: Mercury enters Gemini at 02:22 Tuesday
2019 Aug. 2 Rashi: Mercury enters Cancer at 20:45 Friday
2019 Aug. 8 Rashi: Mars enters Leo at 19:16 Thursday
2019 Aug. 16 Rashi: Venus enters Leo at 11:09 Friday
2019 Aug. 17 Rashi: Sun enters Leo at 03:31 Saturday
2019 Aug. 26 Rashi: Mercury enters Leo at 04:37 Monday
2019 Sept. 9 Rashi: Venus enters Virgo at 16:10 Monday
2019 Sept. 10 Rashi: Mercury enters Virgo at 19:28 Tuesday
2019 Sept. 17 Rashi: Sun enters Virgo at 03:32 Tuesday
2019 Sept. 24 Rashi: Mars enters Virgo at 21:02 Tuesday
2019 Sept. 29 Rashi: Mercury enters Libra at 03:24 Sunday
2019 Oct. 3 Rashi: Venus enters Libra at 19:43 Thursday
2019 Oct. 17 Rashi: Sun enters Libra at 15:32 Thursday
2019 Oct. 23 Rashi: Mercury enters Scorpio at 13:41 Wednesday
2019 Oct. 27 Rashi: Venus enters Scorpio at 23:01 Sunday
2019 Nov. 4 Rashi: Jupiter enters Sagittarius at 18:46 Monday
2019 Nov. 7 Rashi: Mercury enters Libra at 05:24 Thursday
2019 Nov. 10 Rashi: Mars enters Libra at 03:53 Sunday
2019 Nov. 16 Rashi: Sun enters Scorpio at 14:20 Saturday

2019 Nov. 21 Rashi: Venus enters Sagittarius at 01:52 Thursday
2019 Dec. 5 Rashi: Mercury enters Scorpio at 00:03 Thursday
2019 Dec. 15 Rashi: Venus enters Capricorn at 07:28 Sunday
2019 Dec. 16 Rashi: Sun enters Sagittarius at 04:57 Monday
2019 Dec. 25 Rashi: Mars enters Scorpio at 10:58 Wednesday
2019 Dec. 25 Rashi: Mercury enters Sagittarius at 05:15 Wednesday
2019 Jan. 1 Rashi: Venus enters Scorpio at 10:12 Tuesday
2019 Jan. 14 Rashi: Sun enters Capricorn at 09:21 Monday
2019 Jan. 20 Rashi: Mercury enters Capricorn at 10:36 Sunday
2019 Jan. 29 Rashi: Venus enters Sagittarius at 12:58 Tuesday
2019 Feb. 5 Rashi: Mars enters Aries at 13:17 Tuesday
2019 Feb. 6 Rashi: Mercury enters Aquarius at 23:40 Wednesday
2019 Feb. 12 Rashi: Sun enters Aquarius at 22:18 Tuesday
2019 Feb. 24 Rashi: Mercury enters Pisces at 22:22 Sunday
2019 Feb. 24 Rashi: Venus enters Capricorn at 12:14 Sunday
2019 Mar. 14 Rashi: Sun enters Pisces at 20:09 Thursday
2019 Mar. 14 Rashi: Mercury enters Aquarius at 23:29 Thursday
2019 Mar. 21 Rashi: Venus enters Aquarius at 18:14 Thursday
2019 Mar. 22 Rashi: Mars enters Taurus at 05:34 Friday
2019 Mar. 23 Rashi: Rahu enters Gemini at 03:07 Saturday
2019 Mar. 23 Rashi: Ketu enters Sagittarius at 03:07 Saturday
2019 Mar. 29 Rashi: Jupiter enters Sagittarius at 10:32 Friday
2019 Apr. 11 Rashi: Mercury enters Pisces at 18:53 Thursday
2019 Apr. 14 Rashi: Sun enters Aries at 04:38 Sunday
2019 Apr. 15 Rashi: Venus enters Pisces at 15:34 Monday
2019 Apr. 22 Rashi: Jupiter enters Scorpio at 15:45 Monday
2019 May 3 Rashi: Mercury enters Aries at 07:32 Friday

2019 May 6 Rashi: Mars enters Gemini at 21:22 Monday
2019 May 10 Rashi: Venus enters Aries at 09:35 Friday
2019 May 15 Rashi: Sun enters Taurus at 01:30 Wednesday
2019 May 18 Rashi: Mercury enters Taurus at 14:04 Saturday
2019 June 1 Rashi: Mercury enters Gemini at 14:46 Saturday
2019 June 4 Rashi: Venus enters Taurus at 01:49 Tuesday
2019 June 15 Rashi: Sun enters Gemini at 08:07 Saturday
2019 June 20 Rashi: Mercury enters Cancer at 16:56 Thursday
2019 June 22 Rashi: Mars enters Cancer at 13:52 Saturday
2019 June 28 Rashi: Venus enters Gemini at 16:03 Friday
2019 July 16 Rashi: Sun enters Cancer at 19:03 Tuesday
2019 July 23 Rashi: Venus enters Cancer at 03:18 Tuesday
2019 July 30 Rashi: Mercury enters Gemini at 02:22 Tuesday
2019 Aug. 2 Rashi: Mercury enters Cancer at 20:45 Friday
2019 Aug. 8 Rashi: Mars enters Leo at 19:16 Thursday
2019 Aug. 16 Rashi: Venus enters Leo at 11:09 Friday
2019 Aug. 17 Rashi: Sun enters Leo at 03:31 Saturday
2019 Aug. 26 Rashi: Mercury enters Leo at 04:37 Monday
2019 Sept. 9 Rashi: Venus enters Virgo at 16:10 Monday
2019 Sept. 10 Rashi: Mercury enters Virgo at 19:28 Tuesday
2019 Sept. 17 Rashi: Sun enters Virgo at 03:32 Tuesday
2019 Sept. 24 Rashi: Mars enters Virgo at 21:02 Tuesday
2019 Sept. 29 Rashi: Mercury enters Libra at 03:24 Sunday
2019 Oct. 3 Rashi: Venus enters Libra at 19:43 Thursday
2019 Oct. 17 Rashi: Sun enters Libra at 15:32 Thursday
2019 Oct. 23 Rashi: Mercury enters Scorpio at 13:41 Wednesday
2019 Oct. 27 Rashi: Venus enters Scorpio at 23:01 Sunday

2019 Nov. 4 Rashi: Jupiter enters Sagittarius at 18:46 Monday
2019 Nov. 7 Rashi: Mercury enters Libra at 05:24 Thursday
2019 Nov. 10 Rashi: Mars enters Libra at 03:53 Sunday
2019 Nov. 16 Rashi: Sun enters Scorpio at 14:20 Saturday
2019 Nov. 21 Rashi: Venus enters Sagittarius at 01:52 Thursday
2019 Dec. 5 Rashi: Mercury enters Scorpio at 00:03 Thursday
2019 Dec. 15 Rashi: Venus enters Capricorn at 07:28 Sunday
2019 Dec. 16 Rashi: Sun enters Sagittarius at 04:57 Monday
2019 Dec. 25 Rashi: Mars enters Scorpio at 10:58 Wednesday
2019 Dec. 25 Rashi: Mercury enters Sagittarius at 05:15 Wednesday

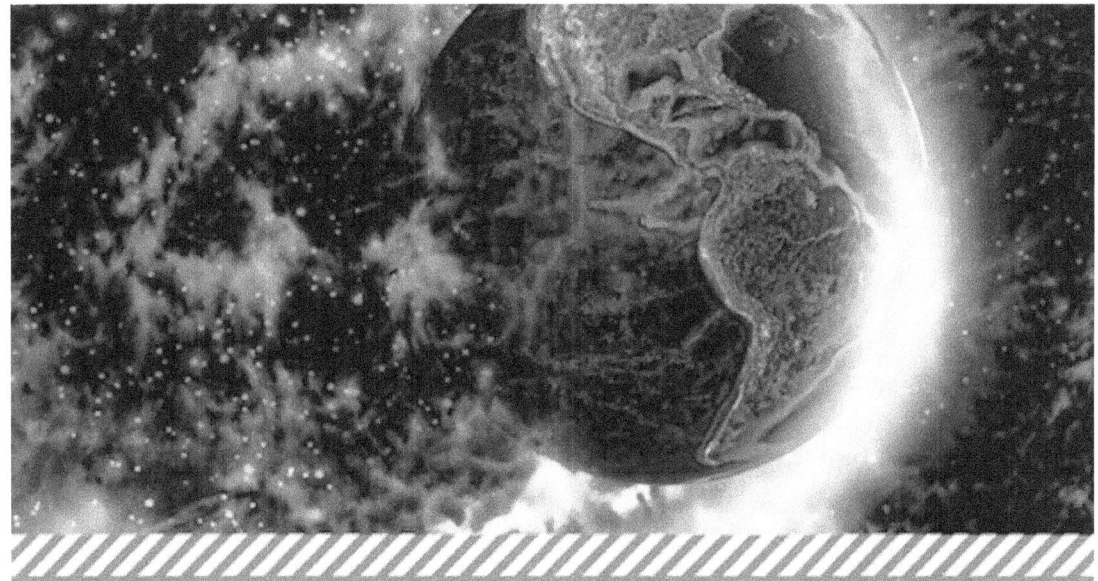

KARAKAS AND SIGNIFICATIONS

Karaka Qualities: Each planet, sign or house signifies certain characteristics.

Below is a quick reference of what each planet represents in the chart.

Sun: Soul, self, father, government, one's own self, ego, royalty, status, overall physique/body, authority, employers, superiors, bosses, circulatory system and heart, heat, power, prestige, the ego, the Right eye, fame and electricity, confidence, independence, actualizing goals, honored, respect, freedom, creativity, living in wooded areas, ulcers, poor vision (afflicted), pompous.

Jupiter: Husband, children, teacher or gurus, elder brother/siblings, banking, respect, family, fortune, body fat, holy places, donation, attorney, counselor, minister, teacher, humanitarian, judge, those who inspire us and give us meaning, devotion, tradition, values, purpose, hope, justice, sense of meaning, judgment, purity, knowledge, wisdom, devotion, philosophy, learning, wealth, scriptures, the higher mind, optimism, overconfidence, spiritual knowledge, good deeds, worship, charity, philanthropy, pilgrimages, community, religious discourses, expansion of consciousness, higher status, and expansion in general.

Moon: Mother, one's own heart, desire, instinct, memory, fertility, bedrock of support, one's mind (emotional), feeling, love of home and family, the Queen, cycles, receptivity, emotions, mind, the Moon, the Left eye, liquid, fluids, water, moisture, heart, sleep, happiness, travel, milk, pearls, imagination, good listener, intuitive, compassion, kindness, emotional nurturing.

Mars: Younger brothers, the fighter, the athlete, surgeon, courage, valor, anger, desire, weapons, strength, scandal, controllers, burns, police, military, boyfriend, warrior, surgery, accidents, competition, flexibility, strategy, skill, adversity, war, defense, action, inner vitality gushing for objective expression, creative initiative, dynamism, growth, movement, change, martial arts, scientific discoveries, full of initiative, love of adventure, childlike joy, animal passion, reckless, suffering, injury, explosions, agitation, outbursts, bloodshed, abortion.

Rahu: Paternal grandfather, metal working, machines, analysis, gambling, unorthodox, foreign things, detachment, ambition, growth, creative/artistic, material success, learning futility of the material world, unexpected fortunes, victimized by overpowering forces, shadowy maneuverings, Karmic axis, tinged with dissatisfaction, emptiness, mysterious, fears and phobias, foreign travel, addictions, dejection leads to transformation, pollution, bad dreams, fright, manic-depression, snake bite, accidents, poison, skin disease, harsh speech, arguments, liar, deceiver, traveling, theft, wickedness, smoke, fog, widow, cheating, loss, manipulation, one's material destiny, material karma; chronic conditions, qualities to be developed in this lifetime, attachment; foreign influences, deceptions, delusions.

Ketu: Maternal grandfather, magnifies, spiritual teacher of moksha, computers, technology, detachment, Moksha, consumption, pain, wounds, dogs, birds, astrology, interested in enlightenment, Divine wisdom, occult knowledge, opens the portals of hidden mysteries, reveals deeper truths of life, travel to foreign countries, always wants to change life direction, renunciation, takes away what it has given in its 7 year period, creates disillusionment, unsettled, questions reality of life, creates emotional knots, emotional distortions, dwell on past mistakes, isolation, past life, blindness, introspection, imprisonment, humiliation, spending time with undesirable people, hard to diagnosis diseases, cancer, infections, prone to wrong surgeries, non-materialistic.

Venus: Wife, mistress, girlfriend, one's ability to relate, love, marriage, things you love, wealth, women, senses, pleasures, comforts, indulgences, conveyances, buying/selling, wine and food, politics, partners, business, relations, lovers, beloveds, those we want to share our happiness with, educator, Spiritual Minister, vehicles, clothing, jewelry, accessories, design, art, interior decorating, beauty, perfumes, gems, sexual pleasure, vanity, laziness, creativity, flowers, massage, music, dance, poetry and expression, diplomacy, ministers, lawyers, feminine, affairs, jealousy, social clubs, celebrations and festivals, attractive appearance, grooming, wish-fulfillment, physical comforts, sexual play, balanced sensual gratification and luxurious living, painting, kidneys, fertility and reproduction.

Mercury: Maternal uncle, friends, the Prince, business, comic writer, communicator, education, communication, speech, business and accounting, intelligence, math, logic, writing, astrology, publishing, memory, analytical thinking, politics, drama, neighbors, hobbies, games, duality, social activities, one's own mind, sharp intellect, curiosity, exploration, monetary rewards, reading, relatives outside the immediate family, science, joking, respiration.

Saturn: Elders, employees, hard-working, authority figures, longevity, karma, death, life, time, struggles, old age, work, enemies, health, perseverance, catastrophic events, inheritance, insurance, transformation, change, unexpected breaks, stress, the mysteries, responsibilities, energy loss, letting go, transitions, slow progress, escapism, surrendering, expenditures, foreign travel, Moksha, labor, clocks, adversity, service, disease, poverty, trouble, losses, theft, servants, dishonor, imprisonment, grief, oil, agriculture, west direction, focus, lessons, justice, steady and dependable, seeking enlightenment through isolation and restraint, adversity and prosperity, limitations, setbacks, returns, delays, lost things, concentration, introspection, meditation, support, work in hospitals, prisons, ashrams, monasteries.

Signs and House - Polarity

Aries/Libra or 1st house/7th house
This is the basic relationship axis, where Aries and the 1st house represent "*self*" and Libra and the seventh house represent "*other*." Where Aries, the 1st house is about self-assertion and Libra the 7th house is about compromise. People born with planets in both Aries and Libra or both the 1st and 7th house need to learn the balance between these two needs and it is the perpetual dance of Mars wanting to be the hero and go it alone and Venus and Libras who always have to do it together.

Wherever there is an Aries, there is also a dominant energy toward major activity in life. Aries are actually very emotional because it is the sign before Taurus, where emotions are full. I actually find many talented artists come out Aries, particularly if they have Venus placed here as the sign brings out their creative talent.

Wherever Libra falls in your chart in any rising ascendant or Varga chart, it brings blessings of prosperity and Lakshmi, the grace to end conflicts. Venus has trouble with Mars. Mars creates by wanting to fight and express its ego in the world and leave its mark and gain status. The Shakti of Venus is to end conflict to bring prosperity, growth and fulfill desires and help distribute resource. Still the dark side is intense psychological brooding, particularly in Chitra or Swati nakshatras where there is never happiness. Artistic creativity has to replace sexual energy for balance to prevail here.

Taurus/Scorpio or 2nd house/8th house
This polarity deals with material manifestation (Taurus and the 2nd house) versus spiritual transformation (Scorpio and the 8th house). While Taurus and the 2nd house deal with matter, personal values, material goods, possessions, and security, Scorpio and the 8th house rules the destruction of material (Ketu), change and transformation.

Ketu is so often forgotten as the secondary owner of Scorpio, with its mystical and spiritual nature wanting to wander in search of enlightenment, which is so opposed to the earthiest sign of Taurus and its desire to bathe in the sense and accumulate more. When Rahu goes through Taurus and Ketu through Scorpio, this opposition will be strongest. We will see this transit in **September 2020 - March 2022.**

If we see Scorpio in any part of a chart, it is connected to the 8th sign of the zodiac and deep past life karma, which can bring deep suffering to one's life. Planets placed in Scorpio may experience deep cruelty from the darker side of Mars and may seem rather fallen. Scorpio is co-owned by Ketu, the mystical, headless wonder that takes us toward enlightenment and the key in Scorpio is finding spirituality and transformation to transform that dark energy.

Ketu may want to take everything from us to point us toward moksha, so it sometimes can create poverty and loss that is completely opposite the material abundance that Taurus brings. Scorpio anywhere in the chart even when blessed by Jupiter or Mars in its own sign can still cause deep problems that are hard to remedy. Still, I think Jupiter and the grace of the Guru can bring the most support to Scorpios and provide the grounding need to balance out the dominance of the space element that Scorpios have.

Gemini/Sagittarius or 3rd house/9th house
This is a mental axis, where Gemini and the 3rd house represent the "*lower mind*" and Sagittarius and the 9th house represent the "*higher mind*" and the wisdom that spirituality and religion brings to the table.

Gemini and the 3rd house rule curiosity and logical thinking. Sagittarius and the 9th house rule a broader way of thinking — the quest for the meaning of why we are here in is the search for the Divine. Inherent in this conflict is the opposition between the logic of Mercury and the 3rd house and the faith and dogma of Sagittarius. It is playing out strongly now between the US sign of Sagittarius and the war with the media represented by Gemini with transiting and weak Saturn in Sagittarius fueling the decaying flames.

Planets placed in Gemini anywhere in the chart need to be creative or they get stuck in idleness. Hence when you see a planet anywhere in the chart connected to Gemini, you need to recommend being active and focused and then the planet will blossom. This sign may also show the path or direction in life, so it is a key signature in people charts for giving them focus towards their life purpose and may reveal the focus that the person needs to take to move forward in their life.

The 9th natural sign of the zodiac brings lessons around belief, dogma and blind faith. The Shakti of Sagittarius is that planets placed here show dogmas and rules but will bring luck if we follow our dharma and will bestow deep wisdom if we can follow our path and purpose. The curse of Sagittarius is that it will create war and conflict in order to uphold its belief and fundamentalist values. The US being Sagittarius rising is a difficult example of this. Sagittarius has problems with Vishnu and Mercury, so it has difficultly with communications in relationship.

Cancer/Capricorn or 4th house/10th house
The private life, domesticity, the need for a home base, and nurturing (Cancer and the 4th house) versus the public life, career, reputation, and accountability (Capricorn and the 10th house). Attachments and love are ruled by Cancer and the 4th, while achievements, rewards, and punishments are ruled by Capricorn. This is the archetypal conflict between being out in the world and wanting to be secure at home.

Ketu moving into Capricorn in September of 2017 and Rahu moving into Cancer will stir this desire more over the next 1.5 years starting in September and probably create a peak in housing prices as the desire for home and security increases while Ketu will create less of an attachment to work and rising in one's career during that transit.

The Shakti of Cancer is to bring the blessings of Divine Mother or Gauri to our lives. Planets placed here show our best friend, those who can provide healing and care for us.

Wherever Capricorn appears as a rising sign in a Varga chart or in other places of the sign, there is no joy but hard work, which creates deep, suffering. If you have Capricorn rising in the D-10 chart or if you are Aries rising where Capricorn rules the 10th, this may seem even stronger.

The 10th natural sign of the zodiac owned by Saturn is challenged with joy and experience deep toil, lack of hope and faith, receive little support except through their own efforts and experience great pain and suffering. There is little awareness and sometimes planets placed here have no choice but to toil and work hard in order to move out of their pain or to cover it up. The weakness for Capricorn is Jupiter, as it needs to learn integrity and ethics in business practice or suffer like Capricorn rising Bernie Madoff did with his investment Ponzi schemes.

Leo/Aquarius or the Conflict between 5th and 11th house
We are always juggling the balance between individual status, fame (Leo and 5th house) and humanitarian service and groups (Aquarius and 11th house). Leo and the 5th house rule creative self-expression and the boost to the individual ego that we receive through pleasure and romance, while Aquarius and the 11th house rules groups and service to humanity. It seems that we are always fighting between ourselves and our personal glory and the need to serve society and do humanitarian work for selfless service.

Rahu transiting Leo and Ketu in Aquarius has stirred this pot over, but it ended last September. Ketu in Aquarius caused us to run away from groups and in favor of personal advancement.

The Shakti of planets placed in Leo show what we know, naturally learn, read or where our hidden talents are to express knowledge. If you have Mercury in Leo, then you have the power to express great knowledge and are a great teacher or speaker. Leo brings the blessings of Lord Shiva and the desire to transcend into the infinite and merge with the Universal transcendental soul, Shiva.

Aquarius is the 2nd most difficult sign to have anywhere prominent in one's chart as it ruled by Saturn and Rahu, which rules suffering and is the seat of desire. Rahu gives and then takes away so that we are reminded that we are here to find the Divine.

Aquarius is on the opposite side of the zodiac from Leo, the giver of light and it tends to take away the material and it creates great pain and suffering from the losses that arise here. Aquarius is a bitter enemy with the moon and mother so issues around maternal care, nurturing and food become prominent. Whatever rising sign in any Varga chart has planets in Aquarius creates suffering and loss in this area. Devotion to Shiva and to meditation and offerings to Shiva, dispel the suffering of Aquarian Karma.

Virgo/Pisces or the conflict between the 6th and 12th houses
This polarity is the service axis, and it deals with the balance between day-to-day

functions and routines, physical health, work and the need for order (Virgo and the 6th house), spiritual health, transcending the material world, and the infinite (Pisces and 12th house). Virgo and the 6th house rules our tools and techniques that we use to deal with day-to-day life, while Pisces and the 12th house rule the tools that we use to deal with our spirituality and our desire for Moksha and to find God. We are often at odds between the drudgery of going to work every day and our desire for our highest calling to realize God.

Whenever a planet appears in Virgo in any sign of the zodiac it means where we need to be better, improve or be pure. Being the natural 6th house of the zodiac, it means that we need discipline around regular work, health and diet to prevent illness and we also need to develop skills to work with people so that we do not develop enmity with co-workers at work. The challenge is Saturn and wanting too much perfection in the world and being too hard oneself and one's weaknesses. There can be too much self-deprecation or a continual focus on seeking perfection. I have Virgo rising in the D-9 chart and I am amazed that these qualities are at the core of my soul's journey. Key words to remember are purity and improvement.

Pisces is the natural 12th sign of the zodiac is connected to Moksha and enlightenment. The Shakti is to bring the blessings of Saraswati, the goddess of wisdom that brings Knowledge of the Self. Planets placed here anywhere in any of the charts show great talents and knowledge. But being the natural 12th house, it requires dedication to service and sacrifice to bring out its power. Pisces rising has difficultly with the Sun, the natural 6th house from Pisces so father issues and issues with authority and bosses become a natural problem.

NAKSHATRA (LUNAR MANSIONS): SHAKTI POWER AND KEY MEANINGS

Special thanks to Dennis Harness, Komilla Sutton and Prash Trivedi and their works for helping me to quickly compile this information.

1. Ashwini: (Ketu) - Rajasic - Horse - Quick Starter - Power to heal and reaching one's goal - sets things in motion.

2. Bharani: (Venus) - Rajasic - Power to clean impurities - Death - Justice - Discipline - Truth - Creative and sexual.

3. Krittika: (Sun) - Rajasic - Power to burn negativity to get to the truth - Cutting energy to heal or destroy - Monumental deeds and achievements.

4. Rohini: (Moon) - Rajasic - Power to foster growth and creation - Desire - Love - Affinity - Creativity - Very devotional - Desire for Moksha.

5. Mrigashira: (Mars) - Rajasic - Power to give fulfillment and searching for liberation - Radiant beauty - Feminine Attributes - Maternal.

6. Ardra: (Rahu) - Rajasic - Power to make gains through life through effort - Striving for material - Cleansing emotional storms - Forgiveness - Compassion - Emotion - Redemption.

7. Purnavasu: (Jupiter) - Rajasic - Divine ability to bring light into Darkness - Energy - Intelligence - Renewal - Good fortune - Re-creation.

8. Pushya: (Saturn) - Rajasic - Power to create spiritual energy - Nurturing - Prospering - Blooming - Most auspicious star.

9. Ashlesha: (Mercury) - Rajasic - Power to inflict poisonous venom - Very mystical - Addictions to sensory world - Esoteric knowledge - Secrets - Sexual desire.

10. Magha: (Ketu) - Tamasic - Power to leave the body - Power - Nobility - and strong material drive.

11. Purva Phalguni: (Venus) - Tamasic - Skills in the fine arts and a love of pleasure - Motivation is Kama or pleasure - Power of creative procreation.

12. Uttara Phalguni: (Sun) - Tamasic - This is the "*social worker*" - Always helping the friend in need - Power in healing arts and counseling fields - Motivation is moksha or spiritual liberation.

13. Hasta: (Moon) - Tamasic - Very mental, intellectual nature - Power to manifest what one seeks and place it in their hands - Great dexterity and are skilled with the healing arts and with handicrafts.

14. Chitra: (Mars) - Tamasic - Successful artisan types - Power to accumulate merit in this life - Artistic beauty - Motivation of Kama, or desire.

15. Swati: (Rahu) - Tamasic - The Self-Going Star - Power to scatter like the wind. Very intellectual - Excellent communication skills - Priest/Priestess - Restless - Independent - Freedom loving - Motivation of artha or attainment of wealth.

16. Vishakha: (Jupiter) - Tamasic - Spiritual initiation - Deep connection with one's soul purpose - Need for patience on the path - Self-interest - Power to achieve many and various fruits in life.

17. Anuradha: (Saturn) - Tamasic - Ability to gather people together for social and spiritual activities - Friendship - Power of worship - Tenacity and discipline when needed.

18. Jyeshtha: (Mercury) - Tamasic - Motivation is materialism. Power to rise, conquer, and gain courage in battle - Superior power - Preeminent - The creative eccentric.

19. Mula: (Ketu) - Satvic - Mystical - Power to ruin or destroy and break things apart - All branches of learning (philosophy, science, teaching) - Place of the galactic center - Strong sensual or kama nature.

20. Purva Ashadha: (Venus) - Satvic - Power of invigoration - Protection of dependents - Kindness - Courage - Victory - Motivation of moksha, or spiritual liberation.

21. Uttara Ashadha: (Sun) - Satvic - Later victory - Power for unchallengeable victory. Humanitarian vision to see all races as equal - Becoming ONE - Absorption - Lonely.

22. Sharvana: (Moon) - Satvic- Shravana: The Star of Learning - Brilliant mind - Capacity to study other cultures and spiritual dimensions - Respectful listener - Scholar - Teacher - Meditator - Motivation is material success, artha or wealth - Power to provide connection with others.

23. Dhanishtha: (Mars) - Satvic - Symbol is the drum, indicating a love of music. The "*kingly star*" due to the fame and wealth that can occur - Highly altruistic - Power to give abundance and fame.

24. Shatabisha: (Rahu) - Satvic - The hundred healers - Protection - Shielding - Independent nature and autonomy - Love for travel and adventure.

25. Purva Bhadrapada: (Jupiter) - Satvic - Two faced man symbol - Cut through negativity to get to the truth. Can see both sides of an issue - Power to raise a spiritual person up in life - Successful in the business world - Contrition - Atonement -

Motivation toward artha, or prosperity.

26. Uttara Bhadrapada: (Saturn) - Satvic - The Warrior Star - Power of "*bringing the cosmic rain*" - Motivation of Kama, or healthy pleasures.

27. Revati: (Mercury) - Satvic - The Wealth of Spiritual Knowledge - Protector - Nurturer of others on their life journey - Motivation of moksha - Power of nourishment symbolized by milk - Spiritual growth and development of psychic abilities.

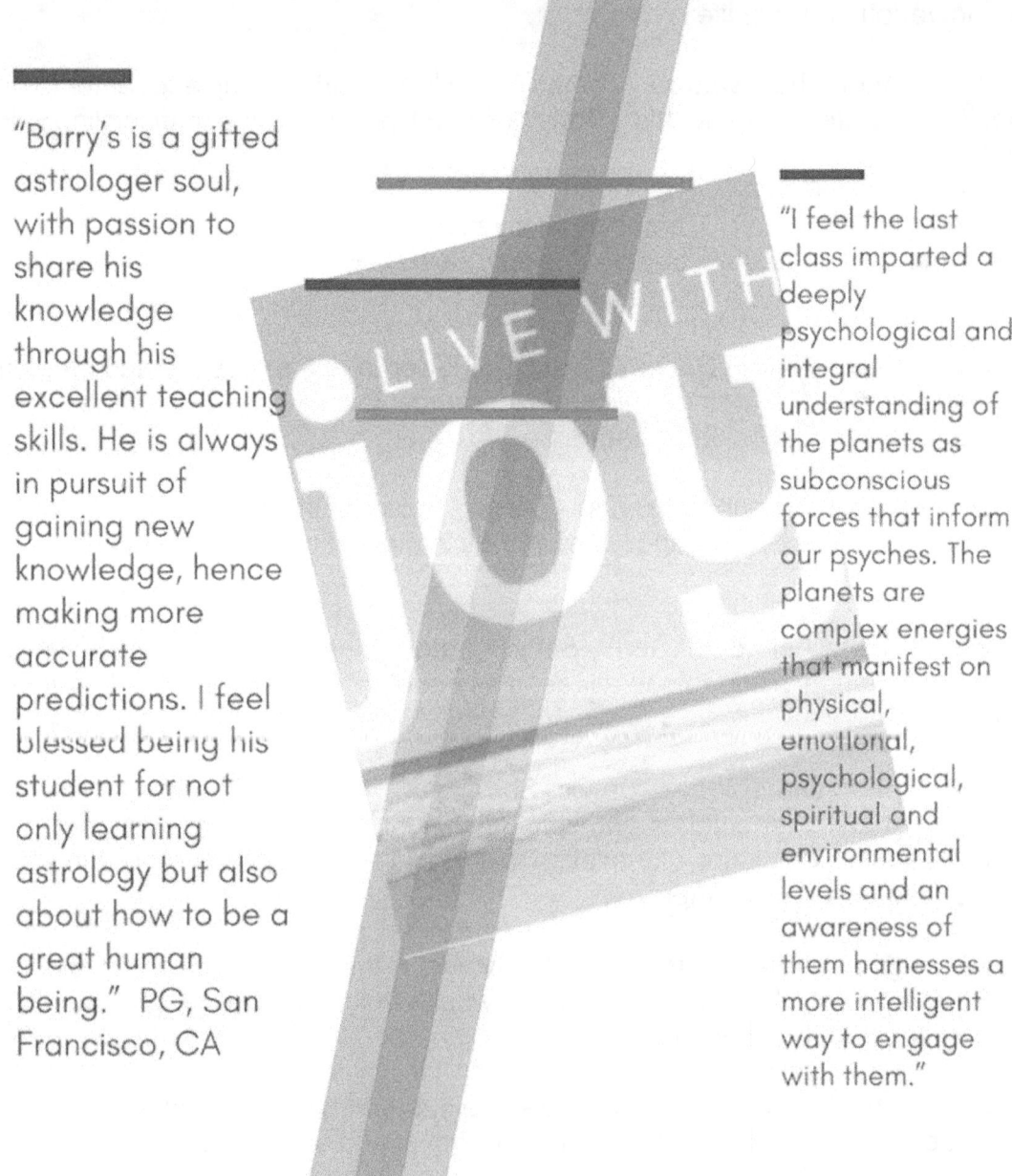

"Barry's is a gifted astrologer soul, with passion to share his knowledge through his excellent teaching skills. He is always in pursuit of gaining new knowledge, hence making more accurate predictions. I feel blessed being his student for not only learning astrology but also about how to be a great human being." PG, San Francisco, CA

"I feel the last class imparted a deeply psychological and integral understanding of the planets as subconscious forces that inform our psyches. The planets are complex energies that manifest on physical, emotional, psychological, spiritual and environmental levels and an awareness of them harnesses a more intelligent way to engage with them."

AUTHOR BIOGRAPHY: ABOUT BARRY ROSEN

Barry Rosen has been practicing Vedic astrology since 1987. He has visited and studied in India on 4 occasions and has spoken numerous times at the American Council of Vedic Astrology Conferences in Sedona, AZ since 1999 and also the British Association of Vedic Astrologers in London since 2006. He has been involved in Vedic culture since 1973 and is a long-time meditation and yoga teacher and a published poet.

Recently, he has been pioneering research in other areas of Vedic astrology including Vedic Astro-locality, the effects your current physical location have on your chart, connecting astrology to hatha yoga for therapeutic purposes and developing transformational healing work to move through karma and the spiritual dimensions of Vedic astrology. He is a Neo-Vedic astrologer and uses the outer planets. He is particularly interested in Jaimni astrology and the soul's journey through the physical world and its karma and purpose and has taken live seminars in London with Sanjay Rath.

For questions, please contact Barry by email barry2@fortucast.com or call Fortucast at 800-788-2796.

APPLIED VEDIC ASTROLOGY COURSE

VEDIC ASTROLOGY AND PSYCHOLOGY: HIDDEN PSYCHOLOGICAL PATTERNS

MOVING BEYOND MENTAL BLOCKS AND KARMA
SUNDAYS, 3:00-5:00 PM STARTS JUNE 3, 2018

HTTP://WWW.APPLIEDVEDICASTROLOGY.COM/WEBINAR-SPIRITUAL-ASTROLOGY-ASTROLOGY-KARMA/

LIVE WEBINAR OR DROPBOX RECORDINGS

CREDIT CARDS & PAYPAL ACCEPTED CALL FORTUCAST 928-284-5740 EXT. 5000 OR 5983

LEARN WITH BARRY ROSEN

VEDIC ASTROLOGY ONLINE COURSES - LIVE OR BY WEBINAR REPLAY!

APPLIEDVEDICASTROLOGY.COM

DO YOU WANT TO KNOW MORE?

- HOW TO REMOVE MONEY BLOCKS AND RELEASE YOUR MONEY KARMA
- THE SECRETS OF THE HOUSES
- THE SECRETS OF TIMING RELATIONSHIPS AND MARRIAGE
- THE SECRETS OF TIMING YOUR LIFE EVENTS
- FINDING YOUR SOUL'S DESTINY
- USING VEDIC ASTROLOGY TO DISCOVER PSYCHOLOGICAL PATTERNS AND HOW TO REMEDIES CAN HELP
- NATAL CHART READING: FOUNDATION COURSE
- ...AND MORE!

Visit www.appliedvedicastrology.com to browse our products and course offerings, plus sign up to receive our e-newsletter and other exclusive offers!

CREDIT CARDS ACCEPTED BY PHONE AT 928-284-5740 ext. 5000 or 5983
For Questions: Email barry2@fortucast.com
Special invoicing available if you do not use PayPal.

GET A VEDIC ASTROLOGY READING!

928-284-5740 EXT 5000 OR 5983
BARRY2@FORTUCAST.COM
APPLIEDVEDICASTROLOGY.COM

ASTROLOGY READINGS WITH BARRY!

APPLIEDVEDICASTROLOGY.COM

VEDIC ASTRO-LOCALITY
Plan your next vacation spot or residential move!

928-284-5740 EXT 5000 OR 5983
BARRY2@FORTUCAST.COM
APPLIEDVEDICASTROLOGY.COM

VISIT THE WEBSITE TO LEARN MORE!

"BARRY'S IS A GIFTED ASTROLOGER SOUL, WITH PASSION TO SHARE HIS KNOWLEDGE THROUGH HIS EXCELLENT TEACHING SKILLS. HE IS ALWAYS IN PURSUIT OF GAINING NEW KNOWLEDGE, HENCE MAKING MORE ACCURATE PREDICTIONS. I FEEL BLESSED BEING HIS STUDENT FOR NOT ONLY LEARNING ASTROLOGY BUT ALSO ABOUT HOW TO BE A GREAT HUMAN BEING." PG, SAN FRANCISCO, CA

COMING SOON!
ASTRO-YOGA 2: SIGNS, SEQUENCING AND THERAPY

APPLIED VEDIC ASTROLOGY READINGS BY BARRY ROSEN

RELATIONSHIP COMPATIBILITY

COMPANY ASTROLOGY
Overview of your company's cycles and outlook.

VEDIC NATAL CHART
Overview of your life-purpose - Major areas of concern are addressed here and overview of the year.

CAREER COUNSELING/LIFE PURPOSE/SPIRITUAL READING
Uncover your life purpose and career path towards creating an income and put all the elements together using periods and transits.

NEWBORN CHILD READING
Get your complete "owner's manual" for your young one and become a better parent to help guide your child through life's hurdles.

FINANCIAL AND INVESTMENT
Psychological and money tendencies. Barry will analyze the best sources for income, as well as, debt, savings, and investments.

Applied Vedic Astrology

APPLIEDVEDICASTROLOGY.COM

STUDY LIVE WITH BARRY ROSEN'S VEDIC ASTROLOGY COURSES

COURSE

WINTER/SPRING 2018 to learn how the Planets Impact Your Chart and Influence Your Life Direction! Learn from an Industry Expert!

Sign up!
http://www.appliedvedicastrology.com

Starts Saturday, January 13th - February 10th, 2018: 3:00-5:00 PM CST (Chicago time) LIVE webinar via GoToMeeting or Video Recordings available through DROPBOX $195.00 Classes are 2 hours in length

SECRETS OF VEDIC RELATIONSHIPS AND COMPATIBILITY: MINI-CLASS

How to develop relationships skills with the planets and mining the depths of the 7th house to reveal its secrets about romance and death!

- How you can better understand the martial sacrifice and sexual consummation in your own relationship by studying the Upapada or AL12 - what meaning does that hold for you in your chart and are there actions you can take to improve your relationship(s) or prepare for future relations?
- How you can learn about the astrology of alternative sexuality and gay relationships from the chart.
- How you can use the tools in this course to time your own relationships and marriage (and that of your friends and family members)!
- How you can learn to match and compare your Moon with your partners Moon, your Venus with your partners Venus and your Rising Signs for comparability - the cornerstone of relationships!
- How I will teach you about "Martian Blemishes" and touch on "Kuja Dosha" and the karmic impact that Rahu and Ketu have your relationships! This is a key factor when studying the implications of relationship compatibility.
- How you can read your own D-9 Navamsha Chart for marriage and relationships interpretations.

APPLIEDVEDICASTROLOGY.COM

928-284-5740 ext. 5000 or 5983

LIVE WEBINAR VIA GOTOMEETING OR VIDEO RECORDINGS AVAILABLE THROUGH DROPBOX $195 CLASSES ARE 2 HOURS IN LENGTH

Applied Vedic Astrology

SECRETS OF THE NAKSHATRAS: PROFOUND PSYCHOLOGICAL AND PREDICTIVE MAGIC

COURSE

Starts February 25, 2018 - May 6th, 2018 10 (2 hour classes)

Sign up at:
http://www.appliedvedicastrology.com/secrets-nakshatras-profound-psychological-predictive-magic/

o Do you understand the puppet strings that pull on your psychology?
o Do you know that past life influences produce current patterns that are STILL playing out in this lifetime?
o Do you know that the zodiac includes 27 lunar mansions or constellations, called Nakshatras that influence our emotions and trigger events to produce in our lives?

Learn about these symbols, archetypes and relationships of the Nakshatras, influenced by the Moon and how they impact our psychological and spiritual experiences to gain insight on what the karmic lessons the planets are teaching you.

APPLIEDVEDICASTROLOGY.COM

928-284-5740 ext. 5000 or 5983

LIVE WEBINAR VIA GOTOMEETING OR VIDEO RECORDINGS AVAILABLE THROUGH DROPBOX
$295.00
CLASSES ARE 2 HOURS IN LENGTH

www.ingramcontent.com/pod-product-compliance
Lightning Source LLC
Chambersburg PA
CBHW081158230426
43666CB00016B/2849